Overcoming Heterosexism and Homophobia

Between Men ~ Between Women

Lesbian and Gay Studies

Lillian Faderman and Larry Gross, Editors

Overcoming Heterosexism and Homophobia

Strategies That Work

Edited by James T. Sears and Walter L. Williams

Columbia University Press

New York

Columbia University Press
Publishers Since 1893
New York   Chichester, West Sussex
Copyright © 1997 Columbia University Press
All rights reserved
"Making Allies of Co-Workers: Educating the Corporate World"
Copyright © 1993 Brian McNaught, reprinted from *Gay Issues in the
Workplace* (chapter 6, "A Model Workshop") by permission of
St. Martin's Press.
Library of Congress Cataloging-in-Publication Data
Overcoming heterosexism and homophobia: strategies that work / edited
 by James T. Sears and Walter L. Williams.
      p.   cm. — (Between men—between women)
   Includes bibliographical references and index.
   ISBN 0-231-10422-7 — ISBN 0-231-10423-5 (pbk)
   1. Homophobia—United States—Prevention. 2. Heterosexism—United
States—Prevention. 3. Behavior modification—United States.
4. Motivation (Psychology)—United States.   I. Sears, James T.
(James Thomas), 1951–   . II. Williams, Walter L., 1948–   .
III. Series.
   HQ76.3.U50994   1997
   306.76'6—dc21   96-50483
                                                                CIP

Casebound editions of Columbia University Press books are printed
on permanent and durable acid-free paper.

Printed in the United States of America

c 10 9 8 7 6 5 4 3 2 1
p 10 9 8 7 6 5 4 3 2 1

Contents

Overcoming Heterosexism and Homophobia

Walter L. Williams

Introduction

This book has resulted from the confluence of like-minded researchers who originally came together in the late 1980s through our activist involvement in the Campaign to End Homophobia. James T. Sears, a principal academic scholar in the campaign and a leading researcher on homosexuality in the field of education, established and edited *Empathy*, an interdisciplinary journal for persons working to end oppression on the basis of sexual identities. He and I were introduced by Warren Blumenfeld, another leading thinker in the campaign, who had resonated to my anthropological finding (Williams 1986): a major factor in the acceptance of sexual diversity and gender variance in nonhomophobic cultures is that those cultures have established specific ways that *heterosexuals* gain benefits from such acceptance. Growing out of this theoretical approach, Blumenfeld edited a pathbreaking book, *Homophobia: How We All Pay the Price* (1992), for which he asked me to write the final chapter (Williams 1992). This book focused on the hidden costs of homophobia to heterosexuals in the United States, in terms of emotional repressions, damaged family relationships, social institutions, and public policy.

About the same time, Sears asked me as a native Southerner to write the introduction for his book *Growing Up Gay in the South* (1991), and he and I started working together on *Empathy*. We soon realized that we thought alike about the need to go beyond merely studying homophobia and instead should encourage research that tries to find out which strategies and techniques are most effective in reducing this prejudice. We were inspired by the pioneering work of the same researchers, including John De Cecco, who as editor of the *Journal of Homosexuality* has promoted such scholarship and in 1984 edited a special issue on homophobia, Suzanne Pharr, whose 1988 book clarified the links between homophobia and sexism, Michael Stevenson, whose 1988 study evaluated the effectiveness of different strategies in reducing heterosexism, and the many articles on the subject by Gregory Herek (1991) and others.

Impressed with Sears' inclusive, multicultural, and feminist perspectives on challenging heterosexism for all gay, lesbian, bisexual, and transgender persons, in 1993 I invited him to come to Los Angeles to be a visiting scholar at the ONE Institute Center for Advanced Studies, of which I am director. Following a bruising media confrontation with antigay Christian fundamentalists in South Carolina, he was happy to relocate to the University of Southern California for a semester, where I was his faculty sponsor at the USC Center for Feminist Research.

I was teaching a course at USC on "Overcoming Prejudice" that focuses on effective strategies and techniques for reducing racism, sexism, heterosexism, anti-Semitism, and other forms of prejudice and institutionalized discrimination. It was while Sears was living as a guest at my house that semester, in our wide-ranging discussions about these topics, that the idea for this edited book developed. We both felt the need to encourage those activists and scholars who have actually been out in the trenches, struggling to reduce heterosexism in multiple contexts, to give others the benefits of what they had learned.

With his focus on educational strategies, Sears took the initiative to gather for this volume an impressive group of schoolteachers, college educators, and workshop leaders who have many years of experience in changing homophobic attitudes in classroom settings. I focused on bringing in social scientists who have similarly impressive experience in reducing heterosexism within grassroots multicultural communities and in socioeconomic institutions. We asked the authors to summarize in brief form their findings about what techniques are most effective, which ones are not effective, what mistakes should be avoided, and where we go from here. All the chapters are original essays written especially for this volume, except for one chapter that is an adaptation from Brian McNaught's excellent book, *Gay Issues in the Workplace*, printed by permission of St. Martin's Press.

Because of our desire to include many topics, we as editors are well aware that much more needs to be written about each of the subjects than the space permitted for each chapter and we are thankful to the authors for being cooperative in condensing their chapters so everything could fit. We also realize that many other topics need to be covered, and we hope that other books will follow this one. For example, a book could be written devoted solely to evaluating the efforts of groups working in the courts, like Lambda Legal Defense, the gay and lesbian rights project of the American Civil Liberties Union, and lawyers working with the Hawaii Equal Marriage Rights Project.

The Overemphasis on Political Strategies

Early on we as editors made a decision not to include political and legal strategies within this volume. We feel that so much attention has been focused on political issues that other significant areas of social change are being relatively ignored. During the 1980s and early 1990s, the strongest focus of American national gay and lesbian organizations has been on political lobbying and on campaign contributions to sympathetic heterosexual politicians. This political trend has had a significant impact and reached its peak with the election of pro-gay president Bill Clinton. Yet several recent failures on the national level, from the gays in the military fiasco and the 1994 congressional elections to Clinton's 1996 public statements against legalizing same-sex marriages, have shown the limits of top-down political change.

Many politicians who are privately supportive might not take progressive public actions simply because of fear of being voted out of office in the next election. Heterosexual politicians who were elected with gay support, from President Clinton on down, typically back off from pro-gay positions when faced with public resistance. Huge amounts of money pour into the coffers of radical right organizations like the Christian Coalition whenever their well-designed publicity campaigns stress an antihomosexual theme. In such a situation, when jobs are on the line and money is involved, it is pointless to think that either the radical right politicians or more liberal politicians will suddenly see the need to push strongly for an end to discrimination. We cannot, consequently, depend solely on a national political strategy. A political approach cannot be effective without addressing prejudicial attitudes and institutionalized discrimination in the general population. We are suggesting that efforts to lobby national political leaders, when the cultural level of acceptance of lesbian and gay Americans is so pitiable across the nation, may be a poor choice for our limited resources.

What the national lesbian, gay, bi, and transgender community has not adequately addressed is the need to evaluate various strategies for reducing heterosexism and to decide at some fundamental levels where we should put our resources. Decisions about money are too often made haphazardly, usually on the verge of a crisis. Our greatest weakness is that we have allowed the radical right to set the stage for battle, as we have merely reacted to their initiatives and political attacks. We do not mean to suggest that leaders should be avoiding all political battles, and certainly it is necessary to advance on several fronts at once, to change attitudes, institutions, and politics. But our movement has not asked the basic questions about where our resources will be most effective in accomplishing lasting social change. We need systemic study to learn where we can get the most bang for our buck.

In order to learn these answers, it is necessary to search widely. As a movement, we can no longer depend solely on the shoot-from-the-hip guesses of leaders of the national lesbian and gay organizations. Certainly they have a valuable perspective, based on their years of political activism, and we need a multiplicity of approaches that include crisis management. But the dominant perspective of the lesbian and gay movement has been severely hampered by a limited perspective focusing almost entirely on politics.

A crucial vantage point can be provided by researchers who are aware of wider responses to social problems. Depending on their area of training, researchers may discover important lessons by interviewing those on the local level who have actually managed to accomplish change, as represented by the chapters in this book. We need researchers to do intensive interviews of individuals who were previously prejudiced but have become more pro-gay. How did these changes occur and how might we use these lessons to reduce heterosexist prejudice among other people? Researchers are also needed to search documentary historical sources, to do statistical analysis to discern long-range trends, and to investigate the experiences of other nations and cultures. Social scientists offer a major resource for understanding the mechanisms by which societal change occurs. Yet this resource has not been adequately mobilized in the campaigns to reduce heterosexism.

Partly this is the fault of academics themselves. Many tenured full professors who are gay or lesbian continue to cower cowardly in the closet. Others devote their considerable skills to every conceivable subject except prejudice, miserably failing our community and our movement. With some notable exceptions most academics who do deal with homosexuality have focused on investigation of supposed "causes" of individual sexually variant behaviors and have ignored the investigation of individual prejudices. Thanks to recent research we know far more about the varied ranges of sexual behaviors of sexual minorities than we know about authoritarian persons who resist acceptance of such variance. We have seen much more theoretical attention paid to the social constructions of homosexual identities than to theories explaining heterosexist discrimination.

That emphasis in academia may be about to change. In an important conference held in 1994 and co-sponsored by the University of Chicago and the American Psychological Foundation, a group of fifty invited researchers working in lesbian and gay studies met to decide the top priorities for future research. The catalyst for this conference was a bequest by Wayne Placek, a gay man who had been inspired in the 1950s by visionaries at Los Angeles's ONE Institute, America's first homophile educational foundation. Upon his death in 1992 Placek left instructions in his will that his entire estate be used to promote research that would be of direct benefit to the gay and lesbian community.

James Sears and I were part of the group of scholars who met to decide the best use of this generous bequest. After much discussion and many debates, over the course of three days, a consensus emerged that academics need to take a more direct role in providing a research base on which activist groups could make their strategic decisions. The right wing recognizes the importance of long-range thinking and heavily funds several think tank research centers that set the stage for the right's dramatic impact on the United States in the 1980s and the 1990s. In response other groups, including feminists, environmentalists, and progressives, have begun developing their own research centers. In sharp contrast, however, the gay and lesbian movement does not even have one single operating think tank. Through the years ONE Institute has been practically the only gay organization trying to address this need, with its International Gay and Lesbian Archives providing the research base upon which a major think tank can be built.

Thankfully, other organizations are finally beginning to respond. The Institute for Gay and Lesbian Strategic Studies was founded by activists like Greg Scott and Ann Northrup, along with academics like Lee Badgett and me, specifically to bring these two groups together and to raise funds in support of research to reduce heterosexism. As one of its projects, this organization has provided valued critical advice and financial support assisting publication of this volume. Also the National Gay and Lesbian Task Force is developing its policy institute as a research arm. This is most needed, since activist organizations like NGLTF are so busy fighting the fires on the front lines that they often have little opportunity to step back from the fray. Sometimes, instead of fighting fires, it is necessary to ask whether the most effective strategy might be to find out what sets them off to begin with.

An example of the value of research to deal with pressing issues is the 1992 publication of *Hate Crimes: Confronting Violence Against Lesbians and Gay Men,* a book coedited by Gregory Herek, an academic researcher, and Kevin Berrill, an official at NGLTF. This book is a model of what can be accomplished by academics and activists who work closely together. Further research needs to be done with case-controlled studies, demonstrating which strategies and techniques are most effective in neutralizing perpetrators of hate crimes and other homophobic activities. We also need more research on our enemies in the radical right. How can we learn from their successes and turn the techniques they have used to our advantage?

Research-based long-term strategic thinking can provide valuable perspective about deciding where to best utilize our resources. This is already occurring on a political level, where research has shown the value of giving more attention to state and local campaigns for public office. A good example of an effective coordinated plan of action has been spearheaded by the Gay and Lesbian Victory Fund, which has developed a more refined strategy for getting lesbians and gay men elected to local office. Victory Fund researchers analyze candidates and locales that have the best chances for success; the fund then collects money nationally to focus on these local races. This research-based organization has been remarkably successful in helping to elect more openly lesbian and gay candidates and has published an important guidebook for other potential candidates (DeBold 1994). The governmental focus of this excellent book is another reason why James Sears and I decided to concentrate the essays in our volume on strategies outside of politics.

As shown by the following chapters, it behooves activists to seriously consider focusing on strategies for changing attitudes, socioeconomic institutions, and the media. At the beginning of the next millennium our biggest impact on society may well be made outside politics. The Placek conference reached the conclusion that the most important research topics needing to be addressed focus on changing heterosexist prejudice and discriminatory behavior. That is, how can we best change attitudes, on a societal or individual level, toward a more positive acceptance of lesbians, gay men, bisexuals, and/or transgender persons? If we can promote these changes, to reduce the misguided fear and loathing that exists and to encourage attitudes of understanding and respect, then politics will also change in response.

Existing research has already demonstrated that the single most effective way to change homophobic attitudes is through one-to-one personal contacts of individuals with whom others share an ongoing association. Thus we need research to suggest the best ways to encourage more lesbigay persons to come out to their relatives, friends, and co-workers and to engage in repeated dialogue about heterosexism.

As emphasized by the essays in part 1 of this book, this *repeated* one-to-one discussion is more effective than all the parades, protest marches, political lobbying, workshops, and educational lectures put together. We cannot have a major impact on social attitudes until more bisexual, lesbian, gay, transgender people, and our supporters take our pro-diversity viewpoint into our workplaces and into the livingrooms of our relatives and friends, where we can overcome stigmatizing generalities and interact as individuals. Those persons can then be encouraged to radiate this antiprejudicial influence further through society.

Besides attitude change through individual-to-individual interaction, the authors in this volume present valuable case studies showing how to change institutions like schools, churches, law enforcement agencies, and industries. While a top-down approach may not always work well in politics, it does seem to be more effective in hierarchical institutions like corporations. If the boss can be convinced to establish and enforce policies prohibiting discrimination, that will go a long way to change the atmosphere in a workplace for lesbian and gay employees. In a situation where prejudiced workers understand they might lose their job if they engage in discrimination, most will adjust their behavior in order to advance their career. Cutting down on prejudicial behaviors, ranging from joking to violence, leads to a gradual decline in prejudicial attitudes as well. Whether we are talking about private businesses or public institutions like schools, police departments, and the military, a crucial element is to have the support of the institution's top administrators. Once that is gained, other efforts to reduce heterosexism can be more effective.

The essays in this volume also show the critical importance of the mass communications industry in shaping public attitudes. Activist groups like the Gay and Lesbian Alliance Against Defamation, Hollywood Supports, and the Lesbian and Gay Journalists Association have had an enormous impact on editors, film producers, television directors, and media executives. Building on these groups' success, it is therefore important to encourage lesbians and gays to take jobs working for radio, television, and film production companies as well as for major daily newspapers and publishers of popular magazines and books. The big media employers are important not only because they reach larger audiences but also because smaller businesses in the same fields usually follow their bigger competitors' trends. Having groups of open employees who will stand up to prejudice and engage in one-to-one dialogue with their co-workers and supervisors will do more than anything else to lessen homophobic rhetoric and present more positive depictions of transgender, bisexual, lesbian, and gay people in these media.

Besides the data featured in the essays in part 5, additional research is needed to understand the effective techniques used by other media activist groups as well as employee groups at other corporations and universities that have enacted antidiscrimination policies and domestic partner benefits. These groups' struggles can be a model for action at other workplaces.

In the "Overcoming Prejudice" class I teach at the University of Southern California I discuss historical examples of social change movements that have had a dramatic impact on changing prejudices on the basis of race, class, religion, ethnicity, and sex. We need to examine more deeply the great social change movements of American history in the nineteenth and twentieth centuries: the antislavery and civil rights movements, the labor movement, the feminist movement, and the early lesbian/gay movement itself. These progressive movements need to be studied to understand both their successes and their mistakes in bringing about public policy changes on both political and social levels. Even more to the point are those small minority groups that have accomplished dramatic reductions in prejudice against great odds. During the nineteenth century discrimination against Irish Americans, Mormons, Jewish Americans, and other ethnicities was rampant, yet these prejudicial attitudes have declined considerably in the twentieth century. While prejudice toward these groups has hardly disappeared, within only half a century other groups like Japanese Americans and some specific Native American tribes have made profound changes in their positions in society.

Much of the progress of minority groups like these have been based on their economic advancement. How can economic development be further encouraged throughout the lesbian/gay/bisexual/transgender community, especially for groups within our community that have been economically marginalized? How can our community centers and business/professional groups take more of a lead in promoting entrepreneurial, skills training, savings plans, and financial investment programs? While much more attention to these workplace and economic issues is needed, some of the essays in this volume begin to address these topics.

Only two of the essays in this book discuss heterosexism outside the United States. Realizing this limitation, James Sears and I are now working to develop projects that highlight effective techniques being used in other nations. Sears is coediting, with Debbie Epstein of the University of London, an anthology of original essays focusing on efforts in the United Kingdom, Australia, the United States, and other Anglophone countries. I am developing an interactive list server on an Internet World Wide Web site of the ONE Institute International Gay and Lesbian Archives entitled "Overcoming Heterosexism: International Perspectives." I want to hear from readers of this book and others who can write of their own experiences and knowledge of progress being made in different nations around the world. Others who read these suggestions can respond, to develop a truly multicultural interaction for tangible advances around the globe.[1]

We see this volume as being just one step in the larger important effort to challenge heterosexism and homophobia. For their unflagging commitment to this project and their careful editing, we are deeply grateful to Ann Miller and Susan Pensak at Columbia University Press, to the series editors, Lillian Faderman and Larry Gross, and to the authors who have taken time from their activism to write down the benefits of their research and experiences for others' benefit. Each reader of this book can hopefully be inspired to take her or his own steps to help overcome heterosexism and to develop even more effective strategies beyond the suggestions provided by the pioneering authors of these essays.

NOTE

1. For information on joining this interactive list server on the Internet, locate the ONE Institute Web site, http://www.usc.edu/Library/oneigla, or write to Professor Walter L. Williams, Anthropology Department, University of Southern California, Los Angeles, CA 90089–0032. Include your E-mail address and a statement of the locale and nature of your experience and/or knowledge of effective strategies and techniques that have been used in reducing heterosexism within a specific context.

REFERENCES

Blumenfeld, W. J., ed. 1992. *Homophobia: How We All Pay the Price*. Boston: Beacon.

DeBold, K., ed. 1994. *Out for Office: Campaigning in the Gay Nineties*. Washington, D.C.: Gay and Lesbian Victory Fund.

De Cecco, J., ed. 1984. *Homophobia: An Overview*. New York: Haworth.

Herek, G. M. 1991. "Stigma, Prejudice, and Violence Against Lesbians and Gay Men." In J. Gonsiorek and J. Weinrich, eds., *Homosexuality: Research Implications for Public Policy*. Newbury Park, Cal.: Sage.

Herek, G. M., and K. T. Berrill, eds. 1992. *Hate Crimes: Confronting Violence Against Lesbians and Gay Men*. Newbury Park, Cal.: Sage.

Pharr, S. 1988. *Homophobia: A Weapon of Sexism*. Little Rock: Women's Project.

Sears, J. T. 1991. *Growing Up Gay in the South: Race, Gender, and Journeys of the Spirit*. New York: Haworth.

Stevenson, M. R. 1988. "Promoting Tolerance for Homosexuality: An Evaluation of Intervention Strategies." *Journal of Sex Research* 25:500–11.

Williams, W. L. 1986. *The Spirit and the Flesh: Sexual Diversity in American Indian Culture*. Boston: Beacon.

—— 1992. "Benefits for Nonhomophobic Societies: An Anthropological Perspective." In W. J. Blumenfeld, ed., *Homophobia: How We All Pay the Price*. Boston: Beacon.

PART I

Foundational Issues

James T. Sears

Thinking Critically/Intervening Effectively
About Heterosexism and Homophobia:
A Twenty-Five-Year Research Retrospective

On any spring midafternoon the following events may occur. As three elementary school students play tag, one calls another "faggot"; a talk radio listener worries about his twelve-year-old daughter, who has yet to outgrow her "tomboy stage"; a stand-up comic begins his five-minute routine about gays in the military with a shower joke; a woman in her mid-teens chooses to have a baby, "proving" her heterosexuality to family and friends; two lesbian mothers remove themselves from any school involvement at their middle-school child's request; a toughened youth engages in consensual sex, then grabs a nearby bookend and batters his partner; a college student puts aside same-sex feelings and buries himself in his coursework; an outstanding employee for a large public relations firm chooses to place a photo of her former college boyfriend at her desk rather than one of her current female partner of three years; a middle-aged father returning from his long business trip refrains from embracing his two young sons. These vignettes represent various manifestations of homophobia and heterosexism. Some are subtle, some covert; a few are malicious; most are insidious. All of them are damaging to a society characterized by diversity and championed as just.

Professional organizations have acknowledged such damage and have taken various actions. The National Education Association and the Association for Curriculum and Supervision have advocated school policies to reduce harassment of lesbian and gay students or to provide supportive services for such students. Accreditation agencies including the Council on Social Work Education, American Medical Association, National Council on the Accreditation of Teacher Education, and the American Law Association have mandated or encouraged the integration of content relating to lesbian and gay issues in the professional curriculum. Municipal and state governments have adopted nondiscrimination statements on the basis of sexual orientation and businesses, ranging from AT&T to American Express, have undertaken employee training on lesbian/gay issues.

As more professional organizations, governmental units, and businesses adopt these policies and call upon consultants to translate them into practice there is an increasing need for effective strategies and targeted resources for use in overcoming homophobia and embracing sexual diversity. Based on a growing body of social science research and extensive professional experiences, contributors to this volume document effective interventions to reduce heterosexist prejudice and homophobic behavior. Avoiding generalities, these authors discuss specific pedagogical methods as well as political and economic strategies that have been marshaled often in working with a specific cultural or occupational group. These groups include law enforcement personnel, elementary school teachers, medical students, prospective social workers, news media as well as persons associated with the film and television industries, college and high school students, clergy, corporations, and members of various cultural groups such as African Americans, Latinos, Asian Americans, and persons of Jewish heritage.

Before focusing on these specific cultural and occupational groups, however, part 1 of *Overcoming Heterosexism and Homophobia* examines foundational principles. Collectively, the first four chapters situate homophobia and heterosexism within psychological, cultural, and educational contexts. Yep examines how we can apply principles of persuasive communication for attitude change. Bridgewater explores how our psychological understanding of prejudice and coming out translate to the reduction of homophobic behavior and heterosexist attitudes. In Williams's chapter we look at models from non-Western cultures and social change movements within our society that have reduced prejudicial attitudes and behaviors.

In this chapter I review research approaches to understanding homophobia and heterosexism. There is a critical need for studies, particularly over the long term, using qualitative and quantitative methods. I then review strategies that researchers have found effective in reducing these twin plagues. We also need to focus homophobia education to forms of prejudice reduction that are culturally and occupationally sensitive, emotionally and behaviorally based, and grounded in the larger social and historical context.

First, I will define our use of the concepts heterosexism and homophobia, review the major research instruments and designs that have been used to assess homophobia and heterosexism, and summarize the major findings generated from this research.

Heterosexism and Homophobia: Evolving Definitions

Definitions and Related Concepts of Homophobia

Earlier, at the outset of the Stonewall Rebellion, George Weinberg popularized the concept of homophobia in this nation's first national newsweekly, *GAY*. He later expanded on this in his well-received book, *Society and the Healthy Homosexual* (1972). His definition was quite specific: "the dread of being in close quarters with homosexuals ... the revulsion toward homosexuals and often the desire to inflict punishment as retribution" (4, 129). The classification of this condition as a "phobia in operation as a prejudice" was critical to Weinberg's definition: "The phobia appears as antagonism directed toward a particular group of people. Inevitably, it leads to disdain of those people, and to mistreatment of them" (7–8). Weinberg further observed:

> Volumes have been written on homosexuality, its origins and its development. This is because in most western civilizations, homosexuality is itself considered a problem; our unwarranted distress over homosexuality is not classified as a problem because it is still a majority point of view. Homophobia is still part of the conventional American attitude. (4)

During the past twenty-five years the concept of homophobia has been integrated into the social science literature, commonly cited by activists, and appropriated by policy makers and the judiciary. Legal codes have gradually changed, first removing homosexuality as a crime and later categorizing a violent act motivated by homophobia as a "hate crime." The term has evolved to less clinical use, referring to overt violence such as physical assault and verbal harassment, to psychological battering resulting in fear of self-disclosure or the absence of same-gender intimacy, to social and political offensives ranging from state referenda to legislative initiatives that have fostered and reinforced antigay sentiments and behaviors.

The related concept of internalized homophobia has come to mean the conscious or subconscious adoption and acceptance of negative feelings and attitudes about homosexuals or homosexuality by gay men and lesbians. The manifestation of these negative feelings are evidenced in fear of discovery, denial, or discomfort with being homosexual, low self-esteem, aggression against other lesbians and gay men as well as exaggerated gay pride or rejection of all heterosexuals.[1] Other concepts such as "biphobia" (Hutchins and Kaahumanu 1991:6) and "transphobia" (Denny 1994) usefully extend our thinking about sexual prejudice.

Definitions and Related Concepts of Heterosexism

As editors, we define *homophobia* as prejudice, discrimination, harassment, or acts of violence against sexual minorities, including lesbians, gay men, bisexuals, and transgendered persons, evidenced in a deep-seated fear or hatred of those who love and sexually desire those of the same sex.

There is a subtle pervasive uneasiness with persons whose sexual identity is nonheterosexual (Herek 1986b, 1995; Jung and Smith 1993; Rothblum and Bond 1996). The exclusion of gay men and lesbians from mainstream media (as outlined in the chapters by Barrett and Nardi), the assumption that heterosexual lifestyles are preferable, or that lesbians and gay men do not marry or have children (as discussed in the Vennard and Hulsebosch/Koerner chapters), the inclusion of homosexuality only in the discussion about HIV/AIDS (Sears 1992b), and the heterosexual-only support services in the schools or the harassment faced by lesbian students (as detailed by Sattel/Keyes/Tupper and Marinoble) illuminate the pervasive influence of heterosexism.

Viewing heterosexism as "one component of the broader and overlapping ideologies of sexuality and gender," Gregory Herek (1990:319) distinguishes between two manifestations. "Cultural heterosexism" is the stigmatization, denial, or denigration of nonheterosexuality in cultural institutions ranging from the church to the courthouse. "Psychological heterosexism" is a person's internalization of this worldview, which erupts into antigay prejudice. Here, we define *heterosexism* as a belief in the superiority of heterosexuals or heterosexuality evidenced in the exclusion, by omission or design, of nonheterosexual persons in polices, procedures, events, or activities. We include in our definition not only lesbians and gay men but other sexual minorities such as bisexuals and transgendered persons as well.

Heterosexism and Homophobia:
Research Constructs and Designs

During the quarter-century since the Stonewall rebellion *homophobia* has evolved from a psychologist's construct to a marcher's chant. There also has been an expansion of research devoted to understanding the attitudes and feelings about homosexuality, the sources for these, their relationship to behaviors, and the likelihood of change. In this section I highlight differing forms of inquiry or research designs that have been used to study these areas; the results of these and other studies are discussed in the following section.

Our understanding of homophobia and its origins has developed from Weinberg's description of it as an irrational and dysfunctional prejudice rooted in a speculative list of five "motives" (religion, repressed envy, fear of being homosexual, threat to values, and existence without vicarious immortality) to Herek's more complex model (1984a, 1984b, 1985, 1986b, 1987) in which homophobia serves four rational functions detailed by Paul Van de Ven in this volume. Measurements, too, have progressed from a simple nine-item Homophobic Scale, developed by Ken Smith (1971) as part of a larger questionnaire on issues of interest to college students, to the construction of scales, with sophisticated tests for reliability and validity, differentiating between attitudes and feelings (MacDonald 1974; MacDonald and Games 1974; Hudson and Ricketts 1980) or between responses to lesbians and gay men (Herek 1988, 1994). During this interim such measures have also been administered to a variety of occupational groups.[2]

What conclusions can we draw from these research designs developed since 1971?[3] While measures have become more refined and our understanding of factors contributing to homophobic beliefs have become more complex, the bulk of studies on homophobia have focused on subjects affiliated with universities (primarily undergraduates from public institutions) who are primarily Euro-American and disproportionately drawn from the middle class or upper middle class. Studies have tended to draw upon an urban population, but with little focus on race and ethnicity. While most researchers have focused on heterosexual respondents, many have not sought to differentiate on the basis of sexual identity. Further, few researchers have acknowledged or designed measurements to gauge differences in response to lesbians and gay men, and fewer have differentiated between heterosexism and homophobia.

Most studies employ some type of experimental or survey design. Although a number of researchers have disentangled attitudes and feelings, there has been little attention to assessing behavioral outcomes. Equally disconcerting is the use or reporting of reliability, validity, and statistical measures and methods, which too often have been flawed. Finally, there have been no studies conducted on the relationship of the attitudes and feelings of heterosexuals or homosexuals toward bisexuals or transgendered persons.

Experimental and Quasi-Experimental Research Studies

In evaluating the effectiveness of various educational interventions such as panel discussions (detailed in the last section of this essay as well as in the Myers/Kardia chapter), some form of experimental design is commonly used.[4] These studies often fuse one or more different "treatment groups" and, generally, a "control group" to assess the impact of an antihomophobia unit.[5]

Some measure(s) of homophobia have been administered before and after experimental treatment. Two common measures used in experimental studies have been the Modified Attitudes Toward Homosexuality (MacDonald and Games 1974), a thirty-item instrument, and the Index of Homophobia (Hudson and Ricketts 1980), a scale of a person's reactions toward homosexual encounters and homosexual persons.[6] These instruments assessed subjects' attitudes toward homosexuality or their feelings toward lesbians and gay men, respectively.

Here we can think of attitudes as a set of cognitive beliefs about homosexuals and homosexuality, whereas feelings may be thought of as deep-rooted emotional reactions to homosexual situations or persons. Examples of attitudinal survey items are "Homosexuality is unnatural"; "Homosexual marriage should be made legal"; and "I would not want homosexuals to live near me." Examples of items that tap respondents' feelings, particularly anxiety, are "I would feel nervous being in a group of homosexuals"; "If I saw two men holding hands in public, I would feel disgusted"; and "I would feel comfortable if I learned that my best friend of my same sex was homosexual."[7]

Recently, others have developed more sophisticated measures. Frequently used is Herek's (1988, 1994) Attitudes Toward Lesbians and Gay Men (ATLGM), a twenty-item rating scale that includes an equal number of statements regarding gay men and lesbians and taps the cognitive dimension (e.g., "Lesbians just can't fit into our society") and the dimension of feeling ("I think male homosexuals are disgusting"). Another promising instrument to measure the affective component of homophobia is a fifteen-adjective checklist developed by a pair of Swedish researchers (Ernulf and Innala 1987; Innala and Ernulf 1992).

While most studies have focused on homophobia, a few have addressed heterosexism or internalized homophobia. For example, in a study of graduate students preparing for the counseling profession, Glenn and

Russell (1986) illustrate heterosexist beliefs through students' evaluation of a fifteen-minute audiotape role play of a counseling interview with a female client whose depression was affecting a "significant relationship" with a partner variously identified as "Doug," "Diane," or "Chris." Here most of the subjects used male pronouns when discussing their client's relationship with "Chris," recommending strategies appropriate for a heterosexual relationship.

Another group of researchers have examined the relationship between levels of internalized homophobia among homosexual Catholic men, some of whom were members of Dignity, an organization of gay Catholics (Wagner et al. 1994). While others have examined the levels of internalized homophobia among gay men (e.g., Frederick 1995), victimized lesbians and gay men (Otis and Skinner 1996), and HIV+ gay men (e.g., Nicholson and Long 1990), this was the first study to examine how religious affiliated groups can reduce internalized homophobia.

Survey Studies

The most common form of empirically based studies on heterosexism and homophobia are survey based.[8] While such studies have sometimes sampled nonstudent adults (e.g., Britton 1990; Dupras 1994; Gallup 1995; Mahaffey and Marcus 1995; Taylor 1982), they have generally focused on undergraduate students.

One of the more interesting survey studies reported questionnaire data on sexual beliefs, attitudes, and experiences among male and female undergraduates vis-à-vis homophobia. Here the researchers (Aguero, Bloch, and Byrne 1984) found that the most negative respondents were those who both expressed negative feelings and the belief that homosexuality was learned.

While data analyses in this form of inquiry tend to be descriptive, some researchers have chosen more sophisticated statistical techniques. Ernulf and Innala (1987), for example, employed factor analysis to compare male and female Swedish undergraduates' attitudes toward homosexuality. This analysis yielded two distinct constructs thought to underlie homophobia: homophobic anger (contempt and disgust toward homosexuals) and homophobic guilt (dread or discomfort of homosexuality). Extending their work to several cross-national populations (Innala and Ernulf 1992), they included a third factor, positive feelings. Also, in a series of four hypothetically linked surveys examining reactions to homosexuals, Gallup (1995) employed regression analysis. Here concerns about contact with children explained much of this negative reaction with parents of children expressing more homophobia than childless parents.

Ethnography and Case Studies

Focusing on individuals and searching for the construction of meanings, some researchers have relied on ethnography or case studies (e.g., Herdt 1987; Sears 1991; Williams 1986). These studies, however, have been limited in focus and scope. There have been no case studies or ethnographies, for example, on the homophobe, although there are several interview-based materials on violent antigay youth (Collins 1992; Weissman 1992).

Researchers using an ethnographic design often have focused on lesbians or gay men or their personal and professional struggles. Most of these studies are student dissertations or theses underscoring the impact that heterosexism and homophobia have upon issues of disclosure and identity development.[9] An exception is Pat Griffin's work (1992) detailing various disclosure strategies employed by lesbian educators while describing the role that the participant researcher can play in "empowering" these professionals.

Other studies have focused on the degree of heterosexual bias or homophobia in texts, including sociology (Phillips 1991), health education (Pollis 1986; Whatley 1992), and educational administration (Sears 1993). While these studies have found some advances in how homosexuality is discussed, textual coverage remains weak and biased.

Unique are empirically based studies complemented by qualitative data.[10] For example, Bleich (1987) analyzed short stories about a conversation with two persons about homosexuality written by first-year college students, Sears (1992a) asked more than one hundred prospective teachers to write short narratives, and Herek (1987) analyzed more than two hundred undergraduate essays to identify various functions served by students' advocacy of antihomosexual attitudes.

Generalizations

Clearly, scholars have become more sophisticated in their theoretical contexts and research designs during the past quarter-century. We need, however, to devote greater attention to relationships among feelings, beliefs, and behaviors, to develop greater precision in both the measures and definitions for heterosexism and homophobia, to seek more representative samples, and to employ a greater variety of research designs—particularly studies tracking persons over extended periods of time.

Despite these areas of needed improvement, findings from these studies warrant three generalizations. First, there are significant relationships among demographic variables (e.g., gender, race, degree of religiosity, age, and geographic residence), personal beliefs and traits (e.g., sexual conservatism, racism and sexism, authoritarianism), and heterosexism/homophobia. Second, homophobic and heterosexist attitudes, feelings, and behaviors are discrete, albeit related, phenomena. Third, heterosexism and homophobia can be reduced through purposive intervention.

In the next two sections, I elaborate on these generalizations.

Components of Heterosexism and Homophobia: General Findings

Demographic Variables and Personality Traits

One of the more extensive areas of research in lesbian and gay studies is on adult attitudes toward homosexuality or toward homosexuals. These studies often report the relationships between attitudes and personality traits such as degree of religiosity, authoritarianism, and gender role or demographic variables like gender, race, age, and geographic residence.

A reasonable generalization based on the research relating to demographic factors is that those harboring negative attitudes about homosexuality are also more likely to reside in the Midwest, the South, or to have grown up in rural areas or in small towns. They, too, are more likely to be male, older, and less well-educated than those expressing more positive attitudes.[11] Most research studies also have demonstrated that adult males often harbor more intense homophobic attitudes or feelings than females, are more concerned about male homosexuality than lesbianism, and are more disturbed by lesbianism than are heterosexual females.[12] While there are ambivalent data regarding racial and ethnic differences in attitudes about homosexuality and toward homosexual persons than others, it is certainly true that being both gay and a person of color results in greater vulnerability to antigay harassment and a more complex set of issues in coming out.[13]

There are also relationships between ideological beliefs, personality traits, and homophobia. People with negative attitudes often hold more conservative religious ideology, more traditional attitudes about gender roles, more negative sexual attitudes or sexual guilt, greater social prejudices, and more likely express authoritarian beliefs than those holding positive attitudes.[14]

These findings, of course, are subject to qualification and should not be used to generalize about specific individuals. For example, while males generally are more homonegative than females,[15] men working as public school counselors express more positive feelings than their female counterparts (Sears 1992a). If one assumes that these counselors hold less traditional gender role attitudes, this finding complements other research that shows traditional gender role attitudes having a more direct relationship on male attitudes toward homosexuality than one's gender (Kerns and Fine 1994; Stark 1991). And, as students move from high school into college, progressing through their university studies, homophobic attitudes lessen (Kurdek 1988; Van de Ven 1994). Further, while African American prospective teachers attending one teacher education program were more likely to express negative attitudes toward homosexuality than Euro-American students, there was no relationship between respondent's race and the feelings he or she expressed toward gay men and lesbians (Sears 1992a). Moreover, despite the strong relationship between religiosity and homophobia, black church attendance was not related to homophobic beliefs, and middle-age African Americans (the civil rights generation) were more liberal than those born into earlier generations (Seltzer 1992).

Attitudes, Feelings, and Behaviors

If we are to intervene effectively to reduce heterosexism and homophobia, then we must recognize the interrelationships between homophobic attitudes, feelings, and behaviors. Few research studies over the past quarter-century have examined all three, although several have looked at varying combinations.

For example, in examining the attitudes and feelings of people in the helping professions toward homosexuality and homosexual persons, a clear heterosexual bias is evident.[16] Similarly, the behavioral component has been studied in relationship to friendship patterns, antigay violence, interpersonal interactions, self-report antigay behaviors, and professional activities. Here those with less negative feelings or attitudes are more likely to have had associations or friendships with gay men or lesbians, although prior associations are not necessarily related to less aggressive behavior toward gay men; males who conform to masculine stereotypes generate more violent homophobic responses than do those gay men who appear effeminate.[17]

Other behavioral measures include nonverbal behavior, same-sex touching, anticipated liking or interaction, social distance, commitment to action, and self-presentation.[18] Research on the impact of heterosexism or homo-phobia in the work setting underscore the complex relationships between feelings, attitudes, and behaviors.

One experimental study, for example, examined the impact of sexual dis-closure where subjects, with various levels of homonegative attitudes, judged and interacted with a co-worker (Kite and Deaux 1986). Here, "intol-erant" male subjects rated their partner more negative and recalled less information about their "homosexual" partner than those expressing greater tolerance. However, even tolerant males demonstrated more negative behav-ior toward their partner when informed of his homosexuality than those with similar scores who were unaware of their partner's sexual identity. Most important, tolerant males who learned of their partner's homosexuality after an initial interaction demonstrated less negative behavior; there was no change in the behavioral patterns for intolerant subjects regardless of when they learned of their partner's sexual orientation.

While persons in positions to evaluate others may claim objectivity, per-sonal bias affects professional judgments.[19] In two other experimental stud-ies subjects asked to evaluate a person's application for either an elementary teaching job (Ellis and Vasseur 1993) or graduate admission into education or fine arts (Jackson and Sullivan 1989) recorded more negative ratings for similarly qualified homosexual applicants. Another finding of the latter study was that emotional responses exerted a more powerful influence on these behaviors than cognitive beliefs. Similarly, Sears (1988, 1992a) found that while most school counselors claimed an ability to set aside personal prejudices and assume a professional relationship with their homosexual clients, many report meager if any supportive professional behavior.

In a related study Sears (1992a) examined how personal feelings and atti-tudes translated into professional activity by asking nearly two hundred prospective teachers for a specific written response to a classroom scenario wherein a discussion about current events turns to AIDS and several homo-phobic comments are made by students. While only a few respondents agreed with the most negative comments, most chose to respond to the stu-dents' negative statements about AIDS, ignoring homophobic comments. Despite the fact that two-thirds of the respondents had indicated (through an earlier segment in the survey) that they would discipline a student for making such derogatory comments, only 6 percent actually did so when pro-vided the opportunity.

Given these research findings, any intervention directed toward overcoming heterosexism and homophobia should be based on twin principles: thoughtful integration of strategies and materials that link attitudes and feelings with behaviors and careful attention to the target audience. To what degree are educational interventions implementing these principles and how effective, in general, are particular strategies?

Effectively Reducing Heterosexism and Homophobia

While we know quite a lot about various persons' attitudes and feelings about homosexuality, there have been few evaluations of the effectiveness of particular strategies (Croteau and Kusek 1992; Stevenson 1988).[20] What are the critical elements related to doing homophobia education? Since there are relatively few studies on the effectiveness of particular educational interventions, it is difficult to specify these with precision. Clearly, however, those involved in homophobia reduction must (1) integrate the intellectual, emotional, and behavioral domains and (2) tailor their interventions to meet various sociocultural backgrounds, addressing specific functions served by the maintenance of homophobic or heterosexist beliefs.

Integrating Cognition, Affect, and Behavior

Seldom do intervention strategies target thought, feeling, and action. While most legal and legislative strategies have focused on the behavioral component and the opponents of "special rights for homosexuals" have employed tactics that exploit the emotional, many educational strategies have focused on the cognitive component (attitudes).

The cognitive component predominates interventions such as speaker panels, guest lectures, videotape presentations, and case study analysis. A common procedure is to couple presentation of information (e.g., facts that challenge stereotypes such as the presumed effeminacy of gay men) with presentation of personal stories by lesbians or gay men.

While studies routinely support the effectiveness of panel presentations to reduce prejudicial attitudes, of greater interest is the differential impact of panel presentations.[21] For example, one study of an interactive panel composed of two gay men and three lesbians resulted only in attitudinal change among women (Green, Dixon, and Gold-Neil 1993). Male participants, including those with prior gay acquaintances, evidenced no change.

Although the effectiveness of such intervention strategies is now taken for granted, the lack of methodological rigor in these empirically based studies is troubling. The variety of panel configurations (ranging from openly gay to nongay speakers) and the range of subject matter (e.g., expert informa-tion, personal coming out stories) makes generalizing across studies diffi-cult. Furthermore, there is often the absence of control group, the use of a preexisting group as a control, or the reliance on a single attitude scale as the measure of outcome. Two noted exceptions are the experimental designs of Reinhardt (1994) and Bateman (1995). Reinhardt studied the impact of a speaker panel intervention on undergraduate self-report measures of homo-phobia that included knowledge, feelings, and behaviors. Here the interven-tion reduced cognitive and affective homophobia but exhibited no effect on behavior. Bateman used a combination of a video, article, and "reason analy-sis," finding them effective in reducing negative attitudes. In this volume Cramer's and Wallick/Townsend's research overcome some of these methodological shortcomings.

Other researchers have examined the creative combination of interven-tion strategies coupled with the use of audiovisual resources, which have been somewhat effective in reducing homophobic attitudes.[22] For example, the combination of extensive reading (accompanied by a list of questions to consider), class viewing of a video produced by a gay youth project, and stu-dent-led small group discussions reduced homophobic attitudes among those male first-year education students who initially reported relatively high negative attitudes (Clift 1988). No significant change, however, was found for women or those already expressing relatively positive attitudes— again underscoring the importance of differential intervention strategies.

In an earlier study by Cerny and Polyson (1984) the use of two seventy-five-minute lectures, two explicit films about the sexual relationships of a lesbian and gay male couple, and a forty-five-minute small group discussion framed by several "structured hypothetical situations" reduced homophobic attitudes among males and females. Another study (Wells 1989) examined the impact of four seventy-five-minute class sessions on sexual orientation within a thirty-session undergraduate course on human sexuality. Using lec-tures, class and small group discussion, a lesbian-gay panel, affirming slide presentations and a film (*Pink Triangles*) as well as explicit films depicting gay and lesbian relationships, students increased in their awareness and acceptance of homosexuality. Attitudinal change among women was greater.

While the preceding studies did not separate out the impact of traditional lecture from the use of audiovisual material, Walters (1994) did find, in two human sexuality courses where one group received lectures on homosexual-ity and homophobia while the other not only heard the lectures but viewed a seventy-minute slide presentation of scenes from film and theater such as *The Children's Hour* and *Kiss of the Spider Woman*, that their combined use was more effective in reducing homophobic attitudes.

Another important factor often neglectd by researchers is the instructor. What impact does the instructor's gender, race, or sexual identity have on changing participants' attitudes, feelings, or behaviors? How do more subtle qualities of an instructor such as authenticity, caring, and empathy or more obvious ones such as knowledge have? Should the instructor disclose his or her sexual identity and, if so, when? While some essayists have pointed to the importance of these qualities and actions, few have examined their impact on homophobia education.[23]

In one study Anderson (1991) found that following a short presentation of factual material to randomly divided groups of 244 undergraduate students the presumed sexual identity of the presenter affected change in homophobic attitudes. Students who were informed that the presenter was homosexual expressed more negative attitudes toward homosexuality.

Presentations generally allow the instructor to distance her- or himself from position or positionality. Instructor disclosure is a classroom barrier that few gay and lesbian educators—even at the college level—have chosen to cross (Sears 1996). Yet, as Bridgewater notes, the impact of "coming out" to persons who already know, respect, and like the person making the disclosure is significant—whereas learning the sexual identity of a person to whom one has only a fleeting or formal relationship, such as panel participants, has less impact. It is here that the essays of Brunner, Cramer, and Roy, included in this volume, offer valuable insight.

Teaching techniques generally fail to move from the psychology of the other to the phenomenology of self. This element, however, is tapped through role-playing, psychodramas, and journal writing.[24] There have been few published studies that have documented their effectiveness. *Overcoming Heterosexism and Homophobia* includes chapters by Mager and Sulek, Brunner, and Russell that provide some documentation.

One documented effective intervention was a case study of an undergraduate seminar on prejudice and conflict that used a pink triangle exercise to facilitate an understanding of the difficulties facing lesbian and gay students (Chesler and Zuniga 1991). Following students' voluntarily wearing a pink triangle for one day, each wrote a two- to three-page paper of their experiences and personal feelings. At the next class, through small and large group discussions, students linked their own fears, anxieties, and personal encounters to larger issues embedded in social prejudice, conformity, conflict management, and social control.

An experimental study (Serdahely and Ziemba 1984) also reported a decrease of homophobic scores among undergraduates enrolled with a median or higher initial score. One unit on homosexuality within a human sexuality course (the control group experiencing no such unit) consisted of reading a chapter on homosexuality, doing two two-person role-playing exercises with each participant assuming the role of a gay person, and participating in a small group discussion that refuted common myths about homosexuals.

Only a few studies, however, have correlated these programs with attitudinal change over extended periods of time.[25] For example, using a three-day workshop for counselor trainees that included lecture, case studies, role plays, videotapes, and small group discussion with lesbian and gay men as co-presenters, Rudolph (1988) found that those who participated were more accepting than their control group counterparts—even after eight weeks had passed. Similarly, using a gay clergy video and a lecture, Goldberg (1982) demonstrated an immediate reduction of negative attitudes, although in this study subjects returned to "normal" levels within five weeks (also see Nevid 1983).

No studies have investigated the impact of educational interventions on behavior. Some studies of educational interventions, however, have demonstrated their effectiveness in modifying participants' behavioral intentions.[26] For example, Patton and Mannison (1994) assessed the degree of change in attitudes toward homosexuality following exposure to lecture, films, readings, and a guest speaker in a semester-long human sexuality course. Subsequent behavioral change was measured by a problem situation of the termination of a gay teacher. Comparing pre- and postquestionnaire responses with open-ended response to problem situations, they found only moderate change in attitudes (one-third remained negative) and no change in feelings. There was, however, a greater shift "towards positive, supportive action on behalf of a gay or lesbian colleague" (Patton and Mannison 1994:193). As educators and researchers, we must emphasize change of behavior rather than the change of attitudes with undocumented behavioral change. While it certainly would be desirable to change the attitudes of homophobic or heterosexist individuals, it is critical that their behavior—be it the acts of a violent homophobe in a darkened alley or of an uninformed heterosexist in a counseling office—change.

We must also pay greater attention to the culture. Race, ethnicity, religion, and occupation largely define our identity, our beliefs, and our status in society. Associations and identities formed on the basis of race and ethnicity, values sanctioned by houses of worship and their representatives, and roles and relationships experienced within our occupation form a bedrock of beliefs about sexuality and sexual diversity.[27] Yet, as Williams notes in this volume, the importance of considering "culture" as a critical factor in developing strategies to overcome heterosexism and homophobia has yet to be fully appreciated. Given the increasingly multicultural composition and focus of public schools and the increasing demand in the private sector ranging from the corporate boardroom to the police squad room for programs on diversity, it is essential that we study and implement those "best practices" found most effective with particular groups. This is not to argue that certain foundational principles apply across work and ethnic cultures or that everyone within a particular group reacts similarly. It is, however, an acknowledgment that the search, development, and implementation of universally applied principles generally ignores that these are themselves products of particular cultures.[28]

In order to develop and implement educational materials, teaching strategies, and programs that reduce homophobic and heterosexist attitudes, feelings, and behaviors, one also must understand the function(s) served by their maintenance and the process of psychological change (Herek 1991, 1995; Ficarrotto 1990). For example, what are the functions served by brandishing homophobic comments in the locker room or by resistance among police officers to gay positive messages? In *Overcoming Heterosexism and Homophobia* several contributors focus on these unique cultures and occupational groups. In the process they highlight effective strategies targeted at the often unarticulated functions served by the maintenance of homonegative attitudes, beliefs, or behaviors.

Some of the chapters in this volume can be understood within the context of Gregory Herek's seminal work. For example, Blumenfeld explicates how change can result from more positive interactions with lesbians and gay persons who share a common Jewish heritage. The Sattel/Keyes/Tupper, Reyes/Yep, and Stewart chapters underscore the importance of peer relationships with significant others in fostering positive attitudes among coaches, Asian Americans, and police officers. McNaught, Emert/Milburn, and Hulsebosch/Koerner explicate how to disassociate personal beliefs (and the importance some people hold in expressing these in civil contexts) from professional behaviors in the corporation, counselor's office, or elementary

school. And the contributions of Crew and Nugent illustrate how to overcome negative attitudes that insulate clergy from personal insecurities.

As homophobia educators we need to borrow from the work, experience,
and knowledge of those involved in anti-oppression work and sexuality education.[29] The acknowledgment that these various areas overlap—politically,
personally, and pedagogically—is central to anti-oppression work. We must
also complement the well-designed sexuality education programs, workshops, and courses that address sexual orientation as a substantive area,
effectively reduce sexual guilt and conservatism, and enhance comfort levels
in discussing sexuality. Collaboration with allied groups as well as closer
working relationships between academics and activists (evidenced in the
newly formed policy research centers of the National Gay and Lesbian Task
Force and the Institute for Gay and Lesbian Strategic Studies) can maximize
our efforts and impact.

During the past twenty-five years researchers, educators, and activists
have made substantive progress. As researchers have developed more refined
instruments and modes of analyses, educators have become more aware of
the importance of focusing on the particular needs of their target audience
and activists have become more effective in translating antidiscrimination
and antiharassment practices into public policy. *Overcoming Heterosexism
and Homophobia* builds upon these experiences while raising new questions,
documenting effective interventions, and highlighting additional areas for
future research and practice.

NOTES

1. See, for example, Burns, "Internalized Homophobia"; Frederick, "Intern-
alized Homophobia, Gender Roles"; Lehne, "Homophobia Among Men";
Malyon, "Psychotherapeutic Implications"; Margolies, Becker, and Jackson-
Brewer, "Internalized Homophobia"; Nungesser, *Homosexual Acts, Actors, and
Identities*; and Shidlo, "Internalized Homophobia."

2. Educators have been studied by Crumpacker and Vander Haegen,
"Pedagogy and Prejudice"; and Sears, "Educators, Homosexuality, and
Homosexual Students"; social workers by Smoot, "Homophobia Among College
Students"; Tate, "Homophobia Among Rural and Urban Social Work Students";
and Weiner, "Racist, Sexist, and Homophobic Attitudes"; counselors by
Rudolph, "Counselors' Attitudes Toward Homosexuality"; and Sears, "Educa-
tors, Homosexuality, and Homosexual Students"; nurses and physicians by
Douglas, Kalman, and Kalman, "Homophobia Among Physcans and Nurses";
Larkin, "Attitudes of Female Registered Nurses"; Matthews, Booth, Turner, and

Kessler, "Physicans' Attitudes Toward Homosexuality"; Scherer, Wu, and Haughey, "AIDS and Homophobia Among Nurses"; Smith, "Homophobia and Attitudes Toward Gay Men"; mental health workers by DeCrescenzo, "Homophobia"; and students preparing for these and other professions by Dressler, "Survey of School Principals"; Kelly et al., "Medical Students' Attitudes"; Maddux, "The Homophobic Attitudes"; and Tate, "Homophobia Among Rural and Urban Social Work Students."

3. My observations are based on the following analyses of the research literature. A content analysis of major articles published in counseling psychology journals between 1978 and 1989 (Buhrke, Ben-Ezra, Hurley, and Ruprecht, "Content Analysis and Methodological Critique"); two meta-analyses, one of research articles examining sex differences in attitudes about homosexuality (Kite, "Sex Differences in Attitudes Toward Homosexuals") and another of studies using various homophobia instruments (Schwanberg, "Attitudes Toward Gay Men and Lesbian Women"); a critical analyses of the conceptual, definitional, and normative limitations of the homophobia construct (O'Donohue and Caselles, "Homophobia"); and my computerized literature search using the terms *homophobia, heterosexism, attitudes, homosexuals, bisexuals,* and *transgender,* conducted on five data bases (Sociological Abstracts, Dissertation Abstract, Pscyhological Abstracts, Education Abstracts, and ERIC), as well as a review of bibliographies of major research studies.

4. Experimental studies, if properly designed, allow for questions of causality to be addressed. Distinguishing features of this research design include random assignment of subjects and/or treatment, the use of a control group, and hypotheses and data analyses techniques specified before implementing the design.

5. Examples of such studies include exposing low and high "homonegative" males to slides of landscapes and various sexual activities (Shields and Harriman, "Fear of Male Homosexuality"); subject selection of interview questions based on a hypothetical one-page résumé of a gay or nongay applicant to a sixth-grade teaching position (Ellis and Vasseur, "Prior Interpersonal Contact"); and subjects' initial therapeutic assessments based on a detailed case history varied by the client's gender and sexual identity (Garfinkle and Morin, "Psychologists' Attitudes"). Other examples of experimental studies are Cerny and Polyson, "Changing Homonegative Attitudes"; Cramer, this volume; Goldberg, "Attitude Change Among College Students"; Pagtolun-An and Clair, "An Experimental Study"; Rudolph, "The Effects of a Multimodal Seminar"; Serdahely and Ziemba, "Changing Homophobic Attitudes"; Van de Ven, this volume; Wells, "Teaching About Gay and Lesbian Sexual and Affectional Orientation."

6. See, for example, Krulewitz and Nash, "Effects of Sex Role Attitudes"; Shields and Harriman, "Fear of Male Homosexuality"; Pagtolun-An and Clair, "An Experimental Study"; Wells, "Teaching About Gay and Lesbian Sexual and Affectional Orientation"; Duncan, "Effects on Homophobia"; Greendlinger, "Authoritarianism."

7. According to the authors of the Index of Homophobia scale (Hudson and Ricketts, "A Strategy for the Measurement of Homophobia," p. 360), scores of less than twenty-five evidence "high grade non-homophobics," and those who score between twenty-five and fifty are considered "low grade non-homophobics." Persons whose scores lie between fifty and seventy-five are regarded as "low grade homophobics," and "high grade homophobics" score above seventy-five. The Modified Attitudes Toward Homosexuality scale (Price, "High School Students' Attitudes Toward Homosexuality") uses a nine-point Likert-type format, with higher scores indicating more negative attitudes (MacDonald et al., "Attitudes Toward Homosexuality"; Sobel, "Adolescent Attitudes Toward Homosexuality"). For more information regarding the reliability and validity of these instruments, as well as the specific wording of each instrument, see Sears, "Attitudes, Experiences, and Feelings of Guidance Counselors."

8. Researchers have used a variety of instruments to assess homophobia, including Smith's ("Homophobia"; Hellman et al., "Childhood Sexual Identity") Homophobia Scale (e.g., Lumby, "Homophobia"), Hudson and Ricketts's ("A Strategy for the Measurement of Homophobia") Index of Attitudes Toward Homosexuals Scale (e.g., Lance, "The Effects of Interaction with Gay Persons"; Ficarrotto, "Racism, Sexism, and Erotophobia"; Pain and Disney, "Testing the Reliability"; Tate, "Homophobia Among Rural and Urban Social Work Students"), the Heterosexual Attitudes Toward Homosexuality Scale (Larsen, Reed, and Hoffman, "Attitudes of Heterosexuals Toward Homosexuality") found in these authors and others' work (e.g., Whitley, "The Relationship of Sex-Role Orientation"), and Herek's ("Attitudes Toward Lesbians and Gay Men"; "Assessing Heterosexuals' Attitudes") Attitudes Toward Gays and Lesbians (e.g., Britton, "Homophobia and Homosociality"; Harry, "Sports Ideology"; Simon, "Some Correlates"), and Nungesser's (1983) Homosexuality Attitudes Inventory (e.g., Frederick, "Internalized Homophobia, Gender Roles"; Shidlo, "Internalized Homophobia").

9. See, for example: Clark, "Cohabiting the Classroom Closet"; Doyle, "A Naturalistic Study"; Fischer, "A Study of Educators' Attitudes Toward Homosexuality"; Fogarty, "Passing as Straight"; Scala, "Heterosexism in the Classroom"; Smith, "An Ethnographic Study"; Talburt, "Troubling Lesbian Identities"; White, "Portrait of an Artist"; and Woods, "The Contextual Realities."

10. Some researchers have gleaned data from brief interviews (D'Augelli and Rose, "Homophobia in a University Community"; Sears, "Educators, Homosexuality, and Homosexual Students"), nonverbal cues (Cuenot and Fugita, "Perceived Homosexuality"), short stories (Bleich, "Homophobia and Sexism"), and brief written or oral reactions to vignettes (Cramer, this volume; Geasler et al., "A Qualitative Study"; LaSalle, "Exploring Campus Intolerance"; Luhrs, Crawford, and Goldberg, "The Presence of the Defensive Function"; Patton and Mannison, "Investigating Attitudes Toward Sexuality"; Weiner, "Racist, Sexist, and Homophobic Attitudes").

11. Britton, "Homophobia and Homosociality"; Bruce et al., "Students' Atti-

tudes"; Herek, "Beyond 'Homophobia' "; Herek and Glunt, "Interpersonal Contact"; Roese et al., "Same-Sex Touching Behavior"; Seltzer, "The Social Location."

12. Gallup, "Have Attitudes?"; Herek, "Heterosexuals' Attitudes"; Kite, "Sex Differences in Attitudes Toward Homosexuals"; Pettinger, "A Survey"; Reiter, "Developmental Origins"; Schatman, "The Prediction of Homophobia Attitudes"; and Wells, "Heterosexual University Students' Perceptions." More equivocal data regarding the relationship between gender and attitudes toward homosexuality is found in the meta-analysis of Oliver and Hyde, "Gender Differences in Sexuality." Similarly, Whitley ("The Relationship of Sex-Role Orientation," "Sex Differences in Heterosexuals' Attitudes") has found heterosexual men reporting more positive attitudes toward lesbianism than women.

13. See, for example, Alston, "Attitudes Toward Extramarital and Homosexual Relations"; Baker, "A Survey of Attitudes"; Comstock, "Victims of Anti-Gay/Lesbian Violence"; Ernst, Grancis, Nevels, and Lemeh, "Condemnation of Homosexuality"; Gutierrez and Dworkin, "Black Gay Men"; Herek and Capitanio, "Black Heterosexuals' Attitudes"; Icard, "Black Gay Men"; Irwin and Thompson, "Acceptance of the Rights of Homosexuals"; Loiacano, "Gay Identity Issues"; Mays, Cochran, and Rhue, "The Impact of Perceived Discrimination"; Marsiglio, "Attitudes Toward Homosexual Activity"; Nyberg and Alston, "Analysis of Public Attitudes"; Sears, "Educators, Homosexuality, and Homosexual Students," "Black-Gay or Gay-Black?"; and Seltzer, "The Social Location of Those Holding Antihomosexual Attitudes." The assertion, however, that African Americans, for example, tend to be more homophobic than Euro-Americans is based largely on anecdotal generalizations (e.g., Clarke, "The Failure to Transform"; Lorde, *Sister Outsider*; Gomez and Smith, "Taking the Home Out of Homophobia"; Philip, "Gay Issues") and meager empirical data often drawn from studies with mixed results (e.g., Marsiglio, "Attitudes Toward Homosexual Activity"; Seltzer and Smith, "Race and Ideology"; Seltzer, "The Social Location"). My own research is ambivalent on this issue; I am more inclined to agree with Icard, "Black Gay Men," p. 24, who concludes: "None of the individuals interviewed stated that he or she thought the Black community as a whole was less accepting of gay men and lesbian women than the White community was as a whole." This position has received additional empirical support in a recent national probability telephone survey of nearly four hundred African American heterosexual adults. Here, despite the widespread negative attitudes toward homosexuality among black heterosexuals (more among men than women), these attitudes appears no more negative than those found among whites. Of particular interest for those seeking to reduce homophobia was that, in contrast to studies among white heterosexuals, personal contact with a gay man or lesbian was not a particularly powerful predictor of homophobia among African Americans.

14. Researchers reporting one or more relationships cited here are Agnew et al., "Proximal and Distal Predictors"; Aguero, Bloch, and Byrne, "The Relationships Among Sexual Beliefs"; Black and Stevenson, "The Relationship of Self-

Reported Sex-Role Characteristics"; Britton, "Homophobia and Homosociality"; Bhugra, "Homophobia"; Ficarrotto, "Racism, Sexism, and Erotophobia"; Greendlinger, "Authoritarianism"; Herek, "On Heterosexual Masculinity," "Heterosexuals' Attitudes"; Herek and Glunt, "Interpersonal Contact"; Kunkel and Temple, "Attitudes Toward AIDS and Homosexuals"; Levant et al., "The Male Role"; Marsiglio, "Attitudes Toward Homosexual Activity"; Newman, "Including Curriculum Content"; Patel, Long, McCammon, and Wuensch, "Personality and Emotional Correlates"; Seltzer, "The Social Location of Those Holding Antihomosexual Attitudes"; Stark, "Traditional Gender Role Beliefs"; and VanderStoep and Green, "Religiosity and Homonegativism." In one study that underscores the power and potential of educational interventions designed to reduce homophobia in persons' proximal attitudes, feelings, and behaviors using advanced statistical techniques, the attitudes of nearly three hundred undergraduates toward homosexuals were examined in light of both "distal family" (e.g., social class) and "distal individual" (e.g., dogmatism) variables vis-à-vis proximal individual (e.g., attitudes toward women) and proximal individual-situational (e.g., friendship with gays, attitudes toward other races) factors. In this study researchers found that the proximal factors accounted for the major portion of variance in predicted homophobia whereas those more distal variables contributed little additional variance to an individual's level of homophobia (Agnew et al., "Proximal and Distal Predictors").

15. Problems in wording of the questions confounds this generalization (Whitley, "Sex Differences in Heterosexuals' Attitudes") as does the methodological entanglement between gender and gender role (Kerns and Fine, "The Relation Between Gender and Negative Attitudes").

16. See, for example, Casas, Brady, and Poterotto, "Sexual Preference Biases in Counseling"; Davison and Wilson, "Attitudes of Behavior Therapists Toward Homosexuality"; DeCrescenzo, "Homophobia"; Douglas, Kalman, and Kalman, "Homophobia Among Physicans and Nurses"; Friedman, "An Examination of Attitudes"; Garfinkle and Morin, "Psychologists' Attitudes"; Gartrell, Kraemer, and Brodie, "Psychiatrists' Attitudes Toward Female Homosexuality"; Hochstein, "Pastoral Counselors"; Larkin, "Attitudes of Female Registered Nurses"; McQuoid, "Attitudes Toward Homosexuality"; Pauly and Goldstein, "Physician's Attitudes in Treating Male Homosexuals"; Sears, "Educators, Homosexuality, and Homosexual Students"; Wisniewski and Toomey, "Are Social Workers Homophobic?" One exception is a survey of random sample New York public school psychologists that found all expressing positive or neutral attitudes and only one-quarter categorized as homophobic (Pettinger, "A Survey").

17. Agnew et al., "Proximal and Distal Predictors"; Anderson, "The Effects of a Workshop"; Bateman, "A Treatment Strategy"; Comstock, *Violence*; D'Augelli and Rose, "Homophobia in a University Community"; Ellis and Vasseur, "Prior Interpersonal Contact"; Gentry, "Social Distance," "Development of Scales"; Herek and Glunt, "Interpersonaal Contact"; Maddux, "The Homophobic Attitudes"; Patel, Long, McCammon, and Wuensch, "Personality and Emotional

Correlates"; San Miguel and Millham, "The Role of Cognitive and Situational Variables"; Schneider and Lewis, "The Straight Story"; Weiner, "Racist, Sexist, and Homophobic Attitudes"; and Wells, "Heterosexual University Students' Perceptions."

18. Studies using one or more of these measures are Cuenot and Fugita, "Perceived Homosexuality"; Gross et al., "Disclosure of Sexual Orientation"; Gurwitz and Marcus, "Effects of Anticipated Interaction"; Kite and Deaux, "Attitudes Toward Homosexuality"; Garfinkle and Morin, "Psychologists' Attitudes"; Roese et al., "Same-Sex Touching Behavior"; Shaw, Borough, and Fink, "Perceived Sexual Orientation"; Van de Ven, "Comparisons Among Homophobic Reactions." There have also been experimental field studies examining the prevalence of homophobic behavior in the marketplace, ranging from differential treatment by store clerks for gay and straight shoppers (Walters and Curran, "Excuse Me, Sir?") to hotel reservationists (Jones, "Discrimination Against Same-Sex Couples").

19. See, for example, Ellis and Vasseur, "Prior Interpersonal Contact"; Jackson and Sullivan, "Cognition and Affect"; Lilling and Friedman, "Bias Toward Gay Patients"; Rudolph, "Effects of a Workshop"; and Sears, "Attitudes, Experiences, and Feelings of Guidance Counselors," "Educators, Homosexuality, and Homosexual Students."

20. Based on a review of five data bases (Sociological Abstracts, Dissertation Abstracts, Psychological Abstracts, Education Abstracts, and ERIC) since 1971, using delimitors of *homophobia, attitude change, homosexuality, heterosexism,* and *pedagogy* as well as a review of bibliographies of major research studies.

21. See, for example, Green, Dixon, and Gold-Neil, "The Effects of a Gay/Lesbian Panel Discussion"; Lance, "The Effects of Interaction with Gay Persons," "Changes in Homophobic Views"; Morin, "Educational Programs." In one study, Lance, "Changes in Homophobic Views," administered the Hudson and Ricketts Scale to undergraduate students enrolled in a human sexuality class. The group exposed to a three-hour panel discussion involving four lesbians and four gay men expressed significantly less discomfort with homosexuals than the group that had yet to experience the panel discussion.

22. See, for example, Goldberg, "Attitude Change Among College Students"; Greenberg, "A Study of Personality Change"; and Wells, "Teaching About Gay and Lesbian Sexual and Affectional Orientation," "What Makes a Difference?."

23. See, for example, Wells, "Teaching About Gay and Lesbian Sexual and Affectional Orientation"; and Wright, "Lesbian Instructor Comes Out."

24. Crumpacker and Vander-Haegen, "Pedagogy and Prejudice"; Lankewish, "Breaking the Silence"; Miller, "Fault Lines in the Contact Zone"; Phifer, "Homophobia"; Regan, "Type Normal"; and Warshauer, "Rethinking Teacher Authority."

25. Anderson "The Effects of a Workshop"; Anderson, "The Effect of Sex Educational Media Format"; Cerny and Polyson, "Changing Homonegative Attitudes"; Goldberg, "Attitude Change Among College Students"; Rudolph, "The

Effects of a Multimodal Seminar," "Effects of a Workshop"; and Serdahely and Ziemba, "Changing Homophobic Attitudes."

26. See, for example, Patton and Mannison, "Investigating Attitudes Toward Sexuality; Sears, "Educators, Homosexuality, and Homosexual Students"; and Van de Ven, "Comparisons Among Homophobic Reactions."

27. While, as Williams notes, there have been substantial anthropological studies of sexual constructions, little empirical work examining the interplay between culture and homophobia has been done (e.g., Aki, "Attitudes Toward Homosexuality"; Whitam, "Culturally Invariable Properties"; Whitam and Zent, "A Cross-Cultural Assessment."

28. Stage theory is an example of the problem of such a universalist outlook evident in the stages of moral development articulated by Kohlberg, *The Philosophy of Moral Development*, and challenged by Gilligan, *In a Different Voice*, as gender-biased or stages of sexual identity developed by Cass, "Homosexual Identity," "Homosexual Identity Formation"; and Troiden, "The Formation of Homosexual Identities"; and challenged by Rust, "Coming Out"; Kahn, "Factors Affecting the Coming Out Process"; and Monteiro and Fuqua, "African American Gay Youth," as not applicable to lesbians or persons of color.

29. Bernard and Schwartz, "Impact of a Human Sexuality Program"; Cohen et al., "Assessing the Impact"; Dearth and Casswell, "Comparing Attitudes"; Kirby, "The Effects of a School Sex Education Program"; Sears, *Sexuality and the Curriculum*; Story, "A Longitudinal Study"; and Taylor, "A Discriminant Analysis Approach."

REFERENCES

Agnew, C. R., V. D. Thompson, V. A. Smith, R. H. Gramzow, and D. P. Currey. 1993. "Proximal and Distal Predictors of Homophobia: Framing the Multivariate Roots of Outgroup Rejection." *Journal of Applied Social Psychology* 23(24):2013–42.

Aguero, J., L. Bloch, and D. Byrne. 1984. "The Relationships Among Sexual Beliefs, Attitudes, Experience, and Homophobia." *Journal of Homosexuality* 10(1/2):95–107.

Aki, S. 1995. "Attitudes Toward Homosexuality in Hawai'i (Ethnicity)." Ph.D. diss., State University of New York, Buffalo. Dissertation Abstracts International, 56(10):4018A.

Alston, J. 1974. "Attitudes Toward Extramarital and Homosexual Relations." *Journal of the Scientific Study of Religion* 13:479–81.

Anderson, C. 1981. "The Effects of a Workshop on Attitudes of Female Nursing Students Toward Male Homosexuality." *Journal of Homosexuality* 7:57–69.

Anderson, M. 1991. "The Effect of Sex Educational Media Format and the Sexual Orientation of the Presenter on Attitudes Toward Homosexuality." Master's thesis, Governors State University.

Baker, D. 1980. "A Survey of Attitudes and Knowledge About Homosexuality

Among Secondary School Teachers in Training." Ph.D. diss., Southern Methodist University, Dallas, Texas.

Bateman, J. 1995. "A Treatment Strategy for Changing Preservice Teachers' Attitudes Toward Homosexuality." Ph.D. diss., Indiana University. Dissertation Abstracts International, 56(8):4637B.

Bernard, H., and A. Schwartz. 1977. "Impact of a Human Sexuality Program on Sex-Related Knowledge, Attitudes, Behaviors, and Guilt on College Undergraduates." *Journal of American College Health* 25:182–85.

Bhugra, D. 1987. "Homophobia: A Review of the Literature." *Sexual and Marital Therapy* 2(2):169–77.

Black, K., and M. Stevenson. 1984. "The Relationship of Self-Reported Sex-Role Characteristics and Attitudes Toward Homosexuality." *Journal of Homosexuality* 10(1/2):83–93.

Bleich, J. 1987. "Homophobia and Sexism as Popular Values." *Feminist Teacher* 4(2/3):21–28.

Britton, D. 1990. "Homophobia and Homosociality: An Analysis of Boundary Maintenance." *Sociological Quarterly,* 31(3):423–39.

Bruce, K., J. Shrumm, C. Trefethen, and L. Slovik. 1990. "Students' Attitudes About AIDS, Homosexuality, and Condoms." *AIDS Education and Prevention* 2:220–34

Buhrke, R. A., L. A. Ben-Ezra, M. E. Hurley, and L. J. Ruprecht. 1992. "Content Analysis and Methodological Critique of Articles Concerning Lesbian and Gay Male Issues in Counseling Journals." *Journal of Counseling Psychology* 39(1):91–99.

Burns, B. 1995. "Internalized Homophobia, Self-Esteem, and the Mothering Choice in Lesbians." Ph.D. diss., Georgia State University, Atlanta. Dissertation Abstracts International, 56(12):7078B.

Casas, J., S. Brady, and J. Ponterotto. 1983. "Sexual Preference Biases in Counseling: An Information-Processing Approach." *Journal of Counseling Psychology* 30(2):139–45.

Cass, V. 1984a. "Homosexual Identity: A Concept in Need of Definition." *Journal of Homosexuality* 9(2/3):105–26.

—— 1984b. "Homosexual Identity Formation: Testing a Theoretical Model." *Journal of Sex Research* 20(2):143–67.

Cerny, J., and J. Polyson. 1984. "Changing Homonegative Attitudes." *Journal of Social and Clinical Psychology* 2:366–71.

Chesler, M. A., and X. Zuniga, 1991. "Dealing with Prejudice and Conflict in the Classroom: The Pink Triangle Exercise." *Teaching Sociology* (April) 19:173–81.

Clark, D. 1996. "Cohabiting the Classroom Closet." Paper presented at the Annual Meeting of the American Research Association, New York, April.

Clarke, C. 1983. "The Failure to Transform: Homophobia in the Black Community." In B. Smith, ed., *Home Girls: A Black Feminist Anthology,* pp. 197–208. New York: Kitchen Table/Women of Color.

Clift, S. 1988. "Lesbian and Gay Issues in Education: A Study of the Attitudes of First-Year Students in a College of Higher Education." *British Educational Research Journal* 14(1):31–50.

Cohen, G., C. Byrne, J. Hay, M. Schmuck. 1994. "Assessing the Impact of an Interdisciplinary Workshop in Human Sexuality." *Journal of Sex Education and Therapy* 20(1):56–68.

Collins, M. 1992. "The Gay Bashers." In G. Herek and K. Berrill, eds., *Hate Crimes: Confronting Violence Against Lesbians and Gay Men,* pp. 191–200. Newbury Park, Cal.: Sage.

Comstock, G. 1989. "Victims of Anti-Gay/Lesbian Violence." *Journal of Interpersonal Violence* 4:101–6.

—— *Violence Against Lesbians and Gay Men.* New York: Columbia University Press.

Croteau, J., and M. Kusek. 1992. "Gay and Lesbian Speaker Panels: Implementation and Research." *Journal of Counseling and Development* 70(3): 396–401.

Crumpacker, L., and E. Vander Haegen. 1987. "Pedagogy and Prejudice: Strategies for Confronting Homophobia in the Classroom." *Women's Studies Quarterly* 15(3/4):65–73.

Cuenot, R., and S. Fugita. 1982. "Perceived Homosexuality: Measuring Heterosexual Attitudinal and Noverbal Reactions." *Personality and Social Psychology Bulletin* 8:100–6.

D'Augelli, A., and M. Rose. 1990. "Homophobia in a University Community: Attitudes and Experiences of Heterosexual Freshman." *Journal of College Student Development* 31(6):484–91.

Davison, G., and G. Wilson. 1973. "Attitudes of Behavior Therapists Toward Homosexuality." *Behavior Therapy* 4(5):686–96.

DeCrescenzo, T. 1983–1984. "Homophobia: A Study of the Attitudes of Mental Health Professionals Toward Homosexuality." *Journal of Social Work and Human Sexuality* 2(2/3):115–36.

Dearth, P., and C. Cassell. 1976. "Comparing Attitudes of Male and Female University Students Before and After a Semester Course on Human Sexuality." *Journal of School Health* 46:593–98.

Denny, D. 1994. "You're Strange and We're Wonderful: The Gay and Lesbian Transgender Communities." In J. Sears, ed., *Bound by Diversity,* pp. 47–53. Columbia, S.C.: Sebastian.

Douglas, C., C. Kalman, and T. Kalman. 1985. "Homophobia Among Physicans and Nurses: An Empirical Study." *Hospital and Community Psychiatry* 36(12):1309–11.

Doyle, S. 1995. "A Naturalistic Study of Four Male Homosexual Teachers in Public Schools in the South." Ph.D. diss., Vanderbilt University.

Dressler, J. 1985. "Survey of School Principals Regarding Alleged Homosexual Teachers in the Classroom: How Likely (Really) Is Discharge?" *University of Dayton Law Review* 10(3):599–620.

Duncan, D. 1988. "Effects on Homophobia of Viewing a Gay-Themed Film." *Psychological Reports* 63(1):46.

Dupras, A. 1994. "Internalized Homophobia and Psychosexual Adjustment Among Gay Men." *Psychological Reports* 75(1):23–28.

Ellis, A., and R. Vasseur. 1993. "Prior Interpersonal Contact with and Attitudes Toward Gays and Lesbians in an Interviewing Contexts." *Journal of Homosexuality* 25(4):31–45.

Ernst, F., R. Grancis, H. Nevels, and C. Lemeh. 1991. "Condemnation of Homosexuality in the Black Community: A Gender-Specific Phenomenon?" *Archives of Sexual Behavior* 20(6):579–85.

Ernulf, K., and S. Innala. 1987. "The Relationship Between Affective and Cognitive Components of Homophobic Reaction." *Archives of Sexual Behavior* 16(6):501–9.

Ficarrotto, T. 1990. "Racism, Sexism, and Erotophobia: Attitudes of Heterosexuals Toward Homosexuals." *Journal of Homosexuality* 19(1):111–16.

Fischer, T. 1982. "A Study of Educators' Attitudes Toward Homosexuality." Ph.D. diss., University of Virginia. Dissertation Abstracts International, 43(10): 3294A.

Fogarty, E. 1980. "Passing as Straight: A Phenomenological Analysis of the Experience of the Lesbian Who Is Professionally Employed." Ph.D. diss., University of Pittsburgh, Pittsburgh. Dissertation Abstracts International, 41(6):2384B.

Frederick, R. 1995. "Internalized Homophobia, Gender Roles, Self-Esteem and Fear of Intimacy in Gay Men. Ph.D. diss., Fairleigh Dickinson University. Dissertation Abstracts International 56(9):5169B.

Friedman, L. 1995. "An Examination of Attitudes Toward Gay Men and Lesbians Among Louisian Licensed Professional Counselors." Ph.D. diss., New Orleans. Dissertation Abstracts International 5610):3837A.

Gallup, G. 1995. "Have Attitudes Toward Homosexuals Been Shaped by Natural Selection?" *Ethology and Sociobiology* 16(1):53–70.

Garfinkle, E., and S. Morin. 1978. "Psychologists' Attitudes Toward Homosexual Psychotherapy Clients." *Journal of Social Issues* 34(3):101–12.

Gartrell, N., H. Kraemer, and H. Brodie. 1974. "Psychiatrists' Attitudes Toward Female Homosexuality." *Journal of Nervous and Mental Disease* 159:141–44.

Geasler, M., J. Croteau, C. Heineman; and C. Edlund. 1995. "A Qualitative Study of Students' Expression of Change After Attending Panel Presentation by Lesbian, Gay, and Bisexual Speakers." *Journal of Colleges Student Development* 36(5):483–92.

Gentry, C. 1986a. "Social Distance Regarding Male and Female Homosexuals." *Journal of Social Psychology* 127(2):199–208.

—— 1986b. "Development of Scales Measuring Social Distance Toward Male and Female Homosexuals." *Journal of Homosexuality* 13(1):75–82.

Gilligan, C. 1982. *In a Different Voice.* Cambridge: Harvard University Press.

Glenn, A., and R. Russell. 1986. "Heterosexual Bias Among Counselor Trainees." *Counselor Education and Supervision* 25(3):222–29.

Goldberg, R. 1982. "Attitude Change Among College Students Toward Homosexuality." *Journal of American College Health* 30(6):260–68.

Gomez, J., and B. Smith. 1990. "Taking the Home Out of Homophobia." *Out/Look* 2(4):32–37.

Green, S., P. Dixon, and V. Gold-Neil. 1993. "The Effects of a Gay/Lesbian Panel Discussion on College Student Attitudes Toward Gay Men, Lesbians, and Persons with AIDS (PWAS). *Journal of Sex Education and Therapy* 19(1): 47–63.

Greenberg, J. 1975. "A Study of Personality Change Associated with the Conducting of a High School Unit on Homosexuality." *Journal of School Health* 45:394–98.

Greendlinger, V. 1985. "Authoritarianism as a Predictor of Response to Heterosexual and Homosexual Erotica." *High School Journal* 68(3):183–86.

Griffin, P. 1992. "From Hiding Out to Coming Out: Empowering Lesbian and Gay Educators." In K. Harbeck, ed., *Homosexuality and Education*, pp. 167–96. New York: Haworth.

Gross, A., S. Green, J. Storck, and J. Vanyur. 1980. "Disclosure of Sexual Orientation and Impressions of Male and Female Homosexuals." *Personality and Social Pscyhology Bulletin* 6:307–14.

Gutierrez, F., and S. Dworkin. 1992. "Gay, Lesbian, and African American: Managing the Intergration of Identities." In F. Gutierrez and S. Dworkin, eds., *Counseling Gay Men and Lesbians*, pp. 141–56. Alexandria, Va.: American Association for Counseling and Development.

Gurwitz, S., and M. Marcus. 1978. "Effects of Anticipated Interaction, Sex, and Homosexual Stereotypes on First Impressions." *Journal of Applied Social Psychology* 8:47–56.

Harry, J. 1995. "Sports Ideology, Attitudes Toward Women, and Antihomosexual Attitudes." *Sex Roles* 32(1/2):109–16.

Hellman, R., R. Green, J. Gray, and K. Williams, 1981. "Childhood Sexual Identity, Childhood Religiosity, and 'Homophobia' as Influences in the Development of Transsexualism, Homosexuality, and Heterosexuality." *Archives of General Psychiatry* 38(8):910–15.

Herdt, G. 1987. *The Sambia: Ritual and Gender in New Guinea.* New York: Holt, Rinehart and Winston.

Herek, G. M. 1984a. "Beyond 'Homophobia': A Social Psychological Perspective on Attitudes Toward Lesbians and Gay Men." *Journal of Homosexuality* 10(1/2):1–18.

—— 1984b. "Attitudes Toward Lesbians and Gay Men: A Factor-Analytic Study." *Journal of Homosexuality* 10(1/2):39–51.

——1985. "Can Functions Be Measured? A New Perspective on Attitudes Toward Lesbians and Gay Men." *Journal of Homosexuality* 10(1/2):1–21.

—— 1986a. "On Heterosexual Masculinity: Some Physical Consequences of the Social Construction of Gender and Sexuality." *American Behavioral Scientist* 29(5):563–77.

—— 1986b. "The Instrumentality of Attitudes: Toward a Neofunctional Theory." *Journal of Social Issues* 42(2):99–114.

—— 1987. "Can Functions Be Measured? A New Perspective on the Functional Approach to Attitudes." *Social Psychology Quarterly* 50(4):285–303.

—— 1988. "Heterosexuals' Attitudes Toward Lesbians and Gay Men: Correlates and Gender Difference." *Journal of Sex Research* 25(4):451–77.

—— 1990. "The Context of Anti-Gay Violence: Notes on Cultural and Psychological Heterosexism." *Journal of Interpersonal Violence* 5(3):316–33.

—— 1991. "Stigma, Prejudice, and Violence Against Lesbians and Gay Men." In J. Gonsiorek and J. Weinrich, eds., *Homosexuality: Research Implications for Public Policy*, pp. 60–80. Newbury Park, Cal.: Sage.

—— 1994. "Assessing Heterosexuals' Attitudes Toward Lesbians and Gay Men: A Review of Empirical Research with the ATLG Scale." In B. Greene and G. Herek, eds., *Lesbian and Gay Psychology*, pp. 206–28. Thousand Oaks, Cal.: Sage.

—— 1995. "Psychological Heterosexism in the United States. In A. D'Augelli and C. Patterson, eds., *Lesbian, Gay, and Bisexual Identities Over the Lifespan*, pp. 321–46. New York: Oxford University Press.

Herek, G. M., and J. P. Capitanio. 1995. "Black Heterosexuals' Attitudes Toward Lesbians and Gay Men in the United States." *Journal of Sex Research* 32(2): 95–105.

Herek, G. M., and Glunt, E. 1993. "Interpersonal Contact and Heterosexuals' Attitudes Toward Gay Men." *Journal of Sex Research* 30(3):239–44.

Hochstein, L. 1986. "Pastoral Counselors: Their Attitudes Toward Gay and Lesbian Clients." *Journal of Pastoral Care* 40(2):158–65.

Hudson, W., and W. Ricketts. 1980. "A Strategy for the Measurement of Homophobia." *Journal of Homosexuality* 5(4):357–72.

Hutchins, L., and L. Kaahumanu, eds. 1991. *Bi Any Other Name.* Boston: Alyson.

Icard, L. 1985. "Black Gay Men and Conflicting Social Identities: Sexual Orientation Versus Racial Identity." *Journal of Social Work* 4(1/2):83–93.

Innala, S., and K. Ernulf. 1992. "The Relationship Between Affective and Cognitive Components of Homophobic Reaction: Three Cross-National Replications." Goteborg Psychological Reports, vol. 22, no. 2. Goteborg, Sweden: University of Goteborg.

Irwin, P., and N. Thompson. 1977. "Acceptance of the Rights of Homosexuals: A Personality Profile." *Journal of Homosexuality* 3:107–21.

Jackson, L., and L. Sullivan. 1989. "Cognition and Affect in Evaluations of Stereotypes Group Members." *Journal of Social Psychology* 129(5):659–72.

Jones, D. 1996. "Discrimination Against Same-Sex Couples in Hotel Reservation Policies." *Journal of Homosexuality* 31(1/2):153–59.

Jung, P., and R. Smith. 1993. *Heterosexism: An Ethical Challenge.* Albany: State University of New York Press.

Kahn, M. 1991. "Factors Affecting the Coming Out Process for Lesbians." *Journal of Homosexuality* 21(3):47–70.

Kelly, J., J. St. Lawrence, S. Smith, J. Hood, and D. Cook. 1987. "Medical Students' Attitudes Toward AIDS and Homosexual Patients." *Journal of Medical Education* 62:549–56.

Kerns, J., and M. Fine. 1994. "The Relation Between Gender and Negative Attitudes Toward Gay Men and Lesbians: Do Gender Role Attitudes Mediate This Relationship?" *Sex Roles* 31(5/6):297–307.

Kirby, D. 1980. "The Effects of a School Sex Education Program: A Review of the Literature." *Journal of School Health* 50:559–62.

Kite, M. 1984. "Sex Differences in Attitudes Toward Homosexuals: A Meta-Analytic Review." *Journal of Homosexuality* 10(1/2):69–81.

Kite, M., and K. Deaux. 1986. "Attitudes Toward Homosexuality: Assessment and Behavioral Consequences." *Basic and Applied Social Psychology* 7(2): 137–62.

Kohlberg, L. 1981. *The Philosophy of Moral Development.* San Francisco: Harper and Row.

Krulewitz, J., and J. Nash. 1980. "Effects of Sex Role Attitudes and Similarity on Men's Rejection of Male Homosexuals." *Journal of Personality and Social Psychology* 38:215–28.

Kunkel, L., and L. Temple. 1992. "Attitudes Toward AIDS and Homosexuals: Gender, Marital Status, and Religion." *Journal of Applied Social Psychology* 22:1030–40.

Kurdek, L. 1988. "Correlates of Negative Attitudes Toward Homosexuals in Heterosexual College Students." *Sex Roles* 18:727–38.

Lance, L. 1987. "The Effects of Interaction with Gay Persons on Attitudes Toward Homosexuality." *Human Relations* 40(6):329–36.

—— 1992. "Changes in Homophobic Views as Related to Interaction with Gay Persons: A Study in the Reduction of Tensions." *International Journal of Group Tensions* 22(4):291–99.

Lankewish, V. 1992. "Breaking the Silence: Addressing Homophobia with *The Color Purple.*" In C. Hurlbert and S. Totten, eds., *Social Issues in the English Classroom.* Urbana: National Council of Teachers of English.

Larkin, F. 1989. "Attitudes of Female Registered Nurses Toward Homosexual Men." Master's thesis, University of Lowell, Lowell. Masters Abstracts International, 28(1):110.

Larsen, K., M. Reed, and S. Hoffman. 1980. "Attitudes of Heterosexuals Toward Homosexuality: A Likert Type Scale and Construct Validity." *Journal of Sex Research* 16(3):245–57.

LaSalle, L. 1992. "Exploring Campus Intolerance: A Textual Analysis of Comments Concerns Lesbian, Gay, and Bisexual People." Paper presented at the Annual

Meeting of the American Educational Research Association, San Francisco, April. ERIC Document Service no. ED 349497.

Lehne, G. 1976. "Homophobia Among Men." In D. David and R. Brannon, eds., *The Forty-Nine Percent Majority: The Male Sex Role,* pp. 66–88. Reading, Mass.: Addison-Wesley.

Levant, R., et al. 1992. "The Male Role: An Investigation of Contemporary Norms." *Journal of Mental Health Counseling* 14(3):325–37.

Lilling, A., and R. Friedman. 1995. "Bias Toward Gay Patients by Psychoanalytic Clinicians: An Empirical Investigation." *Archives of Sexual Behavior* 24(5): 563–70.

Loiacano, D. 1989. "Gay Identity Issues Among Black Americans: Racism, Homophobia, and the Need for Validation." *Journal of Counseling and Development* 68:21–25.

Lorde, A. 1984. *Sister Outsider.* Trumansburg, N.Y.: Crossing.

Luhrs, T., I. Crawford, and J. Goldberg. 1991. "The Presence of the Defensive Function as a Predictor of Heterosexual College Students' Affective Responses Toward Gay Men and Lesbians." *Journal of Psychology and Human Sexuality* 4(4):71–87.

Lumby, M. 1976. "Homophobia: A Quest for a Valid Scale." *Journal of Homosexuality* 2(1):39–47.

MacDonald, A. 1974. "The Importance of Sex-Role to Gay Liberation." *Homosexual Counseling Journal* 1(4):169–80.

MacDonald, A., and R. Games. 1974. "Some Characteristics of Those Who Hold Positive and Negative Attitudes Toward Homosexuals." *Journal of Homosexuality* 1(1):9–27.

MacDonald, A., J. Huggins, S. Young, and R. Swanson. 1973. "Attitudes Toward Homosexuality: Preservation of Sex Morality or Double Standard?" *Journal of Consulting and Clinical Psychology* 40(1):161.

McQuoid, D. 1988. *Attitudes Toward Homosexuality: Implications for Responsible Psychotherapy.* La Mirada, Cal.: Biola University. ERIC Document No. ED 298397.

Maddux, J. A. 1988. "The Homophobic Attitudes of Preservice Teachers." Ph.D. diss., University of Cincinnati.

Mahaffey, K., and D. Marcus. 1995. "Correctional Officers' Attitudes Toward AIDS. *Criminal Justice and Behavior* 22(2):91–105.

Malyon, A. 1982. "Psychotherapeutic Implications of Internalized Homophobia in Gay Men." In J. Gonsiorek, ed., *Homosexuality and Psychotherapy: A Practitioner's Handbook of Affirmative Models,* pp. 59–69. New York: Haworth.

Marsiglio, W. 1993. "Attitudes Toward Homosexual Activity and Gays as Friends: A National Survey of Heterosexual Fifteen- to Nineteen-Year-Old Males." *Journal of Sex Research* 30(1):12–17.

Margolies, L., M. Becker, and K. Jackson-Brewer. 1987. "Internalized Homophobia: Identifying and Treating the Oppressor Within." In Boston Lesbian Psychologies Collective, ed., *Lesbian Psychologies: Explorations and Challenges,* pp. 229–41. Urbana: University of Illinois Press.

Matthews, W., M. Booth, J. Turner, and L. Kessler. 1986. "Physicans' Attitudes Toward Homosexuality—Survey of a California County Medical Society." *Western Journal of Medicine* 144:106–10.

Mays, V., S. Cochran, and S. Rhue. 1993. "The Impact of Perceived Discrimination on the Intimate Relationships of Black Lesbians." *Journal of Homosexuality* 25(4):1–14.

Miller, R. 1994. "Fault Lines in the Contact Zone." *College English* 56(4): 389–408.

Monteiro, K., and V. Fuqua. 1995. "African American Gay Youth." In G. Unks, ed., *The Gay Teen,* pp. 159–87. New York: Routledge.

Morin, S. 1974. "Educational Programs as a Means of Changing Attitudes Toward Gay People." *Homosexual Counseling Journal* 1:160–65.

Nevid, J. 1983. "Exposure to Homoerotic Stimuli: Effects on Attitudes and Affects of Heterosexual Viewers." *Journal of Social Psychology* 119:249–55.

Newman, B. 1989. "Including Curriculum Content on Lesbian and Gay Issues." *Journal of Social Work Education* 25(3):202–11.

Nicholson, W., and B. Long. 1990. "Self-Esteem, Social Support, Internalized Homophobia, and Coping Strategies of HIV+ Gay Men." *Journal of Consulting and Clinical Psychology* 58:873–76.

Nungesser, L. 1983. *Homosexual Acts, Actors, and Identities.* New York: Praeger.

Nyberg, K., and J. Alston. 1976. "Analysis of Public Attitudes Toward Homosexual Behavior." *Journal of Homosexuality* 2(2):99–107.

O'Donohue, W., and C. Caselles. 1993. "Homophobia: Conceptual, Definitional, and Value Issues." *Journal of Psychopathology and Behavioral Assessment* 15(3):177–95.

Oliver, M., and J. Hyde. 1993. "Gender Differences in Sexuality: A Meta-Analysis." *Psychological Bulletin* 114(1):29–51.

Otis, M., and W. Skinner. 1996. "The Prevalence of Victimization and Its Effect on Mental Well-Being Among Lesbian and Gay People." *Journal of Homosexuality* 30(3):93–121.

Pagtolun-An, I., and J. Clair, 1986. "An Experimental Study of Attitudes Toward Homosexuals." *Deviant Behavior* 7(2):121–25.

Pain, M., and Disney, M. 1995. "Testing the Reliability and Validity of the Index of Attitudes Toward Homosexuals (IAH) in Australia." *Journal of Homosexuality* 30(2):99–110.

Patel, S., T. M. Long, S. McCammon, and K. Wuensch. 1995. "Personality and Emotional Correlates of Self-Reported Antigay Behaviors." *Journal of Interpersonal Violence* 10(3):354–66.

Patton, W., and M. Mannison. 1994. "Investigating Attitudes Toward Sexuality: Two Methodologies." *Journal of Sex Education and Therapy* 20(3):185–97.

Pauly, I., and S. Goldstein. 1970. "Physician's Attitudes in Treating Male Homosexuals." *Medical Aspects of Human Sexuality* 4:26–45.

Pettinger, J. 1995. "A Survey of School Psychologists' Attitudes and Feelings Toward Gay and Lesbian Youths." Ph.D. diss., State University of New York, Albany. Dissertation Abstracts International 56(5):2945B.

Phifer, N. 1994. "Homphobia: The Theme of the Novel *Jack*." *ALAN Review* 21(2):10–11.

Phillip, M. 1993. "Gay Issues: Out of the Closet, Into the Classroom." *Black Issues in Higher Education* 10(3):20–25.

Phillips, S. 1991. "The Hegemony of Heterosexuality: A Study of Introductory Texts." *Teaching Sociology* 19(4):454–63.

Polis, C. 1986. "Sensitive Drawings of Sexual Activity in Human Sexuality Textbooks." *Journal of Homosexuality* 13(1):59–73.

Price, J. 1982. "High School Students' Attitudes Toward Homosexuality." *Journal of School Health* 52(8):469–74.

Regan, A. 1993. " 'Type Normal Like the Rest of Us': Writing, Power, and Homophobia in the Networked Composition Classroom." *Computers and Composition* 10(4):11–23.

Reinhardt, B. 1994. "Effects of Gay and Lesbian Speaker Panels on Self-Report Measures of Individual Homophobia." Ph.D. diss., Texas A and M. Dissertation Abstracts International 55(10):3143A.

Reiter, L. 1991. "Developmental Origins of Antihomosexual Prejudice in Heterosexual Men and Women." *Clinical Social Work Journal* 19(2): 3–75.

Roese, N., J. Olson, M. Borenstein, A. Martin, and A. Shores. 1992. "Same-Sex Touching Behavior: The Moderating Role of Homophobic Attitudes." *Journal of Nonverbal Behavior* 16(4):249–59.

Rothblum, E., and L. Bond. 1996. *Preventing Heterosexism and Homophobia.* Thousand Oaks, Cal.: Sage.

Rudolph, J. 1988. "The Effects of a Multimodal Seminar on Mental Health Practitioners' Attitudes Toward Homosxuality, Authoritarianism, and Counseling Effectiveness." Ph.D. diss., Lehigh University. Dissertation Abstracts International, 49(7):2873B.

—— 1989. "Effects of a Workshop on Mental Health Practitioners' Attitudes Toward Homosexuality and Counseling Effectiveness." *Journal of Counseling and Development* 68(1):81–85.

—— 1990. "Counselors' Attitudes Toward Homosexuality: Some Tentative Findings." *Psychological Reports* 66:1352–54.

Russell, C., and J. Ellis. 1993. "Religiosity, Gender, Sex Anxiety, and AIDS Attitudes as They Affect Attitudes Toward Homosexuals." Paper presented at the Annual Meeting of the Southeastern Psychological Association, Atlanta, March. ERIC Document Service no. ED 359444.

Rust, P. 1993. "Coming Out in the Age of Social Constructionism: Sexual Identity

Formation Among Lesbian and Bisexual Women." *Gender and Society* 68(1):50–77.

San Miguel, C., and J. Millham. 1976. "The Role of Cognitive and Situational Variables in Aggression Toward Homosexuals." *Journal of Homosexuality* 2(1):11–27.

Scala, A. 1996. "Heterosexism in the Classroom." Ph.D. diss., Columbia University. Dissertation Abstracts International, 57(2):569A.

Schatman, M. 1989. "The Prediction of Homophobia Attitudes Among College Students." Ph.D. diss., University of North Texas. Dissertation Abstracts International, 50(10):4820b.

Scherer, Y., Y. Wu, B. Haughey. 1991. "AIDS and Homophobia Among Nurses." *Journal of Homosexuality* 21(4):17–27.

Schneider, W., and I. Lewis. 1984. "The Straight Story on Homosexuality and Gay Rights." *Public Opinion* 7(1):16–20, 59–60.

Schwanberg, S. 1993. "Attitudes Toward Gay Men and Lesbian Women: Instrumentation Issues." *Journal of Homosexuality* 26(1):99–136.

Sears, J. T. 1988. "Attitudes, Experiences, and Feelings of Guidance Counselors in Working with Homosexual Students." Paper presented at the American Educational Research Association Meeting, New Orleans, April. ERIC Reproduction Document no. ED296210.

—— 1991. *Growing Up Gay in the South.* New York: Haworth.

—— 1992a. "Educators, Homosexuality, and Homosexual Students: Are Personal Feelings Related to Professional Beliefs?" *Journal of Homosexuality* 22(3/4):29–79.

—— 1992b. *Sexuality and the Curriculum: The Politics and Practices of Sexuality Education.* New York: Teachers College Press.

—— 1993. "Responding to the Sexual Diversity of Faculty and Students: Sexual Praxis and the Critically Reflective Administrator." In C. Capper, ed., *Educational Administration in a Pluralist Society,* pp. 110–72. New York: State University of New York Press.

—— 1995. "Black-Gay or Gay-Black? Choosing Identities and Identifying Choices." In G. Unks, ed., *The Gay Teen,* pp. 136–57. New York: Routledge.

—— 1996. "The Institutional Climate for Lesbian, Gay, and Bisexual Education Faculty: What Is the Pivotal Frame of Reference?" Paper presented at the American Educational Research Association, New York City.

—— In press. "Four Approaches to Teaching Sexuality in a Culturally Responsible Manner." In J. T. Sears, ed., *Conversations for an Enlarging Public Square.* New York: Teachers College Press.

Seltzer, R. 1992. "The Social Location of Those Holding Antihomosexual Attitudes." *Sex Roles* 26(9/10):391–98.

Seltzer, R., and R. Smith. 1985. "Race and Ideology: A Research Note Measuring Liberalism and Conservatism in Black America." *Phylon* 46(2):98–105.

Serdahely, W., and G. Ziemba. 1984. "Changing Homophobic Attitudes

Through College Sexuality Education." *Journal of Homosexuality* 10(1/2): 109–16.

Shaw, J., H. Borough, and M. Fink. 1994. "Perceived Sexual Orientation and Helping Behavior by Males and Females: The Wrong Number Technique." *Journal of Psychology and Human Sexuality* 6(3):73–81.

Shidlo, A. 1994. "Internalized Homophobia: Conceptual and Empirical Issues in Measurement." In B. Greene and G. Herek, eds., *Lesbian and Gay Psychology*, pp. 176–205. Thousand Oaks, Cal.: Sage.

Shields, S., and R. Harriman. 1984. "Fear of Male Homosexuality: Cardiac Responses of Low and High Homonegative Males." *Journal of Homosexuality* 10(1/2):53–67.

Simon, A. 1995. "Some Correlates of Individuals' Attitudes Toward Lesbians." *Journal of Homosexuality* 29(1):89–103.

Smith, D. 1985. "An Ethnographic Study of Homosexual Teachers' Perspectives." Ph.D. diss., State University of New York, Albany. Dissertation Abstracts International, 46(1):66A.

Smith, G. 1993. "Homophobia and Attitudes Toward Gay Men and Lesbians by Psychiatric Nurses." *Archives of Psychiatric Nursing* 7(6):377–84.

Smith, K. 1971. "Homophobia: A Tentative Personality Profile." *Psychological Reports* 29:1091–94.

Smoot, L. 1991. "Homophobia Among College Students Majoring in Engineering, Physical Education, Psychology, and Social Work." Master's thesis, California State University, Long Beach.

Sobel, H. 1976. "Adolescent Attitudes Toward Homosexuality in Relation to Self-Concept and Body Satisfaction." *Adolescence* 11(43):443–53.

Stark, L. 1991. "Traditional Gender Role Beliefs and Individual Outcomes: An Exploratory Analysis." *Sex Roles* 24:639–50.

Stevenson, M. 1988. "Promoting Tolerance for Homosexuality: An Evaluation of Intervention Strategies." *Journal of Sex Research* 25(4):500–11.

Story, M. 1979. "A Longitudinal Study of the Effect of a University Human Sexuality Course of Sexual Attitudes." *Journal of Sex Research* 15:184–204.

Talburt, S. 1996. "Troubling Lesbian Identities: Intellectual Voice and Visibility in Academia." Ph.D. diss., Vanderbilt University.

Tate, D. 1991. "Homophobia Among Rural and Urban Social Work Students." *Human Services in the Rural Environment* 15(1):16–18.

Taylor, M. 1982. "A Discriminant Analysis Approach to Exploring Changes in Human Sexuality Attitudes Among University Students." *Journal of American College Health* 31:124–29.

Troiden, R. 1989. "The Formation of Homosexual Identities." *Journal of Homosexuality* 17(1/2):43–73.

VanderStoep, S., and C. Green. 1988. "Religiosity and Homonegativism: A Path-Analytic Study." *Basic and Applied Social Psychology* 9(2):135–47.

Van de Ven, P. 1994. "Comparisons Among Homophobic Reactions of Undergraduates, High School Students, and Young Offenders." *Journal of Sex Research* 31(2):117–24.

Wagner, G., J. Serafini, J. Rabkin, R. Remien, and J. Williams. 1994. "Integration of One's Religion and Homosexuality: A Weapon Against Internalized Homophobia." *Journal of Homosexuality* 26(4):91–110.

Walters, A. 1994. "Using Visual Media to Reduce Homophobia." *Journal of Sex Education and Therapy* 20(2):92–100.

Walters, A., and M. Curran. 1996. " 'Excuse Me, Sir? May I Help You and Your Boyfriend?' Salespersons' Differential Treatment of Homosexual and Straight Customers." *Journal of Homosexuality* 31(1/2):135–52.

Warshauer, S. 1993. "Rethinking Teacher Authority to Counteract Prejudice in Discussions of Gay/Lesbian/Bisexual Representation: A Model of Teacher Response in the Networked Computer Classroom." Paper presented at the Annual Meeting of the Conference on College Composition and Communication, San Diego, April. ERIC Document Service no. ED 360645.

Weinberg, G. 1972. *Society and the Healthy Homosexual.* New York: St. Martin's.

Weiner, A. 1989. "Racist, Sexist, and Homophobic Attitudes Among Undergraduate Social Work Students and the Effects of Assessments of Client Vignettes." Ph.D. diss., Rutgers University. Dissertation Abstracts International, 50(11):3741A.

Weissman, E. 1992. "Kids Who Attack Gays." In G. Herek and K. Berrill, eds., *Hate Crimes: Confronting Violence Against Lesbians and Gay Men,* pp. 170–78. Newbury Park, Cal.: Sage.

Wells, J. 1989. "Teaching About Gay and Lesbian Sexual and Affectional Orientation Using Explit Films to Reduce Homophobia." *Journal of Humanistic Education and Development* 28(1):18–34.

—— 1991. "What Makes a Difference? Various Teaching Strategies to Reduce Homophobia in University Students." *Annals of Sex Research* 4(3/4): 229–38.

—— 1992. "Heterosexual University Students' Perceptions of Homosexual Behavior." *Annals of Sex Research* 5:171–79.

Whatley, M. 1992. "Images of Gays and Lesbians in Sexuality and Health Textbooks." In K. Harbeck, ed., *Coming Out of the Classroom Closet,* pp. 197–211. New York: Haworth.

Whitam, F. L. 1983. "Culturally Invariable Properties of Male Homosexuality: Tentative Conclusions from Cross-Cultural Research." *Archives of Sexual Behavior* 12(3):207–26.

Whitam, F. L., and Zent, M. 1984. "A Cross-Cultural Assessment of Early Cross-Gender Behavior and Familial Factors in Male Homosexuality." *Archives of Sexual Behavior* (October) 13(5):427–39.

White, N. 1995. "Portrait of an Artist as a Young, 'Half-Gay,' Black Man: Case Study of the Identity Development of a College Student Based on His Personal Journals." Master's thesis, University of South Carolina.

Whitley, B. 1987. "The Relationship of Sex-Role Orientation to Heterosexuals' Attitudes Toward Homosexuals." *Sex Roles* 17:103–13.

—— 1988. "Sex Differences in Heterosexuals' Attitudes Toward Homosexuals: It Depends Upon What You Ask." *Journal of Sex Research* 24:287–91.

Williams, W. L. 1986. *The Spirit and the Flesh.* Boston: Beacon.

Wisniewski, J., and B. Toomey. 1987. "Are Social Workers Homophobic?" *Social Work* 32(5):454–55.

Woods, S. 1990. "The Contextual Realities of Being a Lesbian Physical Education Teacher." Ph.D. diss., University of Massachusetts. Dissertation Abstracts International, 51(3):788A.

Wright, J. 1993. "Lesbian Instructor Comes Out." *Feminist Teacher* 7(2):26–33.

Gust A. Yep

Changing Homophobic and Heterosexist Attitudes: An Overview of Persuasive Communication Approaches

Johnny, a six-year old, repeatedly hears his father say, "They should kill those faggots and dykes," when his father sees lesbian and gay issues being discussed on television.

Rosario, an eight-year old, listens to people in her church talk about how the two women in the house across the street—presumably lesbians—should be avoided because they are living in sin and will burn in hell.

Lashana, a ten-year old, laughs when her friends tell nasty jokes about "sissies" and "dykes."

Eric, a twelve-year old, calls his gay uncle's partner "uncle" just like he calls his nongay uncle's wife "aunt." Eric is reprimanded, and his relatives remind him that his nongay uncle's wife is "family" while his gay uncle's partner is "just a friend."

People are not born homophobic or heterosexist. These attitudes are acquired through interaction with others, such as family members, teachers, peers, and friends. They are learned by direct observation and imitation of persons children look up to (like Johnny witnessing his father express his hatred for lesbians and gay men or Rosario listening to people at her church display their heterosexism), by participating in interactions that are perceived as rewarding (like Lashana giving approval to and receiving approval from her friends when she laughs at cruel lesbian and gay jokes), and by experience (like Eric's awareness of the differential treatment his uncle receives in the family).

Homophobic and heterosexist attitudes are, therefore, learned, shaped, and maintained through communication. It is also through communication that such attitudes can be eradicated. To develop effective homophobia reduction programs or campaigns, a thorough understanding of the persuasive communication process is critical. Such programs need to examine *who says what to whom and with what effect*, in other words, they must consider how source, message, and receiver factors interact to produce persuasive effects. Because homophobia and heterosexism are audience-held attitudes, they must be understood first. The purpose of this chapter is to present an overview of persuasive communication approaches that can be used to combat homophobia and heterosexism. To accomplish this, the chapter is divided into three sections. Section 1 defines the concepts of persuasion and attitude. Section 2 discusses several approaches to attitude change and applies them to the eradication of homophobia and heterosexism. Section 3 offers some guidelines and strategies for creating, designing, and implementing communication tactics aimed at combating homophobia and heterosexism.

I. Definitions

Persuasion is a noncoercive deliberate communication (either verbal or by expression) involving the intent to change the mental, emotional, or behavioral state of others. Persuasion may be accomplished either face to face or through the media and may appeal to logic and/or emotions. The fields of social psychology and communication have developed several concepts of persuasion about how people are convinced to change their positions (Perloff 1993; Bettinghaus and Cody 1994; Larson 1995; O'Keefe 1990; Reardon 1991).

Persuasion is a complex communication process. For example, to diminish negative attitudes toward gay people, the persuader needs to consciously develop a specific strategy to convince individuals holding such attitudes that their position is somehow less desirable than the one the persuader is advocating. The persuasive goal is successful if the persuader is able to produce a change in the attitude of the persuadee.

The concept of *attitude* has a long history in the social scientific literature and it has been considered one of the most significant concepts in social psychology and communication (e.g., Allport 1935; Eagly and Chaiken 1993; Zimbardo, Ebbesen, and Maslach 1977). The most commonly used definition of attitude is a psychological tendency that is expressed by a positive or negative evaluation of a particular entity or attitude object (Reardon 1981). For example, a heterosexist attitude is manifested by favoring (positive eval-

uation) heterosexuality (attitude object or entity), while a homophobic attitude is expressed in terms of dislike or hatred (negative evaluation) toward
lesbians and gays (attitude object). Attitudes are (a) learned, (b) enduring,
(c) affective evaluations, and (d) related to human behavior. Since attitudes
are learned through socialization, they tend to be enduring and stable mental dispositions. Attitudes, for the most part, do not and can not change
overnight. Furthermore, attitudes have a strong emotional component in
which persons (like gays/lesbians), objects (like the gay flag), and ideas (like
homosexuality) are evaluated or categorized as good or bad, desirable or
undesirable, strong or weak, moral or immoral, acceptable or unacceptable,
and so on. Finally, attitudes predispose people to act in certain ways; they
influence human behavior.[1]

While attitudes are often used in conjunction with other related terms
such as values, beliefs, and opinions, it is important to note their differences.
Values are standards of conduct; they are ideals the individual strives to carry
out or live by (like equality). Values are more general than attitudes and may
underlie a cluster of attitudes. For instance, equality (a value) for an individual may be associated with attitudes toward alternative lifestyles and the
like. Beliefs are thoughts containing information that individuals possess
about objects and actions. Opinions are verbalized beliefs and attitudes. An
opinion of gay bashers, for instance, will likely contain beliefs ("It is wrong")
and attitudes ("I dislike gay bashers").

II. Approaches to Attitude Change

Several ways of changing attitudes have been documented in the fields of
social psychology and communication. Four such approaches will be discussed here in the context of changing homophobic and heterosexist attitudes: (a) functional, (b) consistency, (c) social judgment, and (d) elaboration likelihood.

The Functional Approach

Why do some people hold homophobic attitudes? Why do some individuals
protest against domestic partnership policies for lesbians and gay men? Why
do other people seem to passionately defend gay rights? The functional perspective to attitude change argues that people hold certain attitudes because
of the psychological function or need they satisfy (e.g., Herek 1987; Katz
1960; Pratkanis and Greenwald 1989; Shavitt 1989). By understanding the
specific function an attitude serves for the individual, attempts can be made

to change it. For example, if a person is homophobic because she or he does not understand homosexuality—fear of the unknown as the reason for holding the negative attitude—then attempts at changing such attitude may be accomplished through educating the person about homosexuality. Psychologists and communication scholars have identified five psychological functions that attitudes serve: (a) knowledge, (b) utilitarian, (c) social adjustive, (d) ego defensive, and (e) value expressive.

The knowledge function maintains that attitudes help people make sense of their world, providing a framework to understand events. Heterosexist attitudes can perform a knowledge function for many people—for example, heterosexuality as the one and only "normal" lifestyle may appear to make human relationships simpler and easier to understand within a context of diverse and complex relationship patterns and lifestyles. In this way such attitudes can help individuals cope with their lack of knowledge of alternate lifestyles.

The utilitarian function states that attitudes help people maximize rewards and minimize punishment. Reward and punishment are individual perceptions and they are not necessarily physical (like social acceptance or feelings of alienation). To illustrate how this function operates, let's consider the case of a young and ambitious college graduate who is essentially indifferent about lesbians and gays. This young woman learns that the company that employed her is ultraconservative and competition for career advancement is very high. She also finds out that holding certain attitudes—like heterosexist biases and homophobic sentiments—may gain the approval of her boss, which may, in turn, assist her in her high career aspirations. To fulfill her goals, she may start changing her originally neutral attitudes to more negative feelings toward lesbians and gays.

The social adjustive function describes how attitudes help people relate to or maintain relationships with important others or reference groups. The expression of homophobic attitudes in certain peer circles, for example, may help the individual gain acceptance by his or her friends (reference group) and reduce a sense of loneliness or isolation.

The ego defensive function maintains that people hold certain attitudes to protect themselves from acknowledging unpleasant or threatening information. Intensely homophobic attitudes can, then, serve this function by protecting the individual from his or her own homoerotic feelings.

Finally, the value expressive function states that attitudes can help people manifest or openly display their core values. For example, members of Parents and Friends of Lesbians and Gays (PFLAG) often carry banners and signs (i.e., "We love our lesbian daughter" and "Hate is not a family value") during demonstrations to express their values (family closeness as well as nondiscrimination).

The functional approach has important implications for individuals and organizations working toward reducing homophobia and heterosexism. According to this perspective, it is important to find out what specific function or psychological need the homophobic or heterosexist attitude is satisfying in the individual before attempts are effectively made to eradicate it. The development and design of communication programs to change such attitudes will necessarily depend on the particular function the attitudes serve for the target individual.

Strategies to change homophobic attitudes will differ if they are held for knowledge, utilitarian, social adjustive, ego defensive, or value expressive reasons. For example, education programs designed to change homophobic attitudes related to (a) ignorance of homosexuality (knowledge function) may provide people with appropriate knowledge and facts; (b) maximization of reward and avoidance of punishment (utilitarian function) may offer perspectives on alternate reward systems; (c) maintenance of harmonious relationships with reference groups (social adjustive function) may need to change reference group norms; (d) protection of the self from unpleasant information (ego defensive function) may offer individuals a supportive and nonjudgmental atmosphere (by friends, counselors, etc.) for them to accept those parts of themselves that they consider undesirable; (e) overt expression of core values (value expressive function) may point out potential problems, conflicts, and inconsistencies in their value system.

Consistency Approaches

Several consistency theories have been developed in the area of attitude change. All follow three fundamental underlying assumptions: (a) people attempt to maximize their sense of internal psychological consistency (attitudes and beliefs); (b) inconsistency in one's thoughts is taken to be an uncomfortable state, therefore, people strive to avoid it; (c) inconsistency leads to attitude change in the direction of reestablishing psychological consistency.[2] A popular consistency approach, Festinger's (1957) theory of cognitive dissonance is perhaps the most important theoretical contribution to social psychology (Eagly and Chaiken 1993).

Following the same basic assumptions of other consistency theories, cognitive dissonance primarily focuses on the relationship between cognitive elements (attitudes, beliefs, opinions, or information) about objects, issues, events, or other people. These elements may be related to each other in one of three possible ways: (a) they might be *irrelevant* , e.g., Jane is homophobic and Jane likes soda pops; (b) they might be *consonant*, e.g., Jane is homophobic and Jane dislikes Candela, an open lesbian; (c) they might be *dissonant*, e.g., Jane is homophobic and Jane likes Candela. Jane is said to be in a state of dissonance because presumably her homophobia is in direct opposition to her liking Candela, who is openly lesbian. Because dissonance is uncomfortable, Jane will attempt to reduce it. However, the way in which she goes about doing so depends on the magnitude of the dissonance.

Magnitude of the dissonance is the individual's perception of the degree of inconsistency that she or he is experiencing. There is a direct and positive relationship between the magnitude of dissonance and the subsequent pressure to reduce it: the greater the dissonance (Jane is very torn between her intense homophobic attitudes and her strong liking for Candela), the greater the pressure to reduce it; the lesser the dissonance (Jane's homophobic feelings and her liking for Candela are mild), the lesser the pressure to reduce it. Put in another way, large amounts of dissonance create great motivational pressure while small amounts of dissonance produce little or no motivational pressure to change attitudes.

Two factors affect magnitude of dissonance. One is the relative proportion of consonant and dissonant elements. As the number of total consonant elements (Jane likes Candela very much; Jane believes that Candela is a good person; Jane believes that Candela is a supportive friend) increases, the degree of dissonance experienced will likely decrease. Conversely, as the total number of dissonant elements (Jane is very homophobic; Jane believes that lesbians and gays cannot be trusted; Jane believes that Candela is out to "convert her," *but* Jane likes Candela very much) increases, the degree of dissonance experienced will also likely increase. The second factor affecting magnitude of dissonance is the importance of the elements. The greater the importance assigned to dissonant elements (Jane strongly believes that lesbians are "bad" people), the more likely the dissonance experienced will increase. On the other hand, the greater the importance assigned to consonant elements (Jane believes that liking Candela depends more on whether she is a good person or a supportive friend), the more likely the dissonance experienced will decrease.

There are two ways of reducing dissonance. The first is by changing the relative proportions of consistent and inconsistent elements by either adding more consistent elements or deleting existing inconsistent elements. For example, Jane might reduce the dissonance associated with liking Candela by adding new consistent or consonant elements ("Candela would make a great friend"; "Candela is nice"; "Candela is trustworthy"; "Candela is ethical") or by deleting existing inconsistent or dissonant elements ("Lesbians cannot be trusted"; "Candela is out to convert me"). The second way to reduce dissonance is by altering the importance of the elements involved. In Jane's case she might decide that liking someone and having a potentially great friend are more important than her beliefs about homosexuality and therefore, change her attitudes toward lesbians and gay men from a less favorable to a more neutral position.

Cognitive dissonance has important implications for strategies to reduce homophobic and heterosexist attitudes. The old adage "Remind the person you are coming out to that you are still the same person you have always been" may actually be based on this approach. In this instance if the recipient of disclosure is not homophobic there is consonance ("I have always liked you" and "I feel OK about homosexuality"); however, if the recipient of disclosure is homophobic, he or she will likely experience dissonance, especially after the discloser notes that there have been no changes in personhood ("I have always liked you"; "You are still the same person you have always been"; "I dislike homosexuals" may be cognitive elements present in the receiver's mind).

Cognitive dissonance also tells the discloser that she or he might have to take it several steps further to ensure that the person listening to the disclosure reduces the dissonance by becoming less homophobic. One approach might be to increase the number of consonant elements that support positive feelings toward lesbians and gays ("You feel OK with your gay and lesbian coworkers"; "Even your old-fashioned parents support gay rights"; "A lot of lesbians and gays have made very meaningful contributions to society") or increase their importance ("Isn't the bond that you have more important than his or her affectional orientation?").

Another approach might be to reduce the number of dissonant elements or decrease their importance ("Does the sexual orientation of the person really matter when there are all these attributes that you admire?"). In sum, strategies to reduce homophobic and heterosexist attitudes, according to cognitive dissonance, should be based on the creation of a dissonant situation for the target listener, to subsequently increase the total number or degree of importance of consonant elements and to decrease the total number or importance of dissonant elements in the listener's mind so that a greater motivational pressure to lessen the negatively held attitudes is produced.

The Social Judgment Approach

Why are some attitudes so much more difficult to change than others? Why is it that sometimes when we try to change someone's mind his or her reaction is the opposite of what was intended? Or, put in another way, why do some people become more homophobic after we have attempted to show that homosexuality is another variation in the human condition? The social judgment approach provides some insights into these questions.

Social judgment would view homophobic and heterosexist attitudes as consisting of a continuum of evaluations ranging from acceptable, noncommittal, to unacceptable positions from the individual person's point of view (Sherif, Sherif, and Nebergall 1965; Sherif and Sherif 1967). The positions on an issue that a person finds agreeable or acceptable are called *latitude of acceptance*. The positions on an issue that an individual finds either neutral or noncomittal are called *latitude of noncommitment*. Finally, the positions on an issue that a person finds disagreeable or objectionable are called *latitude of rejection*. This approach suggests that two people may endorse the same position on an issue but may dramatically differ in their tolerance of alternative positions on the same issue; for example, two individuals may find homosexual acts objectionable but one may feel that homosexuals are acceptable to society if they don't engage in homosexual activity while the other may feel that homosexuality is not acceptable under any circumstances. In this case the two people endorse the same position (homosexual acts are objectionable) but differ in terms of their latitudes of acceptance (for the first person, homosexuality is OK as long as it is never acted out) and rejection (for the second person, homosexuality is never OK).

To the extent that a person has a narrow latitude of acceptance and a wide latitude of rejection (like the second person in the above situation), the individual is considered ego involved. *Ego involvement* refers to how important a particular issue is to an individual. In other words, a highly ego-involved person is one who feels strongly about the topic and is not open-minded to other perspectives on the subject. Needless to say, homophobic people who are highly ego involved (like religious fundamentalists) are not likely to change their attitudes. Attitude change, according to social judgment theorists, is contingent upon the degree of ego involvement of the target person. More specifically, the greater the ego involvement on a particular topic, the lesser the likelihood of attitude change on the same topic and vice versa.

This approach gives us additional insights into ways of changing homophobic and heterosexist attitudes. For example, there is a need to find out the degree of ego involvement people have regarding their attitudes toward lesbians and gays. For individuals who are not highly ego involved, attitude change is more likely. For those who are highly ego involved, this process of change will likely be very difficult. Perhaps not much time and energy should be wasted in trying to change these individuals' attitudes.

There is also a need to find out the target individual's latitudes of acceptance, noncommitment, and rejection so that appropriate persuasive messages and goals can be developed. Going back to the earlier example of two individuals finding homosexual acts objectionable, the first, who believes that homosexuality is all right if it is never acted out, appears to be less ego involved and more likely to change such attitudes when compared to the second, who essentially asserts that homosexuality is never acceptable under any condition. To develop messages to influence the first individual, we need to ascertain what is acceptable and objectionable for him or her; for instance, we might find out that, for this person, homosexuality is OK, homosexual people are OK (latitude of acceptance), having homosexual friends is questionable (latitude of noncommitment), having homosexuals display their affection for each other in public is not OK, and having homosexual behavior acted out in public or in private is never OK (latitude of rejection). To develop effective ways to change this person's attitude, we might consider persuading our target to widen his or her latitude of acceptance by gradually shrinking other areas or attitude positions; more specifically, we might work on persuading him or her that having homosexual friends is OK (changing noncommitment to acceptance) before attempting to tackle the person's feelings about open display of same-sex affection in public (changing rejection to acceptance).

People involved in the creation and design of homophobia reduction programs need to be aware of potential distortions, which are biases that result from the tendency to perceive things from one's own point of view. Such distortions can be closer to one's point of view (*assimilation effects*) or more distant from the person's point of view (*contrast effects*). Therefore, advocating a position that is objectionable to the person will more likely produce a contrast effect while a position that is acceptable to the individual will likely be perceived as more similar to the person's most acceptable position (assimilation). If we attempt to directly change the person's strongly held negative attitudes toward public display of affection between homosexuals in the above example, we are likely to encounter a contrast effect, that is, the person will react in the opposite direction of the intended persuasive outcome by becoming more intensely homophobic.

The Elaboration Likelihood Model

While many religious fundamentalists, for example, are intensely antigay and many human rights activists are decisively pro-gay, the general population is probably somewhere in the middle, varying in degrees of ego involvement and feelings of noncommitment. To put it more simply, a number of people might find homophobia and heterosexism to be peripheral—as opposed to central—issues in their lives. How do we persuade these individuals? As indicated in the previous section, people who feel very strongly about certain issues (high ego involvement) are difficult to persuade, but can they be persuaded? If so, how?

The elaboration likelihood model (ELM) provides us with some answers to these questions (Petty and Cacioppo 1981, 1986). This model proposes that receivers of persuasive communication process messages differently depending on the degree of relevance it has for them. The more a topic is perceived as relevant to us, the greater the likelihood we will think about implications and consequences of arguments and counterarguments on a subject. The degree of relevance of a topic for the receiver affects how persuasion can occur.

Seven principles related to the process of persuasion and attitude change are presented by ELM. First, it proposes that people are motivated to hold the "right" attitudes. People want to perceive themselves as "doing the right thing," for example, holding the correct moral values or voting for a politician who will accomplish what voters want. Because receivers want to be correct in their attitudes, they are likely to find issues closely related to them (e.g., some moral questions) relevant and to engage in message elaboration (thinking through the advantages and disadvantages as well as the implications of their position).

Second, the degree of message elaboration on the part of the receiver depends on a number of factors associated with the situation or context of the communication (like distraction) and internal state of the person (like motivation or receiver involvement). Third, the direction and degree of attitude change are affected by three factors: (a) the persuasiveness of the argument—for example, strong arguments produce more attitude change than weak ones, especially if they are repeated at least three to five times; (b) a set of peripheral cues that tell the receiver what the response ought to be, as in the case of a very attractive person asking you to sign a petition: you follow through with the request on the basis of the petitioner's physical attractiveness; and (c) the amount and type of elaboration on the part of the receiver.

The extent of elaboration determines two primary routes to persuasion: (a) a *central route* in which the receiver carefully examines the proof and validity of the message and (b) a *peripheral route*, which involves a number of basic rules that affect whether or not the receiver will follow the advice of the speaker. These basic rules (Cialdini 1988) include: (a) *credibility* (we follow the advice of a person whom we perceive as believable and competent), (b) *liking* (we tend to comply with requests made by people we like or find attractive), and (c) *consensus* (we follow the advice of others if we perceive that everyone believes in it or is doing it).

Fourth, there are factors that affect the *motivation* or the *ability* of the receiver to elaborate or scrutinize the quality of message arguments. Motivational factors include (a) *receiver involvement* (people tend to scrutinize messages if they are personally involved), (b) *need for cognition* (the receiver's tendency to engage in thinking about particular topics), and (c) *the presence of multiple speakers communicating multiple arguments* (the tendency of people to scrutinize messages if there are several sources presenting multiple arguments for the message claim). Ability factors include (a) *distraction* (the receiver is not completely focused on the message), and (b) *prior knowledge* (the receiver's past exposure to the topic).

Fifth, there are variables (such as holding an attitude for ego defensive reasons) affecting message processing. For example, if a person is homophobic for ego defensive purposes, she or he may not process messages objectively but rather look only for arguments supporting her or his biased position.

Sixth, if a receiver is not motivated to, or not able to, scrutinize message quality, he or she is likely to be persuaded on the basis of peripheral cues; conversely, if a receiver is motivated to, or able to, examine message quality, he or she is likely to be influenced by the quality of the argument.

Last, the outcome of processing a message through the central route will produce attitude changes that are longer lasting and more resistant to counterpersuasion and have greater impact on behavior. In other words, if the persuader can get the receiver to scrutinize or think about the quality of the message, the potential effects of persuasion can be greater and more persistent.

This model suggests that changing homophobic and heterosexist attitudes can occur through two basic routes of message processing on the part of the receiver: (a) peripheral and (b) central. Attitude change through the peripheral route can be accomplished by using credible and likable speakers who create a sense of consensus or social proof; however, reduction of homophobic or heterosexist attitudes, by using such tactics, can produce faster results but are less likely to be permanent. To create more persistent and long-lasting attitude changes in the target individual, it is necessary to get the receiver who has been peripherally influenced to later process the antihomophobic and antiheterosexist arguments through a more central route. In this case, the persuader examines the messages carefully by personally involving the receiver. For example, the persuader might tell the receiver that current statistics indicate it to be very likely for the receiver to either have a family member, a close associate, or a friend who is lesbian or gay. Another approach is to have several sources communicating multiple arguments with the same claim. For example, several trusted individuals could use various arguments to support the claim that homophobia is harmful to everyone.

III. Combating Homophobia and Heterosexism with Persuasive Communication Strategies

Cultural homophobia and heterosexism are pervasive in America today. In *Homophobia: A Weapon of Sexism* Suzanne Pharr (1988) argues that "heterosexism and homophobia work together to enforce compulsory heterosexuality and that bastion of patriarchal power, the nuclear family" (16–17). Heterosexism sets the stage for homophobia to thrive in an environment in which every individual must be heterosexual to enjoy the privileges of power and social acceptance.

Blumenfeld (1992) observes that homophobia is detrimental to everyone—both gay and nongay—for a variety of reasons: (a) homophobia hinders individual growth, creativity, and self-expression by confining people in rigid gender roles; (b) homophobia creates divisiveness and maltreatment of people outside the boundaries of heterosexuality; (c) Homophobia inhibits individuals from forming close personal relationships with members of the same sex; (d) homophobia generally restricts interaction with other individuals in society including family members. (e) homophobia prevents heterosexuals from accepting the contributions of sexual minorities in all domains of life; (f) homophobia hinders appreciation of other forms of human diversity. In spite of such harms, homophobia and heterosexism continue to flourish (Blumenfeld 1992; Chesebro 1994; Comstock 1991; De Cecco 1985; Ehrlich 1981; Herek and Berrill 1992; Morin and Garfinkle 1981; Pharr 1988; Russo 1987; Siegel 1981; Simms 1981).

A homophobic and heterosexist culture appears to be "so normal" that often lesbians and gay men have internalized negative attitudes toward themselves. Those who react to injustice and differential treatment often do so with anger. Although rage may be justified, it does not always lead to the changes these individuals are advocating in their reactive stance.

This chapter proposes a more proactive position in the eradication of homophobia and heterosexism by going back to the roots of these attitudes. Such understanding will allow individuals and organizations to develop specific programs to change these pervasive attitudes. Four approaches to attitude change were discussed in this context, including functional, consistency, social judgment, and the elaboration likelihood model. These perspectives on attitude change primarily focus on the receiver or the target audience.

Four important areas associated with heterosexist attitudes have been identified. First, it is important to collect information about the potential audience to understand what specific psychological functions homophobic and heterosexist attitudes serve for the target individuals. Second, it is essential to understand the cognitive and belief systems of homophobic and heterosexist persons. Third, it is necessary to ascertain how intense their homophobia is and how ego involved these individuals are. Finally, it is important to find out how the target receivers process information and messages related to the topics of homophobia and heterosexism. After understanding the receivers' attitudinal systems, persuasive goals or outcomes can be developed so that the success of the program can be measured. For example, if the majority of the audience is not highly ego involved, greater attitude shifts can be expected.

Once program outcomes are established, multiple persuasive messages can be developed. Such messages should be specifically designed to (a) address the functions that homophobia and heterosexism are serving for the attitude holder, (b) create specific cognitive inconsistencies in the mind of the receiver and ways to reduce the dissonance in the direction of lessening their negative attitudes, (c) increase the receiver's latitude of acceptance by shrinking the regions of noncommitment and rejection, and (d) personally involve the receiver so that he or she will engage in central route processing, which will, hopefully, result in more permanent attitude shifts.

The speaker or source of the persuasive message should also be considered; for example, who can be the most effective speakers for the program? The degree of speaker credibility, trustworthiness, competence, dynamism, and similarity with the target audience are important factors in the communication process. In addition, the effectiveness of homophobia reduction programs should be evaluated to find out what works and what needs to be changed with specific target audiences.

The process of eradicating deeply ingrained homophobic and heterosexist attitudes is a challenging task requiring multidisciplinary cooperation between such fields as communication, psychology, sociology, social work, anthropology, and education, among many others. This multidisciplinary approach can integrate theory, research, and practice to enable individuals, groups, and organizations to take a more proactive stance in dealing with such attitudes and reclaiming the power and equality that belongs to every lesbian and gay man in the world.

NOTES

1. When I say that attitudes are related to behavior, I do not imply that attitudes always predict behavior. There is considerable debate about the relationship between attitude and behavior, however, general consensus indicates that attitudes guide human behavior. See, for example, Fazio, "How Do Attitudes Guide Behavior?"; Fazio and Roskos-Ewoldsen, "Acting as We Feel"; LaPiere, "Attitudes vs. Actions"; and Zanna, Higgins, and Herman, *Consistency in Social Behavior*.

2. This is essentially a group of attitude change theories that has been developed since World War II. Consistency theories have become one of the most fruitful areas of study within the social sciences in general and persuasive communication in particular. This group of theories includes psychological balance (e.g., Heider, *The Psychology of Interpersonal Relations*), congruity (e.g., Newcomb, "An Approach to the Study of Communicative Acts," and Osgood, Tannenbaum, and Suci, *The Measurement of Meaning*), and cognitive dissonance (e.g., Cooper and Fazio, "A New Look at Dissonance Theory," and Festinger, *The Theory of Cognitive Dissonance*), among others.

REFERENCES

Allport, G. W. 1935. "Attitudes." In C. Murchison, ed., *A Handbook of Social Psychology*, 2:798–844. Worcester: Clark University Press.

Bettinghaus, E. P., and M. J. Cody. 1994. *Persuasive Communication*. 5th ed. Fort Worth: Harcourt Brace Jovanovich.

Blumenfeld, W. J., ed. 1992. *Homophobia: How We All Pay the Price*. Boston: Beacon.

Chesebro, J. W. 1994. "Reflections on Gay and Lesbian Rhetoric." In R. J. Ringer, ed., *Queer Words, Queer Images: Communication and the Construction of Homosexuality*, pp. 77–88. New York: New York University Press.

Cialdini, R. B. 1988. *Influence: Science and Practice*. New York: Harper/Collins.

Comstock, G. 1991. *Violence Against Lesbians and Gay Men*. New York: Columbia University Press.

Cooper, J., and R. H. Fazio. 1984. "A New Look at Dissonance Theory." In L. Berkowitz, ed., *Advances in Experimental Social Psychology*, 17:229–66. Orlando: Academic.

De Cecco, J. P., ed. 1985. *Homophobia in American Society: Bashers, Baiters, and Bigots*. New York: Harrington Park.

Eagly, A. H., and S. Chaiken. 1993. *The Psychology of Attitudes*. Fort Worth: Harcourt Brace Jovanovich.

Ehrlich, L. G. 1981. "The Pathogenic Secret." In J. W. Chesebro, ed., *Gay Speak: Gay Male and Lesbian Communication*, pp. 130–41. New York: Pilgrim.

Fazio, R. H. 1986. "How Do Attitudes Guide Behavior?" In R. M. Sorrentino and E. T. Higgins, eds., *The Handbook of Motivation and Cognition: Foundations of Social Behavior*, pp. 204–43. New York: Guilford.

Fazio, R. H., and D. R. Roskos-Ewoldsen. 1994. "Acting as We Feel: When and How Attitudes Guide Behavior." In S. Shavitt and T. C. Brock, eds., *Persuasion: Psychological Insights and Perspectives*, pp. 71–93. Boston: Allyn and Bacon.

Festinger, L. 1957. *The Theory of Cognitive Dissonance*. New York: Harper and Row.

Heider, F. 1958. *The Psychology of Interpersonal Relations*. New York: Wiley.

Herek, G. M. 1987. "Can Functions Be Measured? A New Perspective on the Functional Approach to Attitudes." *Social Psychology Quarterly* 50:285–303.

Herek, G. M., and K. T. Berrill, eds. 1992. *Hate Crimes: Confronting Violence Against Lesbians and Gay Men*. Newbury Park, Cal.: Sage.

Katz, D. 1960. "The Functional Approach to the Study of Attitudes." *Public Opinion Quarterly* 24:163–204.

LaPiere, R. T. 1934. "Attitudes vs. Actions." *Social Forces* 13:230–37.

Larson, C. U. 1995. *Persuasion: Reception and Responsibility*. 7th ed. Belmont, Cal.: Wadsworth.

Morin, S. T., and E. M. Garfinkle. 1981. "Male Homophobia." In J. W. Chesebro, ed., *Gay Speak: Gay Male and Lesbian Communication*, pp. 117–29. New York: Pilgrim.

Newcomb, T. M. 1963. "An Approach to the Study of Communicative Acts." *Psychological Review* 60:393–404.

O'Keefe, D. J. 1990. *Persuasion: Theory and Research*. Newbury Park, Cal.: Sage.

Osgood, C. E., P. Tannenbaum, and G. Suci. 1957. *The Measurement of Meaning*. Urbana: University of Illinois Press.

Perloff, R. M. 1993. *The Dynamics of Persuasion*. Hillsdale, N.J.: Lawrence Erlbaum.

Petty, R. E., and J. T. Cacioppo. 1981. *Attitudes and Persuasion: Classic and Contemporary Approaches.* Dubuque, Iowa: Brown.

—— 1986. *Communication and Persuasion: Central and Peripheral Routes to Attitude Change.* New York: Springer-Verlag.

Pharr, S. 1988. *Homophobia: A Weapon of Sexism.* Little Rock: Women's Project.

Pratkanis, A. R., and A. G. Greenwald. 1989. "A Sociocognitive Model of Attitude Structure and Function." In L. Berkowitz, ed., *Advances in Experimental Social Psychology*, 22:245–85. San Diego: Academic.

Reardon, K. K. 1981. *Persuasion: Theory and Context.* Beverly Hills, Cal.: Sage.

—— 1991. *Persuasion in Practice.* Newbury Park, Cal.: Sage.

Russo, V. 1987. *The Celluloid Closet: Homosexuality in the Movies.* 2d ed. New York: Harper and Row.

Shavitt, S. 1989. "Operationalizing Functional Theories of Attitudes." In A. R. Pratkanis, S. J. Breckler, and A. G. Greenwald, eds., *Attitude Structure and Function*, pp. 311–37. Hillsdale, N.J.: Lawrence Erlbaum.

Sherif, C. W., and M. Sherif, eds. 1967. *Attitude, Ego-Involvement, and Change.* New York: Wiley.

Sherif, C. W., M. Sherif, and R. E. Nebergall. 1965. *Attitude and Attitude Change: The Social Judgment-Involvement Approach.* Philadelphia: Saunders.

Siegel, P. 1981. "Androgyny, Sex-Role Rigidity, and Homophobia." In J. W. Chesebro, ed., *Gay Speak: Gay Male and Lesbian Communication*, pp. 142–52. New York: Pilgrim.

Simms, S. A. 1981. "Gay Images on Television." In J. W. Chesebro ed., *Gay Speak: Gay Male and Lesbian Communication*, pp. 153–61. New York: Pilgrim.

Zanna, M. P., E. T. Higgins, and C. P. Herman, eds. 1982. *Consistency in Social Behavior: The Ontario Symposium.* Vol. 2. Hillsdale, N.J.: Lawrence Erlbaum.

Zimbardo, P. G., E. B. Ebbesen, and C. Maslach. 1977. *Influencing Attitudes and Changing Behavior.* 2d ed. Reading, Mass.: Addison-Wesley.

Dee Bridgewater

Effective Coming Out: Self-Disclosure
Strategies to Reduce Sexual Identity Bias

Gays, lesbians, and bisexuals comprise a *sexual identity minority* targeted for discrimination by American society. Blumenfeld (1992) has postulated that bias based on sexual identity pervades America's culture (social norms, codes of behavior, customs, etc.), institutions (governmental agencies, religious organizations, educational systems, professional affiliations, etc.), and private interpersonal relationships (families, friendship networks, co-workers, etc.). Acts of bigotry are enacted in the form of civil liberty violations, discriminatory treatment in the public sector, and psychological and physical assaults (Blasingame 1992; De Cecco and Elia 1993; Herek and Berrill 1992). This malaise of hostile sentiment and resultant overt forms of discrimination have a negative impact on the lives of gays, lesbians, and bisexuals—causing psychological distress, impinged careers and social interactions, and physical harm (Blumenfeld and Raymond 1993; De Cecco and Elia 1993; Herek and Berrill 1992).

Therefore, it is vital to ascertain and implement strategies that effectively reduce the covert ideology and overt acts of discrimination based on sexual identity in American society. Furthermore, strategies must be instituted that limit, ameliorate, and repair the negative consequences of extant prejudice in the lives of gays, lesbians, and bisexuals. The goal of this chapter is to (1) advocate coming out as a prime method for reducing negative attitudes and acts of prejudice against sexual identity minorities while increasing the well-being of gays, lesbians, and bisexuals and (2) provide strategies of coming out that effectively confront sexual identity discrimination and its detrimental impact.

Blumenfeld (1992) defines coming out as "the process, often lifelong, in which a person acknowledges, accepts, and in many cases appreciates his or her lesbian, gay, bisexual, or transgender identity. This often involves sharing this information with others" (283).

Thus, Blumenfeld delineates two aspects of coming out—disclosure to one's self and to others. This chapter will encompass both these aspects; however, the particular focus will be on coming out to others.

What is the impact of coming out in reducing antigay, antilesbian, and antibisexual bias? Allport (1954) conducted seminal research on the impact of personal contact with a minority group member in reducing prejudice. More immediately relevant research results have demonstrated that individuals who know a gay, lesbian, or bisexual person tend to be less negative in their attitudes than individuals without such personal contact. Herek and Glunt (1993) have summarized much of the previous research in presenting the results of a landmark study using a national random sample and valid assessment procedures. Results of their study indicate that individuals with personal knowledge of at least one gay person were more favorable in their attitudes than those who knew no openly gay person. Further, this trend was consistent across subgroups and was true even for those individuals who have been traditionally found to be negative in their attitudes. These results add further support to the conclusions of other researchers who have reported that coming out is a potent (perhaps the most potent) method of reducing antigay, antilesbian, and antibisexual beliefs (Davis 1992; Garnets and Kimmel 1993; Gonsiorek and Weinrich 1991; Klein 1993).

What makes coming out such a powerful force for attitudinal change? Poll results indicate that only 30 percent of Americans actually know an openly gay person (Herek and Berrill 1992). Thus, 70 percent of America relies on secondhand accounts to form their opinions about gays. Similarly few Americans know an openly lesbian (de Monteflores 1993) or bisexual person (Blumstein and Schwartz 1993). Thus, most Americans develop attitudes about sexual identity minorities from acquaintances who know no openly gay, lesbian, or bisexual person and/or from media portrayals that can be inaccurate, sensationalized, or negative (see the essay by Nardi in this volume).

Therefore, actually knowing a self-acknowledged gay, lesbian, or bisexual individual replaces unsubstantiated myths about the Unknown Other who engages in homosexual activity with a human reality—a person. It is for this reason that the coming out of gays, lesbians, and bisexuals constitutes a grassroots movement in eroding discrimination against sexual identity minorities.

The remainder of this chapter is devoted to proposing a process to facilitate the decision about whether to come out and presenting coming out strategies to promote positive outcomes if the gay, lesbian, or bisexual person chooses to disclose. The first step is self-awareness.

Self-Assessment

The choice to disclose one's sexual minority identity is a landmark event in the life of an individual (Cass 1979; Troiden 1989; Klein 1993). Coming out is a rite of passage signifying a further integration of one's self-designation as gay, lesbian, or bisexual with one's external social world and, thus, is truly a transformational act (Herdt 1992). Is the person ready? One vital factor in deciding is the level of self-acceptance the individual has achieved in his or her identity as a gay, lesbian, or bisexual. The process of establishing a sexual identity is complex and lengthy for every human being. When the person's sexual identity is met with widespread societal hostility and bias, the developmental process is particularly arduous (Blumstein and Schwartz 1993; de Monteflores 1993; Troiden 1989). Therefore, the major consideration an individual must make in deciding to come out is, "Where am I in my own self-acceptance."

Seeking help from gay, lesbian, and bisexual affirmative friendship networks, organizations, and/or mental health professionals who are affirmative in their clinical approach could be valuable in facilitating an individual's positive gay, lesbian, or bisexual identity. Furthermore, those supportive others could help the individual ascertain if he or she is ready to disclose (Klein 1993; Troiden 1989).

Another factor to consider in the deliberation of coming out is the expertise of the gay, lesbian, or bisexual on sexual identity issues. Although the interpersonal relationship seems primary in reducing bias against sexual identity minorities (Blumstein and Schwartz 1993; Herek and Glunt 1993), a secondary, didactic aspect factor needs to be noted. As stated earlier, it is most likely that the heterosexual person to whom disclosure is made will have little firsthand, accurate information about gay, lesbian, or bisexual people. Therefore, the individual who comes out needs to make an effort to obtain accurate information so that she or he can dispel any fallacies and myths. *Is It a Choice? Answers to Three Hundred of the Most Frequently Asked Questions About Gays and Lesbians* by Eric Marcus is a comprehensive source of basic information. *The Bisexual Option* by Fritz Klein offers a wealth of information as well as contact information for bisexual organizations.

Finally, the individual gay, lesbian, or bisexual must assess the actual impact coming out will have on his or her life. What are the legal, professional, psychological, and physical safety repercussions connected with coming out? Coming out might cause disruptions in familial relationships, discrimination on the job, or psychological and physical violence (Garnets and Kimmel 1993; Herek and Berrill 1992; Blumstein and Schwartz 1993; and Klein 1993). Thus, the potential for negative repercussions from coming out are real.

Is it worth it? The individual must analyze the costs against the potential gains. People who have come out report a sense of greater freedom and political empowerment, a deeper sense of integration in life, the overcoming of career impingements, and a more developed social sphere.

Coming Out Strategy Assessment

Coming out is a public statement of one's sexual identity geared to reduce the negative effects of prejudice in the life of the person who is disclosing. This reduction can take two forms: (1) an intrinsic reduction in negative attitudes within the person to whom disclosure is made; or, 2) a reduction and/or containment in discriminatory acts perpetrated by the person.

These two hoped-for consequences call for two different coming out strategies. The person contemplating disclosure must establish a realistic goal—intrinsic attitudinal change or extrinsic behavioral containment. This decision is based on the ideological bent of the person to whom the gay, lesbian, or bisexual is contemplating disclosure. Just as there is no one way to be gay, lesbian, or bisexual, there is also no one way to be antigay, antilesbian or antibisexual. I propose that there are diverse antigay, antilesbian, and antibisexual orientations, ranging from the more benign to the more virulent (Herek and Berrill 1992).

Assessment of the Other Person

The individual contemplating disclosure must determine if the person to whom she or he might disclose simply has benign heterosexist attitudes or engages in virulent homo/biphobic discrimination. If the person is more benign, then attitudinal change would be a realistic goal. If the person is more homo/biphobic, then containing antigay, antilesbian, and antibisexual behaviors would be a more realistic goal.

A second factor needs to be assessed in deciding one's disclosure strategy. What are the dynamics of the relationship between the individual contemplating disclosure and the person to whom she or he is contemplating coming out? How close and emotionally charged is this relationship? If the person has a stronger, more favorable attitude and a longer continuity of interaction with the gay, lesbian, or bisexual, it is likely that the person would have a greater motivation to relinquish his or her biased attitudes (Herek and Glunt 1993). Inversely, if the relationship is marked by little emotional attachment or continuity, it is likely little motivation to change exists (Herek and Berrill 1992).

Two scenarios will be the prime foci of discussion: (1) the situation in which the person classifies as low in her or his bias orientation (heterosexist) and high in relationship commitment (motivated) and (2) the situation in which the person is high in her or his bias orientation (homo/biphobic) and low in relationship commitment (not motivated). Some incidental comments on the remaining two situations in which the person is low in both bias and commitment and high in both bias and commitment will be made.

The Strategy of Inherent Attitudinal Change

If an individual does not have a powerful personal commitment to homo/biphobic beliefs and has an intimate relationship with the gay, lesbian, or bisexual who has come out, the possibility of inherent attitudinal change is likely to exist (Blumenfeld and Raymond 1993). Commonsensically, in this case scenario there is little resistance to and a high motivation for change. How can the person contemplating coming out ascertain if a mild bias is the mindset of the specific person to whom he or she might disclose? The prime indicator would be the person's observed behaviors. Does he or she *persistently* make antigay, antilesbian, or antibisexual jokes and/or slurs? Does he or she subscribe to deeply held values of religious or secular groups that promote antigay, antilesbian, or antibisexual agendas? Has he or she repeatedly mentioned (or has the person observed) any acts of overt discrimination? It should be noted that this is an ambiguous situation, the inference being that the person is relatively benign in his or her attitudes from an absence of biased actions. The situation becomes less ambiguous if an overt affirmative behavior is observed.

Since the relationship is an intimate one, the individual contemplating disclosure probably has a sense of the person's beliefs; however, if the gay, lesbian, or bisexual feels he or she has too little data to assess the person's position, a "testing of the waters" is suggested. The person could mention a gay-, lesbian-, or bisexual-related issue from the popular media (e.g., a referendum on equal civil rights for sexual identity minorities) in a nonopinionated manner and observe the person's response. Does she or he respond in an ambiguous or affirmative fashion, or is the response hostile to gays, lesbians, or bisexuals?

In making her or his assessment, it is important for the person contemplating coming out to be as precise as possible in ascertaining the specific attitude of the person to whom she or he might disclose. Negative attitudes toward gays, lesbians, and bisexuals have been globally conceptualized as general ideological bias against sexual identity minorities; however, this is too broad a conceptualization for the individual contemplating coming out. What is the person's precise attitude toward individuals who have the specific demographics of the individual who is coming out? If the individual is a gay male, what are the person's attitudes toward gays; if a lesbian, what are the attitudes toward lesbians; if a bisexual female or bisexual male, what are the attitudes toward bisexual women or bisexual men?

Finally, the gay, lesbian or bisexual needs to assess the nature of his or her relationship with the person. Is the person a family member, friend, coworker? What needs to be established is a sense of how strong the bond is in the relationship. The stronger the bond, the more likely the person will be willing to work through any psychological conflict that coming out might generate (Garnets and Kimmel 1993).

Overall, the individual contemplating disclosure must assess the strength of the other person's pervasive negativity to one of the specific sexual identity minority groups—gays, lesbians, or bisexuals. Then the individual contemplating coming out must estimate the other person's positivity to him or her as an individual. Finally, the individual contemplating disclosure must compare this generic negative reaction to gays, lesbians, or bisexuals with the specific positive reaction to him or her as an individual. The less negative the pervasive disregard for a particular sexual identity minority, and the more positive the regard for the specific individual disclosing, the more likely the person would be to change his or her attitudes. Sometimes it can be a fine call. The individual contemplating disclosure may want to talk it over with friends, knowledgeable acquaintances from the gay, lesbian, or bisexual communities and/or trusted counselors.

If the individual feels that the orientation of the person and the quality of the relationship are such that an inherent attitudinal change can occur, it is suggested that one come out in a fairly direct manner: "I am gay/lesbian/bisexual." As stated earlier the individual can then offer her or his willingness to discuss the person's concerns, making it clear that the issue at hand is working through any possible biased attitudes on the person's part and affirming that the individual is comfortable with his or her own gayness/lesbianism/bisexuality.

At this point the individual must follow the lead of the person to whom he or she has disclosed. How willing is the person to proceed, and in what way? If the person is fairly open, the gay, lesbian, or bisexual can then invite the person to become more integrated into her or his gay, lesbian, or bisexual social network. A suggested guide in this process would be the gay, lesbian, or bisexual person's memories of his or her own coming out process of increasing self-acceptance. What was it like as she or he became more comfortable with her or his sexual identity and became more integrated socially with gays, lesbians, or bisexuals? Recalling that process could make the person more empathic in being patient while facilitating greater acceptance and interaction on the part of the person to whom he or she has disclosed. Do not get discouraged by a negative initial response; when given time to think about the situation, many people will gradually become more comfortable and accepting.

As this process unfolds, it would be appropriate for the individual to simultaneously and constructively confront the person on any unconscious biased behaviors they may be committing. Pointing out the person's use of noninclusive language (*wife/husband* rather than *spouse/partner*) or the person's laughter at homo/biphopic jokes can serve a consciousness-raising function. Also, if and when the person is ready, the individual might invite him or her to be more active in demonstrating support for gays, lesbians, and bisexuals—confronting people he or she knows on remarks denigrating to nonheterosexuals, advocating affirmative policies for sexual identity minorities at work, and talking with their relatives about the inconsistency of sexual identity prejudice with democratic values, for example.

As a last note, the possibility exists that when confronted with an openly gay, lesbian, or bisexual individual, the person may respond in an overt homo/biphobic manner. If the person to whom disclosure is made "doesn't take it too well," a strategy of containment is offered.

The Strategy of Containment

If a person is highly homo/biphobic and has little motivation to change, it is unlikely that he or she will forego his or her negative beliefs (Blumenfeld and

Raymond 1993). Also, it is likely that she or he will be resistant to limiting her or his acts of discrimination (Herek and Berrill 1992). Therefore, it would be unrealistic for the individual to establish a goal of inherent attitudinal change with such a person. An attempt to limit and/or contain the negative impact of the person's acts of discrimination by making the person accountable for his or her actions would be more realistic. Commonsensically, the greater the negative consequences of homo/biphobic actions, the more likely a person will abstain from such acts.

Determining if a person is homo/biphobic is a less ambiguous situation than the heterosexist scenario discussed above. It is likely that the homo/biphobe will be more overt in committing observable biased comments and/or discriminatory acts (Blumenfeld 1992; Herek and Berrill 1992; Klein 1993). The individual contemplating disclosure will also be aware of the bond strength of the relationship, which would provide an index of the person's motivation to change.

If the individual ascertains that the person to whom he or she will disclose is fairly homo/biphobic and that the relationship is not marked by a close emotional bonding, a fairly indirect coming out is suggested: "I am offended by discrimination against gays/lesbians/bisexuals." It is important to come out first as a person who is affirmative of gays/lesbians/bisexuals and then, when appropriate, to come out personally as gay, lesbian, or bisexual. In this way the issue is made unambiguously clear. Prejudice is the salient point. Specifically, the person must understand that sexual identity discrimination is intolerable.

Interactions should be directed against the behaviors of the homo/biphobe and not toward attitudes. The individual who has come out can state that everyone has a right to his or her beliefs but no one has a right to discriminate. It must be emphasized that it is most effective for the person to avoid engaging the homo/biphobe in her or his biased belief system. Herek and Berrill (1992) have discussed the psychological and functional needs certain people have to adhere to antigay attitudes and commit antigay acts. Such homophobic individuals maintain a sense of personal well-being in part through their antigay orientation. A confrontation on such deeply held beliefs could be taken as a threat and thus exacerbate the homo/biphobe's biased acts (Herek and Berrill 1992).

The individual might cautiously address the belief system of the homo/biphobe to point out inconsistencies. For example, if the person has a religious or ethical belief in the equality of all people, the individual could point out the inconsistency of the person's discrimination against sexual identity minorities with his or her conviction to egalitarianism. The resulting cognitive discomfort might cause the person to restrict his or her biased actions.

However, the most effective tack would lie in establishing an environment in which the homo/biphobe is held accountable for her or his actions. Depending on the setting, the individual can point out that the person's actions are causing a disruption in the family or friendship network or are decreasing productivity on the job. It should be noted that there might be an initial hostile reaction, causing the homo/biphobe to increase his or her discriminatory behaviors. Therefore, the more containment pressure placed on the homo/biphobe, the better. It would be wise for the individual to enlist informal and formal support systems to join in confronting the homo/biphobe on hisorher behavior. Family members, friends, and coworkers who voice protests against the homo/biphobe's actions would add containment support. Also, the reality of supervisors, company arbitrators, and lawyers threatening possible reprimands, job dismissal, and other legal and/or financial repercussions can be a powerful motivator for inhibiting discriminatory actions.

The individual needs to determine the support network he or she has available and may wish to employ in confronting the homo/biphobe. Do not go it alone. It could be appropriate for the individual to establish a hierarchy of people to whom she or he chooses to disclose. One may choose to disclose to individuals who are more positive in their beliefs, using the attitudinal change strategy stipulated above. Some of these individuals could then serve as members of a support network to aid in containing the biased behaviors of the homo/biphobe. Consulting with supervisors or other pertinent support staff on the work setting's policies and legal redress to sexual identity bias would also be advised before the individual discloses on the job.

If the relationship between the gay person and the homo/biophobe is highly committed, on the other hand, the homo/biphobic person may be sufficiently motivated to change her or his biased attitudes. This often happens to parents, relatives, and close friends of lesbians, bisexuals, and gay males. Their concern for the person who has come out to them forces them to rethink their prejudices. If this happens, the gay, lesbian, or bisexual person can employ the attitudinal change strategy stipulated above.

A final scenario needs to be discussed. All gays, lesbians, and bisexuals know individuals who express mild heterosexist views but are not personal intimates. Anyone—no matter what their sexuality—might feel the need to confront this heterosexism for political reasons. If the lesbian, gay, or bisexual feels motivated to come out, the attitudinal change strategy would be appropriate; however, this might necessitate an increase in interpersonal interactions to have more of an effect. If that is not possible, the alternative is to enlist the intervention of another person (for example, a supervisor, co-worker, relative, or friend who is close to them) in confronting them. Heterosexism needs to be challenged wherever it exists, but it is more effective when some kind of personal relationship is involved.

All too many lesbians, gay males, and bisexuals think they have effectively come out when they have merely marched in a Gay Pride parade or confronted some strangers while remaining closeted to those with whom they could really make a difference: their close friends, relatives, and co-workers. It is only by coming out to the people to whom we are closest that significant change can occur. Prejudice against sexual identity minorities is a deep-seated aspect of American culture. Biased actions are a subsequent widespread result of this ideology. Coming out can have a potent impact in eroding these attitudes and in limiting biased acts against gays, lesbians, and bisexuals. However, it is vital for the individual who comes out to choose an effective strategy of disclosure. This choice must be based on the realistic goal of changing inherent belief systems or containing biased behaviors vis-à-vis the person to whom the gay, lesbian, or bisexual discloses. Ultimately, the most important goals are overcoming heterosexism and increasing the well-being of the individuals who have come out. What force could be more powerful in ending discrimination against sexual identity minorities than a national community of happy and fulfilled gay, lesbian, and bisexual individuals?

REFERENCES

Allport, G. W. 1954. *The Nature of Prejudice.* Reading, Mass.: Addison-Wesley.
Blasingame, B. M. 1992. "The Roots of Biphobia: Racism and Internalized Heterosexism." In E. R. Weise, ed., *Closer to Home: Bisexuality and Feminism,* pp. 47–54. Seattle: Seal.
Blumenfeld, W. J., ed. 1992. *Homophobia: How We All Pay the Price.* Boston: Beacon.
Blumenfeld, W. J., and D. Raymond, eds. 1993. *Looking at Gay and Lesbian Life.* Boston: Beacon.
Blumstein, P. W., and P. Schwartz. 1993. "Bisexuality: Some Social Psychology Issues." In L. D. Garnets and D. C. Kimmel, eds., *Psychological Perspectives on*

Lesbian and Gay Male Experiences, pp. 168–84. New York: Columbia University Press.

Cass, V. C. 1979. "Homosexual Identity Formation: A Theoretical Model." *Journal of Homosexuality* 4:219–36.

Davis, P. 1992. "The Role of Disclosure in Coming Out Among Gay Men." In K. Plummer, ed., *Modern Homosexualities: Fragments of Lesbian and Gay Experience*, pp. 75–86. New York: Routledge.

De Cecco, J. P., and J. P. Elia, eds. 1993. *If You Seduce a Straight Person, Can You Make Them Gay? Issues in Biological Essentialism Versus Social Constructionism in Gay and Lesbian Identities.* New York: Haworth.

de Monteflores, C. 1993. "Notes on the Management of Difference." In L. D. Garnets and D. C. Kimmel, eds., *Psychological Perspectives on Lesbian and Gay Male Experiences*, pp. 218–47. New York: Columbia University Press.

Garnets, L. D., and D. C. Kimmel, eds. 1993. *Psychological Perspectives on Lesbian and Gay Male Experiences.* New York: Columbia University Press.

Gonsiorek, J. C., and J. D. Weinrich, eds. 1991. *Homosexuality: Research Implications for Public Policy.* Newbury Park, Cal.: Sage.

Herdt, G., ed. 1992. *Gay Culture in America: Essays from the Field.* Boston: Beacon.

Herek, G. M., and K. T. Berrill, eds. 1992. *Hate Crimes: Confronting Violence Against Lesbians and Gay Men.* Newbury Park, Cal.: Sage.

Herek, G. M., and E. K. Glunt. 1993. "Interpersonal Contact and Heterosexuals' Attitudes Toward Gay Men: Results from a National Survey." *Journal of Sex Research* 30(3):239–44.

Klein, F. 1993. *The Bisexual Option.* New York: Harrington Park.

Marcus, E. 1993. *Is It a Choice? Answers to Three Hundred of the Most Frequently Asked Questions About Gays and Lesbians.* San Francisco: Harper.

Troiden, R. R. 1989. "The Formation of Homosexual Identities." *Journal of Homosexuality* 17:43–73.

Weinberg, G. 1973. *Society and the Healthy Homosexual.* Garden City, N.J.: Doubleday/Anchor.

Weise, E. R. 1992. *Closer to Home: Bisexuality and Feminism.* Seattle: Seal.

Walter L. Williams

Multicultural Perspectives on Reducing Heterosexism: Looking for Strategies That Work

The dominant perspective of the lesbian and gay movement has been severely hampered by a focus limited almost entirely to the United States in the last half of the twentieth century. It is necessary to get away from what Gore Vidal has called "the dictatorship of the present," the limits of the here and now. While many activists have benefited from important lessons and inspiration from the recent African American civil rights movement and from the feminist movement, a wider perspective can be gained by also analyzing the successes of other groups that have confronted and reduced prejudice. For example, within the last two centuries Japanese Americans, Jewish Americans, Mormons, Irish Americans, and others have made substantial progress in reducing prejudice against their groups. Meaningful lessons can be learned from the historical experience of each of these groups as well as from the antislavery movement, the women's suffrage movement, the labor movement, and even the early lesbian/gay movement itself.

Another particularly valuable source of learning is to focus on cultures (either in the past or the present) that do not discriminate against sexual and gender diversity. What are the characteristics of such societies and how do they incorporate same-sex eroticism into their worldviews without feeling threatened by this reality? These questions especially apply to cultures that recognize and value same-sex marriages and families. Such a multicultural understanding can give significant insights for contemporary efforts to legalize same-sex marriages and to recognize domestic partner benefits, child custody, foster care, and adoption.

I have written elsewhere (Williams 1986, 1992a) about the acceptance of same-sex relationships in Native American cultures. In contrast to male-dominant cultures, many aboriginal American societies treated women with high respect and prestige. In such gender-egalitarian cultures there is nothing wrong with a "feminine" male taking on aspects of women's roles or a "masculine" female becoming a hunter and warrior. The fact that people differ in their gender styles and their sexual inclinations is accepted as an elemental reality of the sacredness of life. Specifically, this gender and sexual variance is seen in many Native American religions as a gift from the spirit world, of great benefit to families, to friendships, and to society as a whole.

While Native Americans offer some of the world's best examples of non-homophobic cultures, we can learn other lessons from several new studies that investigate homosexuality in Asia. While these cultures are not gender egalitarian, they do offer examples of ways by which male-male love can be accepted. Unfortunately, because only a few brief reports have so far been published on Asian female homosexuality, conclusions have to be made primarily from books that have focused on males. A high priority needs to be given to encourage lesbian researchers to do fieldwork among women in other cultures, so as to improve our knowledge of female sexual variance worldwide.

In the meantime, we can point to some pathbreaking recent books. One of the most interesting, by anthropologist Serena Nanda (1990), focuses on effeminate or androgynous males in India who occupy an alternative gender role, distinct from either men or women. This *hijra* role is different from a transsexual role in the West. Western ideology, uncomfortable with ambiguity, strives to eliminate in-between categories by forcing every person to conform to one of only two gender roles.

On the other hand, Nanda points out, before British colonialism exported alien Western homophobia to India traditional Hindu ideology not only accommodated the reality of ambiguity and diversity among different personality types but also conceptualized androgynous persons as special sacred beings. Hindu mythology makes frequent reference to combined man/woman beings. The reputation of hijras as religious figures, combining both man and woman, thus provided them with social respect. That respect has declined sharply because of the impact of British colonialism, but among many traditional Hindus, even today, hijras are seen as representatives of the Hindu goddess Bahuchara Mata, which endows them with ritual power.

Nanda suggests that religion is a crucial factor in a culture's acceptance of homosexuality and gender variance. Sexual/gender nonconformists are socially accepted when a religion offers (1) a specific explanation for such difference, (2) formalized traditions for such persons in ritual, (3) a recognition that there are many different paths to personal fulfillment, enlightenment, or salvation, and (4) the idea that such nonconformists cannot resist following their own true nature and are fated to be the way they are.

This is similar to my own research findings among traditional Native North American cultures, where gender nonconformists are seen as making special contributions to society that are different than what the average person does. These might be as a religious leader, a healer, a teacher, or as a person of prestige (Williams 1986, 1992b). Androgynous "Two Spirit Persons," who are conceived as combining both the spirit of man and the spirit of woman, are given social prestige precisely because of their difference from the average person. The differences are *emphasized* and thus are seen as providing society something positive, some benefits that it would not gain if everyone were the same.

The acceptance of those who are most different, the androgynous gender-blenders, makes social acceptance easier for all homosexually inclined people in such societies. In an atmosphere where that culture's version of drag queens or butch dykes are valued as exceptional persons, little notice is taken of masculine males or feminine females who prefer a partner of the same sex. Homosexuality is not controversial, neither socially nor politically. In such cultures people involved in same-sex relationships are not denigrated, subjected to violence, or forced to hide. Instead, they are integrated into their extended family and community and often acknowledged with special social and religious positions (see Williams 1986 and 1992a).

The implication here is that, rather than trying so hard to blend in, we should be emphasizing our uniqueness. The dominant message propounded by the radical right in the 1980s was that everyone *should* be the same. That desire for sameness, for "being normal," has a strong attraction for people living in a diverse society that is going through great changes. The gay rights movement has not given society a positive message to counter that desire. All we have done is to beg for equal rights, appealing for justice. Unfortunately, such appeals are not persuasive for many people.

Why should heterosexuals support gay rights? What's in it for them? One effective strategy is to show how homophobia hurts heterosexuals (see Blumenfeld 1992). Another is to draw on the Native American and South Asian traditions of religious respect for differences among people. If everyone were the same, these religious teachings suggest, then society would lose out on the creativity and aliveness that different perspectives help to bring about. If we want society to advance, we need to do everything we can to promote independent thinking and creativity. Mindless conformity is, economically as well as emotionally and intellectually, a dead-end road. The lessons to be drawn here are important for a multicultural understanding of homophobia and what must be done to overcome it. It is not enough for a religion to be "tolerant" of gender diversity and sexual variation; it must also provide specific recognition for such diversity.

We can see this clearly in the case of Thailand, whose national religion of Buddhism makes Thailand one of the most nonhomophobic nations in the world. Peter Jackson (1989) did research on homosexuality while living in Thailand for several years. He quotes extensively from a magazine advice column for homosexuals that has appeared in several Thai mass-market publications since the early 1970s. This columnist reprints letters from homosexually inclined Thais from throughout the country and then offers them advice from an accepting pro-gay perspective. This column has had a major impact in helping general readers see things from a gay and lesbian point of view. This example offers American activist groups the idea that we should be trying to influence supermarket tabloids and other mass-market periodicals to include gay-authored advice columns, as an influential tool for reducing heterosexism in America. While openly gay columnists like Deb Price and Gabriel Rotello have been a positive influence for readers of American newspaper editorial pages, an even bigger impact could be made through advice columns.

While suffering from the same kinds of male dominance found in most other areas of mainland Asia, Thai culture is not afflicted by the kind of institutionalized homophobia that is seen in America. Besides the lack of religious homophobia, there are no laws against homosexuality, and the Thai government does not try to repress people's private sexual behavior. Androgynous gender-mixing queens (called *kathoey*), butch lesbians (called *Tom*), intergenerational man-boy relationships (translated as "love child"), and bisexuals are all well known and accepted. Individuals of these types, as well as gender-conforming homosexuals, seldom experience job discrimination, police harassment, antigay violence, or any of the manifold evidences of homophobia that are common occurrences in America.

Yet gays and lesbians still experience problems in Thailand. These problems come almost entirely from two sources: unstable relationships and pressures from the person's family to marry heterosexually. Such pressures from relatives occur mainly because of the high value attached to having children. Those who are exclusively homosexual are not discriminated against; they are rather pitied because they are seen to be childless.

One thing that is necessary, in order to improve gay status in the Thai cultural context, is for gay households to adopt children. In contrast to Anglo-American culture, which fosters individual autonomy, Thai culture fosters intergenerational interdependence. People are encouraged to have children in order to have someone to provide for them in their old age. In this context, perhaps gays should focus on getting children. Much of the social stigma against gays in Thailand is not based on any idea of sinfulness or sickness but simply on the fact that they exist outside the family structure and thus will be left alone and unprovided for in their old age.

At this point, stable lesbian and gay households do not often exist in Thailand, since most unmarried persons live with their parents. When they get old, in turn, they need children to take care of them. In third world societies without governmental welfare support systems for the infirm and aged, and without adequate economic resources for most individuals to dependably set aside enough money to support themselves in their old age, people survive by their reliance on kin. My research on Native American androgynous two-spirit persons (Williams 1986) leads me to feel that one of the most important reasons why such persons are so socially accepted in their communities is that they have traditionally been seen as the logical persons to provide care for their young nephews and nieces and as adoptive parents for orphan children. This has two beneficial social functions: to provide caring households for orphans and gay/lesbian teenagers, and to provide care for elderly nonreproducers.

This perspective implies that third world gays and lesbians should not necessarily look only to a Western-style romantic relationship for their long-term good but should also strive to fit themselves into a kinship system. Whether single or coupled, they can do this by providing economic and emotional support for their siblings' children and/or by adoption. Given the massive numbers of homeless children in many third world countries, lesbian and gay individuals as well as same-sex couples could thus fulfill an important beneficial economic role for their society. The adoption issue is clearly a crucial one for the future of gay communities in the third world, if not in America as well. In the United States, as our population ages and as there are fewer young people to help support and take care of the baby-boom elderly, an anthropological perspective suggests that gay and lesbian political leaders should therefore emphasize adoption rights as a prime gay issue.

Thai attitudes toward sexuality of youth also differ from those in the West. Concerning homophobia, Jackson explains its absence in Thailand as being due to child-rearing techniques that emphasize "having fun" as a high value, while children are not exposed to antihomosexual rhetoric. Thai youths therefore grow up without much sexual inhibition. In contrast, an American child's absorption of popular antisexual, homophobic, and transphobic attitudes leads them to view lesbians and gays as disgusting and sinful. Among those youths who later develop sexual attractions to someone of the same sex, such feelings are often met with alarm and self-hatred. To reestablish their self-identity as "good people," such insecure individuals may lash out against open gays and lesbians. That is, homophobia may arise because of a person's fearful reaction to their own repressed homosexual feelings.

If there is not much sexual repression in one's childhood, there will not be much homophobia. This view suggests that homophobia is primarily learned in the home and the school and must be changed at those levels. As long as parents are fearful that their children might turn out to be lesbian or gay, and as long as other social influences do not challenge these prejudices, a change in attitude will be difficult.

What this suggests is that the same techniques which Parents and Friends of Lesbians and Gays (PFLAG) has used to overcome homophobia among parents of older children also need to be employed with parents of young children as well. When I ask my heterosexual students how they would react if one of their children turned out to be lesbian or gay, most report that they have never even thought of that possibility. We need to exert more influence on professionals who work with young parents or write child-rearing books to get them to address such issues. If parents know that their homophobic expressions could exert great psychic harm on their child, this might have the effect of getting at least some parents to inhibit their homophobia in front of their children. If such expressions are inhibited, then young people will less likely absorb prejudicial attitudes.

Jackson also suggests that Thai people are so accepting of homosexual behavior because they have strong traditional values that people should be able to "follow your own heart" (1989:108), that people should mind their own business and avoid open confrontation. This implies that gay leaders in America can best challenge homophobia in the United States by appealing to traditional American values. Ideas coming to mind include values like freedom of expression and freedom of individual choice. American ideas that people should not psychologically repress themselves can be used to highlight the damage done to children by repression of their sexuality. Greater publicity of suicides among gay youth, of violence against gay people, and of discriminatory laws (no immigration rights for gay spouses, lack of the legal right of marriage and adoption, lack of employee benefits, etc.), can be shown to violate traditional American notions of fair play and equal opportunity.

In Thailand the absence of homophobia as a public issue has traditionally meant that there is little need for a politicized gay movement. That may change if Thai people adopt more Western values and homophobic discrimination increases. But, for now, outside of some isolated Western-influenced incidents, that does not appear to be the case. The contrast in America shows that if there were not so much discrimination against homosexuals a politicized gay movement would likely never have arisen. In a nonhomophobic society there is no reason for sexuality to become political. It's just part of life. No doubt an urban gay subculture would still have existed, just as an urban gay subculture has grown dramatically in Bangkok since the 1970s. But it would not have become politicized.

This cross-cultural evidence shows that we can build our communities socially and economically, even if progress is not being made on a political level. Even if we suffer political defeats, a strong lesbian and gay community can still keep growing through nonpolitical means. For example, the most significant advances for lesbian and gay equality in the 1990s have been made in the workplace, especially in intellectual environments like computer-related fields, publishing, and universities. Well-managed corporations realize that homophobia leads to a less productive workforce. Another important development is with the newly expanded international reach of lesbian and gay perspectives on the Internet. This computerized form of worldwide communication allows an immediate means for sexual minorities to reach other readers to whom we might not otherwise have had access. Combined with a new gay openness on television, film, and in popular music (though unfortunately not yet in talk radio), and with famous media celebrities making many pro-gay public statements, substantial cultural changes are occurring outside the political arena.

It can be argued that a major mistake made by the various civil rights movements since the 1960s has been the overwhelming focus on government as the leading agent of change rather than on grassroots organizations and individuals trying to change social and economic institutions from within. That is, if we have influence within our families, neighborhoods, local social groups, and workplaces as open lesbian, gay, bisexual, and transgender people, combined with the mass media and corporate America on our side, then homophobic political initiatives will fall on increasingly deaf ears. We might decide, for tactical reasons, to support political initiatives to get people discussing the issue of sexual discrimination, but let's be very clear that our larger goal is to change attitudes.

We learned from the government's nonresponsiveness to the AIDS epidemic that we cannot merely retreat into our queer ghettos and pay no attention to the larger society. We should build strong vibrant communities that genuinely show compassion for our people, but we also must spread our cultural influence outward. We must never forget that the "straight" mainstream contains a lot of queer people, whether adults hiding in their straightlaced closets or youths just coming into their own identities.

Japan is another nation from which we can learn important lessons. With a history of acceptance of same-sex love, Japan deserves to be ranked (along with the cultures of ancient Greece and the American Indians) as one of the world's most important examples showing how a society can incorporate homosexuality into the core of its social organization (Watanabe and Iwata 1989). As premodern Japan's population reached an optimal point for the land available on the small island in the Edo era, there was pressure to reduce population growth. Abortion, infanticide, and encouragement of nonreproductive forms of sexual expression were demographically useful means of keeping the population stable. The expansion of the nonhomophobic Buddhist religion into Japan encouraged this trend, and early European explorers reported with horror the common social acceptance of same-sex love (ibid).

However, Japan's climate of social acceptance changed in the early twentieth century. As industrialization revolutionized Japan, and made a need for more population to provide a growing labor force, prejudice emerged against nonreproductive forms of sexuality. Once Japan embarked on an expansionist military policy after 1900, even more people were needed to man the armies and navies and to staff the large economic and political bureaucracies necessary for administering an empire. In this context the Japanese began to favor pro-procreative and antihomosexual policies imported from the West. The requirements of being a good citizen in an expansionist state meant that men were expected to sublimate their desires in favor of their jobs, while women were pressured to bear and raise more children for the growing workforce. So many Japanese people were killed during World War II that a cultural inclination to reproduce even more children took hold in Japan after 1945. Coupled with the importation of Western homophobia during the American occupation, Japan rejected its heritage of respect for sexual variance in favor of more rigid gender and sexual roles for men and women. Only recently has an emerging gay and lesbian movement begun to challenge this trend in Japan.

A multicultural perspective, from studies of Japan, Thailand, India, and Native American cultures, can thus supply many ideas as to how we might best go about attacking antigay prejudice and discrimination. Activists and scholars alike cannot afford to restrict our knowledge to the American gay and lesbian movement alone. By looking at these examples from other cultures, it is clear that any attempt to reduce antigay prejudice must promote nonhomophobic religions and gender egalitarianism, integrate uncloseted gays and lesbians into extended families, stress adoption of homeless children, and emphasize the need to restrict overpopulation. Besides continuing to build alliances with feminist and civil rights groups, we as individuals and as a community must reach out and make alliances with the world's nonhomophobic religious, pro-family, adoption, and population control groups in particular. They are our natural allies, and we need to point out to them that we can contribute significantly to the accomplishment of their goals.

As mentioned in the introduction, as part of the World Wide Web site of the ONE Institute International Gay and Lesbian Archives I am developing an Internet page, "Overcoming Heterosexism: International Perspectives," that will focus on effective strategies and techniques to reduce heterosexism in different cultures. The extent to which we can drop our cultural blinders and pay attention to what is going on in other nations around the world will make a crucial difference in the campaign against homophobia and heterosexism.

REFERENCES

Blackwood, E. 1984. "Lesbian Behavior in Cross-Cultural Perspective." M.A. thesis, San Francisco State University.
—— 1985. "Breaking the Mirror: The Construction of Lesbianism and the Anthropological Discourse on Homosexuality." *Journal of Homosexuality* 11:1–18.

—— 1986. *The Many Faces of Homosexuality: Anthropological Approaches to Homosexual Behavior.* New York: Harrington Park.

Bolton, R. 1994. "Sex, Science, and Social Responsibility: Cross-Cultural Research on Same-Sex Eroticism and Sexual Intolerance." *Cross-Cultural Research* 28:134–90.

Boswell, J. 1994. *Same-Sex Unions in Pre-Modern Europe.* New York: Villard.

Bullough, V. 1976. *Sexual Variance in Society and History.* Chicago: University of Chicago Press.

Carrier, J. 1995. *De los Otros: Intimacy and Homosexuality Among Mexican Men.* New York: Columbia University Press.

Conner, R. 1993. *Blossom of Bone: Reclaiming the Connections Between Homoeroticism and the Sacred.* San Francisco: Harper.

Cory, D. W. 1956. *Homosexuality in Cross-Cultural Perspective.* New York: Julian.

Dover, K. J. 1978. *Greek Homosexuality.* Cambridge: Harvard University Press.

Duberman, M., M. Vicinus, and G. Chauncey, eds. 1989. *Hidden from History: Reclaiming the Gay and Lesbian Past.* New York: New American Library.

Dynes, W. et al., eds. 1990. *Encyclopedia of Homosexuality.* New York: Garland.

Eskridge, W. N. 1996. *The Case for Same-Sex Marriage.* New York: Simon and Schuster.

Evans-Pritchard, E. E. 1970. "Sexual Inversion Among the Azande." *American Anthropologist* 72:1428–34.

Grahn, J. 1984. *Another Mother Tongue: Gay Words, Gay Worlds.* Boston: Beacon.

Gregersen, E. 1983. *Sexual Practices: The Story of Human Sexuality.* New York: Franklin Watts.

Hardman, P. 1990. *Homoaffectionalism.* San Francisco: ONE Institute Press and GLB Press.

Harry, J., and M. Singh Das, eds. 1980. *Homosexuality in International Perspective.* New Delhi: Vikas.

Hart, D. 1968. "Homosexuality and Transvestism in the Philippines: The Cebuano Filipino Bayot and Lakin-On." *Behavior Science Notes* 3:211–48.

Heiman, E., and C. Van Le. 1975. "Transsexualism in Vietnam." *Archives of Sexual Behavior* 4:89–95.

Herdt, G. 1981. *Guardians of the Flute: Idioms of Masculinity.* New York: McGraw-Hill.

—— 1984. *Ritualized Homosexuality in Melanesia.* Berkeley: University of California Press.

—— 1987. *The Sambia: Ritual and Gender in New Guinea.* New York: Holt, Rinehart, and Winston.

Hinsch, B. 1990. *Passions of the Cut Sleeve: The Male Homosexual Tradition in China.* Berkeley: University of California Press.

Jackson, P. A. 1989. *Male Homosexuality in Thailand: An Interpretation of Contemporary Thai Sources.* Elmhurst, N.Y., and Amsterdam: Global Academic.

Lewin, E., and W. Leap, eds. 1996. *Out in the Field: Reflections of Lesbian and Gay Anthropologists.* Urbana: University of Illinois Press.

Morris, R. J. 1990. "Aikane: Accounts of Hawaiian Same-Sex Relationships in the Journals of Captain Cook's Third Voyage (1776–1780)." *Journal of Homosexuality* 19:21–54.

Murray, S. O. 1992a. *Oceanic Homosexualities.* New York: Garland.

—— 1992b. "The 'Underdevelopment' of Gay Homosexuality in Mexico, Guatemala, Peru, and Thailand." In K. Plummer, ed., *Modern Homosexualities.* London: Routledge.

—— 1995. *Latin American Male Homosexualities.* Albuquerque: University of New Mexico Press.

Murray, S. O., and W. Roscoe, eds. In press. *Islamic Homosexualities.* New York: New York University Press.

Nanda, S. 1990. *Neither Man Nor Woman: The Hijras of India.* Belmont, Cal.: Wadsworth.

Parker, R. 1991. *Bodies, Pleasures, and Passions: Sexual Culture in Contemporary Brazil.* Boston: Beacon.

Ratti, R, ed. 1993. *A Lotus of Another Color: The Unfolding of the South Asian Gay and Lesbian Experience.* Boston: Alyson.

Robertson, C. 1989. "Art Essay: The Mahu of Hawaii." *Feminist Studies* 15: 313–26.

Robertson, J. 1992. "The Politics of Androgyny in Japan: Sexuality and Subversion in the Theater and Beyond." *American Ethnologist* 19:419–42.

Sankar, A. 1986. "Sisters and Brothers, Lovers and Enemies: Marriage Resistance in Southern Dwangtung." In E. Blackwood, ed., *The Many Faces of Homosexuality: Anthropological Approaches to Homosexual Behavior.* New York: Harrington Park.

Schalow, P. 1990. "Introduction." In I. Saikaku, ed., *The Great Mirror of Male Love,* pp. 1–46. Trans. P. Schalow. Stanford: Stanford University Press.

Schmitt, A., and J. Sofer, eds. 1990. *Homosexuality and Islam.* New York: Haworth.

Schneebaum, T. 1988. *Where the Spirits Dwell: An Odyssey in the New Guinea Jungle.* New York: Grove.

Wafer, J. 1991. *The Taste of Blood: Spirit Possession in Brazilian Candomblé.* Philadelphia: University of Pennsylvania Press.

Watanabe, T., and J. Iwata. 1989. *The Love of the Samurai: A Thousand Years of Japanese Homosexuality* . Trans. D. R. Roberts. London: Gay Men's Press.

Weston, K. 1991. *Families We Choose: Lesbians, Gays, Kinship.* New York: Columbia University Press.

—— 1993. "Lesbian/Gay Studies in the House of Anthropology." *Annual Review of Anthropology* 22:339–67.

Whitam, F., and R. Mathy. 1986. *Homosexuality in Four Societies.* New York: Praeger.

Williams, W. L. 1986. *The Spirit and the Flesh: Sexual Diversity in American Indian Culture.* Boston: Beacon.

—— 1991. *Javanese Lives: Women and Men in Modern Indonesian Society*. New Brunswick, N.J.: Rutgers University Press.

—— 1990. "Male Homosexuality in Thailand." *Journal of Homosexuality* 19:126–38.

—— 1992a. "Benefits for Nonhomophobic Societies: An Anthropological Perspective." In W. J. Blumenfeld, ed., *Homophobia: How We All Pay the Price*. Boston: Beacon.

—— 1992b. "A Cross-Cultural Perspective on the Relationship Between Male-Male Friendship and Male-Female Marriage: American Indian and Asian Examples." In P. Nardi, ed., *Men's Friendships*. Newbury Park, Cal.: Sage.

—— 1996. "Being Gay and Doing Fieldwork." In E. Lewin and W. Leap, eds., Out in the Field: Reflections of Lesbian and Gay Anthropologists. Urbana: University of Illinois Press.

—— 1997. "Social Acceptance of Same-Sex Relationships in Families: Models from Other Cultures." In A. D'Augelli and C. Patterson, eds., *Lesbian, Gay, and Bisexual Identities in Families*. New York: Oxford University Press.

PART II

Working with Ethnic Groups and Family Members

Eric Estuar Reyes and Gust A. Yep

Challenging Complexities: Strategizing with Asian Americans in Southern California Against (Heterosex)Isms

In an editorial in the newsletter of Asians and Friends–Washington (AFW), *Silk Road*, Nicolas F. Shi argues that demonstrative behavior and slogans such as "We're not Uncle Bens, we're sticky rice" are divisive, racist, and "not in step with the other marchers" at the 1994 Stonewall 25 March.[1]

In a counterargument, Don Miguel Crisostomo notes the 1987 murder of Vincent Chin, a young Chinese Man, by two unemployed autoworkers in Detroit who mistook him for a Japanese individual, the brutal beating of Loc Minh Truong in Laguna Beach, and the oppressive exploitation and eroticization of Asian Pacific sexuality such as *Miss Saigon,* and the continued battle for culturally competent HIV/AIDS services for Asian Pacific LGBS as examples of why we must express our rage and anger.[2]

These identity negotiations by Asian and Pacific Islander lesbians, bisexuals, transgendered people, and gay men display the complexity of our struggles for social change. These struggles for changes in representation and power in political, social, economic, and cultural spheres are far from unified and coherent. Mediations are further complicated by how differently individuals locate themselves in perceived and imagined communities whether comprised of only Asians and Pacific Islanders (API), people of color (POC), mainstream lesbian, gay men, bisexuals, and transgendered people (LGBT), or some combination of singular or multiply racialized, sexualized, classed, and gendered individuals.[3] Indeed, within this discussion we have sought out the perspectives of individuals in Southern California with the explicit understanding that although these perspectives speak from this region, the ideas presented here *may* have relevance to the racialized situations of Asians and Pacific Islanders throughout the United States. This is not the definitive study of APIS and heterosexism, but it is another moment in the strategic struggle for social change against discrimination and oppression.

Heterosexism and homophobia circulate along with other processes of racial, sexual, economic, and nationalist discriminations within Asian American communities. The ongoing discussions of closets and invisibility prevalent in lesbian and gay studies are not new to APIS or POC in the United States. Closets of scaled invisibility have been and continue to be discussed, whether analyzed as transnational networks, ethnic enclaves, ghettos, or individual separate safe spaces. However, the complexity of our living spaces as multiply closeted and concealed cannot be discerned by examining how to live in three different communities, the gay/lesbian community, the ethnic minority community, and the predominantly heterosexual White mainstream society, and somehow then adding them up.[4] This approach neglects the possibility of an ethnic minority LGBT community and assumes that communities are rigidly defined objects with impermeable borders. Here we argue that communities, like identities, are less objects to describe and measure, but flexible spaces wherein identities are mediated and positions established in relation to each other as processes of identity and community formation. For multiply marginalized individuals, challenging the process of community building based on narrow identity definitions is an underlying tactic toward opposing the oppression of discriminations such as racism and heterosexism. Indeed, the terms *Asian American* and *Asian and Pacific Islander* reduce the vast diversity of specific Asian and Pacific Islander ethnicities to a common linguistic site regardless of sometimes disparate and uncommon histories and agendas.[5] The central argument of this essay points to these contradictions and suggests that the process of constructing spaces in which these contradictions can be worked through is of paramount importance.

Further, Asian American communities do not exist in a vacuum, and neither do individual APIS live solely in one particular community, ethnic or otherwise. Our many communities dwell within and on the simultaneous landscape of our lived and imagined neighborhoods, cities, and countryside. How these various sites generate separate and often intervening and conflicting demands on multiply marginalized individuals create the political dilemmas of prioritizing oppressions. What is different is not only our various API communities but also who is asking and from what position are they speaking. All of us as educators, regardless of our individual or collectively constructed differences, need to examine our positionality as we experience and teach others about these oppressions within, between, and outside our daily communities. With this in mind, and with such complex interplay of sites, we realize that we cannot completely explore the myriad diversity of API communities. Nor could we in this short essay represent the tactical positions of all LBGT individuals of API heritages across the United States. Nevertheless, we hope that this small window will help generate spaces to confront the various oppressions within all our communities.

To facilitate this essay we spoke with several individuals of various Asian/Pacific backgrounds in the Southern California region to discuss issues of homophobia and heterosexism within our communities and where they worked and lived. The people with whom we spoke ranged in sexual orientation, gender, age, ethnicity, generation, and degree of working engagement with API and/or LGBT communities.[6] In these discussions we asked individuals about their backgrounds and provided them with the definitions of heterosexism and homophobia as outlined in the introduction to this book. We then asked individuals how they defined heterosexism and homophobia and how they experienced or observed these issues in their work in Asian American communities. Finally, we asked them how they confronted these manifestations and what tactics did they employ in their struggles. Again, Southern California is not emblematic of the Asian American experience, if there truly is one, but hopefully these ideas will suggest something useful for other locales. In the following essay we present framing discussions, suggest some tactical actions, and conclude with reflective comments on the complexity of heterosexism and homophobia in Asian and Pacific Islander communities.

Discussions

The individuals we spoke with expressed divergent conceptualizations of homophobia and heterosexism. According to Eric Wat, a student affairs officer working at the Asian American Studies Center at the University of California at Los Angeles, heterosexism is manifested by individuals through uncontested actions and a widely accepted belief system that showcases heterosexuality as the norm. Shella Aguilar, co-chair of the Los Angeles Asian and Pacific Islander Sisters (LAAPIS), noted that heterosexist individuals ignore the existence of lesbians and gay men and deny us our basic civil rights. Sachiko Reece, a licensed psychotherapist and advisory board member for the Asian Pacific AIDS Intervention Team (APAIT) in Los

Angeles, maintained that homophobia is a reaction to a challenge to one's heterosexist worldview in which the person experiencing the threat externalizes his or her discomfort by attacking the trigger of those feelings (i.e., an individual identified as a lesbian or gay male). Steven Shum, director of the Lesbian, Gay, and Bisexual Resource Center at the University of California at Riverside, noted that heterosexism is a matter of unrecognized privilege and assumptions that we act and live by. Diep Tran, a member of the Vietnamese Lesbian, Bisexual Women's Support Network and APAIT staff member, was more direct in saying that heterosexism is basically incompetence of (having a certain) knowledge. More than just belief, heterosexism is a way of acting, thinking, and materializing what matters from a specific (heterosexist) position.

The identity closets that others, not necessarily non-APIS or non-POC, create for us as API LGBTS also came up repeatedly. Steven Shum recalled how (API and non-API) people generally assume that he is simply a very open-minded Asian man working with gay men as opposed to thinking of him as a gay Asian man in that position. Eric Wat also noted that when he comes out (to his students), he experiences the feeling that he is betraying his Asian ancestors as much as heterosexist presumptions. Diep Tran reported similar conflated assumptions in noting how many of the Vietnamese social service workers she has worked with assume she has solely a working relationship with Vietnamese gay men. Recall the opening quote, in which Nicholas F. Shi argues against public and vocal display of desire between APIS as racist and counterproductive to the LGBT agenda and Don Miguel Crisostomo argues that, because of oppression on the economic, political, cultural, and institutional scale, this particular tactic of affirmative same-race desire is necessary. Identity closets of race, sexuality, gender, and class collide as Shi and Crisostomo speak from different positions in relation to an assumed same but different gay male identity.[7] Indeed, these examples illustrate the ways in which identity is not simply a reflection of skin color or personal history but a relation in difference that is socially constructed. Further, we argue that the complexity of racialized, gendered, and sexualized identities needs to be critically examined and perhaps tactically deployed for certain situations.

Visible Education

The primary strategy of visibility within API/POC and non-API/POC contexts challenges the universal heterosexist closet. Shella Aguilar suggested that API queers need both visibility and representation. Invisibility of API LGBTS perpetuates ignorance about API, gender, and lesbian and gay issues in both LGBT and API/POC communities. Shella Aguilar observed that she is first perceived as an Asian woman and a heterosexual object and her lesbian sexuality is conveniently rendered invisible within the Pilipino, API, and women's communities. She noted how Pilipino co-workers will talk about her in Tagalog while she is in the same room, assuming that because she is second generation she can not understand the laughter and guarded glances, even though she can. Visible representation as physical presence does not immediately translate into a deheterosexualized relationship between individuals. However, without her presence and visibility as an *out* Pilipina *and* lesbian, sexuality and the subsequent awkward moments in which opportunities emerge for individuals to challenge heterosexist assumptions would not have occurred.

To foster a more complex engagement with API LGBTs, we as APIs and others must encourage educational processes across scales of action, whether located within or between the relationships of individuals, groups, institutions, or social movements. Sachiko Reece recommended working with people at the individual and family levels. For example, in her psychotherapeutic practice she increases her clients' awareness of their heterosexist biases and offers a safe atmosphere to discuss and examine alternatives to heterosexuality. Shella Aguilar suggested that educating individuals or groups within API communities can potentially increase their awareness of lesbian and gay issues. She further noted that this educational process should be culturally and linguistically appropriate. In other words, in designing programs we must consider language ability, immigration history, social, political, and economic status, and specify API ethnicity, whether Korean, Pilipino, Vietnamese, multiple ethnicity, Laotian, Cambodian, and so on. On the individual level, J Craig Fong, chief policy analyst in the Los Angeles Gay and Lesbian Center, stated that direct confrontation with ignorance can provide heterosexist individuals with an opportunity to examine their biases and assumptions. For example, if individuals make statements such as "There are no gay Asians" or "Queers make us (Asian Americans) look bad," Fong suggested they be confronted with factual information and "lose face" by highlighting their ignorance, intolerance, and prejudices.[8] Implicit in all these educational tactics is the support, challenge, and fostering of the right of individuals to determine their own specific identities and to work toward differing positions within our various communities.

As Eric Wat states,

> Being out, present, and vocal as a gay Asian man through my daily teaching, I'm breaking stereotypes of invisibility. Students don't expect a gay man to speak about the API community and an API man to talk about the gay community. They assume gay men are not part of the API community, but that [only heterosexual] men are part of the community. It's sort of a sympathetic exclusion.

Eric Wat emphasizes the condescension implicit in assumed separate spaces and how visibility confronts these "sympathetic exclusions" by shattering constructed invisibilities, with education engaging the individual at a scale in which the processes (of ignorance) that construct those invisibilities can be dismantled.

Everyday Practice

Oppressive processes based on sexuality, like other dominating processes such as racism and sexism, are intricately linked to cultural practices—the everyday of how we live our lives, not necessarily as groups but also as individuals in relation. One possible site of this practice is how a sense of community and family serves to gender and heterosexize our obligations and expectations. In an example that specifically regards the Chinese community, J Craig Fong noted that "the family is everything.[9] In his opinion, there is an unchallenged expectation that male individuals in the family have the duty to carry out the family name and take care of the family. Fong suggested that being a good son implied not only upholding the respect of the family name but also having children, especially sons, to preserve generational continuity. Fong reasoned that because the family and community are paramount in most Asian/Pacific cultures, self-asserting and individualistic tactics such as "I am gay, and this is my life to live" are constructed as antifamily and equated with an ethnic betrayal of the unsaid collective trust for generational reproduction and community preservation. This weaving of familial duty with the heavy responsibility of generational continuity suggests one dimension of the perpetuation and reinforcement of heterosexism and sexism through familial and community patriarchal gender role expectations in Chinese American communities. We would qualify Fong's point by noting that this may not reflect *all* Chinese families, communities, or individuals, especially as Fong may be specifically referring here to the position of Chinese gay males in Chinese American communities.

On a different scale, J Craig Fong proposes that the best hope to combat heterosexism is to form an API LGBT culture by creating, teaching, disseminating, and encouraging new traditions through social, artistic, philosophical, and literary expressions of queer API experiences.[10] He also stressed the importance of "holding a flashlight to provide young people with illumination to appreciate multiple perspectives and with space to change so that younger generations can develop a strong and empowered sense of gay identity that is both self-validating and self-asserting." Fong raises the need for cross-generational queer communities, but we would add that "traditions" new or old inherently bind us to some identity construct and we should be careful of how "new" is sometimes just another version of "old" oppressions. In other words, he calls for the fostering of a Queer API Space, to which we would add that the process and close attention to it may be more important than its object goal.

Within this space the voices and experiences of APIs of various sexualities and ethnicities can be nourished by collectively shared expressions of the complexity of our particular situations. Yet the intricacy of our simultaneous and separate contexts intrudes as we try to decide what is "safe and nurturing" when media representations of API women and men, regardless of sexuality, continue to "orientalize" APIs as over/undereroticized and exoticized?[11] Who are these cultural representations for? How does cultural representation create or preclude the space for API LGBTs to even exist?

Visibility and education certainly address part of these oppressive processes, but only through creating space of and for API LGBTs can there be a place for API LGBTs in our various contexts. For example, through challenging orientalist cultural productions such as the musical *Miss Saigon*, local activists in New York were able to forge alliances with API and POC groups and, in so doing, construct a space for individuals of many differences to meet and work together.[12] In these API-specific LGBT spaces we construct a space where we can discuss, plan, and work on issues such as coming out to our heterosexist families, explore the possibilities of relationships with other APIs, produce API-specific media representations, and investigate the specificity of being LGBT-identified and Korean, Pilipino, mixed heritage, and so on.[13] Through the practice of meeting, organizing, discussing, and sharing meals, API LGBTs generate a place from which API LGBTs can confront heterosexisms both within and across API (and non-API) communities.

Alliances

The HIV/AIDS crisis has not bypassed the API communities, and its impact has affected us in as many ways as gender, ethnicity, race, class, immigration history, and language abilities serve to mediate the degree to which we can access knowledge, power, and, unfortunately not so simply, health services. All our discussants and we ourselves have at one time or another worked as volunteers, service providers, or advocates for HIV/AIDS services for APIs that are API culturally competent and linguistically appropriate. Through this work we encountered forms of sexisms, classisms, and racisms intertwined with heterosexism and homophobia, with the added thread of AIDSphobia. For example, Diep Tran noted that the intervention of condom distribution at a Vietnamese community event highlighted the conflation of homophobia, heterosexism, and AIDSphobia as the event sponsor, a Vietnamese community-based organization, cited "litter concerns" to dissuade Diep Tran from distributing brochures on safer sex and condoms. Shella Aguilar also pointed out that individuals from other API organizations assume that as a lesbian she focuses only on AIDS and ignores other issues with which lesbians are identified such as the rights of lesbians to adopt children, child care, and legal rights. Similarly, in a recent Women and HIV Conference in Los Angeles, Aguilar noted that lesbian issues were assumed to be included in women's issues.

Yet tactical interventions can challenge these intertwined oppressions. Diep Tran noted that many Vietnamese individuals aligned with Vietnamese community-based organizations are less likely to challenge the policies and perspectives of the organization, as the community and the organization are perceived to be the same entity. Thus, to challenge the organization is to challenge the community and risk a kind of community banishment. To deal with this dilemma Diep Tran has tried to create other networks of Vietnamese lesbian and bisexual women such as the Vietnamese Lesbian and Bisexual Women's Support Network. In other words, she attempted to develop a separate space in which she and others can work through issues of sexuality and Vietnamese ethnicities and from which to challenge the issue of sexuality and gender in the general Vietnamese, API, and non-Vietnamese/API community.

Shella Aguilar concentrates her coalition work on action- and issue-oriented alliances. For example, she is called upon as LAAPIS co-chair to participate on many organizing committees for events such as Lesbian Visibility Month and the API Lesbian, Gay, and Bisexual Community Event for Asian Pacific Heritage Month. She further noted that inclusion in the planning process for any activity, political or otherwise, at the beginning is the critical difference between token and inclusive participation. Both Diep Tran and

Shella Aguilar were adamant in their tactic of collective action. Yet both realized that, working in a minority within a minority within a minority, they needed to create alliances with other groups with other agendas. What is possible is often limited by "external" processes that shape the ways disparate agendas can meet. In another example API HIV/AIDS service providers like the Asian Pacific AIDS Intervention Team in Los Angeles have created multiethnic, issue-focused alliances between both API community-based organizations and other POC organizations. These alliances are not only designed to address broad isms but are also project- and action-oriented. In other words, this suggests that empowerment through education and cultural practices on the individual level can be complemented by collective action on organizational and institutional levels through tactical coalition building.[14]

However, these tactics reveal an important distinction between organizing for either "local" or "global" objectives. Tran's organizing of a separate group is an example of organizing local for local, where local becomes an identity closet that affirms the construction of unconnected closets while occluding the broad oppressive process that makes these closets necessary. Yet when the group redirects its efforts outward into the Vietnamese and non-Vietnamese community, the process becomes organizing local for global. *Global* does not mean universal, but local struggles must tactically engage in certain situations with other struggles—heterosexisms, sexisms, and classisms—that circulate across groups regardless of identity. To facilitate this form of local-for-global action, we turn to the following suggested activities.

Actions

- Create an API-specific coming out group, with mentoring to youth by experienced LGBT persons
- Create a POC-specific coming out group
- Create and support API-specific LGBT social and political groups by and for API LGBTs, building an in-group extended family feeling and an API LGBT culture.
- Create and implement educational workshops on API ethnicity, gender, and sexuality issues for local API/POC and non-API/POC organizations, local schools, and LGBT organizations, especially the media and HIV/AIDS service organizations[15]
- Demand API/POC language and cultural specificity when designing educational materials and programming

- Demand API/POC LGBT representation in the planning and implementation of API, POC, and LGBT political, social, economic, and cultural activities from the very beginning
- Support API/POC and API/POC LGBT cultural productions through sharing resources, attendance, and encouraging more programming of underrepresented artists
- Challenge orientalized API media representations and foster more complex representations of APIs and POC LGBTS
- Focus on issue-oriented and goal-focused alliances that bring various groups and individuals together
- Provide information about our various differences to students through, for example, community panel discussions, internships and other community work, a wide variety of books and magazines for local libraries, and access to the ever-growing number of web sites on the Internet such as those for Asian American and/or LGBT students.[16]

Speculations

They (non-apis or non-poc) are open to listening, but not necessarily action.
—Shella Aguilar

I (had) hoped, as an out gay api, flocks of other queer apis would come out here in Riverside. I realize what a fiction that is and that it takes more organizing.
—Steven Shum

Shella Aguilar's and Steven Shum's comments illustrate some of the limitations of visibility and representation as tactics against heterosexism and homophobia.

Our discussions with participants centered on the issue of marginalization based on sexuality, but each discussant raised issues of racism, sexism, language, and immigration histories as well. Through these discussions major themes emerged that may mirror to lesser or greater degree the particular situation in API communities in the continental United States. These major themes included the dilemma of prioritizing oppressions, the difficulties of "choosing" communities, the ongoing need to confront stereotypes of orientalized Asians and Pacific Islanders, and the struggle to be seen and *heard* within various communities of ethnicity, gender, class, and sexuality. Finally, the tactics we offer center on our ongoing struggles for visibility and representation, education and practice within all of our communities, creating cultural space and developing tactical alliances while critically examining and changing the social processes by which we endeavor for these goals.

The struggle for local and global actions against oppressions including those based on nationalist, gender, heterosexual, class, and racial discriminations is not simple. For Asian Americans this struggle is further complicated by the issue of critical mass and the question of how many individuals does a "community" make? Outside of major urban centers there simply may not be enough Asian Americans who identify as APIs to form an API-specific coming out group, for example. Yet how can we ask individuals to act as representative of a community when that community is itself a fractured concept? We return to the issue of the complexity of negotiating identity and positions. When we confront issues of heterosexism and homophobia as members of multiple communities, we must consider not only the singular oppression at hand but the context in and through which we and others perpetuate these various oppressions in our daily lives as participants, educators, and activists. The struggle is just that—a struggle—which requires moving from listening to action. Successful action necessitates courage and patience.

NOTES

We thank the participants for sharing their views, our anonymous reviewers for their comments and several readers who helped us with final revisions including Karin Aguilar-San Juan, Milton Kimura, and Stephanie Tai.

1. Rice Roundtable, "Editorial." *InformAsian: Newsletter of the Gay Asian Pacific Support Network, Los Angeles* (October 1994), 8(10):1, 4.

2. Ibid., p. 4.

3. For the purpose of brevity, we will use API referring literally to Asian and Pacific Islander individuals in order to acknowledge the difference locations and self-identification between Asians and Pacific Islanders. However, within this broad term API we are also referring to *Asian Americans*, the term that is commonly used for all individuals in the United States who identify or are identified with Asian or Pacific Islander heritages.

4. E. S. Morales, "Ethnic Minority Families and Minority Gays and Lesbians," in F. W. Bozett and M. B. Sussman, eds., *Homosexuality and Family Relations* (New York: Haworth, 1990), p. 220.

5. For a succinct discussion on the racial terms for Asians and Pacific Islanders, see J. Kehaulani Kauanui and J. H. J. Hans, "Asian Pacific Islander: Issues of Representation and Responsibility," in S. Lim-Hing, ed., *The Very Inside: An Anthology of Writing by Asian and Pacific Islander Lesbian and Bisexual Women* (Toronto: Sister Vision, 1994).

6. We talked with a total of six individuals, three female and three male. Ethnic and generational backgrounds follow: two second-generation Chinese males, one first-generation Chinese male, one first-generation Japanese woman, one second-generation Pilipina woman, and one first-generation Vietnamese woman. All agreed to waive anonymity.

7. Other issues to consider are the class dimensions of those who have the resources to attend national events such as Stonewall 25 and generational difference in terms of age and immigration history.

8. Note that *queer* is not universally embraced by API LGBTs.

9. Fong speaks specifically to the Chinese American experience, not to the API experience in general. For further insights into sexuality and family relations in Asian America, see A. Y. Hom's "Stories from the Homefront: Perspectives of Asian American Parents with Lesbian Daughters and Gay Sons," in R. Leong, ed., *Asian American Sexualities: Dimensions of the Lesbian and Gay Experience*, pp. 37–49 (New York: Routledge, 1996).

10. For examples of API LGBT writings, see *APA Journal—Witness Aloud: Lesbian, Gay, and Bisexual Asian/Pacific American Writings* (Spring/Summer 1993), 2:1; R. Leong, ed., *Asian American Sexualities: Dimensions of the Lesbian and Gay Experience* (New York: Routledge, 1996); S. Lim-Hing, ed., *The Very Inside: An Anthology of Writing by Asian and Pacific Islander Lesbian and Bisexual Women* (Toronto: Sister Vision, 1994); and R. Ratti, ed., *A Lotus of Another Color: An Unfolding of the South Asian Gay and Lesbian Experience* (Boston: Alyson, 1993).

11. For a discussion on "orientalization" and exoticized API eroticism, see R. Fung's "Looking at My Penis: The Eroticized Asian in Gay Porn," in Bad Object-Choices, ed., *How Do I Look? Queer Film and Video*, pp. 145–60 (Seattle: Bay Press, 1991), and M. F. Manalansan, "(Dis)Orienting the Body: Locating Symbolic Resistance Among Filipino Gay Men," *Positions, East Asia Cultures Critique—Circuits of Desire* (Spring 1994) 2(1):73–90.

12. See Y. Yoshikawa's "The Heat is On *Miss Saigon* Coalition: Organizing Across Race and Sexuality," in K. Aguilar-San Juan, ed., *The State of Asian America* (Boston: South End, 1994).

13. In areas like Los Angeles, San Francisco, and New York with large populations of APIs, several API ethnic-specific groups, both organized and informal, have emerged in, for example, the Pilipino, Vietnamese, and Korean communities.

14. For more discussion on alliances within API communities, see K. Aguilar-San Juan's "Linking the Issues, From Identity to Activism," in Aguilar-San Juan, *The State of Asian America*.

15. For a listing, or more information, on API LGBT and/or HIV/AIDS organizations, contact the Living Well Project, 1841 Market Street, San Francisco, CA 94103, (415) 575–3939, X 320 or 321.

16. For example, see the extensive web page by Stephanie Tai at http://www.tufts.edu/stai/QAPA/resources.html.

REFERENCES

Aguilar–San Juan, K., ed. 1994. *The State of Asian America, Activism, and Resistance in the 1990s*. Boston: South End.

APA Journal—Witness Aloud: Lesbian, Gay, and Bisexual Asian/Pacific American Writings (Spring/Summer 1993) 2:1.

Bad Object-Choices, ed. 1991. *How Do I Look? Queer Film and Video*. Seattle: Bay.

Bozett, F. W. and M. B. Sussman, eds. 1990. *Homosexuality and Family Relations*. New York and London: Haworth.

Lim-Hing, S., ed. 1994. *The Very Inside: An Anthology of Writing by Asian and Pacific Islander Lesbian and Bisexual Women*. Toronto: Sister Vision.

Manalansan, M. F., 1994. "(Dis)Orienting the Body: Locating Symbolic Resistance Among Filipino Gay Men." *Positions, East Asia Cultures Critique*. Special issue: *Circuits of Desire* (Spring) 2(1):73–90.

Okihiro, G. Y., M. Alquizola et al., eds. 1995. *Privileging Positions: The Sites of Asian American Studies*. Pullman: Washington State University Press.

Ratti, R., ed. 1993. *A Lotus of Another Color: An Unfolding of the South Asian Gay and Lesbian Experience*. Boston: Alyson.

Rice Roundtable. "Editorial." *InformAsian: Newsletter of the Gay Asian Pacific Support Network, Los Angeles* (October 1994) 8(10):1, 4.

Lourdes Arguelles and Manuel Fernández

Working with *Heterosexismo* in Latino/a Immigrant Los Angeles: Reflections on Community Background, Processes, and Practices

Heterosexismo in Latino communities in the United States is embedded in everyday life. Sexual minority Latinos/as deal with issues of discrimination, violence, and scorn as intensely and as extensively as other sexual minorities. The ways in which heterosexismo is expressed and dealt with, however, greatly differs within these populations and compared to other U.S. minorities.

This brief essay pursues a beginning interpretation of Latino/a low-wage workers and their personal dependents in Los Angeles, based on our own research as Latino/a queer scholars and activists. We also suggest strategies that we find useful in working within this community to develop what cultural theorist Antonia Darder (1995a) has called a solidarity of difference.

Significant Cultural and Sociopolitical Backgrounds

Scholars and practitioners tend to treat U.S. Latinos/as as homogeneous peoples and pay little or no attention to the material conditions of their existence. The meaning and complexity of critical background experiences such as colonialism and neocolonialism, border crossings, rerooting/resettlement efforts, and the multiple actual and imaginary return migrations are mostly absent from mainstream theorizing on Latino/a gender and sexualities. The vast differences in the "class of origin" and the "class of resettlement" among Latinos/as and their implications in understanding heterosexismo in our communities also continue to be ignored in these theoretical efforts.

Life narratives provide an important way to view subjects from the perspective of the people themselves. The following narratives describe the importance attributed to some of the class variables left out by scholars.

José Manuel, the scion of a prerevolutionary Cuban bourgeois family and an activist in the gays of color community, describes his experience:

Cuban society is *machista*, but if you grew up with money and power the norms of the poor man did not apply. True, we often were forced to marry and have children against our wishes, but we also had our own lives. We could have all kinds of sex in the island and in the other countries where we often traveled. We were very Americanized, so we had a very U.S. view of sexuality, but with more freedom to experiment than your average American. Coming to the U.S. was a downer because my family lost all its money, and being a refugee you had to be very careful. It took me years to get an education and money to be able to come out. I find that upper-class Latinos have always been able—as most upper-class people all over the world—to do more with their sexuality than the middle classes. When you are middle class you depend on a job for your daily meal. In my work in the gay community I find Latinos of upper-class backgrounds—and there are a few of those around— freer with their sexuality. They have been able to get away with more things back home and so there is a certain freedom you get accustomed to. I look for them to help me out working with middle-class and poor Latinos and try to make them relate to those who come from other classes. If they commit what one of my mentors calls "class suicide," they can lead here.

Carmen, José Manuel's sister, however, believes that upper classness in her country of origin hindered her ability to be a lesbian there. For her, exile did not impact on her sexual practices and identity in the same way that it did on her brother. She puts it briefly: "Women in Cuba had one duty: marry. Certainly that was the case in my family. As a result, our virginity was very valuable and closely guarded. I kept my sexual longings to myself until I came to the U.S. and split from everybody except from José Manuel."

Xochil, a lesbian from a Guadalajara middle-class family, currently studying in an L.A. community college, comments on the importance of the class origin factor in her coming out process:

My father is a university professor in Mexico. He works at a private university. If I had come out in Guadalajara he would have probably lost his job because his boss is very Catholic. It would have been me or his job. Here in L.A. I am a lesbian. In Guadalajara I am straight and letting people believe I am waiting for the right man. My folks are in no hurry for me to get married because they want me to finish my education first.

Among working-class men and male peasants in Mexico and other parts of Latin America very particularized conceptions of sexuality have been constructed. In these settings a "homosexual" is the male who is penetrated during same-sex intercourse, while the male who penetrates does not compromise his "straight" identity. In his study of sexual behavior among lower-middle- and upper-lower-class males in the northwestern regions of Mexico, Carrier (1995) found that the incidence of sex with males was extremely high among young unmarried males. These males cannot have sexual relations with their girlfriends or most other women because "good" women are supposed to remain virginal until they get married. On the other hand, they cannot afford "bad" women (prostitutes) either, because prostitutes are too expensive. These men learned from an early age that "homosexual," sexually passive males are available as sexual outlets, ready to satisfy their sexual urges, and that this is acceptable, as long as it is not acknowledged publicly (ibid.:16, 188). This construct is also reinforced by the fact that homosexually identified males would culturally avoid having sex with other "homosexual" males. In working-class communities in Honduras, *locas* (queens) would normatively pursue sex with *hombres* ("straight" men; Fernández 1995). As Mario, from San Pedro Sula, told one of the authors: "I would never have sex with another loca. It's not right that two locas go to bed together. It has to be an hombre and a loca." This greatly differs with U.S. mainstream notions in which a "homosexual" male is the one who gets physically or romantically involved with other males, regardless of what role or sexual position he plays.

In such a cultural context strategies to reduce heterosexismo are quite different from those addressed to Anglo-Americans. The stigma is attached to the act of being penetrated, rather than to the sex act itself. This shows the crucial importance of challenging misogynist attitudes against women along with heterosexism. As Lancaster (1992) explains, in Nicaraguan society things related to passivity, to receiving, are feminine and therefore tend to be stigmatized. On the other hand, things related to activity, to giving, are masculine and therefore not stigmatized but conferred with honor. "When one 'uses' [penetrates] a *cochón* [homosexual male in Nicaragua], one acquires masculinity; when one is 'used' as a cochón, one expends it. The nature of the homosexual transaction, then, is that the act makes one man a machista and the other a cochón. The macho's honor and the cochón's shame are opposite sides of the same coin" (Lancaster 1992:242–43). The loca is the object-shame of the relationship hombre/loca because "she" is the penetrated one. On the other extreme, the *macho* male is the subject-honor. He is the one who performs the penetration. He is the agent, the subject, the user, the penetrator. Both women and locas are the objects, the used ones, the penetrated.

Despite the deconstruction of such categories (see Murray 1987:192, Murray 1995:52; and Edelman 1994), we continue finding representations of the macho penetrator/the loca penetrated among Latinos in the United States. Rubén, an undocumented worker from Baja California living in Los Angeles, confirms the prevalence of the emphasis on penetration thesis in his community: "There are two types of men: those who penetrate and those who are penetrated. Those who penetrate are machos. They penetrate every-thing, including animals. Those like me who like to be penetrated are *mari-cas, jotos,* and we have a very hard time. The only ones who can escape are jotos with money, money, money."

The conventional scholarship of gender and sexuality commonly divides U.S. Latinos/as on the basis of traditional notions of acculturation and assimilation, which tend to be based on one-dimensional attitudinal and behavioral indicators and emphasize length of stay. Though it can be said that U.S. Latinos/as as well as other immigrants born and educated in the United States typically tend to exhibit a higher level of cultural integration than foreign-born Latinos/as, barriers arising from parental ideologies firmly opposed to assimilation into the U.S. mainstream or into marginal co-cultures within the mainstream cannot be ignored.

Suyi, the daughter of Salvadoran refugees, suggests some of the complex-ities of growing up in her household in the Pico-Union area of Los Angeles and trying to engage in political work with a Chicana lesbian group:

> My parents were activists on the left in El Salvador. They were very progres-sive politically as well as culturally. My father was tortured and almost killed by Mano Blanca [a right-wing Salvadoran terror group reputed to have been financed by the U.S.]. Unfortunately, they had to seek refuge in the country [U.S.] that brought so much pain into their lives. So they try their best for us not to assimilate into this society, even into those parts that are fighting against the mainstream. It's funny . . . they mind less that I am a lesbian than that I work with Chicanas. They believe Chicanos have capitalistic values and are too American.

Socioeconomic status (SES) in the United States seems to be an important factor in determining levels of cultural integration as well. In their study on sexual behaviors among Puerto Rican males in New York, reseaches found that Puerto Rican men who have sex with men of higher SES tended to identify as "gay" and "bisexual," while the ones of lower SES tended to identify as "drag queens" and "straights": the dichotomy loca/hombre (Carballo-Diéguez and Dolezal 1994:61–63).

Narratives from Guatemalan Latinos in Los Angeles support a strong relationship between SES in the United States and sexual/gender identity. Braulio's statements illustrate some of the dimensions of this connection: "I have sex on and off with this Mexican man. He has a good job, a beautiful car, and a very expensive home. No one would dare call him a 'loca.' He calls himself 'gay,' although he is the one who penetrates me most of the time."

Another factor is religiosity. Catholicism and fundamentalist Protestant Christianity are often portrayed as the only religions in the U.S. Latino/a reality. We need to understand the cultural traditions of bireligiosity rooted in the colonial experience of Latino societies, where the religion of the conqueror and indigenous and/or slave spiritualities coexisted in creative tension. The reclaiming and further development of *Santería*, *Espiritismo*, and other Latino/a syncretic religious traditions characterized by the use of erotic ritual practices offers one of the most potentially important strategies for reducing heterosexismo within Latin (and also non-Latin) communities in the United States. Yet such religions are ignored by most researchers and practitioners working on Latino/a gender and sexuality.

Ramón, a Guatemalan undocumented worker in Los Angeles, comments on the importance of such noninstitutional spirituality in his love life: "I have met many men at the house of the *curandero* [healer]. We take medicine and pray together and love together. Under the guidance of Don Alicio we help each other out." Clara, a Mexican immigrant adds: "To be able to communicate with gods that think and act sometimes like you and me is very important. These gods and goddesses love men and women. It doesn't matter. The love and the attraction is the important thing. The smells, the music, the food are also very important in a place where you live so alone and so afraid."

Heterosexismo Processes in the U.S.

U.S. Latinos/as, particularly Latino/a workers in Southern California, are living in a context of intense economic, ethnonational, and sexual violence. The current restructuring of the California economy in general and the Los Angeles economy has led to a situation in which exploitation in the labor intensive sectors of the agricultural, garment, and tourist industries (where the majority of Latinos are employed) has been intensified. Low pay, long hours, two or three jobs, crowded living conditions, and extremely unhealthy workplace environments are the daily fare of Latino/a workers documented as well as undocumented. In this economic context the need for strong male bodies in Latino/a everyday life has been reinforced, as has the notion that heterosexual penetration performance is the best expression of healthy maleness. Chino explains the reinforcement and expansion of traditional Latino notions of maleness and its effects on parental practices: "My son has to be even stronger than I am if he is to make it here. No more of this that my wife says he needs to rest and to eat well. He needs to show me he is becoming a man. He is already twelve and the sooner he gets into the women he will know what it takes. He has to survive here."

For undocumented laborers, the need for a strong male body is also manifested at times in the relinquishing of gender change plans. A Mexican laborer who has wanted a female body since he was very young remarked: "I cannot even think of taking female hormones now. I need this strong macho body to eat."

The demands of the economy are not the only socializing agents of the configuration of traditional and emerging immigrant genders and sexualities. Other economic factors also enter into play, such as the reinforcement of the experience that U.S. homosexual identities are the prerogative of the upper classes. For Latino males, working for affluent and openly gay and lesbian employers in this country often fans the flames of class envy, gender hatred, and heterosexismo. Manuel, an undocumented Salvadoran worker in a West Hollywood restaurant owned by gay men sums it up: "They have the money. They treat us badly and they are not even men. They dress like women, even shave their legs, and they think they can push us around. I want to kill them for forcing us to clean the floors on our knees. That's women's work . . . their work."

Sandra, a cleaning lady working for affluent lesbians, however, has learned to appreciate the lives and choices of her employers. She attributes her increased acceptance of lesbians to her ability to work free of gender abuse: "They have helped me a lot when I needed help. I prefer to work for them because they don't abuse me or go after me sexually. At first I thought that could be a problem, but it hasn't. I am safer with them. . . . Even if they would try it with me I can handle it."

In a climate of increased anti-immigrant sentiment and initiatives as well as of constant raids of homes and workplaces by the "La Migra," as the Immigration and Naturalization Service (INS) is referred to by the immigrant Latino, the performance of what are deemed "acceptable" gender and sexual identities is given, according to many Latinos/as, greater importance than back home. Lydia, an undocumented Salvadoran living in Pomona, comments: "I thought coming here I would be freer to choose who I wanted to have sex with but with La Migra breathing down our necks, who wants to be different and have more people hate you and turn you in?" Cristina, a documented Mexican lesbian living in Los Angeles adds: "I have papers and I have two more years to become a citizen. I don't want them to have an excuse to deny me my rights so I don't go out much with my lover. That's hard because I like to be out all the time. Maybe when I get my citizenship I will. People here are always looking at you in the streets and acting funny. Imagine if I hold hands with her."

Latinos/as in the United States are immersed in a high intensity media market where the use of heterosexual bodies, sexist relations, and homophobic messages to sell products, political messages, or future existence is a consistent practice. In addition, the Latino/a popular cultural products that are most accessible to the lower socioeconomic rungs of the immigrant market such as telenovelas or serial melodramas reinforce these sexist and homophobic practices. Elena, a Salvadoran worker recently arrived in Los Angeles, states:

> I feel bombarded by so many TV and radio programs and ads everywhere. In my town we had two radio stations and one movie a week. Sometimes I feel I am just going under. . . . I also feel so ugly in spite of everything I do to fix myself. . . . I am afraid that my lover is going to leave me one day. . . . She has been here longer . . . and can keep up. I cannot keep up. Back home you did not have all these discussions about homosexuals and people being nasty to us right on TV."

Work with Heterosexismo

How do we work with heterosexismo in the context of these immigrant working-class Latino/a communities in Los Angeles and other areas in the twenty-first century? We do so by framing our work in a critical reading of the interaction between significant country of origin background variables, border crossing and rerooting/resettlement experiences, and materials from dreams and other realms of the cultural imaginary. We also work with different levels and types of experiencing, including those frequently devoid of conceptual thinking, for example, ritual processes. In this context we have found the following strategies effective in ensuring conditions where authentic dialogue on gender and sexuality concerns and the neutralization of the violence and pain endured by working-class Latino/a sexual minorities can be enabled. We have also found these strategies helpful in assisting us to mark the first steps toward a solidarity of difference among Latino/a queers and nonqueers.

1. Working in the Context of a Political Economy of Heterosexismo   The importance of taking the social situation as the beginning point cannot be stressed enough. This approach, particularly when anchored on a standpoint theory that privileges the perspectives of those experiencing conditions of inequality and subordinate relations, has been instrumental in our work in facilitating a reflective apprehension of the dynamics of heterosexismo in Latino/a immigrant communities.

We thus begin our work by conducting a political economic analysis of the group we will be working with and by delving into microlevel processes that are shaped by political economic conditions. Recent work by young Latino/a scholars exploring key dynamics utilizing both macro- and micromethods of analyses and anchored in standpoint theory have been extraordinarily inspiring in this respect (Cantu 1995). Narrative methodologies have been critical in this work. These approaches significantly depart from conventional ethnographies in both epistemology and method (Arguelles n.d.).

Our goal in immersing ourselves in the political economy of the peoples we are working with is to apprehend their daily reality in a thorough fashion rather than in a fragmented isolated way and to be able to evaluate both the possibilities and limitations of our strategic interventions. This grounding, for example, permits us to more effectively identify the various moral economies within a community and critical points of intervention from which to challenge the moralization of the heterosexual self and the demoralization of the nonheterosexual other. In the words of Guacho, a Mexican worker:

> I am very different than I was in my country. Here if you give me a hand, even if you are a *maricón*, I take you as a friend. I am able to do this because a lot of the *viejos* [elders] are not around. I take you as a friend because I need you and you need me in this war. If you prove you are fighting with me and that your ways are not going to bring me more problems with the *gabachos* [whites], it's a deal."

2. Expanding Latino/a Street Popular Culture   This strategy differs from notions that encourage sexual minorities to perform and/or highlight roles based on industrial family, gender, religious, and sexual forms wrongly associated with Latin American traditional systems of kinship, mutual aid, and caring. It also differs from attempts to preserve and cultivate cultural memory through the traditions of corridos and cuentos [Latin American traditional genres of epic song and storytelling] rooted in popular traditions of heterosexismo.

Instead, our work seeks to use in very specific contexts popular forms such as *rasquashismo* (Ybarra-Fausto 1991), a uniquely working-class aesthetic of Mexican origin that transforms utilitarian articles into sacred or aesthetic objects, for example, by putting bottles, curtains, etc., in Catholic-like altars or by decorating "low rider" automobiles with candles and curtains (see the chapter on East Los Angeles's aesthetics in Lipsitz 1990).

We have found that enabling queer artists of working-class immigrant origins and destinations to take rasquashismo into the streets in order to appropriate, critique, and subvert dominant gender and sexual ideologies can be effective in generating authentic and often humorous dialogue. Two students of one of the authors used rasquashismo focusing on sexual orientation in their East Los Angeles community. They put a picture of two male lovers in a *rasquashe* frame (a wooden frame with the Mexican flag, among other things). In the picture the lovers were embracing, and below was written the word *jotos* (faggots). And this was put in a sort of altar in exhibit on the street. They took the street over. As the two students commented: "People were amused, and after days of hard work who does not want to be amused? One elderly woman even said to me she wished she was younger to see my point more fully. We laughed together a lot and no one seemed upset. Latinos seem to accept things on the street more easily than in enclosed spaces." The students found community members admiring of Latinos who are willing to take the streets without fear. Pablo explained his reactions to the students' queer street rasquashismo project: "They had no fear that that is strange among Latinos."

3. Cultural Work with Sacred Traditions and Rituals   Queer Latinos/as and queer Latino/a culture often play a major role in Afro-Caribbean and indigenous spiritual traditions in Latin America, which, as we have noted, include erotic practices in their ritual life.

In Cuban Santería transgendered spirit beings or *orichas* are perceived as extraordinarily powerful. As a result, many houses of Santería allow and encourage the commingling of "godchildren" (metaphorically adoptive children as part of a fictive kinship system) of variant sexualities. In addition, houses of Santería often provide support and assistance in the form of networking to immigrants. In the same line, Afro-Brazilian *Candomblé*, being itself a stigmatized tradition within Brazilian mainstream society, has provided gender variant, socially stigmatized people a niche and a social network (Wafer 1991; Fry 1995:194).

A bonus resulted from one of the authors' work with a particularly well-known house of Santería in Los Angeles that offered to provide safe space for recently arrived immigrants. Mireya, a Cuban worker without documents who lived in the house for two months, reported:

> The *padrino* [godfather, *santero*] is homosexual. At first I was scared. . . . Even in Cuba I was scared of santeros, and when I found out that he was homosexual I was even repelled. As the days passed I began to admire him. Something in me connected with Santería . . . something deeply Cuban in me. I began to see him as a person who had made a choice on how to live his life and who was spiritually very powerful. I am now a very good friend of his partner and an initiate. I go to the house now and reconnect with my land and the drums.

Our work around the Day of the Dead, a celebration of syncretic origins that is also observed by Latinos in California in its traditional Mexican form, has resulted in compassionate dialogue between Latino/a sexual minorities and majorities. In her fall classes one of the authors has for years included a celebration of a Day of the Dead. Community peoples and students are invited to participate in what cultural theorist Alicia Gaspar de Alba (1995) has called a commemoration for the "wetback with amnesia" that every Latino/a is in danger of becoming. Participants in these events have openly and often tearfully embraced each others' difference under the shadow of death. Raúl, a second-generation Chicano observed: "In death we finally realize we are the same. It is strange that we cannot realize it in life. This Day of the Dead is an annual jog to my memory so I do not impose my macho self on others throughout the year."

René, a former client of one of the authors, has commented on the differences between the Days of the Dead celebrations he attended in Mexico and those he attends now: "I felt very strange because in my family's altars we only had pictures of the 'blood family,' like dead parents, grandparents, and so on. But when Ramón said that our lovers and our friends who had died of AIDS were the 'true blood brothers,' it made sense." For the first time, René put a photograph of his deceased lover in an altar during a Day of the Dead celebration in San Diego one week before his own death (Arguelles and Rivero 1995).

Sharing the contemplation of impermanence in these rituals often brings a level of communion between queer and nonqueer Latinos not experienced elsewhere. This sharing involves more than intellectual acceptance and understanding. The effects are frequently long-lasting. Maruja told us: "Since we had this celebration two years ago [the Day of the Dead] I feel homosexuals are my brothers and sisters. I feel it. I cannot explain it."

4. *Latino/a Queer Class-Based Coalitional Politics*   We have found that linking queer politics with class-based politics is essential in working with heterosexismo in Latino/a working-class communities in the sociohistorical context of 1990s Los Angeles and surrounding communities. Antiheterosexist intervention strategies abstracted from daily immigrant struggles are often met with derision. A comment by Salvador, a Mexican worker living in Ontario, to a student of one of the authors illustrates this point: "When I see them maricones doing something for me I will think that they are human . . . and not like people to be abused. Right now my only experience is seeing them trying to fuck everyone in this factory."

Doing something with and for undocumented workers and their families is an opportunity that has been taken by some Latino/a queer activists and missed by others. José was one of the activists who took the opportunity to work against Proposition 187, the California anti-immigrant initiative approved in 1995. He campaigned door-to-door in Pomona seeking to register new Latino/a voters. On his lapel were both a Mexican flag and a pink triangle. Reflecting on his campaign experiences, he said to one of the authors:

> They would ask me about the pink triangle and I would tell them I was gay and the meaning of the triangle. Only two men got upset. The rest, about two hundred men and women, were very polite and nodded when I made the links between the antigay groups and the racist groups behind Prop. 187. One man embraced me and told me to be very careful. He even advised me not to knock on his neighbor's door because he feared for my safety.

The man said of his neighbor: "He is an old Mexican that has forgotten where he came from. He is for Prop. 187." José continued, "I did [knock at his neighbor's door], but I removed my triangle at his request." Finding a common enemy, a strategy advocated in antiprejudice reduction strategies (see Walter L. Williams's "Multicultural Perspectives on Reducing Heterosexism: Looking for Strategies That Work" in this volume), seems to have worked well for José.

5. *Exploring Pedagogies for Latino/as Working with Heterosexismo*   Work with heterosexismo in working-class Latino/a immigrant communities presupposes the development of critical, passionate, and mindful pedagogies. These pedagogies are essential to help move work with heterosexismo in our communities—particularly in highly exploited community sectors such as those of working-class peoples at the lowest rung of the class structure—beyond the traditional oppositions between straight majorities and nonstraight minorities as well as beyond assimilationist models of mirroring heterosexuality for survival purposes.

These pedagogies need to inform workers about reliable ways to identify and challenge structures of oppression and exploitation that are common to queer and nonqueer Latinos/as. They also need to inform these workers on how to work within communities and enable the recovering/reconstructing of cultural memories and the development of queer-nonqueer dialogues, allegiances, and bonds.

Heterosexismo will undoubtedly survive us. Our task in this sociohistorical context seems then to be to prepare and work for the long haul.

REFERENCES

Arguelles, L. N.d. "On Method: Narratives in the Politico-Economic Study of Immigration."

Arguelles, L., and A. M. Rivero. 1995. "Working with Gay/Homosexual Latinos with HIV Disease: Spiritual Emergencies and Psycho-Therapeutic Treatments." In A. Darder, ed., *Culture and Difference: Critical Perspectives on the Bicultural Experience in the United States*, pp. 155–68. Westport, Conn.: Bergin and Garvey.

Cantu, L. 1995. "The Peripheralization of Rural America: A Case Study of Latino Migrants in America's Heartland." *Sociological Perspectives* 38(3):399–414.

Carballo-Diéguez, A., and C. Dolezal. 1994. "Contrasting Types of Puerto Rican Men Who Have Sex with Men (MSM)." *Journal of Psychology and Human Sexuality* 6(4):41–67.

Carrier, J. 1995. *De los Otros: Intimacy and Homosexuality Among Mexican Men.* New York: Columbia University Press.

Darder, A. 1995a. "Introduction—The Politics of Biculturalism: Culture and Difference in the Formation of Warriors for Gringostroika and the New

Mestizas." In A. Darder, ed., *Culture and Difference: Critical Perspectives on the Bicultural Experience in the United States,* pp. 1–20. Westport, Conn.: Bergin and Garvey.

—— 1995b. *Culture and Difference: Critical Perspectives on the Bicultural Experience in the United States.* Westport, Conn.: Bergin and Garvey.

Edelman, L. 1994. "The Mirror and the Tank: AIDS, Subjectivity, and the Rhetoric of Activism." In L. Edelman, *Homographesis: Essays in Gay Literary and Cultural Theory,* pp. 93–117. New York: Routledge.

Epps, B. 1995. "Proper Conduct: Reinaldo Arenas, Fidel Castro, and the Politics of Homosexuality." *Journal of the History of Sexuality* 6(2):213–83.

Fernández, M. 1995. "Honduras: Somos Varones Homosexuales; Entrevista con Osvaldo." Part 1: *De Ambiente* (December 1994–January 1995), vol. 8; part 2: *De Ambiente* (February–March 1995), vol. 9.

Fry, P. 1995. "Male Homosexuality and Afro-Brazilian Possesion Cults." In S. O. Murray, ed., *Latin American Male Homosexualities,* pp. 193–220. Albuquerque: University of New Mexico Press.

Gaspar de Alba, A. 1995. "The Alter-Native Grain: Theorizing Chicano/a Popular Culture." In A. Darder, ed., *Culture and Difference: Critical Perspectives on the Bicultural Experience in the United States.* Westport, Conn.: Bergin and Garvey.

Lancaster, R. N. 1992. "Subject Honor, Object Shame." In R. Lancaster, *Life Is Hard: Machismo, Danger, and the Intimacy of Power in Nicaragua.* Berkeley: University of California Press.

Lipsitz, G. 1990. *Time Passages: Collective Memory and American Popular Culture.* Minneapolis: University of Minnesota Press.

Murray, S. O. 1987. *Male Homosexuality in Central and South America.* San Francisco: Instituto Obregón. Gai Saber Monograph 5.

—— 1995. *Latin American Male Homosexualities.* Albuquerque: University of New Mexico Press.

Wafer, J. 1991. *The Taste of Blood: Spirit Possession in Brazilian Candomblé.* Philadelphia: University of California Press.

Ybarra-Fausto, T. 1989. "Rasquashismo: A Chicano Sensibility." In *Chicano Aesthetics: Rasquashismo,* p. 5. Phoenix: Movimiento Artístico del Río Salgado.

Sylvia Rhue and Thom Rhue

Reducing Homophobia in African American Communities

Many prominent African Americans have been at the forefront of the struggle to reduce homophobia, from civil rights activists like Coretta Scott King and Jesse Jackson to media figures like Oprah Winfrey and Bill Cosby. Pioneering African American mayors of several cities have built solid support in lesbian and gay communities, and no voting bloc in the United States Congress has a more consistent pro-gay stance than the Black Congressional Caucus. Nevertheless, there is no unified opinion in the African American community in opposition to heterosexism. A 1995 survey of black heterosexuals' attitudes toward lesbians and gay men found that while homophobia is no more prevalent among blacks than among whites, the survey's directors concluded that in the African American population "negative attitudes toward homosexuality are widespread" (Herek and Capitanio 1995:95).

There are limitations to the belief that people who have experienced oppression will be more sympathetic to others who have also been oppressed. Just as a web of racism ensnarls many gays and lesbians, a web of homophobia entraps many African Americans. While homophobia has been challenged by some political leaders and prominent individuals, expressions of antigay sentiment within African American institutions and among many individuals are not at all uncommon. For example, a Bible-quoting black Baptist minister, apparently forgetting how the Bible has been used to justify American slavery through the sons of Ham story, had to be censured and removed from San Francisco's Human Rights Commission because he proclaimed that homosexuals deserve God's scorn. Members of the Nation of Islam routinely characterize gays and lesbians as the consequence of a degenerate white society. Intellectuals writing about the black family dismiss gays as a strain of disfunctionality within the black community resulting from racism. Black comedians on television raise howls of laughter from delighted audiences with demeaning caricatures of lisping, limp-wrist swishers dragging across the stage. Black teenagers commonly insult each other with anti-gay labels, while rap singers denounce "faggots" in their lyrics with impunity.

The objection to homosexuality is in some respects a reflection of the general American fear and misunderstanding of same-sex orientation, but it is heightened by problems specific to American blacks: family disintegration in the inner city, emasculation of black males through racism, miseducation, crime, and incarceration. Howard University professor Ron Simmons, who has written insightfully on black/gay issues, hypothesizes that

> in the African-American community, "homophobia" is not so much a fear of "homosexuals" but a fear that homosexuality will become pervasive in the community. Thus, a homophobic person can accept a homosexual as an individual friend or family member, yet not accept homosexuality. This is the attitude that predominates in the African-American community. The motivation for homophobia is "heterosexism"—the belief that heterosexual sex is good and proper, and homosexual sex is bad and immoral.
>
> (Simmons 1991:211)

There is, of course, no single source of homophobia among blacks. Broadly, the sources of black attitudes toward gays and lesbians can be traced to the interaction of (1) patriarchal assumptions about the nature of society, (2) religious beliefs publicized in Christian churches and the Nation of Islam, (3) writings on the condition of the black family and community by some scholars and intellectuals, and (4) aspects of popular culture and entertainment. We will examine each of these four sources separately.

Patriarchy

Homophobia in African American communities cannot be explored without a critical analysis of patriarchy, the system in which homophobia lives. Patriarchy can be defined as "the manifestation and institutionalization of male dominance over women and children in the family and the extension of male dominance over women in society in general" (Lerner 1986:239). Patriarchy is the father of racism, sexism, and homophobia, and the story of African America, indeed, of Africa itself, is wrapped, packaged, and inextricably tied up with our relationship with, response to and struggles against those edifices of our oppression, the masonry of our misery.

Patriarchy maintains racism through its inherent structure of hierarchical power with whites on top and blacks on the bottom. Sexism, the system by which women are kept subordinate to men, is the axle upon which the wheel of patriarchy turns and homophobia is the linchpin that holds it together. In *Homophobia: A Weapon of Sexism*, Suzanne Pharr states,

> Homophobia works effectively as a weapon of sexism because it is joined with a powerful arm, heterosexism. Heterosexism creates the climate for homophobia with its assumption that the world is and must be heterosexual and its display of power and privilege as the norm. Heterosexism is the systemic display of homophobia in the institutions of society. Heterosexism and homophobia work together to enforce compulsory heterosexuality.
>
> (1988:16, 17).

The oppressions are connected, chain-linked together by male supremacist power, control, and values.

There are many progressive African American men who see those interconnections and fight against them. But their voices are hardly heard above the din of the black male supremacists who, true to patriarchy, have agreed that there is a hierarchy of oppression, with racism as the major tyranny and all other problems, like sexism and homophobia, being of minor concern, peccadilloes of the powerless, inconsequential and not worthy of the work of real men. Black male supremacists never call themselves "black male supremacists"; they call themselves brothers, fathers, friends, lovers, ministers, rap singers, athletes, writers, filmmakers, politicians, and husbands. Many of them are women.

In a racist world where benefits are scarce, black men cling to whatever power and privilege male supremacy affords them, just as whites, in the maintenance of racism, cling to the benefits and rewards of white skin privilege. Both systems must utilize a nihilistic logic to survive. The overt results of the trauma and treachery of these power dynamics are evident in the violence of American society, in poverty, drug abuse, spousal abuse, broken families, broken hearts, desperation, despair, and dreams deferred. Homophobia exists and exhibits itself in African American communities in much the same way that it manifests itself in the dominant Euro-American culture. Homophobia is ingrained in our psyches through myth and media, church and state, politics and perception, and it is created and re-created within every system of public discourse.

Yet homophobia in African American communities also has its own unique flavors and sets of consciousness. It is the black minister who feels free to give a homophobic sermon and is shocked to find immediate confrontation by his congregation. It is also the minister who gains nationwide prominence in his work with gospel music but lives and suffers silently with AIDS in a glass closet.

Homophobia in African American communities is a schizophrenic phenomena coexisting in a community that has historically been known to know all (because "Nobody Knows The Trouble We've Seen"), to forgive all because we have been given no quarter, and to embrace all because we are the last stop at the gate of humanity. This same community can also be quite intolerant, rigidly fixed in its beliefs, and defiantly conservative.

There is a river of sexual terror that pushes past the walls of reason and baptizes us in a flood of homosexual panic. James Baldwin talked about this in an interview with Richard Goldstein (cited in Goldstein 1989:178).

> GOLDSTEIN: *Have you any sense of what causes people to hate homosexuals?*
> BALDWIN: *Terror, I suppose. Terror of the flesh. After all, we're supposed to mortify the flesh, a doctrine which has led to untold horrors. This is a very Biblical culture, people believe the wages of sin is death. In fact, the wages of sin is death, but not the way the moral guardians of this time and place understand it.*
> GOLDSTEIN: *Is there any particularly American component of homophobia?*
> BALDWIN: *I think Americans are terrified of feeling anything. And homophobia is simply an extreme example of the American terror that is concerned with growing up. I never met a people more infantile in my life.*

The Christian Church

Homophobia in African American communities is inextricably linked to the black church. African American scholar Eric C. Lincoln has stated, "There is no distinction between the black church and the black community. The church is the spiritual face of the black community, and whether one is a 'church member' or not is beside the point (cited in Sears 1991:60). The black church has been the bulwark, the fortification, the defense, the center, the backbone, the sanctuary, the Alpha and Omega of the African American community in America. A mixture of African and European theologies, it was brewed in the bosom of slavery, born, bred, and bled through generations of hope, history, and hysteria.

Inside it is not just a church. It is, as one African American scholar noted, an "African village," with the minister in the role of the chief and the congregation as the villagers. And just as it takes "an entire village to raise a child," it can take an entire church (village) to convince that child that he or she is worthy or unworthy. For it is in the church that we hear what it means to be. For African Americans the church actually became the substance of things hoped for, the evidence of things not seen. Therefore, to question, to reject, to deny this collective bond of community and renewal known as "the church" has for many been the crux of our anguish. For lesbian and gay black folk, the church has been the cross upon which our truth has been nailed. Our burden has been the way our hearts beat. Seemingly out of sync with Scripture, some have felt out of sight from God.

And today, we see the spectacle of black ministers marching hand in hand with white male supremacists, marching for hate, taking public stands against lesbian and gay rights. The radical right is fueled, funded, and fanaticized by powerful, rich white males who have demonstrated a genius for manipulating the media, framing the issues narrowly to their broad agenda, and raising money by capitalizing on people's fears and ignorance. The radical right produced a video entitled "Gay Rights/Special Rights." *BLK*, the black lesbian and gay magazine, printed the text of the black participants in that video:

> Four anti-lesbian and gay African-Americans speak on camera in "Gay Rights, Special Rights." They are Emanuel McLittle, Publisher, "Destiny" magazine; Lester James, Regional Director, Traditional Values Coalition; Cheryl Coleman, Public Affairs Representative, and Jan Rice, Committee of Public Affairs. The following is a complete transcript of their comments, in the order they appear in the video.

> McLITTLE: *Now homosexuals are using not only the language, but they are beginning to insist the statutes—the laws—all of the advantages gained by civil rights leaders such as Martin Luther King be now applied to homosexuals.*
>
> JAMES: *Frankly, there is a movement in this country that threatens to undermine and belittle the entire civil rights efforts of the 1960's.*
>
> COLEMAN: *This Civil Rights Amendment would completely neutralize the Civil Rights Act of 1964. What it will do, is that it will say that anyone, anyone with any type of sexual preference (which would include everyone) would be protected under this law. So therefore there would be no protection for minorities, specifically.*
>
> JAMES: *The high-handed attempt on the part of (the) gay and lesbian movement to hijack the 1994 Civil Rights Act in order to give national credence to their immoral lifestyle is an offense to black America.*
>
> McLITTLE: *There are few people willing to stand up and rebut this whole notion that there is any kind of comparison to the sexuality of homosexuals*

and the skin tone of black people. It is a horrendous lie. Black people are not born choosing to be black. The homosexuals, on the other hand, choose their homosexual lifestyle.

RICE: *Their high income, their education, their current status in society, compared to the mean or the median, income in minority families today—there is just no comparison. So for them to want protection under this law and to try to further beat down the minorities and further lessen their chances of equal protection and equal chances at jobs, I just think is ludicrous.*

MCLITTLE: *The homosexual lobbyists, the homosexual groups in this country are well-funded, well-connected to powerful politicians.*

RICE: *Our intent is to see that everyone is treated fair and equal and they are being treated equal under the law as a citizen of America. But their behavior should not dictate special preference for them.*   (Zarembka 1994:19).

The Nation of Islam

Homophobia is not restricted to black Christians. The Nation of Islam has consistently demonstrated high-profile homophobic rhetoric. The infamous Nation of Islam minister Khalid Abdul Muhammed, shot while speaking at the University of California at Riverside in 1994, has advocated the murder of lesbians and gay men. But it is the charismatic Minister Louis Farrakhan, heir to Elijah Muhammed himself, after Malcolm X, who commands the greatest respect among the nation's followers and many non-Muslims. In explaining "decadent" white America's influence over African Americans before an Oakland audience in 1990, Farrakhan advocates the enforcement of Old Testament and Koranic laws to govern black America. Turning his attention to gays, he said,

> Now brother, in the Holy world you can't switch. [Mimicking an effeminate man] No, no, no . . . in the Holy world you better hide that stuff 'cause see if God made you for a woman, you can't go with a man. . . . You know what the penalty of that is in the Holy land? Death. . . . They don't play with that. . . . Sisters get to going with another sister—both women [are decapitated]."
>
> (cited in Simmons 1991:222)

Minister Farrakhan referred to secular reasons for male homosexuality in a 1983 speech delivered to a Morgan State University audience, insisting that

> those of you—who are homosexual—you weren't born [that] way brother— You never had a strong male image. These are conditions that are forced on black men. You're filling up the jails and they're turning you into freaks in the jails.   (Simmons 1991:213)

Black homophobes use the same code words, the same distortions, the same arguments, but with a black twist. They have been able to tap into black religious folks' terror and fantasies about gays and lesbians who are painted and perceived to be affluent, white, effeminate degenerates claiming to be oppressed and clamoring for "civil rights." Civil rights are "black territory" and "privileged white male sissies" are felt to be moving in on our turf. There is much indignation when the civil rights struggle is compared to the struggle for gay rights.

Cornel West, professor of African American studies and the philosophy of religion at Harvard University addresses this:

> There is always deep sensitivity among black people about any movement that seems to displace black suffering. But that's also narrow and truncated, and to me it's inexcusable to completely downplay genuine suffering among gay brothers and lesbian sisters in the name of making black suffering central. (cited in Waller 1994:90)

The Reverend Peter Gomes, minister of Harvard University's Memorial Church and openly gay African American theologian, is convinced that, within several years, lesbian and gay rights will be seen as natural as civil rights for African Americans do today. In a recent profile in *10 PERCENT*, Gomes is described as being

> comfortable employing the analogy of the lesbian and gay rights movement to the civil rights movement of the early 60's, he is adamant about the consistency of the parallel. . . . Gomes sees rising homophobic fundamentalism as a strictly fin-de-siecle phenomenon, the last gasp of a doomed movement: "I frankly regard its venomousness and potency as a sign not of strength, but of its recognition that this is a do-or-die operation, and it's likely to die."
> (cited in Thorpe 1994:39, 70)

The radical right and their cohorts of black homophobes fly in the face of the reality of the mainstream leadership of Jesse Jackson, Coretta Scott King, Benjamin Chavis, Maxine Waters, Angela Davis, Cecil Williams, James Lowery, and countless others who stand with the lesbian and gay movement knowing that the arc of the moral universe bends toward love and social justice.

Intellectuals and Scholars

The state and nature of the black family became a subject of wide and intense debate in the early 1970s, partly in response to a study authored by

Harvard professor Patrick Moynihan, later to become a Democratic U.S. senator from New York. Professor Moynihan's controversial 1970 report, *The Black Family in America*, in large part blamed the breakdown of the black family on single-parent, out-of-wedlock births. A large number of black scholars and intellectuals came to the defense of the black family, pointing to its extended network, flexibility over the decades, and survival in spite of racism. But many of these same intellectuals were far less scholarly when it came to explaining homosexuality in the black community. Among the most prominent of these scholars were Nathan Hare and Robert Staples, who began the *Black Scholar*, widely read by black intellectuals throughout the country. Dr. Hare and his wife, Julia, who also ran workshops to help black heterosexual couples, wrote an influential book in 1984 entitled *The Endangered Black Family: Coping with the Unisexualization and Coming Extinction of the Black Race.*

Arguing that people are alienated and set apart from their "natural origins" in a decaying society like America where "there emerges a breakdown in child-rearing and socialization. . . . Without a solid core to their personalities, children grow up confused—developing problems of identity, most notably that of gender confusion. Homosexuality accordingly will proliferate" (cited in Simmons 1991:212). They have asserted that the preponderance of white female schoolteachers in child centers, nurseries, and primary schools forcing black boys to play with blonde dolls leads to homosexuality. Further, they believe that "there is no need to engage in endless debates about the pros and cons of homosexuality. . . . Homosexuality does not promote black family stability . . . and historically has been a product largely of European society" (cited in Simmons 1991:212).

Robert Staples, in his book *Black Masculinity*, believes that "the nation's prisons are the main places where homosexual preferences are evident—because of the unavailability of women" (cited in Simmons 1991:213). He contends that lesbianism is on the increase as a result of "a shortage of black men—or the conflict in male/female relationships" (ibid.). Other lesser-known nationalist intellectuals such as Molefi Asante and Haki Madhubuti (Don L. Lee) repeat themes of prison-induced, white culture-induced effeminacy in, respectively, *Afrocentricity: The Theory of Social Change* (1980) and *Black Men. Obsolete, Single, Dangerous? The Afrikan American Family in Transition: Essays in Discovery, Solution and Hope* (1978).

The poet and playwright Amiri Baraka, a.k.a. LeRoi Jones, represents one of the more conflicted figures in literary circles when writing about homosexuality. His plays *The Toilet* and *The Baptism* characterize gays as "faggots" and weak. His "Civil Rights Poem" opens by calling Roy Wilkins "an eternal faggot. His spirit is a faggot" (cited in Simmons 1991:217). This obsession with "faggots" crops up again and again in his writing. In his essay "American Sexual Reference: Black Male" he writes that "most American white men are trained to be fags . . . their faces are weak and blank . . . that red blush, those silk blue faggot eyes" (ibid.). His autobiographical novel, *The System of Dante's Hell*, reveals the tortured manner with which the main character suppresses his homosexual feelings, although there is no mention of this period of his life in *The Autobiography of LeRoi Jones.*

Popular Culture

American culture is not conceivable without African American influences. Cornel West has argued that "black culture is unimaginable without James Baldwin and Audre Lorde" (cited in Waller 1994:90). While these openly gay and lesbian writers blew the hinges off the closet door, homophobia and heterosexual imperatives have demanded the dilution, distillation, and/or disappearance of the true sexual orientations of those who have been so influential in creating American culture. Therefore, black divas who love women must always sing love songs to men or never be heard again, gay and lesbian actors perpetuate the myths of heterosexuality for stage and screen or risk losing their careers, black, gay, lesbian, and bisexual athletes play it "straight" or get out of the game, ad nauseam. Vito Russo, author of *The Celluloid Closet*, points out that "the big lie about lesbians and gay men is that we do not exist" (1987:vii).

While lesbian and gay sensibilities are becoming more conscious and more visible, generally speaking, the culture of the closet continues. When Alice Walker's *The Color Purple* was released, it caused a nationwide paroxysm of homophobic hysteria in the black community, mainly from black men. A great wailing went up against Walker for "airing our dirty laundry" regarding black male brutality toward women. Calvin C. Hernton, writing in *The Sexual Mountain and Black Women Writers*, states, "The belief that men should be all-powerful and that women should be weak is at the foundation of all patriarchal ideology, which is clearly depicted in *The Color Purple*. Patriarchy is 'good' because men are sacred, and matriarchy is 'bad' because women are profane" (1987:12).

Black male critics advanced the belief that watching *The Color Purple* could make girls become lesbians. Fear and terror were in the air. The kiss between Celie (played by Whoopi Goldberg) and Shug shook the foundations of patriarchy for a mere nanosecond and men's knees trembled. It took Whoopi Goldberg years to live down playing the part of Celie, with its lesbian context.

Walker allowed the Black Women's Forum (in Los Angeles) to premiere the movie and it was picketed by the Black Psychologist's Association of Los Angeles (and others.) The protesters carried signs that spelled out the "sins" of *The Color Purple*. Listed on the picket signs were the words *incest* and *rape* and *lesbianism*. When some demonstrators were asked if they had even seen the movie, they answered, "No." *The Color Purple* was the first time a kiss between two black women was ever shown on film. The resultant frenzy is a telling account of how homophobia is a certain kind of madness. Hernton summed it up:

> The bricks and arrows hurled at Alice Walker and her novel are motivated by the same old concern as to how the black writer should portray black people. People from different backgrounds with different sensitivities, ideologies and class leanings will respond differently to the same work. Jealousy and envy are also part of the motivations. However, more than with any other black-authored work so far, *The Color Purple* seemed to have driven some people literally crazy.   (Hernton 1987:33)

Homophobia has also been evident in African American popular magazines. When the Black Gay and Lesbian Leadership Forum wanted to advertise their 1990 conference in *Essence* magazine, the magazine rejected the ad. The forum sued *Essence* for sexual discrimination. After much behind-the-scenes maneuvering, *Essence* not only went on to publish the ad but later ran an article on a mother and her lesbian daughter as well. That daughter turned out to be Linda Villarosa, senior editor for *Essence*. The article received more mail response than any article in the publication's history. In the avalanche of letters only a handful were negative, while hundreds complimented the magazine for tackling the subject of lesbianism. *Essence* went on to publish other gay- and lesbian-oriented articles. *Ebony* magazine, in contrast, feels free to publish stories with homophobic intent. The May 1994 issue of *Ebony* featured a cover story on singer Tony Braxton, written by Muriel Whetstone, who informed her readers: "The scuttlebutt shaking through the grapevine is that when Tony appeared on The Arsenio Hall Show, she somehow indicated that she preferred women rather than men. The stinging, hurtful rumor, she says, 'is absolutely false!' " Whetstone went on to call the rumor a "nasty innuendo." *Ebony* magazine has not yet responded to or published letters of protest for the negative and homophobic tone of the article.

Racism, sexism, and homophobia congealed into a festering farce of stupidity and denial in the United States Senate hearings on gays in the military. Even though women are six times as likely as men to be "witch-hunted" and discharged for the accusation of homosexuality, and even though African American women are a high percentage of the targeted group—African American Sergeant Perry being a pioneer in legal precedent—white men took center stage on both sides of the debate. Heterosexual men described their horror at what might happen if gay men looked at them the way straight men look at women. They talked of abhorrence and revulsion if they were to be touched by a man—how it would be too much to bear. Even though it was not articulated as such, the gays-in-the-military debate pointed out the real purpose and function of homophobia: (1) to keep females endlessly accessible and in service to men physically, sexually, erotically and emotionally, and (2) to "protect men from the sexual aggression of men" (Stoltenberg 1989:131). As Stoltenberg went on to say,

> Homophobia keeps men doing to women what they would not want done to themselves. . . . Cultural homophobia keeps men's sexual aggression directed towards women. Homophobia keeps men acting in concert as male supremacists so they won't be perceived as an appropriate target for male-supremacist sexual treatment. Male supremacy requires homophobia in order to keep men safe from the sexual aggression of men.   (131)

Homophobia, the linchpin of patriarchy, is integral to the system of male supremacy.

Strategies for Combating Homophobia

Come Out   The most important thing lesbians, gays, bisexuals, and transgender persons can do, individually for themselves and to enhance the level of integrity in life, is to come out of the closet. Studies show that people are less likely to be homophobic or vote against us when they know gays or lesbians personally.

Be Confrontive   Cut off the church music, refuse to play the organ, and send the tenor section home! Black folk don't respect timidity, and African American lesbian and gay people are best equipped to confront homophobia in African American communities. Black people are much more apt to listen to and hear a black lesbian or black gay man as opposed to a white gay or lesbian person. We have to make sure the public face of the gay and lesbian community is multicolored and multicultural. We must find our allies in the larger black communities and work with them in their efforts to fight homophobia. We are commissioned to confront those in the black community who attack us, hate us, and disrespect our lives. Black gay and lesbian student and academic groups need to confront homophobic scholars on campus. Challenge homophobic editors of black studies journals. We are an integral part of the African American community, with a shared history and family connection. Tell them proudly that our humanity is not debatable.

Learn How to Deal with the Media   It is important to be media savvy. Learn how to utilize the media, how to write press releases, letters to the editor, op-ed pieces, and letters to television producers. Sit down with editors and talk to them. The Gay and Lesbian Alliance Against Defamation can give pointers on how to deal with the media.

Encourage African American Artists to Treat Us with Respect   Bill Cosby, Oprah Winfrey, Patti Labelle, and other prominent black media figures have been our staunch allies. Write them and encourage them to continue. Eddie Murphy, Arsenio Hall, and Will Smith have changed their homophobic stances after they were confronted and forced to grow up. African American artists have profound influence on how we are perceived and how we are treated. We cannot continue to allow rap singers to recommend gay bashing.

Build and Maintain the Institutions That Nourish Us   If a black organization or leader publicly supports us, support them and let them know how much it means to you. Gay-led black churches are few and far between; consider starting one in your community. Get involved in AIDS organizations or other service groups. We need to create our own spaces in the African American community.

Build Alliances of Openly Lesbian-Gay Groups   Join with other African American service organizations: assist child breakfast programs, tutor youth, help the elderly, work with battered women, get involved.

Speak the Truth About Our Lives   Bisexuality is black America's best kept secret. It is a larger closet than homosexuality. Respect the fact that bisexuality is also an orientation and homophobia also keeps bisexuals "straight-jacketed."

Learn to Discuss the Bible with Authority   Certain Bible texts have been used to create, justify, and maintain antigay and lesbian beliefs, attitudes, and laws. In order to discuss the Bible with the knowledge you need, you would benefit from reading the following books: *Christianity, Social Tolerance, and Homosexuality*, by John Bosewell, *Stranger at the Gate*, by Rev. Mel White, *Rescuing the Bible From Fundamentalism*, by Rev. John Spong, and *What the Bible Really Says About Homosexuality*, by Daniel Helminiak. Remind our brothers and sisters that the Bible has been used to justify slavery, segregation, and Jim Crow. It is the basis of apartheid and the theory of the "Curse of Ham" that doomed us to be "hewers of wood and drawers of water."

Adopt a Church Program   Start meetings in your local churches to discuss homophobia in African American communities. To facilitate these discussions obtain the film *All God's Children* by calling (800) 343–5540 or write Dr. Sylvia Rhue, 3145 Geary Boulevard, Box 421, San Francisco, CA 94118, for speaking, training, and consultation.

Tell the Story   We must tell the story of our gay, lesbian, and bisexual heroes. We must be aware of and keep alive the memories of James Baldwin, Langston Hughes, Audre Lorde, George Washington Carver, A. Phillip Randolph, Bayard Rustin, Lorraine Hansberry, and other lesbian, gay, and bisexual African Americans who forged so many paths.

Utilize the Following Letter   An Open Letter to the African American Community from Members of the Family:

We are African Americans, African-rooted and American-grounded. Everyday you are living, working, playing, struggling for justice, and praying side by side with us in our various black communities. We are members of the Family.

And as family members, we are concerned with the amount and degree of homophobia that exists in our community. Homophobia doesn't appear in our homes, churches and workplaces as some casual tourist, but it has entrenched itself into our daily lives as surely and as insidiously as its parasitic hatetwin, racism. They are both chronic mental illnesses that plague our communal psyches and do great harm to our external realities. Both stem from a kind of visual insanity that telegraphs fear and hatred of difference. Both are counterfeit concerns that result in immature terror.

James Baldwin called homophobia "an extreme example of the American terror that's concerned with growing up." Baldwin connected the dots between the nexus of sex and race and suggested that we all grow up.

We gay, lesbian, bisexual, and transgendered African Americans who sit with you at the banquet table of our resplendent heritage suggest that is high time for a national discussion on this matter of homophobia. The dialogue can begin anywhere we gather: in our homes, at work, in our churches—in our hearts, but it has to begin now.

REFERENCES

Goldstein, R. 1989. "Go the Way Your Heart Beats: An Interview with James Baldwin." In Q. Troupe, ed., *James Baldwin: The Legacy*, pp. 178–85. New York: Simon and Schuster.

Herek. G. M., and J. P. Capitanio. 1995. "Black Heterosexuals' Attitudes Toward Lesbians and Gay Men in the United States." *Journal of Sex Research* 32(2): 5–105.

Hernton, C. C. 1987. *The Sexual Mountain and Black Women Writers*. New York: Anchor.

Lerner, G. 1986. *The Creation of Patriarchy*. New York: Oxford University Press.

Pharr, S. 1988. *Homophobia: A Weapon of Sexism*. Little Rock: Womens Project.

Russo, V. 1987. *The Celluloid Closet: Homosexuality in the Movies*. 2d ed. New York: Harper and Row.

Sears, J. T. 1991. *Growing Up Gay in the South: Race, Gender, and Journeys of the Spirit*. New York: Harrington.

Simmons, R. 1991. "Some Thoughts on the Challenges Facing Black Gay Intellectuals." In E. Hemphill, ed., *Brother to Brother*, pp. 211–28. Boston: Alyson.

Stoltenberg, J. 1989. *Refusing To Be A Man*. New York: Anchor/Doubleday.

Thorpe, D. 1994. "Keeping the Faith at Harvard." *10 Percent* (March/April), 2(7):36–39, 70–71.

Waller, J. 1994. "Go West." *Out* (October), p. 90.

Whetstone, M. 1994. "Toni Braxton Talks About Men, Sudden Stardom, and the Undying Rumor." *Ebony* (May), 49(7):134–41.

Zarembka, A. 1994. "Debunking the 'Minority Status' Lie." *BLK* (March), 5(3):19.

Warren J. Blumenfeld

Homophobia and Anti-Semitism:
Making the Links

Throughout history we find agent or dominant groups (sometimes called majorities) depicting or representing target groups (sometimes called minorities) in a variety of ways in order to maintain control or mastery. Myths and stereotypes are expressed in proverb, social commentary, literature, jokes, epithets, and pictorial depictions, among other forms. We are now seeing this played out yet again. In 1994, for example, in testimony to the U.S. Senate, Joseph Broads, a professor at the George Mason University School of Law, urged lawmakers to defeat the proposed Employment Non-Discrimination Act that would have included lesbians and gays as a protected category, saying: "It will result in special privileges for an elite group that has unjustly played the victim card to advance" (Roehr) Upon hearing this, Senator Paul Wellstone (D-Minn.), barely controlling his rage, responded: "As a Jew, I have a real problem with what you say. That is precisely the kind of argument that has been made . . . in behalf of the worst kind of discrimination against Jewish people" (Roehr).

This incident highlights what many of us have noticed for some time—the many clear and stunning connections between historical representations and oppression of Jewish people and lesbian/gay/bisexual/transgender (LGBT) people. Jewish people and LGBT people have suffered the injustices of oppression and are, or at least can be, natural allies. However, primarily in the West, a dominant Christian and heterosexual cultural hegemony has prevented such alliances from forming to the degree to which they can.

Among the various available prejudice/oppression-reduction strategies is the formulation of coalitions between and within social groupings targeted for oppression. One method I have used is an interactive workshop whose purpose is to help participants link the various strands of oppression (in this case homophobia/heterosexism and anti-Semitism), with the eventual hope that this understanding will aid in the enhancement of alliances where they currently exist and the building of alliances where none has existed previously. Going beyond the concept of empathy, in which one walks in the shoes of another, linking oppressions allows participants to travel the journey in their own shoes while walking side by side (and even hand in hand) in solidarity with members of other social groups.

Qualifications

Sexual identity (in this instance lesbian, gay, and bisexual) and religious/ethnic identity (in this instance, Judaism), is *NOT* the focus of my workshop. Instead, I concentrate on forms of *oppression:* homophobia/heterosexism and anti-Semitism.

By highlighting the parallel representations and manifestations of oppression of Jews and LGBTs, I am not asserting (or even attempting to imply) that members of these groups encounter oppression similarly. The experiences of Jewish people under institutional and societal anti-Semitism and those of gays, lesbians, bisexuals, and transgendered persons under forms of homophobia/heterosexism are often very distinct.

Indeed, also *within* these groups, experiences differ. Many social identity factors influence experience, most notably biological sex, race, class background, age, geographic residency, degree of assimilation into the dominant culture, and historical context. The realities of Jews in the United States today, for example, are not identical with those of their European ancestors of the 1930s. Societal reactions to lesbians, gay males, bisexuals, and transgendered people have changed somewhat from the days of greater repression before the advent of a visible modern rights movement. In addition, experiences certainly differ between individuals within a given time frame.

While unique in many respects, I believe that the many forms of oppression run parallel and, at points, actually intersect. A primary goal of my workshop is to unearth some of the intersections between homophobia/heterosexism and anti-Semitism, for I believe it is at these points of intersection that the potential for the development of alliances is greater.

In addition, though I have chosen to discuss here these two specific forms of oppression for comparison, I believe all the various spokes on the wheels of oppression are connected to varying degrees. Therefore, I have conducted workshops linking other forms of oppression, for example, racism and homophobia/heterosexism, racism and anti-Semitism, and sexism and racism, among others. By limiting my discussion here to anti-Semitism and homophobia/heterosexism, no assumption should be made that these are the only forms of oppression that are in some way connected.

A Workshop Outline

To increase diversity and enhance the efficiency of the workshop as well as to make it a more enjoyable experience for me personally, I have chosen to facilitate workshops with a co-facilitator. For this particular workshop, I have worked with either a heterosexual Jew or a lesbian, gay, or bisexual Gentile. Depending on the participant composition and duration of the workshop, I include a number of activities combining affective (feeling) and cognitive (informational) components.

Agenda

I first welcome the participants, and begin by displaying and discussing the workshop agenda, which I write on the chalkboard or on a large sheet of newsprint paper: "Welcome," "Opening Activity," "Facilitator Introduction," "'What We Have Heard' Activity," "Caucus Groups," "Lecturette," "Jewish and LGB Panel," "Taking the Next Step," "Closing Activity," "Evaluation." I then ask participants to introduce themselves from their seats, telling their names and where they live (or what they are studying, if an educational or classroom group, or their occupation or position, if in a workplace setting).

Icebreaker Activity I then facilitate an "Icebreaker" activity, usually one that involves movement of some sort, to help reduce anxiety and set a comfortable welcoming tone. One way to do this, if the room is large, with plenty of open space, is to conduct a "Forced Choice" exercise in which I ask participants to form two groups to respond to questions developed by Bradley Cohen for a 1990 workshop at the Medical Foundation of Boston. The first question is neutral: "I am more like a *museum painting* or more like *graffiti*?" All those who are more like a museum painting join in one group, graffiti in another. I tell participants where each group will meet in the room.

Once they have chosen their groups, participants are to discuss with others members of their group the reasons for believing they are more like graffiti or more like a museum painting. Following this, I ask a few members from both groups to share with the larger group why they chose the way they did. Some of the responses have included, for a museum painting: "I am rather formal, self-contained; I like to follow the rules (stay within a framework); I am classy; I like to remain indoors." And for graffiti: "I like to break the rules; I am spontaneous, unstructured, rebellious; I like to be outdoors; I change from day to day; I am not concerned with material things; I am spiritual."

If time allows, I repeat the exercise with another of Cohen's questions, connected directly to the workshop topic: "I believe that anti-Semitism and homophobia (or oppression in general) is more like a *snowball* or more like a *dust ball*?" Again, have participants divide into two groups and process activity. Some responses have included, for snowball: "It begins small but over time gets bigger and bigger; it can deeply hurt and wound when thrown at you; it can eventually be reduced or even melted away after shedding light and heat on it." And for dust ball: "Though it may be invisible at times, it is virtually everywhere; some people never see it; it is filled with microscopic disease-laden organisms; when you seem to clean it away, it somehow always returns; one has to remain ever vigilant for its return; there are things we can do to reduce the dust in our environment."

If the room configuration, size of the group, or time considerations do not permit the effective running of this activity, an alternate "Icebreaker" option is to have participants divide into pairs and, after a brief period in which they get acquainted, each person in turn introduces her or his partner to the rest of the group, giving the partner's name and where they currently reside and, if they are willing, a surprising or interesting thing about themselves that not many other people may know.

Goals, Guidelines, Assumptions, Working Definitions

I display (on the board or on large sheets of newsprint paper) the workshop "Goals," "Guidelines," "Assumptions," and "Working Definitions."

Goals   "To discover the interconnections between homophobia and anti-Semitism through the sharing of personal histories and factual information" and "To have some fun."

Guidelines   "Anonymity" (though participants can discuss the workshop with others once they leave, I ask them not to use names or other identifying characteristics of the participants). "Respect for Ideas." (no attacks or blaming, we agree to disagree, and, closely linked to that ...) "Try On" (I ask participants to consider new ideas that might contradict their current beliefs or opinions, without immediately rejecting them or becoming defensive).

"Personalize Knowledge" (speak from personal experience and do not speak for anyone else). "Share Air Time" (allow others to speak). "Value Risk Taking and Expressing Emotions" (feelings are OK to express in the workshop). "Take Care of Personal Needs" (for example, participants can go to the rest room without seeking permission; also, they can choose not to take part in any workshop activity in which they do not feel comfortable).

Assumptions   "Homophobia and anti-Semitism are two separate and distinct forms of oppression." "Homophobia and anti-Semitism are not identical, but have some common links." (At this point, I emphasize that the focus of the workshop is on the interconnections between forms of *oppression*, and NOT between sexual identity and religious/ethnic identity.) "Other forms of oppression also have common links." "Homophobia and anti-Semitism are pervasive throughout the society." "They are not our fault; we are not to blame, but we must accept responsibility for them within ourselves." "These forms of oppression hurt all people." "Working to end homophobia and anti-Semitism is a lifelong process."

The first three points listed under "Assumptions" are extremely important and should therefore be emphasized throughout the workshop to lessen potential resistance from some workshop participants who may be having difficulty accepting the premise that these two forms of oppression are in any way linked.

Working Definitions   *Homophobia* is the fear and hatred of those who love and sexually desire those of the same sex. Homophobia, which has its roots in sexism, includes prejudice, discrimination, harassment, and acts of violence brought on by that fear and hatred (Blumenfeld 1992b). *Anti-Semitism* (sometimes called *anti-Jewish oppression*) is the systematic discrimination against, denigration, or oppression of Jews, Judaism, and the cultural, intellectual, and religious heritage of the Jewish people (Lerner). For the purpose of the workshop *Heterosexism* is defined as the system of advantages bestowed on heterosexuals. It is the institutional response to homophobia that assumes that all people are or should be heterosexual and therefore excludes the needs, concerns, and life experiences of LGBTS (Blumenfeld 1992b). A parallel word I use is *Christianism,* which, particularly in the West, I define as the assumption that everyone is or should be Christian and therefore excludes the needs, concerns, and life experiences of people who do not define themselves as Christian.

Facilitator's Introduction

To take the connections between anti-Semitism and homophobia/hetero-sexism out of the realm of abstraction and make them real, I tell the participants how these forms of oppression have affected my life by recounting the following personal anecdote:

> One day, when I was very young, I sat upon my maternal grandfather Simon's knee. Looking down urgently, but with deep affection, he said to me, "Varn" (he always pronounced my name "Varn"), "you are named after my father, Wolf Yusel Mahler, who was killed in Poland by the Nazis along with my mother and most of my thirteen brothers and sisters." When I asked why they were killed, he responded simply, "Because they were Jews." Those seemingly simple words have reverberated in my mind, haunting me ever since.
>
> In this country my own father suffered the effects of anti-Jewish prejudice. One of only three Jews in his high school, many afternoons he returned home injured from a fight. To get a decent job, his father, Edmond, was forced to anglicize the family name, changing it from Blumenfeld to Fields.
>
> My parents did what they could to protect my sister and me from the effects of anti-Jewish prejudice, but still I grew up with a constant and gnawing feeling that I somehow didn't belong. The time was the early 1950s, the so-called McCarthy Era—a conservative time, a time when difference of any sort was held suspect. By the time I reached the age of seven or eight, I was increasingly becoming the target of harassment and attack by my peers who perceived me as someone who was different. Names like "queer," "sissy," "little girl," "fag," were thrown at me like the large red ball the children hurled on the school yard in dodgeball games. Not knowing what else to do, my parents sent me, beginning at age five and lasting for over seven years, to a child psychiatrist because they feared I might be gay (or, to use the terminology of the day, *homosexual*). And, as it turned out, their perceptions were indeed correct.
>
> My journey of coming out over successive years was often difficult and painful, though, looking back, I conclude that it has been worthwhile in that is has been the prime motivator for the work I am doing. Though I have experienced a double stigma growing up gay and Jewish, I truly believe that I am twice blessed."   (Blumenfeld 1992a)

What We Have Heard

To begin to bring out the parallel representations of Jews and LGBTs, I facilitate an activity that I call "What We Have Heard." In front of the entire group I write on the board, and then discuss in greater detail, the three categories of things we have heard about oppressed groups in general. These categories are 1. Nothing, 2. Positive/Factual Information, 3. Misinformation and Stereotypes. I relate some of the things I heard growing up about LGBT people, and then things I heard about Jews.

I next have participants break into small groups of six to eight members. Considering the three categories, within the groups participants are to brainstorm the things they heard growing up, one-half of the groups focusing on what they heard about Jews, the other half focusing on what they heard about LGBTs. Each group chooses a recorder who writes down the responses. After fifteen to twenty minutes, I ask the whole group to reconvene. I ask the recorders from the groups focusing on Jews to read their lists of things heard by group members. I facilitate the same process for things heard about LGBTs.

I ask participants to analyze these terms to determine if they can see any parallels and, if so, what these parallels are.

(Note: Whenever we discuss societal representations of targeted groups, there is always the potential that some destructive and hateful words and stereotypes can surface. I therefore conclude this activity by asking participants to pair up and discuss with a partner the feelings that came up for them during this activity. When I reconvene the group, I allow individuals time to relate their feelings to members of the large group.)

Caucus Groups

If small group facilitators are available, and depending on the needs of the participants, I save time for caucus groups to form (a Jewish group, a gay/lesbian/bisexual group, or separate lesbian, gay, , or bisexual groups, for example). Since some workshop participants may define as both Jewish and bisexual/gay/lesbian, the participants can choose which group to attend.

The purpose of the caucus group is to allow an opportunity for members of similar social identities to engage in open dialogue and "check in" with one another, before returning to the larger group.

Lecturette: Parallel Representations of Jews and LGBTs

From the previous workshop activity, and from my research, I present, in brief "lecturette" form, a number of interconnections in societal and historical representations of Jews and LGBT people. Additional information I give in the form of handouts, which participants take with them for future reference. I divide this information into five basic categories, which I print on the board or on newsprint paper: "Religious Condemnations," "Immature Developmental Stage," "Immutable Biological Types," "Abuse and Recruitment of Children," and "Domination and Destruction of 'Civilized' Society" (for a summary of this research see Blumenfeld 1996).

Jewish/LGB Panel

To further emphasize the interconnections, I offer participants the opportunity to speak from their own experiences. I ask for the following individuals to volunteer for a panel: two Jews (one male and one female), one lesbian or bisexual female, and one gay or bisexual male. The panelists are seated next to one another in front of participants. I guide them, one at a time, to answer the following questions, focusing, as much as possible, from a single identity perspective. I write the questions on newsprint paper, which I place on the floor in front of the panelists.

1. What do you love about being a Jew/lesbian/gay male/bisexual female/ male)?
2. What is difficult about being a _____?
3. What do you never want to see or hear said about_____ again?
4. What do you want from your allies to support you?

To protect the emotional safety of the panelists, no questioning of panelists' experiences by workshop participants is permitted. After each panelist has answered the four questions, I ask the workshop participants to choose a partner and discuss among themselves what they learned and what feelings came up for them during the panel. Panelists remain seated in front of the group and choose a partner from the panel to discuss the feeling that came up for them during their presentation.

I reconvene the larger group and allow participants to give appreciations to panel members (one to two minutes) without the panelists responding. These might include acknowledgments of what the panelist said or some other appreciation of the panel members.

I conclude with thanking the panelists by recognizing the emotional risks they took. I instruct the workshop participants not to discuss with the panelists without their consent the information and feelings that came up, although they may continue to give panelists appreciations afterward.

Taking the Next Step

I have participants break into groups of six to eight members and answer the following questions, which I write on the board or on newsprint paper. If time permits, I ask participants first to take a few minutes by themselves to write their responses to the questions and then join with their group members. The questions are:

1. What can we do as individuals, as groups, and as institutions to increase Jewish and lgbt visibility and reduce anti-Semitism and homophobia/heterosexism?
2. What can we do as individuals, as groups, and as institutions to strengthen alliances between Jews and LGBTs?

Each group chooses a recorder to write participants' responses. After about twenty to thirty minutes I reconvene the group. Recorders in turn read from their lists of responses. I write these responses on the board or on newsprint paper. I conclude this activity by asking participants to choose one or two actions they will take to reduce oppression and/or build alliances and, if they feel comfortable, to stand and commit this to the group.

Closing Circle

I close the workshop by asking participants to form a large circle. I ask them, if they wish, to either share one thing they learned or found surprising about the workshop or to offer an appreciation.

Evaluation

I ask participants to complete a workshop evaluation form by answering the following questions:

1. What were the high points of the workshop for you?
2. What would you recommend we change when we run this program again?
3. Some things I learned about myself are:
4. Some things I learned about others in the group are:
5. Additional comments:

Analysis

Evaluation of the workshop has varied widely, with representative responses ranging from, "You have crystallized for me what I have seen, read, and felt for a long time!" to "How dare you say that anti-Semitism has any links with homophobia!" I have not submitted these evaluations to "scientific" investigation, and my analysis is purely anecdotal. However, I have observed that generally gay, lesbian, and bisexual Jews see the strong links between these two forms of oppression, while many, though by no means all, of the heterosexual Jewish workshop participants and, to a lesser extent, the LGBT Gentiles seem—at least initially—a bit more reluctant to accept this basic thesis. The degree of acceptance is further influenced, for heterosexual Jewish participants, by their religious teachings on a continuum, with Orthodox and Conservatives more resistant and Reform and Reconstructionists more willing to accept the interconnections. Likewise, LGBT Gentiles who have a greater foundation in Jewish history and familiarity with Jewish culture seem more accepting of this premise than those who do not. Throughout the workshop, however, many participants who previously might not have considered the connections, begin to see the parallels.

Conclusion

As a final note, I remind workshop participants about a central tenet of Jewish tradition—*tukkun olam*: the transformation, healing, and repairing of the world into a more just, peaceful, and nurturing place. In the final analysis, we are most certainly all in this together. We cannot allow the theocratic right to revise history and to frame the terms of the debate. I say, then, let us go out and work together for *tikkun*. Let us transform the world.

REFERENCES

Blumenfeld, W. J. 1992a. "A Letter to My Great-Grandfather on Being Jewish and Gay." *Empathy* 3(1):83–86.
—— 1992b. *Homophobia: How We All Pay the Price*. Boston: Beacon.
—— 1996. "History/Hysteria: Parallel Representations of Jews and Gays, Lesbians, and Bisexuals." In B. Beemyn and M. Eliason, eds., *Queer Studies: A Lesbian, Gay, Bisexual, and Transgender Anthology*, pp. 146–62. New York: New York University Press.
Lerner. M. 1992. *The Socialism of Fools: Anti-Semitism on the Left*. Oakland, Cal.: Tikkun.
Roehr, B. 1994, August 7. "Hope, Fear, and Loathing: Landmark ENDA Hearings in the U.S. Senate." *In Newsweekly*, p. 10.

Eileen Durgin-Clinchard

A Three-Legged Stool:
PFLAG's Support, Education, and Advocacy

Parents, Families, and Friends of Lesbians and Gays is an organization made up of chapters, groups, and representatives located around the world, predominantly in the United States but also in eleven other countries (Australia, Belgium, Canada, England, France, Holland, Germany, Israel, New Zealand, Russia, South Africa). It is a grass-roots support/self-help group and social movement. Its three-part mission: to *support* the needs of parents and friends of lesbians and gay men who were having difficulty understanding and dealing with the sexual orientation of their children, to *educate* them and others, and to *advocate* equality for their gay and lesbian children.

Basic to the emotional well-being of gay and lesbian people is the need for support in the face of a homophobic society. Explicit in the PFLAG mission is also the need for advocacy of lesbian and gay people's civil rights. There are those who come to PFLAG as a vehicle for advocacy, and they too need the support of a safe haven when they have found themselves targets of prejudice and heterosexism.

In its structure and organization, and in its raison d'être, PFLAG is representative of many self-help/mutual aid groups. It is also a very real homophile organization. Its paradoxical aspect for many of the parents and family members has been the need to deal with both the stigma that society has placed upon their lesbian and gay loved ones and the perceived stigma upon themselves from the point of view of their own homophobia, and yet to recognize in an open and affirming way the pull to join the civil rights movement for gay, lesbian, and bisexual people.

From its inception PFLAG recognized the need to balance its activities and programs, to walk the thin line between frightening away those in need of support and depressing those who come in need of a vehicle for change. For these reasons PFLAG may be unique among support groups.

Many self-help groups begin with support as a major goal and evolve into outward extensions of education and advocacy as the individuals become aware that the "problem" is outside of themselves and needs to be addressed by the larger community. Katz and Bender (1990) quote Frank Reissman's use of the term *prepolitical* to describe most self-help groups. "Although there has been a significant increase in their advocacy orientation, self-helpers are largely pre-political.... An advocacy focus may appear as the self-helpers discover the external causes of their problems" (Katz and Bender 1990:255). Katz and Bender point out that the term *advocacy* must be used discriminately, noting that some self-help groups eschew advocacy or any form of political activity. Reissman used the term in the sense of social action, which coincides with the use of the term in this paper. As one of its initial purposes PFLAG specifically identified seeking civil rights, a legislative goal, for lesbian and gay people.

Combating Heterosexism

So what do they do about it? Buy a stool—a three-legged one—and climb up on it. Chapters concerned about combating heterosexism attempt the delicate task of programming for all three aspects of the PFLAG mission: support, education, and advocacy. Providing members with opportunities to be involved in all three aspects is a criteria for chapter affiliation with PFLAG. The key is providing opportunities and information and recognizing that there are no clear-cut lines of demarcation. The individuals who come to PFLAG come at their own stage of understanding, their own degree of readiness to absorb whatever is offered, and their own comfort range.

Combating heterosexism is a process that requires learning. Adults as well as children learn in a variety of ways: We know that (1) a certain degree of tension is necessary, but not so much that the learner is overwhelmed; (2) personal contact with lesbian, gay, and bisexual people reduces prejudice; (3) learning will not take place without new information to modify or replace the old that is being redefined or discarded.

Tools of Change

Some people require a lot of information delivered in a variety of formats;

others say, "Just tell me what to read." Chapters of PFLAG make use of the following tools.

Newsletters   Newsletters are mailed to members, others suggested by members, helping professionals, gay-friendly clergy, people who phone for information, college and university offices of student affairs, lesbian- and gay-managed bookstores and other places of business, organizations with diversity statements inclusive of sexual orientation, and exchanged with other PFLAG chapters. Preparing newsletters, whether to twenty or thirty addresses or to hundreds, involves numerous chapter members in a variety of ways, giving additional opportunity for interaction over routine tasks.

Helplines   Telephone helplines are a key part of the PFLAG network. All PFLAG affiliates are listed in the national directory. In newly started chapters a helpline may be a phone in someone's home or an answering machine from which calls are collected by a remote. Larger, more established chapters may have a number of volunteers scheduled to respond to calls they collect. In the early stages of a chapter, with less than a dozen members, the phone may also serve as preliminary to a newsletter, to pass on news, to arrange rides with one another, and for continued communication.

Programs   Monthly meetings that address a variety of subjects and audience needs are a vital component of chapters. "Programs" may be a member sharing remarks about a book from the library or showing a video borrowed from an established chapter or saved from television. With growth, programs may become more regularly organized by an informal committee on a month-by-month basis or planned months in advance. A variety of members need to be involved in planning, suggesting, and leading or introducing the program. Panels, guest speakers such as clergy, political candidates, school personnel, counselors, presentations by gay male and lesbian couples, parents, youth, and seniors are all appropriate. Programs are the heart of the educational component and serve to keep the interest of members who are not yet fully drawn in to planning and participating in the chapter in other ways.

Brochures   Brochures invite new people to come to PFLAG. Typically a brochure contains the PFLAG mission statement, time and location of the meetings and a phone number for more information, and frequently a list of suggested readings. A nationally produced PFLAG brochure is available, with space reserved for local information. Placing brochures in appropriate places is a short-term task that can involve newly connected people meaningfully.

Library   A small library of books, videos, copies of relevant articles, and lists of current events are collected over time, available for check out, and may serve as a drawing card for people as yet too shy to seek out these informative materials. Books can be traded or book sales of new and used books arranged. Gifts to the PFLAG library and donation projects for public or school libraries are both outreach/advocacy and internal education. Regional directors and the national PFLAG office are sources of information on booklists and other suitable material. Some chapters have developed major book donation projects to libraries statewide and in sets individuals may purchase to give to schools.

Short-term Tasks   Short-term tasks are important as soon as new people are comfortable and willing. When individuals reciprocate the support they receive they learn more themselves and begin to internalize the positive messages to which they have been exposed. This requires that veteran members of the chapter be willing to let go and appropriately delegate tasks to newcomers that are meaningful as well as mundane. Efficiency is not the point; reciprocity is.

Liaison Persons   Lesbian and gay organizations welcome connections with PFLAG and generally appreciate the participation of parents, family members, and friends to enter. Members are encouraged to examine the policies of other civic and social organizations to which they belong. Nongay organizations, particularly those with nondiscrimination policies inclusive of sexual orientation, are a step along the road to advocacy. These organizations may not have put this policy into practice. Someone who recognizes the opportunities, as well as the challenges of living their philosophy, is often a catalyst for broader views and actions.

Letter Writing   Informing its members about topics of concern and listing addresses are part of PFLAG practice. Letter-writing time, while some browse through books at a meeting, is an easy way to express support, opposition, or thanks to policy makers on legislation, school board policies, television and radio shows, newspapers, and so on. Involve the general membership by brainstorming for additional recipients of letters.

Small Groups   Dividing into small groups at monthly meetings allows for both the diversity of needs and the opportunity for sharing stories. Confidentiality is stressed. Planning for different needs is important, even when groups are small. Some come to PFLAG as activists seeking a vehicle for change; others need a long time before they reach that point. Education is the bridge. Members' varied stages offer informal modeling of support and action.

Celebrating   There are many opportunities for celebration in the gay/lesbian/bisexual community. Joint holiday events, potluck meals, or Thanksgiving turkey in a family atmosphere planned by PFLAG members invite participation by all. Gay Pride celebrations and Coming Out Day are obvious times for coming together. Increasingly we celebrate union and marriage ceremonies and the advent of youngsters into lesbian- and gay-headed families. Celebration adds joy to the soul and lifts the spirit.

Outreach   Chapter members of PFLAG serve as panel members and speakers to other organizations, college classes, and teacher staff development workshops. Newer members of PFLAG may not do speaking but are invited to attend for moral support and to observe.

Two themes are (1) the sense of self-empowerment through early active involvement and (2) the emphasis on reciprocity. Provide multiple opportunities, over time, for meaningful involvement at levels the individual finds comfortable, not mere busywork.

Smaller and newer chapters do not do all these things at once but develop gradually. Some larger chapters sponsor others, supplying help, attending their meetings for a while, and including news and announcements in the larger chapter's newsletter. Much of the success of chapters exists because of the intuitive responses of a few of the leaders, while others must consciously learn to work in ways that empower others. Collaborative group efforts in starting a chapter, with regional director support, is most likely to ensure continued involvement of the participants and their growth.

How Do These Activities Combat Heterosexism?

Engagement by an individual in these processes allows greater opportunity for internalizing the new knowledge. Familiarity with the issues faced by gay and lesbian people is gained. These processes build interaction among all who come to PFLAG.

Advocacy, education, and support sound like neat parcels, but in reality they are an interdependent web. Clearly there are individuals who are publicly out as parents, individuals who are supporters of lesbian and gay rights—as activists who lobby—who make statements to the media and are interviewed. At the other extreme are those who do not seem to be able to move past being fearful that someone they know might come to a PFLAG meeting. But most people can take action in small and important ways. Consider the following statements I have heard from PFLAG members over the years.

- "I leave PFLAG cards with the helpline number on it at various places, like in library books and on the laundromat bulletin board."
- "I put brochures at several agencies and where I work."
- "I phoned/wrote my senator to oppose any amendment Jesse Helms makes. I told him that he is a bigot and we don't want his bigotry brought against any group."
- "I heard a negative joke—you know, using "fag"—at coffee break and didn't know what to say. Next time I'll ask why that was funny."
- "I attended a school board meeting in support of our PFLAG president when she spoke about the needs of gay/lesbian/bisexual students."
- "I visited with my minister/pastor/rabbi about PFLAG and volunteered to meet with other parents confidentially or take them with me to their first PFLAG meeting."
- "I made a phone call to a radio call-in show when they were giving false information about what gays do. I told them that according to FBI statistics 97 percent of child molestations were perpetrated by heterosexual men, not gay men."

When the above quotations were given to workshop participants, as small steps in the direction of advocacy, I found that they identified these statements as falling into all three categories, support, education, and advocacy. What one person feels is a major step in his or her own coming out process toward advocacy may be perceived as support by someone else, and still another may believe it to be education. The beauty of PFLAG is that this continuum of comfort zones and perceptions is allowed and affirmed. There is recognition that learning to overcome our biases and heterosexism is an ongoing process. Nurturing and reciprocity are the processes that occur in PFLAG chapters.

This reciprocity, first documented by Reissman and often cited by others, has become known as the "helper therapy principle." Reissman wrote, "Helping others is a two-way situation since it not only assists the beginner in his first efforts but also aids the helper who derives from his efforts something which is essential" (1965:28). In my years of experience in PFLAG, and in my research, this principle has been directly expressed. People speak of how good it feels to be able to hear other's stories and know that by sharing their own stories they help someone else.

External catalysts to spark the formation of PFLAG chapters are all too prevalent today. With increased media attention and accompanying visibility of PFLAG there is growing interest in starting PFLAG chapters, particularly in areas hardest hit by groups who would legislate discrimination.

Families and nongay friends have their feet in both camps. They form the bridge that can lead to greater acceptance and understanding of a human diversity that cuts across all races, ethnic groups, religious beliefs, and functional abilities. Individuals' skills and knowledge of their communities are involved at every step, creating the potential for an atmosphere conducive to acceptance within PFLAG. Not a panacea, PFLAG is the only nongay organization whose sole focus is the elimination of heterosexism in whatever form. The need is greater than ever before for the energy and education that PFLAG delivers through its local affiliates, supported by their national office.

NOTE

Regional directors, an international coordinator, a public directory of all affiliates, and publication lists are available from: PFLAG National Office, 1101 14th Street, NW, Suite 1030, Washington, DC 20005, (202) 638–4200, fax (202) 638–0243.

REFERENCES

Durgin-Clinchard, J. E. 1993. "Characteristics of Selected Local Chapters of Parents and Friends of Lesbians and Gays That Have Been Identified as Strong or Successful." Ph.D. diss., University of Nebraska, Lincoln.

Katz, A. H., and E. I. Bender. 1990. *Helping One Another: Self-Help Groups in a Changing World.* Oakland: Third Party.

Reissman, F. 1965. "The 'Helper' Therapy Principle." *Social Work* 10(2):27–32.

Jane E. Vennard

Anger to Advocacy:
Support Groups for Nongay Spouses

However nongay spouses find out about the sexual orientation of their partners, the disclosure is often traumatic and has long-term implications. When parents, siblings, or children find out their sons or sisters or parents are gay, lesbian, or bisexual, there is shock, anger, and sadness, but the parent/child or sibling relationship can remain intact and often deepens and strengthens because secrets are no longer present. On the other hand, when a spouse comes out within a marriage, the marriage relationship often ends in divorce. If the partners remain married, the marriage as lived before disclosure is irrevocably altered. Even when the couple was honest from the beginning of the marriage and had discussed sexual orientation and its impact on the marriage, there comes a time when the nongay spouse is faced with an issue she or he had not expected.

When married men and women begin to face the crucial questions of their sexual orientation, there are many places they can go for help and support. The homosexual spouse comes out into a supportive community of other lesbian, gay, transgender, and bisexual people who are finding pride and dignity in who they are. In contrast, many nongay spouses feel invisible. Most have never heard of a marriage like theirs. Although they may have gay and lesbian friends, they have likely not encountered former husbands and wives. More than two million lesbian and gay and bisexual people are married or have been married (Buxton 1994:327), but nothing definitive was written about the experience of the nongay spouse until 1989 (Gochros).

These women and men, so long ignored, can become instrumental in the struggle against homophobia and heterosexism. But nongay spouses cannot be enlisted in the gay rights movement until their own pain has been addressed. Without understanding and support, the nongay spouse's anger at the loss of the marriage, bitterness of betrayal, and grief of shattered dreams is misplaced. Sexual orientation becomes the culprit. Nongay spouses often become homophobic. They then teach their children from this place of pain, fear, and misunderstanding.

With support, nongay spouses can eventually become a powerful force in educating others about homophobia and heterosexism. They have known intimately the coming out process of another. They have seen and experienced the pain that a heterosexist society has caused a loved one. They have felt the prejudice and discrimination of homophobia. Nongay spouses stand in a unique place to teach the true meaning of full acceptance of all sexual orientations.

Concerns of the Nongay Spouse

The best support for nongay spouses comes from other nongay spouses. This support may be had through a telephone call, an exchange of letters, a meeting in a coffee shop, or a more formal support group that meets regularly with a trained facilitator. (Federation of Parents, Families, and Friends of Lesbians and Gays [PFLAG], at P.O. Box 27605, Washington, D.C. 20038–7605, (202) 638–4200, will provide a connection to the Spouse Network, which helps individuals and groups locate other spouses living in their area.) The nongay spouse can hear the message he or she truly needs only from a person who has had a similar experience: you are not alone; you did not cause this; you are not crazy; you will survive.

You Are Not Alone

The isolation of the nongay spouse is hard to break. Many simply go into their own closets and never tell anyone the cause of their distress or the reason for ending their marriages. When the topic of gay/straight marriages is discussed on talk shows or addressed in "Dear Abby" advice columns, the response is always the same. The phone lines and mails are flooded with people saying, "I thought I was the only one. Thank God you've broken the silence." Many referrals to the Spouse Network and to spouse support groups come from the gay and lesbian and bisexual community. Some nongay spouses call the hot line themselves and find a group. Others are sent by their gay and lesbian partners.

Educating helping professionals to understand the special needs of nongay spouses is important. Although a therapist, a social worker, or a clergy person may directly hear the story of a nongay spouse, more often the gay, lesbian, or bisexual person is the one seeking help, talking, exploring, and struggling with the coming out process. What a gift it would be for the person helping her or him to be aware enough to say, "And what of your spouse while you are going through this? Is she or he getting support? Let me give you a name that might help." Nongay spouses may need to be gently pulled from their closets by people who recognize their existence, understand their issues, and have resources available. Connecting a nongay spouse with a support group or another nongay spouse can be a lifeline for healing and wholeness.

You Did Not Cause This

Many nongay spouses have no knowledge of homosexuality before it shows up in their marriage. They are awash with the myths and misconceptions of a homophobic culture. "If I were more of a man, she would not have left me for a woman." "He told me I was frigid; this must be my fault." "If only I had been more sexually attractive, aggressive, receptive, alluring, experienced." "If only I . . . "

Some nongay spouses blame themselves for their partners' homosexuality. Nongay spouses need good, clear, up-to-date information about homosexuality. They need to know beyond the shadow of a doubt that they did not cause their partners' sexual orientation. They need to understand the long, slow process that gays and lesbians face in coming out. Although a person may come out in the middle of a marriage, the husband or the wife has not caused the basic sexual orientation of his or her partner.

You Are Not Crazy

Many people exploring their sexual orientation are unable to name who they are becoming. One day they believe they are straight, another day bisexual, another day homosexual. One moment they are alive with the possibilities of self-discovery, the next moment overcome with shame and guilt. One day they are ready to tell the world of their discovery and another day they demand absolute secrecy. This is the rollercoaster of the coming out process. The nongay spouse finds her/himself along for the ride.

Nongay spouses are also on their own tumultuous journeys, but they are alone. To watch someone you love developing her or his sexual identity can be an exhilarating experience. But that process can lead to the end of the marriage. To watch one's mate bloom into new opportunities creates gladness. At the same time, the nongay spouse is angry and fearful about the consequences of these possibilities. During the difficult experience of a partner's coming out, nongay spouses need to be reassured that all their experiences are normal, that their rage is part of the process, that their grief is real, that love may exist side by side with hate. Nongay spouses need to be constantly told, "You are not crazy," for this is a "crazy-making" time.

You Will Survive

Nongay spouses need to witness those who survive the coming out process of a partner. They need to witness others moving on and flourishing. A person who learned only five days before that her spouse is gay can be comforted simply by the presence of another who is three years beyond disclosure and who is finding satisfaction and pleasure in his or her life.

The process of healing and transformation can occur. Just as bisexual, lesbian, or gay partners find transformation in their coming out process, nongay spouses can also claim transformation for themselves. Opportunities emerge out of crisis. When nongay spouses recognize these new possibilities and find the courage to seize them, they may be led in new directions or achieve previously unimagined goals. "Shattered beliefs and assumptions [can] be incorporated into a new belief system," says Amity Buxton. "Then spouses can move forward into what is for many the most rewarding period of their lives, with or without their partners" (Buxton 1994:299). Even in the darkest moments during the coming out process of a husband or a wife the light of possible transformation must be present, for it provides hope in what seems a hopeless situation.

Group Facilitation

Support groups for nongay spouses and former spouses of gay, lesbian, and bisexual people are an effective way to address the four basic issues discussed above. A group may be of any size, ranging from two or three and up to ten or twelve people. Some groups are run by therapists for a set length of time and the participants are charged a fee. More commonly, groups are ongoing and fall under the umbrella of a larger organization such as PFLAG, a community center, the YWCA, or a religious organization. They may be facilitated by members of the organization or trained nongay spouses or former spouses. The advantage of these groups is that they are always available on a monthly basis, and a nongay spouse can attend a meeting soon after she or he has reached out for help.

In my experience, and the experience of other group leaders, the following guidelines are important:

1. Confidentiality is necessary. The group must be safe for the expression of all feelings and experiences. Privacy must be protected.
2. New members need only give their first names and the shortest possible statement about who they are. One group described a woman who came and said nothing until the end of the meeting and then revealed she was a married lesbian who was trying to find ways to help her husband. Her intentions were good, but the group felt "invaded."
3. No one in the group has the answers for another person. This is territory with no map, no right way, no clear answers. Each person needs room to discover the best way and the best timing for his or her situation. The facilitator and other group members are there to provide guideposts that have developed out of their own experiences.
4. All feelings are acceptable and can be freely expressed in the group: anger, fear, disgust, confusion, shame, guilt, love. At the same time, misinformation about homosexuality and homophobic comments must be gently confronted.
5. All religious views must be honored. At this time of loss, holding tight to faith is important. A gentle "not all Christians believe that" could plant the seed of liberation while honoring the experience of the moment.
6. Laughter is encouraged. Along with the tears and pain, some situations are humorous. One group spent a good fifteen minutes tossing ideas around about how to ask a first date if he is gay or she is lesbian. As the suggestions got more outrageous, the laughter increased, and a very real fear held by nongay spouses (that they will fall in love with another homosexual) had been addressed with humor.

Every support group takes on a life of its own, changing, growing, deepening as people arrive and leave, as trust builds, as people move on in their healing process. One-on-one interaction through counseling, brief meetings, letters, or phone calls can be of great help if there is no support group available. But a group of people all struggling with the same issue offers the hope of healing and the possibility of transformation.

Children

Children of homosexual or bisexual parents can become educated, accepting, loving advocates for the end of homophobia and heterosexism (Buxton 1994:85–139, 215–57). To move through their own issues regarding their parents' sexual orientation, the children need strong support. The most crucial support comes from nongay parents, because they share with their children the loss that comes from another's self-discovery. Children tend to follow the lead of the nongay parent in either accepting or rejecting the homosexual parent. Parents strong in their sense of self and their own dignity and worth are able to respond to children's questions and reactions more wisely.

The younger children are when they hear the news that "Daddy is gay" or "Mommy is a lesbian," the better off they are. (Buxton 1994:238). Young children have not developed the stereotypes and prejudices of older children and teens. They accept the information, even if they don't really understand what the words mean.

Older children will need to sort out what they have heard in school and the neighborhood about "fags" and "dykes" and "queers." They will also have to look at the fact of their parent's sexuality, which most children prefer not to do no matter what the sexual orientation. They will have to deal with fears about their own sexuality, "Does this mean I will be gay? I will be a lesbian?" Children who were told at a younger age will also have to address these teenage issues, coming to a new understanding based on their own sexual development.

If children are adults when a parent comes out, there is more possibility of mature compassion. On the other hand, there is also more possibility that the adult children are firm in their homophobia. Because of their age and their independence from their parents, they can distance and not work through their own issues, even when support is offered.

How to tell children about a parent's sexual orientation will depend a lot on the situation. Ideally, both parents are present when the news is broken, so the children see their parents together and coping and both parents are available to respond to questions and concerns. Some parents choose to tell each child separately, others gather the children together. In either case, all children must be told the truth.

When both parents finally discover this truth through the coming out process, decisions can be made in relation to the marriage and the family. Some couples decide to accept the sexual orientations of both partners as a reality in the marriage and to sustain their vows of monogamy. Other couples restructure their families by opening their homes to the lover of the lesbian, gay, or bisexual spouse and seek ways for the three of them to live under one roof in harmony. Still other couples open their marriages so that both partners are free to explore other relationships. Some children can thrive in relationships in which all the adults have freely chosen the new arrangements, the original contract has been rewritten and affirmed, and communication is open and honest among all family members (Whitney 1990).

When the sexual orientation of one of the parents precipitates separation and divorce, divorce issues must be kept distinct from sexual orientation issues. This is very hard to do, for in many cases divorce is happening because of sexual orientation. Since divorce is always traumatic for children, they tend to view whatever causes divorce to be bad. Children then connect being homosexual with being bad. For this reason some parents decide to talk first about separation and divorce issues and explain the sexual orientation issues after a new family pattern of custody and visitations has been arranged.

Whether parents divorce or remain together, the best relationship children can see is one of friendship, respect, and supportive co-parenting. The children know from their own experiences and from watching their parents that change in the family structure is painful and sad. Both parents are obligated in the name of love to provide reassurance and support even when they are in the midst of their own struggles (Ahrons 1994).

Children whose parents have done their own grief work and faced their own homophobia can eventually open to new possibilities and mature in their compassion for those who are different. Many learn to respond to homophobic statements and attitudes with the following kinds of comments: "Yeah, my dad is gay. You want to tell that fag joke to my face?" "I live with my Mommy and Debra. I'm lucky. I have two Mommies and a Daddy too." "My dad is gay. And he's really a good person and a great dad. No way is he going to hell."

Spouses, former spouses, and children of gay, lesbian, and bisexual people are in a unique position to speak out against homophobia and heterosexism. To speak about the right to a fulfilled life for all people takes self-confidence and solid knowledge. These qualities are developed in the nongay spouse when she or he receives strong, trustworthy, compassionate support during the coming out process of the homosexual spouse.

Nongay spouses and former spouses and their children can dispel homophobia and heterosexism by speaking from their own experience. They can become an important social force to expand equality for all people.

REFERENCES

Ahrons, C. 1994. *The Good Divorce: Keeping Your Family Together When Your Marriage Comes Apart.* New York: Harper Collins.

Buxton, A. 1994. *The Other Side of the Closet: The Coming Out Crisis for Straight Spouses and Families.* Rev. ed. New York: Wiley.

Gochros, J. 1989. *When Husbands Come Out of the Closet.* New York: Harrington Park.

Whitney, C. 1990. *Uncommon Lives: Gay Men and Straight Women.* New York: New American Library.

Glenda M. Russell

Using Music to Reduce
Homophobia and Heterosexism

When I first started conducting workshops and seminars, I went prepared with studies and facts and statistics—all the information I could find. This information was necessary and often useful. However, there were times when I had the very real sense that my information was not producing the impact I wanted. Something wasn't hitting home. It took me a while to figure out just what "home" it was I was trying to hit. In retrospect, I was sensing the need to impact the affective or emotional component of people's attitudes around sexual orientation. My intuition suggested that it was in this affective domain of attitudes that many people's homophobic and heterosexist lessons had been planted. I also had the suspicion that, if people could be moved emotionally in relation to homophobic issues, they might be more likely to be moved to action on behalf of those same issues. Having made the decision to try to tap more into the affective dimension of attitudes around sexual orientation, it was an easy next step to introduce music as a focal part of some of my training efforts.

I have used music in a variety of training settings and with a broad range of participants for two decades now. While music is not part of every training I conduct, I use it often. Over the years both formal evaluations and informal feedback have attested to the value of music for participants in these trainings. In evaluation forms, for example, people frequently have mentioned the usefulness of hearing real songs from lesbian, bisexual, and gay people and the importance of having had the opportunity, through those songs, to become aware of and discuss their discomfort with issues related to sexual orientation in a safe environment.

As a training tool music serves to undercut resistances to the material of the training (Cleaver 1989–1990). Music is recognized as a universal language and goes directly to people's emotions. Presenting ideas and imagery about gays and lesbians and about homophobia in the context of a song makes it less likely that those ideas and imagery will be kept distant and remote by the listener. Music allows for active learning to occur (Hamilin and Janssen 1987; Olzak 1981). Participants are invited to wrestle with material in a way that is familiar and personally meaningful. And, perhaps most important, music, "the expressive form closest to the human voice" (Julius 1993:154) touches people at a level that allows them to draw on their humanity and to recognize the humanity in others (Campbell 1988; Humpal 1990, 1991; Kalliopuska and Ruokonen 1986, 1993).

I have used music as part of homophobia-reduction trainings in two major ways: as a medium for imparting content-based information and as a medium for participants to use to access their own emotional reactions.

The use of songs as vehicles for teaching specific information (Bosompra 1991–1992) and for provoking discussion (Cooper 1981, 1988) is hardly a novel idea. We have long known that popular music carries information of many kinds (e.g., Freudiger and Almquist 1978). It only makes sense that teachers and trainers would intentionally use that form in their efforts to convey information. Imparting content within the structure of a song allows it to be carried in a familiar and comfortable medium. The information, designed to influence participants' intellect, comes in a package that typically touches participants' emotions as well. The goal of using music in this way is the exchange of content; the music is seen as a means of facilitating that transfer of content.

Virtually any song about the experiences of lesbians, bisexuals, and gays is a candidate for inclusion in this category. Obviously, however, some songs are better than others, based on quality of the content conveyed as well as on the aesthetic properties of the song. Many of the same songs that are used to convey information also may be used by participants to gain access to their own emotional reactions. What separates these two categories is not so much an exclusive set of songs for each but rather the uses to which the songs are put by the trainer. Consider, for example, Romanovsky and Phillips's song "Straightening Up the House" (1988). On the face of it, the song stands as a humorous description of what two closeted gay men do to "de-gay" their house upon hearing that one of their mothers is about to visit. The amusing details of hiding gay magazines and gay pride shirts is underscored by the need to hide the central love of one's life from one's mother. As such, the song can serve as a good basis for describing the intricacies of a gay person's coming out to his or her family. Alternately, the song can be used to focus participants' attention on the felt experiences of hiding from one's own family. Finally, the song can be used to generate discussions with (primarily) heterosexual participants on how gays, bisexuals, and lesbians withdraw and hide from them and what reactions that hiding evokes in participants.

While it may be that any gay-oriented song is a candidate for inclusion in antihomophobia trainings, there are issues that are frequently addressed in these trainings and some songs that are especially suitable for elucidating those issues.

Manifestations of Homophobia and Heterosexism

Several songs offer descriptions of different manifestations of homophobia and heterosexism. Included among them are two each by Tom Wilson Weinberg—"Day After Dade" (1979) and "Bat Boy" (1993a)—and Romanovsky and Phillips—"Homophobia" (1986a) and "When Heterosexism Strikes" (1991d), as well as "Don't Pray for Me" by Linda Tillery (1977a) and "Feeding the Flame" by Willie Sordillo and Flor de Caña (1990). While most of these songs present a survey of different examples of homophobia, "Bat Boy" is a disturbing song that depicts an episode of violence against two gay men. The song's vivid description of gay bashing allows listeners to connect affectively with the reality of antigay violence. It has been used successfully in trainings with public safety officials, including police officers. "Bat Boy" provides a good segue between facts and statistics about bashing and the psychological effects of bashing.

Discussion can be focused on eliciting a humane picture of the experience of being victimized for one's sexual orientation and on the effects of violent incidents on the gay/lesbian/bisexual community as a whole.

Speaking from a more personal level, Holly Near's song "Simply Love" (1986) challenges the listener to examine her or his own homophobic reactions to the singer's love for a woman. "Simply Love" interweaves the story of two women who share touches, glances, hard work, children, and love with a challenge to the listener: "Why does my love make you shift in your chair?" For groups that have previous knowledge and some agreement to explore their personal feelings about sexual orientation (e.g., some Women Studies classes), the song can be used to focus discussion on participants' reactions to the images as a lesbian couple making a life together. Groups that have accepted Near's challenge have used the song to elucidate aspects of their own discomfort about lesbians and their relationships.

Coming Out

It is not surprising that there is a wealth of songs describing various aspects of the process of coming out, since it is of such fundamental significance for lesbians, gays, and bisexuals. Very personal treatments of coming out at an individual level have been offered by Margie Adam in "Sweet Friend of Mine" (1976), Michael Callen in "Crazy World" (1990), George Fulginiti-Shakar and Eliot Pilshaw in "Welcome Home" (1990), and Meg Christian in "The Road I Took to You" (Keith 1977). This latter song provides an exceptionally strong portrait of the psychic breakthrough that often accompanies a person's coming out. I have used it as a foundation for discussions about the coming out process for mental health professionals and for religious clergy.

David Maddux's "The Other Side of the Door" (Maddux 1992) is one song in a ten-song gay and lesbian choral work, any of which can be used in antihomophobia trainings. This specific song describes the fear and shame of being closeted as well as the liberating quality that awaits one "on the other side of the door." It provides powerful images of the personal fragmentation ("Too many hearts are still in pieces") and interpersonal duplicity ("Few friends know me just as I am / Others see the fraud and the sham") associated with being in the closet. I have asked participants to discuss the song line by line to explicate the psychological and social costs of being closeted. This discussion can be concluded by asking participants to explain what the songwriter might mean by his images of coming out: "futures to explore," "more life than you've ever known before," and "Come out now while your spirit still can soar / On the other side of the door."

At a broader social level, "Friends in High Places" by Tom Wilson Weinberg (1993b) and "Queers in the Closet" by Romanovsky and Phillips (1991c) both emphasize the need for gays, lesbians, and bisexuals from all walks of life to come out. These songs can be very useful as a basis for discussing coming out as a political issue, as they focus on the social and political costs of the closet, especially in cases of powerful and well-known people who are gay or lesbians. This perspective helps participants understand that coming out is not solely a personal decision for the individual. It also carries political implications and therefore is influenced by social and political pressures as well. While this perspective is often valuable, trainers should beware of the danger of participants' being drawn into an interminable argument about outing. I often avoid such arguments by raising the issue myself and giving a brief summary of the rationales for and objections to outing.

Gay and Lesbian Families

Placing gay, lesbian, and bisexual lives in the context of relationships may be an important counteractant to some of the more prominent bases of homophobic attitudes (see, e.g., Herek 1992). One obvious step toward this end is through the use of love songs. There are many love songs from which to choose. Some that have received positive responses in trainings include "In a Restaurant By the Sea" (Bucchino 1986), recorded by Holly Near, "Here Is a Love Song" by Margie Adam (1983), "Amma" by the Washington Sisters (1987), "Would You Like to Dance" by Deidre McCalla (1987), and "Valentine Song" by Meg Christian (1974). This last song suggests the transformative potential of newfound love. Without the otherworldly romance of so many love songs, "Valentine Song" highlights the surprising nature of love: "My love was a love of the moment / Of the strangeness, the thrill / But moments deny a tomorrow / And yet, I love you still." It also underscores both the awakening passions ("And I loved you at first for your wicked eyes / And the laughter that loosens your bones / And your soft curls / And the passions that I've never known") and the growth-enhancing properties of new love ("And I loved you for facing my crazy eyes / And using your strengths to build mine / And learning compassion, and growing more mellow and kind"). The songwriter and the beloved could be of either/any gender. Participants can be asked to listen to the song and generate images when they think of the beloved as male and then to generate another set of images as they consider the song as being sung to a woman. This exercise typically allows participants to become aware of both the limited number and nature of their images of same-sex relationships.

Two songs have been especially useful for exploring facets of gay/lesbian parenthood. Margie Adam's "Babychild" (1982) speaks to the pain of lesbian mothers having to fight for the custody of their children. "Love Is All It Takes" by Romanovsky and Phillips (1991a) is sung as a lullaby to the children of gay and lesbian parents. It provides a springboard for differentiating the negative effects of homophobia and heterosexism from the intrinsic properties of being a child in a gay or lesbian family. I have used this distinction as the focus of discussion for a variety of groups including teachers, family law attorneys, child care workers, and social service professionals.

Gay Youth

It has been important in trainings for personnel in both public and private schools to promote extensive discussions of the role of homophobia and heterosexism in the lives of young people who identify themselves as gay, lesbian, or bisexual or who are wrestling with issues around sexual orientation. Some songs that have been especially useful in generating these discussions are Tom Wilson Weinberg's "Get Used To It" (1993c) and "It's a Boy, It's a Girl" and "Stories," both from David Maddux's choral work, *Boys and Girls with Stories* (1992). Lucie Blue Tremblay's "Peaking" (1989) has been profitably used to bring the emotional reality of youth suicide into focus. This song was written by Tremblay in response to a report of a teen suicide on television. It can serve as the basis for a discussion of the alienation of gay and questioning youth: "There must be something wrong / When you can't get along / 'Cuz you don't belong." Possible solutions to such alienation are the obvious next focus of discussion. Participants should be encouraged to strategize solutions that are directly relevant to their lives and work settings as well as solutions that are more general in scope.

A song that I've relied on countless times to help participants understand internalized homophobia is Romanovsky and Phillips's "Lost Emotions" (1986b). This song offers three vignettes, each describing an interaction between two men: two friends, two brothers, and, finally, two gay lovers. Each interaction is interrupted by prohibitions against same-sex (especially male-to-male) expressions of affection. As the song proceeds from one interaction to the next, the prohibitions become less external in nature and more internalized. "Lost Emotions" can provide a springboard for discussions about the nature and manifestations of the internalization of homophobic attitudes. Alternately, this song can be used to explore the relationship between homophobia and sexism. Ron Romanovsky has suggested that men are taught more about the exploitation of women than about "how to connect with other men on an emotional or spiritual level" because "being emotional, gentle, receptive, and nurturing are [viewed as] strictly female qualities and therefore less valuable, useful, and important" (Sears 1992:73). A discussion pursued from this vantage point offers participants the opportunity to see homophobia in the light of sexism. Male participants in particular often begin to see the costs to them caused by homophobia and sexism.

Stereotypes

Bisexuals, gays, and lesbians, like all oppressed groups, have been subject to a variety of stereotypes. One of the prominent goals of much of antihomophobia education is to replace these stereotypes with more realistic images. In the words of singer Paul Phillips, songs can "challenge people to rethink the things they've been taught by their parents, their churches, their schools, their socializations, and their own communities (Sears 1992:74). The presence and impact of stereotypes can be felt whether or not the stereotypes are addressed directly. I have found it useful to tackle the issue of stereotypes directly. Doing so requires ample time for participants to both recognize and explore the stereotypes to which they have been exposed and be offered more factually based information about bisexuals, gays, and lesbians. Songs that have been of use in confronting stereotypes include "Straight Girl Blues" by Jamie Anderson (1989), "Leaping," recorded by Meg Christian (Fink and Grippo 1977), and "Once Upon a Time" by Romanovsky and Phillips (1991b). Because some of these songs rely on a satirical treatment of stereotypes, it is imperative that trainers work with participants to disentangle the satire from the "truth" of the songs. If the satirical nature of the song is not explicitly acknowledged, there is some danger that participants may take the songs literally. Therefore, it is advisable to use these songs with participants who have the ability to think abstractly and have a sense of humor.

Heterosexual Privilege

One of the most potentially illuminating exercises in trainings is to assist heterosexual participants in developing an appreciation of the benefits they derive at personal and institutional levels simply by virtue of their heterosexuality. Many heterosexual participants have not considered that their sexual orientation affords them a measure of personal safety that others do not enjoy. Nor have many heterosexuals considered that institutional benefits such as the possibility of marriage and custody and survivorship accrue to them solely on the basis of their heterosexual status. The results of a study on heterosexual allies that I have conducted have bolstered my impression that heterosexuals who appreciate their own privilege tend to understand homophobia with a significant degree of depth and sophistication and to be more likely to commit themselves to working against homophobia. Of course, to understand their privilege, heterosexuals need to be open to looking at themselves in addition to learning about lesbians, gays, and bisexuals.

Therefore, I reserve in-depth discussions of heterosexual privilege for groups that already have a basic understanding of oppression and its relationship to sexual orientation.

There are two songs that I've found especially useful for setting up discussions of heterosexual privilege. Tom Wilson Weinberg's (1987) "Wedding Song" illustrates the absence of social supports to relationships that heterosexuals take for granted: "No usher or bridesmaid, no movies or slides made, We're just we" and "No silver service, no hostess or hosting, no bright clever toasting, We're just we." The song's humor allows the listener to be drawn into a description that ends up being quite poignant: gays and lesbians who choose to be in committed relationships do so without the supports that heterosexuals enjoy. "Buried Treasure" by David Maddux (Maddux 1992) is a subtler depiction of heterosexual privilege. It is an understated song about the difficulty of finding happiness in relationships: "We live in a world where true love is perfection / but perfection's the thing that seems always out of reach." Except for one verse, the lyrics are not tied to any particular sexual orientation. That verse, however, is a powerful statement of the impact of heterosexual privilege on same-sex relationships: "We live in a world where man and woman marry, / Is it fair that their voices should hinder our choices, / And make finding love twice as hard?"

Linking Various Oppressions

Without denying the unique aspects of any form of oppression, it is important to understand and, often, to explicate the linkages between different forms of oppression. To that end, I frequently include songs that invite discussions of those interconnections. Meg Christian's "Rosalind" (1977), for example, offers an opportunity to discuss the intersection of racism and homophobia in one interpersonal relationship told from the perspective of a white Southern lesbian. "Brown Like Me" (Millington 1987) by the Washington Sisters portrays the end of isolation in the relationship between women of color. As such, this song may be used to focus discussion on how racism and homophobia intersect at interpersonal and wider social levels. Lindy Tillery's "Freedom Time" (1977b) speaks directly to the experience of the "triple jeopardy" of being African American, female, and lesbian: "If I could tell you just what it's really like / To live this life of triple jeopardy / I fight the daily battles of all my people / Just to sacrifice my pride and deny my strength." Songs such as these are important both because they offer the opportunity to expand participants' understanding of different forms of oppression and because they undermine the tendency to forget that gays, bisexuals, and lesbians come from all races, classes, and religions.

The power of music as a teaching tool in homophobia-reduction trainings can be maximized by following a few steps. First, use the best sound equipment that you can. The better it sounds, the more participants will respond to the music. An inexpensive tape recorder will be less effective than a boom box. If you are conducting trainings, ask if the host group has a tape player.

Second, no matter how good your sound system is, there inevitably will be lyrics that won't be audible for at least some participants. Having written lyrics available allows participants to really work with the songs rather than struggle to hear each word. After experimenting with different modalities, I have decided that the use of an overhead projector is optimal for displaying lyrics. This allows everyone to see the lyrics while still maintaining a group focus. If an overhead projector is not available, copies of lyrics can be distributed to each participant.

Finally, be prepared to discuss whatever songs you use with participants. Starting with general comments or questions does not work as well as commenting on or asking about specific aspects of the song. While the songs may be entertaining in and of themselves, their greatest value as educational tools will be realized only if trainers have planned to focus attention on one or two particular issues raised by the songs and then develop those issues in discussions with participants. I make strategic decisions to forego the use of music when the training is too brief or when the participant group is very formal. Some training contracts do not provide for any format other than a lecture. I also avoid using music when I lack advance information about participants that would indicate whether music would be appropriate or what songs would be useful.

If you do use music in appropriate training situations, it can add to your effectiveness as a trainer. Not only does it convey information, it also allows participants to access and explore their own emotional reactions to issues around sexual orientation and homophobia. Music often operates as a tool to facilitate understanding at a level beyond the purely cognitive. That kind of understanding is frequently associated with changes in attitudes and behavior.

REFERENCES

Adam, M. 1976. "Sweet Friend of Mine." *Songwriter*. Record. Berkeley: Pleiades.
—— 1982. "Babychild." *We Shall Go Forth*. Record. Berkeley: Pleiades.
—— 1983. "Here Is a Love Song." *Here is a Love Song*. Record. Berkeley: Pleiades.
Anderson, J. 1989. "Straight Girl Blues." *Closer to Home*. Cassette. Tucson: Tsunami.
Bosompra, K. 1991–1992. "The Potential of Drama and Songs as Channels for AIDS Education in Africa: A Report on Focus Group Findings from Ghana." *International Quarterly of Community Health Education* 12:317–42.
Bucchino, J. 1986. "In a Restaurant by the Sea." *Singing with You,* H. Near and R. Gilbert. Record. Oakland: Redwood.
Callen M. 1990. "Crazy World." *Feeding the Flame: Songs by Men to End* AIDS. CD. Chicago: Flying Fish.
Campbell, D. G. 1988. "The Cutting Edge: Personal Transformation with Music." *Music Therapy* 7:38–50.
Cleaver, R. 1989–1990. "Harry and Terry: Using Music to Educate." *Empathy* 2(1):29–30.
Christian, M. 1974. "Valentine Song." *I Know You Know*. Record. Los Angeles: Olivia.
—— 1977. "Rosalind." *Face the Music*. Record. Los Angeles: Olivia.
Cooper, B. L. 1981. "Audio Images of the City: Pop Culture in the Social Studies." *Social Studies* 72:130–36.
—— 1988. "Social Concerns, Political Protest, and Popular Music." *Social Studies* 79:53–60.
Fink, S., and J. Grippo. 1977. "Leaping." *Face the Music*, M. Christian. Record. Los Angeles: Olivia.
Freudiger, P., and E. M. Almquist. 1978. "Male and Female Roles in the Lyrics of Three Genres of Contemporary Music." *Sex Roles* 4:51–65.
Fulginiti-Shakar, G., and E. Pilshaw. 1990. "Welcome Home." *Feeding the Flame: Songs by Men to End* AIDS. CD. Chicago: Flying Fish.
Hamilin, J., and S. Janssen. 1987. "Active Learning in Large Introductory Sociology Courses." *Teaching Sociology* 15:45–54.
Herek, G. M. 1992. "The Social Content of Hate Crimes: Notes on Cultural Heterosexism." In G. M. Herek and K. T. Berrill, eds., *Hate Crimes: Confronting Violence Against Lesbians and Gay Men*, pp. 89–104. Newbury Park, Cal.: Sage.
Humpal, M. 1990. "Early Interventions: The Implications of Music Therapy." *Music Therapy Perspectives* 8:30–35.
—— 1991. "The Effects of an Integrated Early Education Music Program on Social Interaction Among Children with Handicaps and Their Typical Peers." *Journal of Music Therapy* 28:161–77.
Julius, D. A. 1993. "Mourning and Melancholia in the Creativity of John Lennon." *Mind and Human Interaction* 4:154–64.

Kalliopuska, M., and I. Ruokonen. 1986. "Effects of Music Education on Development of Holistic Empathy." *Perceptual and Motor Skills* 62:187–91.

—— 1993. "A Study with a Follow Up of the Effects of Music Education on Holistic Development of Empathy." *Perceptual and Motor Skills* 76:131–37.

Keith, B. 1977. "The Road I Took to You." *Face the Music*, M. Christian. Record. Los Angeles: Olivia.

McCalla, D. 1987. "Would You Like to Dance." *With a Little Luck*. Record. Oakland: Olivia.

Maddux, D. 1992. *Boys and Girls with Stories*. Seattle.

Millington, J. 1987. "Brown Like Me." *Understated*, The Washington Sisters. Record. Milwaukee: Iceberg.

Near, H. 1986. "Simply Love." *Singing with You*, H. Near and R. Gilbert. Record. Oakland: Redwood.

Olzak, S. 1981. "Bringing Sociology Back In: Conveying the Sociological Imagination in a Changing Undergraduate Climate." *Teaching Sociology* 8:213–25.

Romanovsky, R., and P. Phillips. 1986a. "Homophobia." *Trouble in Paradise*. Cassette. Berkeley: Fresh Fruit.

—— 1986b. "Lost Emotions. *Trouble in Paradise*. Cassette. Berkeley: Fresh Fruit.

—— 1988. "Straightening Up the House." *Emotional Rollercoaster*. CD. Berkeley: Fresh Fruit.

—— 1991a. "Love Is All It Takes." *Be Political, Not Polite*. CD. Santa Fe: Fresh Fruit.

—— 1991b. "Once Upon a Time." *Be Political, Not Polite*. CD. Santa Fe: Fresh Fruit.

—— 1991c. "Queers in the Closet." *Be Political, Not Polite* CD. Santa Fe: Fresh Fruit.

—— 1991d. "When Heterosexism Strikes." *Be Political, Not Polite*. CD. Santa Fe: Fresh Fruit.

Sears, J. T. 1992. "An Interview with Romanovsky and Phillips." *Empathy* 3(1):72–78.

Sordillo, W., and F. de Caña. 1990. "Feeding the Flame." *Feeding the Flame: Songs by Men to End* AIDS CD. Chicago: Flying Fish.

Tillery, L. 1977a. "Don't Pray for Me. *Linda (Tui) Tillery*. Record. Los Angeles: Olivia.

— 1977b. "Freedom Time." *Linda (Tui) Tillery*. Record. Los Angeles: Olivia.

Tremblay, L. B. 1989. "Peaking." *Tendresse*. CD. Oakland: Olivia.

Washington Sisters, the. 1987. "Amma." *Understated*. Record. Milwaukee: Iceberg.

Weinberg, T. W. 1979. "Day After Dade." *Gay Name Game*. Cassette. Boston: Aboveground.

—— 1987. "Wedding Song." *Ten Percent Revue*. Cassette. Boston: Aboveground.

—— 1993a. "Bat Boy." *Get Used to It*. CD. Philadelphia: Aboveground.

—— 1993b. "Friends in High Places." *Get Used to It*. CD. Philadelphia: Aboveground.

—— 1993c. "Get Used to It." *Get Used to It*. CD. Philadelphia: Aboveground.

PART III

Working with Students

Diane DuBose Brunner

Challenging Representations of
Sexuality Through Story and Performance

In this chapter I attempt to show the impact and limitations of story and performance in revealing diverse attitudes and feelings regarding homosexuality. I chronicle students' reactions toward the gay and lesbian narratives in one text and toward the pedagogy in the course. Although in this essay I refer both metaphorically and literally to performance as the means by which humans articulate sexuality, and though the course deals with all representations of sexuality, here I detail only the portion of the class in which students made references to heterosexism and homophobia.

I teach an undergraduate 400-level literature course composed of thirty-one females and eight males, many of whom come from working-class backgrounds and are the first in their families to attend college. The racial mix in the course is about like it is elsewhere at Michigan State—mostly Euro-American students, a few African American students, an even smaller number of Native American students, and, perhaps, several non-American students (i.e, this term one student is from Turkey). The course is one among many courses offered in the English department that deals with women and ethnic minorities. The enrollment cap is forty-five. Students majoring in English must complete at least one course in women's/ethnic literature.

Unfortunately, the size of the class (thirty-nine) and possibly the subjects under discussion prevented my immediately getting to know these students. Unlike some classes, in which I seem to know a good deal about students' personal lives early in the semester, this class of students seemed rather private. Despite, however, what seemed to be an early effort to remain closed—

at times even aloof—students eventually did open up and show, at least, some of their inner struggles.

During the particular semester under discussion I had chosen the focus for this course: examining difference through story and performance. Literature for the course consisted of biographical and autobiographical accounts of particular lives, including letters, memoirs, several personal narratives written as fiction, and other ethnographic renderings of personal narratives that suggested the pervasiveness of sexism, racism, classism, heterosexism, and homophobia, etc., within schools and the wider society.

The strategies I suggest here are those used to introduce topics and elicit discussion connected with one particular text, *Growing Up Gay in the South: Race, Gender, and Journeys of the Spirit* (Sears 1991). Students' reactions/ responses are to the literature and to the strategies. Responses seem to suggest both the potential and the limitations of self-authoring literature and the *masquerade* for unearthing the repressed shadows of students' individual and collective struggles to construct sexual identities.

The idea of masquerade comes from Judith Butler whose work was integral in helping me to shape the course in terms of both form (discussion, responsive writings, and the performance or masquerade) and content (narratives as literature with the body as a primary theme). In *Bodies That Matter* (1993) Butler distinguishes linguistic self-disclosure (such as that which might occur in written narrative) from performative disclosure. She says subject positions/identities are produced in language through regulatory acts that define and therefore repress so that what is refused continues to determine one's identity (190). Through performance that signifies what *appears* rather than what necessarily *is*, Butler concludes that the masquerade may be the site most likely to permit subjects to transgress identities formed in relation to social and political regulation (1990).

Additionally, Mikhail Bakhtin's (1965, 1973) work on *carnival* culture suggests *re-staging the drama of the body*. Bakhtin's drive to (re)present the sensual body was against the grain of official order in Stalinist Russia and was, indeed, primarily a drive to (re)stage the myth of the official body.

The relationship then between what subjects perceive as a fixed category of meaning designated by relations of power that suggests one gender or one form of sexuality is privileged over another and the *performative* function of the masquerade seems to lie precisely in the latter's potential for (re)articulation of new meanings and possibilities—for political (re)signification. Adding a performative dimension to narrative, whether literally or figuratively, then, might possibly disrupt contained or status quo representations of identity.

I assume that what Bakhtin suggests as carnival may be present during those moments and in those spaces when and where bodies are (re)cast/ (re)staged and (re)understood—moments when, for whatever reasons, symbiosis among individuals occurs despite layers of difference. And I perceive that these changes are contingent upon values that pertain to verbal and nonverbal body literacies. Disruption of a contained order occurs in circumstances that require continual negotiation of social norms in communities of difference that include, among many dispositions, gender and sexuality—moments/situations in which representations of identity are interrogated, dismantled, and possibly (re)cast. (Re)articulations do not easily occur with the individual in isolation; performance requires an actor and a spectator, and both spectator and actor may reside in the performer of any act. The intersection between words and actions is the space of performance; therefore, I assume classrooms are one space where carnival may be invoked and often through circumstances related to reading and discussing literature.

My goal, then, in drawing upon Butler's notions of the performative and Bakhtin's drama of the body to create a literature course in which to challenge heterosexism is more than a suggestion of alternative modalities: modes of teaching, modes of learning, modes of thinking, modes of being. I intended, as Butler suggests, "to establish a kind of political contestation . . . of contemporary relations of power . . . forging a future from resources inevitably impure" (1993:241). Literature became the catalyst through which students began to question sexual identity, and the performance metaphor became the lens through which we examined responses that for some approached a (re)articulation of identity.

My discussion here focuses on students' responses to one book in particular, *Growing Up Gay in the South* (Sears 1991), because the text deals explicitly with the struggle to make and mark sexual identity. Though we read Charlotte Perkins Gilman's *The Yellow Wallpaper* (1973) and *The Letters of Virginia Woolf: 1932–1935* (1979), among other narratives, discussions of these texts did not create the resistance that the gay and lesbian narratives did in Sears's text. In fact, many students did not come to class during the entire five class periods in which we discussed Sears's text. What follows are the particular prompts/strategies I used to evoke response/discussion over the five days we studied Sears's text and my attempts to work with and against the students' resistance to talking about lesbian/gay issues and their own homophobia/heterosexism.

Strategies for Negotiating the Text

Having set aside five class periods for reading and discussing *Growing Up Gay in the South* (and because so many students were absent on the day discussion was to begin on this book), I took the first discussion day to simply have students respond in writing to the five theoretical assumptions on which Sears (1991) based his research: (1) "human beings are diverse sexual creatures," (2) "human beings interpret and reinterpret their lived experiences," (3) "sexual biographies are integrally related to society," (4) "many gay and lesbian activists work within and build upon the history, scripts, and language of the culture within which the movement was born," (5) and "sexual identities can be as oppressive as they are liberating" (18–19). This seemed to me a way into our exploration that would prove to be less threatening than actually having to discuss the text on the first day. Also, if students had not written in their journals, this would provide the opportunity for some reflection on the issues before they spoke (class met on Tuesdays and Thursdays).

In preparation for the next four days' discussion, I told students we would treat chapters like case studies and attempt to problematize issues surrounding each case. I used the organization set forth in the text for pairing cases and issues—what Sears refers to as "vantage points." Discussions were then organized around the following issues (organization differs slightly from the text):

> "homosexuality and Southern communities" [with three cases, one female and two males]; "homosexuality and Southern families in the religious South" [with four cases, three males, one female]; "gender and sexuality in the South" [with three cases, two males and one female]; and "sexuality and adolescence" [with three cases, two males and one female].   (13–17)

When class met again, and before moving directly into discussion of the chapters as outlined by the "vantage points," I used several students' reflections as a springboard for opening discussion. I also wanted to give students an opportunity to ask questions and to check the idiosyncratic nature of students' responses. Vanessa's response, which I asked permission to use and then paraphrased for class, presented the most interesting layering of assumptions and laid a foundation for the day's discussion.

In response to Sears's fifth theoretical assumption, Vanessa wrote that she thought there were too many negative things associated with the recognition of homosexuality or bisexuality for acknowledgment to seem liberating. While seemingly not too extraordinary, Vanessa's response did unearth several assumptions. She reported thinking of homosexuality as a stigma and then further stigmatized by calling the man or woman whose sexual preference/orientation is homosexual a "liberal homo." Additionally, the last phrase of the last sentence—"to justify the enjoyment of being different" may suggest Vanessa assumed that when something is liberating it will also be enjoyable. Vanessa may have been responding to the notion of "sexual rebels" Sears discusses in his first chapter (1991:6–23). In other words, Vanessa may have assumed that the students in Sears's study were homosexual out of some misplaced urge to resist their parents and society, purely for the sake of being different.

Though none of her assumptions seem so unusual compared with the class in general, her response suggests to me that she had only a vague notion of the struggle for sexual identity. Vanessa's assumptions are possibly indicative of her having never given much consideration to the matter one way or another, of simply assuming a *taken-for-grantedness* with respect to sexuality. Again, though not particularly unusual, Vanessa's responses do, at least, reinforce in my mind the need for the kind of study the course and text under question provides.

Vanessa's comments launched further discussion about the larger political movement begun by gay and lesbian men and women. For example, Wendy hesitantly responded to Sears's fourth assumption by suggesting a melting pot approach to American "difference," stating that the theory "rubs [her] the wrong way" and that she doesn't agree the movement is necessarily political.

To begin our discussion of "homosexuality and Southern communities" I asked students to spend twenty minutes discussing in three groups first, what they knew or believed about "the South," and second, this aspect of the South against the backdrop of one of the three cases within today's topic. Though I was not privy to much of this conversation when we came together in the larger group, I tried to solicit at least one comment from a member of each of the three groups. Nevertheless, comments were probably not representative of the group's sentiment and discussion was tentative. Shalico reported that the book helped her better understand sexuality, in general, and more about herself, in particular. Kristin, who grew up in the South, simply agreed with the book's conception of the South; she targeted many places as "oppressive, confining, [and] narrow-minded."

As we discussed the impact of homosexuality on the Southern community, we especially focused on the notion of one's being carefully prepared for a particular role in society. Andrea associated gender roles with labels like heterosexual and homosexual. She stated that if not for those roles possibly "50 percent or more of all people might be gay or, at least, bisexual."

The Time Line

This discussion led to the next class meeting's opening activity. Before our discussion of "homosexuality and Southern families in the religious South" during the third class meeting, I asked students to take a few minutes to prepare a time line, with focal points being ages three, six, twelve, and fifteen. Students recalled what they were reading, watching, and listening to and who they most identified with either in their own communities or in books and other media. Following this, I ask a student to compare his or her time line data with that of a partner.

Anne recalled being twelve and getting into teen romance novels. She discussed a supposed-to-be romance common to such books, even though, as she said, "What I saw around me wasn't exactly fantasy land." Megan remembered that she and her friends did all they could to fit in. She related this need to conform to the pressures with which the kids in the text had to cope and to their pain as well. She said, "I wondered how I would tell people if I were lesbian." One of the reasons for having students focus on their earlier years in this activity is to juxtapose the sexual awareness of many of Sears's participants with students' own awareness at varying stages of development.

Our conversations led us to discuss whether or not Vince's story rang true as told in the section entitled "Vince and the True Tones." Vince suggests that he knew he was homosexual since the sixth grade. Many students found this unbelievable. Nevertheless, in sympathy with Vince, Anne responded that, with respect to wanting to check out library books about gay experiences, when she was fifteen she would have done the same. She expressed outrage at the social control exerted over our minds and how ridiculous it was to fear reading something that will reveal our identities.

At this juncture Essie blurted out that she didn't know how anyone could *know* they were homosexual without first having given themselves a chance to be heterosexual. Essie's comment provoked another student across the room, Michell, to shout back, "What, do you think people decide to be homosexual only after trying heterosexuality?" Michell's reply created the space for a brief digression on biological determinism and what I referred to in the course as religious determinism. Though most students had not read the section of the text in which Sears dealt with social constructionist versus essentialist views of sexuality and the notion of the "biologizing" of homosexuality (1991:417), I referred students to this passage. Before I could complete my remarks, Joel said that before taking this course he believed homosexuality was genetically heritable. However, he now wondered whether we're not born androgynous and then socially directed to a sexual identity. Stacey then commented on the biologization of homosexuality, asking why some communities needed to understand *why* people are homosexual. She went on to say that she is horrified when people call homosexuality a *disease* that can be caught. Kristin echoed, "And *cured.*"

With respect to the religious rhetoric regarding homosexuality, Stacey contributed, "Once I was told I was going to hell for accepting homosexuality." And Kristin followed with a story about her friend Scott, from a devout Baptist family, who believed that he would go to hell because he was gay. Both Stacey and Kristin's responses mark a kind of solidarity with Malcolm's struggle against a religious upbringing that taught the need to "deaden [the] sexual appetite in order to please God" (1991:61).

Several journal responses written for the readings on homosexuality and Southern families in the religious South suggest students' confusion with issues of homosexuality: harassment and lifestyle choice and struggles with same-sex attraction. Karin wrote, "It's hard to stay focused on the facts and issues when my conservative church friends are telling me gay = bad and my best friend is asking me to accept his homosexuality."

Naming Our Forbiddens

Before discussion on the fourth day and in an effort to continue the focus on parental/familial and religious roles as determinants or guides in the formation of sexual identities, and to help students connect these guides with the struggles faced by adolescents, I asked students to briefly respond to the following questions:

> What are you forbidden to do?
> What do you forbid yourself to do?
> What role do you most try to fit into?
> What role are you least able to fit?
> What causes you pain?

Again, I asked students to share their responses. Anne said that she would be afraid to tell if she were lesbian because she knew that would be forbidden by family and church. Kristen thought that she might simply be forbidden to read this book and admited she was even intimitated to buy it and have it sit on her bookshelf. Andrea connected her reaction to the assignment with her readings for this day's discussion on gender and sexuality. She recalled that she had for many years forbidden herself to unravel "the tangled vines" of her own sexual abuse.

From the vantage point of gender and sexuality, with its many layers of discussion on how issues of power prefigure what Sears describes as the "reinterpretation of childhood events to fit into constructed sexual identity" (1991:260), discussions of sexual abuse by older family members became the focal point in this day's discussion. For instance, James believed the discussion on molestation was taken too lightly and said that the men who spoke of being fondled by adults seemed to think it was perfectly natural.

Power Issues

In our fifth class meeting, and before discussion, I gave a minilecture on the issues of power and authority involved in both the production and the ultimate use of personal narrative texts, especially when those texts are from adolescents who, because of their struggles, may perceive themselves as powerless already (class discussion on "sexuality and adolescence"). Lynette wondered whether Sears's participants withheld any information from him during interviews, whether they exaggerated their stories, whether he reported their stories accurately or exaggerated himself. These were important questions, as they link the researcher with the researched and can create interesting dilemmas, ethical and otherwise, for researchers. This minilecture connected also with Sears's chapter on "journeys of the spirit" and helped frame the question of difference in relations of power and how it coalesces within formations of identity.

Though the class continued to have its limitations the entire term, the greatest amount of progress seemed evident near the end of our discussions about the Sears text. Many students began our discussions in complete denial of diverse sexualities: remember Essie's question, "How do these people know they're homosexual, why they didn't even give themselves a chance to be heterosexual"? As students felt more comfortable making their own circumstances known, the tenor of the conversation changed; students began to talk about personal struggles, oppressions, and inequities due to sexuality. A few even admitted moments of questioning their own sexuality, and perhaps an even greater step was when some students who had attempted to seem unbiased admitted their own homophobia/heterosexism. Still others described the way they felt when learning a best friend or roommate of several years was gay. Lauren's comments betray a sentiment I suspect is still deeply embedded within many of my students' attitudes and feelings with respect to issues of normalcy and homosexuality. She described a friend she assumed to be heterosexual when she said, "He just seemed normal." And Kristin displaced her own feelings in her response by shifting the responsibility to Scott, a friend since age eleven. Nevertheless, she reiterated the above sentiment when she pointed out that "intermediate and high school were a living hell for him because he was trying so hard to be what he considered normal and fit in with the other kids."

Issues of what is perceived as *normal* were a part of handed-down sexual representations challenged in this course. What counts and who decides must be addressed in order to begin to help young people understand that all their representations, both sexual and otherwise, are a part of a common stock of assumptions about the way the world works, the way "things are supposed to be." The time line activity was one attempt to try to move students to examine some of the means by which these social and cultural messages are transmitted. Naming our forbiddens was yet another attempt to focus on those we invest with the power to determine codes of behavior. I'm not certain that either had a great impact. Fixed ways of seeing the world offer a good deal of security, and, therefore, this kind of containment is extremely difficult to disrupt.

Yet I do think the texts, the activities, and the conversations may have created a momentary interruption, an interstice, even if students returned to the hegemonic practices of everyday life immediately thereafter. I'd not call this a success, but merely a beginning. Stacey's comment sums up my feelings here. One afternoon after class, well into another book, she confided that she felt as if a gaping wound, open for a long time, had finally begun to heal. Other responses from journals or in-class discussion may have suggested less profound results but do seem to indicate that the strategies and texts have provoked thought in areas, perhaps, which had been given little consideration heretofore.

(Re)staging the Drama of the Body:
A Conclusion

Although the course included an actual performance that followed several pantomime workshops, the notion of masquerade/performance is used here as figuratively as it is literally. Because my essay focuses on classroom conversations that metaphorically (re)stage the myth of the official body by examining hetereosexist mythologies and struggling against the homophobia that such taken-for-grantedness can create, I have excluded detailed discussion of the end-of-term play and its preparation. One student, John, contributed to the final performance in a manner that best exemplified the *shadow play* that had occurred during discussion of the Sears text.

John was so quiet in class that for the first part of the semester, after a period of missing a number of classes in succession, I believed he had dropped the course. When he returned I was amazed; he seldom spoke, and I assumed he was getting nothing from the course. John was among those students who did not attend class during the five discussion days on the Sears text. His attendance remained sporadic until we began to craft the performance. With the help of his group a part of John's narrative became central in the second act, entitled "Refugees: A Story of Awakenings."

John wrote about a "special homecoming" and his own struggle with the (sexual) skin he found himself in. ("The skin we're in" was one of the workshop themes drawn from the coming-of-age story by Lorene Cary, *Black Ice* [1991]; the theme focused as much on race and gender as it did on sexuality.) Though John's narrative was written metaphorically, with allusions to "Jesus in sunglasses," "sinners and retribution," and "loony bins," his lack of support at home and the moral indignation with which his words were met was made clear.

John's story reminds me of what Audre Lorde suggests is the power of language to transform silence into action (1984) and of the power of a common project to transcend differences (1978). John's silence and lack of attendance in the course may have suggested much more than his words did in the final presentation. The common project at the end of the term and the understanding that identity is a performance may have helped John turn his silence into words and action. Sometimes the only community or "home" students can find or (re)define is the one they find with each other over a common project. And sometimes, as in the particular case of this class, students learn that understanding who they are sexually can be as oppressive as it can be liberating (Sears 1991).

For the final course production, students wrote autobiographical narratives that focused on some period in their lives and that seemed especially important for their own constructions of self. Students then worked in teams to script portions of each narrative into a play—a collective autobiography. The play, which they performed on stage before an audience of parents and peers, seemed to uncover—unmask—some of the repressed shadows of both individual and collective struggles to construct sexual and social identities. Using a variety of performative styles such as mime, dance, and traditional acting with dialogue, students dramatized self-discoveries through a coming-of-age motif.

Because students perceive the task as outside the usual (both the task and the stage literally create a new classroom dynamic), they may be more capable of acting outside accepted modes of being. After all, it is acting, and acting is perceived as different from "real" life. Both the stage and the metaphoric dimension allow for wearing a different mask, for social commentary to be produced outside that which is understood as a *given*, and for the disembodied, violated body to be (re)embodied and united with the spirit—a kind of liberatory symbiosis that can mark a transformation of shadow and thus healing.

The potential for transformative—even revolutionary—moments, then, occurs each time we create a space for imagining the unimagined, saying the unsaid, being that which has not been: (re)signifying our politicized subject identities. *But success is never guaranteed.* For the drives, the passions, the subjectivities that might lead to revolution seem, with little doubt, in this society the least valued and most often silenced. In any case, the same culture that already/always seems structured to prohibit transgression of sexual norms nevertheless may produce occasions for ambivalence (of which I saw this class as one) through which those violating ideals might be temporarily layed to rest.

In that regard, then, I perceive the need to assess how much of our work in the institution called school creates shadows and to what extent we are willing to create spaces for potential healing. Indeed, how is such work valued in our departments, our universities, and by our colleagues?

No one was prepared for the response to this play; we were astonished at the support generated among parents, grandparents, and peers. While many spectators seemed taken aback by the language and the explicitness with which students dealt with sensitive subjects, each of us was most affected by the emotional response, which ranged from joy to pain, suggesting that the range of experiences presented in the play were not isolated; students sensed they were not alone in their feelings and experiences. For many, among spectators and participants, it seemed the experience of the play opened topics for discussion that had not been broached before. To my students this was both frightening and encouraging. Both the performance and the collaborative work of preparing for it raised many questions about behaviors and attitudes. Yet, most agreed, they would not forget the experience of joining their stories collectively. I hoped that the continual set of (re)articulations implied by the notion of (re)staging would be an effect students would realize again and again.

I am left with a number of questions from this experiment with narrative theater. Several are similar to those Butler raises. For example, how does such work enable the "reformulation of kinship"? How does it help us redefine home, "not solely . . . [in terms] of whiteness or heterosexual norms, and in all its forms of collectivity" (1993:240)? And how can a redefinition of home, which may include a reasoned consideration of one's sexual identity, serve as a marker of agency and not a consequence that functions within traditional power structures?

The work of this course challenged sexual representations and, in doing so, also challenged homophobia/heterosexism; other sacred assumptions were probably challenged as well. It literally shook things loose, and that, for many students, was disarming. That it was disarming is perhaps the best indication I have that something positive happened.

NOTES

1. The inspiration for developing this course comes from a presentation given by Margo Figgins's students at the Conference on English Education plenary session during the National Council of Teachers of English spring meeting in Richmond, Virginia, 1993.

2. Writing out one's "forbiddens" is an activity Liz Ellsworth and Mimi Orner led in a session at the 1992 Conference on Curriculum on Theory and Practice at Bergamo, Dayton, Ohio.

REFERENCES

Bakhtin, M. 1965. *Rabelais and His World*. Trans. H. Iswolksy. Cambridge: MIT Press.

—— 1973. *Problems of Doestoevsky's Poetics*. Trans. R. Rotsel. Ann Arbor: Ardis.

Butler, J. 1990. *Gender Trouble: Feminism and the Subversion of Identity*. New York: Routledge.

—— 1993. *Bodies That Matter: On the Discursive Limits of "Sex"*. New York: Routledge.

Cary, L. 1991. *Black Ice*. New York: Vintage.

Gilman, C. P. 1973. *The Yellow Wallpaper*. New York: Feminist.

Lorde, A. 1978. *Uses of the Erotic: The Erotic as Power*. Freedom, Cal.: Crossing.

—— 1984. *Sister Outsider*. Trumansburg, N.Y.: Crossing.

Sears, J. 1991. *Growing Up Gay in the South: Race, Gender, and Journeys of the Spirit*. New York: Harrington Park.

Woolf, V. 1979. *The Letters of Virginia Woolf: 1932–1935*. Vol. 5. 6 vols. Ed. N. Nicolson and J. Trautmann. New York: Harcourt Brace.

Donald N. Mager and Robert Sulek

Teaching About Homophobia
at a Historically Black University:
A Role Play for Undergraduate Students

African American students bring many positive attributes to the classroom regarding homophobia. They are typically sensitive to prejudice and hence can be empathic to its other forms. Another strength is self-disclosure and an eagerness "to tell their stories." The instructors often solicit from the class a "call of stories" in the tradition of Harvard University professor Robert Coles's pedagogy. Our students find these "sharings" to be refreshing and nonthreatening. They excel at learning modes that feature performance: verbal debate, dramatizations, role plays, and case studies. Another asset our students bring is that many were raised in multigenerational extended family settings; therefore, unlike students from middle-class nuclear families, these students bring a wider set of observations and contacts about how people actually live their lives and the diversities that occur. These living arrangements foster a dynamic tolerance.

Another feature our students bring is strong religious backgrounds—with Baptist being the most popular group. We also have students who consider themselves Muslim, despite original Christian training. The religious background is not only reflected in the passion they bring to some issues but also in a reluctance to reflect on their own dogmas, an unwillingness, often, to question religious authorities, whether Muslim or Christian. There are also some cognitive gaps our population brings to a course such as "Literature of Social Reflection"; many are not sensitive to or even very aware of feminist thinking; many have a high level of sexual activity—often under peer pressure—and therefore a high anxiety level about sexual topics and a sense of personal vulnerability that is painful to acknowledge or speak about; finally, a majority articulate a fairly pervasive bantering kind of homophobic discourse that they do not even recognize as such, because they believe it to be obvious and natural. Except for a human sexuality course, and a few spots in literature and psychology courses, our course is the only place on campus that attempts to address homophobia in a knowledgeable, nonjudgmental, and informed manner.

In terms of attitudes toward homosexuals and expressions of homophobia, in many respects our students conform to patterns in the African American community as documented by various researchers. How is sexual orientation perceived to relate to race? Carmen Braun Williams (1992) reports that a conference of the Association of Black Psychologists (ABPsi),

> asked what the panelists' positions on homosexuality in the Black community were. The first panelist articulated the need for acceptance of a diversity of sexual orientations. The second panelist remained silent. The third panelist, an avowed Afrocentrist, quite forcefully and disturbingly asserted that homosexuality is: (1) abhorred among African peoples, (2) inconsistent with African values, and (3) most jarring, a "white" disease that all African-American must reject. (46)

Certainly all three positions show up each year during our unit, often positions two and three being voiced by students who are articulate high achievers. Position three, in our experience most often voiced by males, is a "loud" but minority position. Position one is typical of females and speaks for many. It is often combined with a religious caveat: while sexual diversity needs to be met with compassion, homosexuality, after all, is a "Biblical sin" and therefore a matter to be resolved by the individual and the Lord—a view marked by compassion, not acceptance.

Linda Villarosa (1991a) produced a feature article for *Essence* magazine about a gay woman and her mother who share "their journey and emotion from fear to disappointment and anger and finally toward peace and acceptance" (1991a:83). *Essence* was flooded with "an avalanche of mail" and Villarosa produced a follow-up piece six months later that sampled the "avalanche" (1991b:19). Two patterns were apparent: the overwhelming majority of readers had a favorable response to the original article and many shared their own personal stories of coming to terms with the "coming out" of friends, daughters, mothers, or other family members. Our experience with our female students, who often represent three-fourths of the class enrollment, parallels the *Essence* experience. Not only do they show more empathy and compassion than male students, they are more comfortable with the topic of homosexuality.

In "Undoing Homophobia in Schools" Richard A. Friend (1993) reports on an "equity training" program that "fosters in education appreciation of the diversity of school populations and examines individual and collective responsibilities for creating school climates that are 'fair' in outcome as well as practice." As he profiles the training program, he notes resistance.

> Not all participants accept the conceptual linkage of the "isms," particularly with regard to homophobia and racism. Some resist the notion that lesbian, gay, and bisexual students experience targeting . . . in ways similar to racial minority groups. They say sexual orientation is invisible, something one can choose to keep hidden, whereas race is visible and targeting cannot be avoided. (65)

The same point is typically raised by our students. Homophobia is initially seen as a problem faced only by the most "blatant" gays, who could easily avoid it if they "toned down their act."

One of the real discoveries that our students make is that homophobia runs much more deeply and affects actions and attitudes far in excess of teasing an overly "blatant" gay person. At the same time, students are sometimes offended by the gay political agenda, as they understand it from the media, as riding on the coattails of the black civil rights movement. They feel African Americans have earned their rights through a history of brutality and suffering that is somehow trivialized by gays wishing to claim similar rights without a comparable history of suffering. We have seen students incredibly argumentative on this point. Role play helps to see the kinds of suffering that can be generated even on a fictional black campus—for some, a disturbing revelation. As non-African American professors, one way we have opened dialogue on this point is to ask a handful of students to report on Essex Hemphill's essay "If Freud Had Been A Neurotic Colored Woman: Reading Dr. Frances Cress Welsing" (1992), because, as a political activist black gay male his attack on her Afrocentric position situates the debate squarely as a debate among African Americans. To statements by Welsing, a prominent African American psychologist, such as,

> Black psychiatrists must understand that whites may condone homosexuality for themselves, but we as Blacks must see it as a strategy for destroying Black people that must be countered. Homosexuals or bisexuals should neither be condemned nor degraded, as they did not decide that they would be

so programmed in childhood. The racist system should be held responsible. Our task is to treat and prevent its continuing and increasing occurrence.

(cited in Hemphill 1992:55)

Hemphill replies,

Even among the oppressed there is a disturbing need for a convenient "other" to vent anger against, to blame, to disparage, to denigrate. Such behavior is surely as detrimental as any an oppressor can exercise against the oppressed. There is no excuse for such behavior just as there is no credibility for Dr. Welsing's theories regarding sexuality. At best, her views reinforce the rampant homophobia and heterosexism that have paralyzed the Black liberation struggle. She widens the existing breach between Black gays and lesbians and their heterosexual counterparts, offering no bridges for joining our differences. (1992:61)

Finally, Cornel West's insistent linkage of issues of racism, sexism, and homophobia offers a well-argued theologically grounded position of considerable respect; he argues that homophobic attitudes see only part of a person and therefore render that person's humanity less than the wholeness bestowed by the creator (cited in Kazi 1993:28–29).

The Honors College of Johnson C. Smith University, a historically black university in Charlotte, North Carolina, serves about 160 students out of a population of 1,350. Through innovative course designs it provides a core liberal studies curriculum for these students. "Literature of Social Reflection" is such a course, patterned after one designed by Robert Coles, taught yearly in the fall semester by a team of two professors. Typically, forty to fifty students take the course, which meets in a lecture hall. The course meets core curriculum requirements for honors sophomores who form the majority of the class. Robert Sulek is the rector of the Honors College, with specialities in mathematics and the education of the academically talented. Donald Mager is an English professor. The course focuses on eight to ten texts, ranging from Agee's *Let Us Now Praise Famous Men* and Tolstoy's *The Death of Ivan Ilyich* to Baldwin's *The Fire Next Time* and Norman's *'Night Mother*, addressing issues such as poverty, spirituality, death, and moral choices. The texts stimulate freewheeling discussions of personal reflections on social implications. Students are urged to hear the atypical voice and to respect its difference. The course is writing intensive, with almost weekly papers plus rewrites, conferences, and reading logs. The course outline states:

The writers whose books are assigned in this course have struggled a great deal to reconcile scholarly, literate and artistic pursuits with moral concerns. In the course, we will try to compare various modes of social observation; and at the same time to explore the ethical issues that confront those men and women who want to change the world in one way or another, those ordinary people caught in a particular historical crisis, and not least, those who try to make sense of what others initiate politically, struggle with psychologically, endure socially. The fundamental assumption which guides this course is that we cannot achieve self-understanding except in so far as we learn to see ourselves as "the other."

In 1989 we began including a unit addressing homophobia, institutional policy, and social justice. That year it was the culminating experience, taking the last six class hours. The text was *Torch Song Trilogy*. This format was repeated in 1990. Since then, homophobia has been the initial topic, and the text has been *The Education of Harriet Hatfield* by May Sarton. Role play and novel are typically followed later in the semester by other activities. A guest speaker (a member of Parents and Friends of Lesbians and Gays, PFLAG) whose son is gay has spoken of her difficulties, trials, and personal success in dealing with the issues.

Later in the semester, a unit on death and dying focuses on *The Death of Ivan Ilyich* and *'Night Mother* as texts. One piece in this unit is a period given to showing slides taken from the book *Christopher Isherwood: Last Drawings*, which chronicles Isherwood's dying as portrayed by his lifemate Don Bachardy. Isherwood, the well-known novelist, diagnosed in 1986 with terminal stomach cancer, died five months later at home. Bachardy, a well-know graphic designer and portrait artist, did several hundred drawings of Isherwood during his final illness. They were married for thirty-five years. These drawings bring the students to an intimate but not ghoulish encounter with dying; at the same time, the experience is placed in the context of a gay marriage. "Literature of Social Reflection" turns out for many to be a pivotal experience because the course invites students to address fundamental human and social concerns: sexuality, our purpose in life, love, identity, death. What follows is a report of the role play, followed by assessments of it.

The Role Play

The role play involves the entire class over four class periods. The role play situation is fictionalized, based on events that occurred some ten years ago at another college.

Rape Incident and RA Response
Step One: Day 1

At the end of the second day of class the mechanics of role-playing are explained, along with the ground rules. Students receive copies of the following article and are told that each will be assigned a part in the role play at the beginning of the next class.

RA *Excluded from Campus in Gay Discrimination Case*

The Office of Student Life has removed Carlos McVay, senior, from his position as RA in Malcolm X Men's Hall, and has permanently excluded him from the university. He will not graduate with his class in May.

The University Blazer has received the following account from the Office of Student Life. On Friday night, November 1, at about 10:00 P.M., four residents of Malcolm X Hall, all of whom are members of the football team, followed Christian Jones, freshman, to his car in the dormitory lot, then followed him in his car to Buddy's Place, a gay bar. Jones went into the bar. The four students returned to campus and reported the incident to Carlos McVay. McVay immediately called Jones' parents to inform them that their son is gay. Jones returned to the dorm alone at about 1:00 A.M. Saturday. As he unlocked the door to his room, the four men who had followed him earlier jumped him, forced him into his room, and took turns holding him down and allegedly raping him. McVay watched the events. When the four men left Jones' room, McVay again called Jones' parents. He requested that they come get him as soon as possible.

Mr. and Mrs. Jones drove all night and arrived Saturday morning, withdrew their son from the university, and took him home with them. They did not allow him to discuss the episode with university officials. *The Blazer* has tried to reach them by phone, but they refuse to be interviewed and will make no statement.

McVay did not report the incident to campus police or Student Life. On Monday, when the Dean of Student Life learned of the events, she immediately took action to exclude McVay from the university. She interviewed him personally, then ordered him to remove himself and his property from the campus by 5:00 P.M.

No disciplinary action has been taken regarding the four men, because Jones is no longer a student, and has not filed a complaint against them. Reporters from *The Blazer* have had no success in learning their identities. All four will play in the opening line-up for Saturday afternoon's game. When asked, Coach Ramsey said, "The allegations in this affair have no reflection on our football program. These boys have been charged with no infraction of the student code."

In a related story, three women at Marian Anderson Hall, Tonia Davis, Berthea Toomer, and Saphira Troutman, have called for a meeting to form a Gay and Lesbian Support Group. The organizing meeting will be held tonight at 7:30 in the Arts Complex. Toomer is a prominent student on campus, serving as current president of the Christian League and as a member of the homecoming court.

Parts Assigned and Groups Form
Step Two: Day 2

As students come into the lecture hall, they are assigned roles. Assignments are adjusted each year as class sizes and gender compositions vary. No student is allowed to change parts. Roles that share common interests, such as members of a group, however, are informed who the other members are. What follows is a sample of the information each student received on her or his assignment slip.

Football players   Male 1. Jeb Davis, football player, alleged participant in the rape. Only the dean of Student Life and the other three players know his identity.

Gay and Lesbian Support Group   Female 1. Tonia Davis, junior, identifies herself as a lesbian but never shared this information with anyone on campus except two friends, Berthea Toomer and Saphira Troutman. She dates guys as a cover-up. The incident with Christian Jones has made her want to stand up and protest homophobia. Her roommate is Glenda Washington. They have been close friends since freshman year. This is their third year to room together. Tonia does not feel that she should have to change roommates in the middle of the term, hoping that she and Glenda can reach an understanding if other students will just leave them alone to work it out.

Female 2. Berthea Toomer, junior, identifies herself as a lesbian but never shared this information with anyone on campus except two friends, Tonia Davis and Saphira Troutman. She dates guys as a cover-up. The incident with Christian Jones has made her want to stand up and protest homophobia. Her roommate is Elissa Day. They have been close friends since freshman year. Berthea is president of the Christian League, very popular on campus, and is a member of the homecoming court.

The roommates   Female 4. Danielle Pride, junior, is Saphira Troutman's roommate. They have been close friends since their freshman year. This is their third year to room together. When she discovers that Saphira is a lesbian, she feels deeply betrayed. "Why didn't she ever tell me this? I've been living with her and never really knew. It's awful."

The Christian League   Male 5. Jerome Manly, member of the Christian League, votes to have Berthea Toomer removed from office as president and barred from membership. He is the person who calls special meetings of the Christian League to deal with the matter of Toomer's "disgraceful, shocking, and sinful behavior," as he calls it.

Gay students   Male 7. Charlie Grant is a gay student who lives off campus. He has had an active social life but maintains a strict separation of his campus and academic activities from his life off campus. He does not believe that most of his nongay friends suspect he is gay. After the three lesbians hold their meeting to organize a support group, which no one attends, he gets together with four of his gay friends. They phone the women, promising to join them. He says he will even be willing, now, as an open gay male, to meet with university officials.

University officials   Male 12. He is the president of the university and will preside over the meeting of the president's cabinet. At that meeting two items are on the agenda.

1. A decision in response to the dean for Public Relations who has asked how she should reply to the request from *Ebony*.
2. A decision in response to the dean for Student Life who has requested that Danielle Pride, Ellisa Day, and Glenda Washington be granted their request to change roommates.

Other issues that need a formal presidential decision may come before the cabinet during the course of the meeting.

This is but a sample of the role slips. Although the role-assigning process takes half a class session, students typically develop a high level of anticipation and involvement.

Meetings Held, Public Reactions
Step Three: Day 2

After roles are assigned and common interests groups are formed, the following narration is read and copies distributed.

Tuesday 7:30 P.M. The meeting to form a Gay and Lesbian Support group is held in the Arts Complex. Only the three women who called the meeting show up. They sit for an hour and a half with the door to the corridor open. During the time they sit there they count a least two hundred students pass and look in. Some giggle and "act funny." No one comes into the room to speak to them. The campus is quiet as they walk back to Marian Anderson Hall. Each finds that her roommate has moved out for the night.

Wednesday. During the morning, Charlie Grant, Wesley Washington, Jr., Moses McAndrew, Jon Paris, and Antonio Shaw phone the three women who had called the meeting the night before. All five men live off campus. They explain that, like a lot of other gay and lesbian students on campus, they were afraid to come to the meeting; but they heard what happened and now they want to "come out" and give the women their support.

Wednesday. During the day. The roommates of each of the three women demand that they be assigned new rooms. Marian Anderson Hall has a meeting of all women and votes to support their request and take the issue to the student government association (SGA).

Wednesday, 7:00 P.M. The Christian League meets without notifying its president, Berthea Toomer, to debate whether to ask her to resign her office and leave the group. The meeting is called and run by Jerome Manly. The vote is split.

Thursday. National news services pick up the story, including the ABC 7:00 P.M. news. Headlines in papers around the country the next morning (November 8) include the following:

Gay Rights Protests Come of Age at Black Campus
Southern Campus Erupts in Gay Rape Scandal
Football Team Implicated

Friday. *Ebony* contacts the dean of Public Relations to request permission to do a story and take pictures on campus. The dean requests that the president of the university call an emergency meeting of the president's cabinet to decide whether to grant or deny the *Ebony* request.

Friday, 7:30 P.M. SGA meets. Many students attend, voting delegates and nonvoting interested students. It turns into a disorganized shouting contest and no vote is taken on any issue.

Friday, 10:00 P.M. The women of Marian Anderson Hall meet and vote to support the roommates of the three lesbians in their demands to be reassigned to new roommates and to bypass SGA and go directly to dean of Student Life. When the meeting breaks up and the women go back upstairs, they find graffiti spraypainted on the doors of the three rooms. No one knows who did the sprayings.

BULL-DYKE   SATAN WORSHIPER   NO LICKERS HERE!

All weekend the campus is alive with rumors. Secret meetings take place, but the situation does not get better or worse overall. The regular home game is played on Saturday. During the game many students speculate about who the four players might be; no one knows for sure. The team wins, twenty-eight to seven. In his report on the victory a local sportscaster of the 11:00 P.M. news comments, "The coaches seem to want to win so bad they'll even use rapists and queers on their team."

Monday, 8:00 A.M. The three roommates appear first thing in the morning at the dean of Student Life's office with their dorm officers. They tell her about the dorm vote Friday night and demand that she act immediately to give them new roommate assignments. The dean calls the president of the university to request that the president's cabinet take up the matter of the reassignments.

Monday, 9:00 A.M. The president of the university announces to all the deans that the cabinet will meet in emergency session at 3:00 P.M. Monday afternoon. They will consider two issues: the *Ebony* request and the roommate reassignment demand.

Debates, Demands, Controversies
Step Four: Day 2

During the remainder of the second day session students spontaneously meet in groups, debate positions, form proposals, make demands, and negotiate strategies and alliances. These meetings must build on and respond to the events as presented.

Sulek's role, as the play plays itself out, was that of a floating gadfly and an observer-recorder. As gadfly, he sat in on various meetings, whispering suggested responses to various students in order to provoke the maximum airing of issues and points of view. As observer-recorder, he kept track of particularly significant statements and exchanges ("A true Christian does not judge, she shows compassion!" "No, a true Christian obeys God's laws, not man's laws!") and watched for shifts of position and how they were rationalized. Mager's role throughout was facilitator, keeping track of the information flow. Students were highly inventive in wanting to instigate new complications, and he would judge their viability. For instance, one year the students wanted a demonstration of local skinheads to be staged at the campus gates.

Actions and Reactions
Step Five: Days 3 and 4

For two full class sessions students continue the role play in whatever ways they find effective. Groups and individuals call for meetings, make demands, post and publish statements, "crash" meetings, and debate in both open and closed forums—always maintaining the identities of their role assignments. Mager continues to facilitate, Sulek to gadfly and record observations.

The play develops different directions; for instance, one year the Christian League brought in a local minister (a student invented this role) who preached a virulent homophobic sermon, which in turn swayed the SGA to push for antigay measures, whereas the most recent year's role play came to be dominated by a "Hard Copy" style group of reporters who tried to stir up scandal at every turn. At the end of each class Mager summarizes positions and actions to date.

President Speaks
Step Six: Day 5

Each year the class is notified that on day 5 the university president's cabinet will hold a public meeting, at which time it will announce all decisions made regarding the *Ebony* request, the dorm reassignment request, and any other issues that have come up before it in the meantime. The cabinet must explain the rationale for its decisions and then take answers from the audience. This is the final event of the role play.

Decision and Self-Reflection
Step Seven: Day 5

Following the president's cabinet report, discussion is led by the instructors—an analysis and assessment of the experience. Sulek begins the discussion by sharing some of the observations he made as he sat in on groups and meetings. He attempts to tease out contradictions and inconsistencies in stated positions, to probe the rationale for positions, and to explore the implications and consequences that result from individual or group actions, especially as they impact on the lives of others. This is the practice of *social reflection* around which the course is designed. For us the practice of social reflection means posing questions, asking students to explain their positions, hearing the diversity of positions, and asking whether these positions can stand the test of universality or are only self-serving.

The whole class is asked to briefly write about whether social justice was truly served by the president's cabinet's decisions, whatever those are in any given year's play. Further questions are explored in discussion: Was everyone heard? Whose viewpoint was silenced? Whose validity as a person was denied or demeaned? Did your feeling about your role change? Did your opinion about the issues change? What would you have done if you were in the RA's shoes? or the President's shoes? or the shoes of one of the gay or lesbian students? If something like this occurred at our campus, how would we as an academic community handle it? Is there one kind of justice or due process for some people and a different kind for others? Do we sanction such discrepancies? Finally, students are asked to assess shifts in their thinking regarding homophobic acts and statements and ways to confront them in everyday situations.

Assessment and Analysis

How do we assess the pedagogical success of this activity? First, the student self-assessments give us an indication of growth in awareness and their development of frameworks for seeing and responding to homophobia. Often, however, it is not the writing done on the last day of the role play that registers their most passionate reactions but journal pieces or semester-end evaluations of the entire course. One student wrote:

> When I first decided to take "Social Reflections" it was because I needed an extra class to take. . . . After the role-playing I knew that the class would require me to do something that I had in the past tried not to do—reflect. I was going to have to reach deep inside myself and search for "truth." I was going to have to come face to face with an issue like gays that I chose not to.

The previous year, another student said:

> I think the subject that I benefited most from was the Gay/Lesbian unit. I used to have awful thoughts about them. It was ignorance on my behalf, I must admit. But after we were put into situations as either a gay or lesbian person, I began to understand that they are no different . . . but just have a different preference.

The class touched an important issue that is often left unspoken.

But of equal significance is the context of these particular students' experiences as African American students of the 1990s, a generation that at least one commentator, Cornel West (1992), sees as reflecting a nihilism with regard to human ability to effect social betterment. Witness these remarks:

Some students were saying this [the events in the role play] were just made up by Mager and Sulek to create a learning experience. They said nothing like this would ever happen on a black campus. Let's get real, it could happen right here, and people would react and say the same things they did in the play. What makes us think black campuses don't have prejudice? It's never going to change.

Even more bluntly, another stated: "The biggest impact on me was the one about the rape incident. I thought that people tried to be fair when making decisions but not all did. But life is not fair." We have also had to reflect on the question whether homophobia as a discourse or as a set of behaviors is displayed as a singularity among young African Americans. Does our pedagogy, as two non-African American professors, acknowledge or address this singularity?

Because semester-end self assessments by students through writings, conversations, and anecdotal information suggest some positive shifting toward more personal accountability and culpability, the instructors have gauged the overall design of the role play about homophobia to be pedagogically successful. There is also a lessening of fear, ignorance, and prejudice, if student declarations (such as those quoted above) are honest indicators.

We believe the particular strengths that African American students often bring to the classroom mesh well with a role play teaching method. In particular, those with extended family backgrounds often have lived (or at least closely observed) experiences about gays and lesbians that students from more restricted small nuclear families may lack. During discussion and analysis, without exception, every year, students have shared information and anecdotes about gay or lesbian aunts, uncles, cousins, and siblings, and it is not uncommon for one to describe the AIDS death of a loved one and some of the prejudices that person encountered at work or with medical providers. A willingness (even eagerness) to self-disclose is another particular ability our students often display, as these examples show. Finally, because students at our school frequently come from staunch fundamentalist religious backgrounds, for them the competition between righteous judgment and humane compassion often takes a particularly agonizing form. The consequence is often a cleansing/confusing experience followed by some hope/growth feelings. Students generally feel they've learned something about a previously unacknowledged group but, more important (and perhaps frightening), about themselves not only as perpetrators of homophobia but also as victims of rigid gender norms and heterosexist stereotypes.

We continue to use the role play about homophobia as a unit in our course, because we believe it is successful in challenging student notions about gay people, and in helping them to look at their own homophobic behaviors and attitudes. Each year we modify the unit and the role play, but essentially it is presented as described here. We believe our success is due to four factors: (1) the strength of the role play design, which involves every student in dialogic roles with opportunities for real choices and the chance to see consequences of those choices played out, (2) the constant practice of reflective writing, which is a fundamental feature of our course, as it provides students an informal and fairly private medium in which test, think, inquire, and self-assess, (3) the steps we have taken to acknowledge, to be personally informed, and to be sensitive to the singularities relevant to this unit that arise from our students being at a historically black university, and (4) the fact that the gay/homophobia theme is connected throughout the semester to other major course themes (identity, prejudice, love, relationships, death, and grief), thereby inviting students to sustain their reflections over time, rather than to settle for one-shot judgments. For these reasons we believe the role play model, if designed with these four factors in mind, could provide a rich pedagogic tool in a wide number of settings, from classrooms to counseling groups and from young people to older adults.

REFERENCES

Agee, J., and W. Evans. 1960. *Let Us Now Praise Famous Men*. Boston: Houghton Mifflin.

Bachardy, D. 1990. *Christopher Isherwood: Last Drawings*. Texts by Don Bachardy, John Russell, and Stephen Spender. London: Faber and Faber.

Baldwin, J. 1962. *The Fire Next Time*. New York: Laurel/Doubleday.

Coles, R. 1989. *The Call of Stories: Teaching and the Moral Imagination*. Boston: Houghton Mifflin.

Fierstein, H. 1978. *Torch Song Trilogy*. New York: Signet/New American Library.

Friend, R. A. 1993. "Undoing Homophobia in Schools." *Education Digest* 58(6):62–66.

Hemphill, E. 1992. "If Freud Had Been a Neurotic Colored Woman: Reading Dr. Frances Cress Welsing." In E. Hemphill, *Ceremonies: Prose and Poetry*. New York: Plume/Penguin USA.

Kazi, K. F. 1993. "Cornel West Talking About *Race Matters*." *The Black Collegian* (September-October), pp. 24–35.

Morrison, T. 1972. *The Bluest Eye*. New York: Washington Square.

Norman, M. 1983. *'Night, Mother*. New York: Mermaid Dramabook.

Sarton, M. 1989. *The Education of Harriet Hatfield*. New York: Norton.

Tolstoy, L. 1981. *The Death of Ivan Ilyich*. Trans. Lynn Solotaroff. New York: Bantam.

Villarosa, L. 1991a. "Coming Out." *Essence* (May) 21(1):82–84, 92.

—— 1991b. "Readers Respond to Coming Out." *Essence* (October) 22(6):19–22.

West, C. 1992. *Race Matters*. New York: Beacon.

Williams, Carmen Braun. 1992. "Afrocentricity Do or Die?" *Essence* (December) 23(8):46.

Patricia Myers and Diana Kardia

"But You Seem So Normal!":
Multidimensional Approaches to
Unlearning Homophobia on a College Campus

If you are coming to this book as a lesbian, gay man, or bisexual person who has done any work with antihomophobia education—either on a personal or political level—you can probably picture the facial expression that accompanies the quote from the title of this essay, "But you seem so normal!" It is a look that tells you something has happened, something has shifted, and the foundation of homophobia has become a bit shakier. The immense gulf that separates heterosexuality from all other forms of sexual identity has been recogr.ized for the moment as the optical illusion that it is; progress has been made. But what exactly is this progress and how does it come about? The edited volume *Multicultural Teaching in the University* featured a description of strategies used by the Educational Outreach Program (EOP) of the Lesbian-Gay Male Programs Office (LGMPO) at the University of Michigan, one of the oldest, continuous campus-based speakers bureaus in the country (Edwards, Myers, and Toy 1993). "But you seem so normal" extends this earlier work by combining educational theory with evaluations of this program in order to further articulate its impact as a tool to combat homophobia on a college campus. Based on participant feedback, we demonstrate the importance of using a variety of activities and approaches within a single program in order to work effectively with the diversity of needs, assumptions, and experiences represented in a typical student body.

Our interests in the LGMPO and its educational programming are not altogether impartial, since both of us have played key roles in the development of these programs and in their presentation on the University of

Michigan campus and elsewhere. Many people have contributed to the evolution of this program as coordinators of the LGMPO or the EOP and as facilitators of presentations since its inception in 1971. We are unable to recognize these individuals by name, but we wish to acknowledge the tremendous contributions these activists have made to homophobia education at the University of Michigan (Retzloff 1991:118; Toy 1991). We write this chapter from our own experiences and in recognition of these efforts.

We start with a brief overview of the workshop format in the following section. We then introduce pedagogical and attitudinal theory in order to reveal underlying assumptions about the form, process, and content of these educational efforts. While these theories did not explicitly inform efforts to design this program, they provide a useful frame for exploring decisions that were made in the experiential space that is sometimes called "flying by the seat of one's pants" but that usually reflects an implicit integration of theory and experience. Finally, we apply the insights gained from our theoretical consideration to a variety of data sources that reflect the impact of this program on the University of Michigan campus. Throughout this discussion we refer to homophobia rather than heterosexism as the primary focus of these educational efforts. While this program incorporates an explicit critique of heterosexist institutional and societal structures, the EOP is designed to work with individuals as the "unit of change." Based on the definitions of homophobia and heterosexism presented in this volume, we thus interpret these efforts as antihomophobia education.

General Workshop Format

Workshops of the Educational Outreach Program begin with an overview of the university programs and services that is followed by an experiential activity whose principal goals are values clarification and consciousness raising. Exercises ask people to react to contemporary social issues, explore aspects of their identity and socialization, brainstorm slang words or stereotypes, participate in guided fantasies, or role-play scenarios related to the lives of lesbians and gay men.

Exercises are followed by personal stories whereby each facilitator describes an aspect of her or his life as a lesbian, gay man, or bisexual person in a brief, lecturelike format. "Through the personal sharing audience members are moved to see lesbians, gay men, and bisexual people as individuals, distinct from each other, and transcendent of stereotypes" (Edwards, Myers, and Toy 1993:256). Finally, audiences have the opportunity to interact with the facilitators during the question and answer portion of the program, the second half of a two-hour presentation.

Theoretical Background

Feminist Pedagogy

A number of feminist pedagogical principles underlie our interpretation of the Educational Outreach Program workshop content and form. In particular, EOP workshops incorporate feminist values regarding the importance of diversity, the connectedness of various forms of oppression, and the value of empowerment. Feminist pedagogy engages with the implications of difference in various aspects of the classroom including those associated with gender, race, ethnicity, and class. As Audre Lorde has noted, feminism attempts to "identify and develop new divisions of power and new patterns of relating across difference" (1984:123). This commitment is reflected in the facilitators and coordinators of the EOP, the training materials provided, and the educational opportunities sought.

The EOP presentations are designed with an awareness that homophobia is part of a larger system of inequalities, a crucial analytical conclusion of feminism. "Oppression is a process; it is constituted within and through a complicated and dynamic network of asymmetrical power relations. Because oppression is a system of relations, it is both theoretically inadequate and politically self-defeating to treat particular manifestations of oppression in isolation" (Pellegrini 1992:53–54). Within a presentation workshop leaders often discuss the "commonalities and distinctions between homophobia and other forms of individual and institutional oppression" (Edwards, Myers, and Toy 1993:257) as well as stress an understanding of the interconnectedness of forms of oppression as a way of interpreting and articulating experience.

The form of the EOP workshop also demonstrates feminist educational goals. In particular, empowering learners and leaders to actively direct their educational experience is an important feminist educational goal, in that feminist teachers attempt to use their power as teachers to undermine domination rather than reinforce it (hooks 1989:52). For students, empowerment describes the negotiation and sharing of power as everyone engages in the processes of learning and the enhancement of self-esteem for all involved. Lesbians and gay men who facilitate EOP workshops experience the validation of being the "experts" on homosexuality, a shift "from margin to center" (hooks 1984), as well as the encouragement to modify their authoritative positions by creating an informal personal atmosphere that encourages sharing and risk taking from all participants. Audience members are empowered to enter the dialogue with facilitators from their particular perspectives, giving them a chance to have questions answered and values clarified in a supportive atmosphere.

These principles combine into an awareness of the importance of a multidimensional approach to effective educational interventions. For our purposes, acknowledgment of different learning styles, especially in relation to gender, as well as inequities in social power are two important variables considered. Learning that is "close to the heart," that attends to the affective as well as cognitive processes, is in line with feminism's educational objectives and is a critical part of the Educational Outreach Program's values (Thompson and Disch 1992:4).

Attitudinal Change

The importance of a multifaceted approach to educational efforts aimed at homophobia is also supported by psychological theory and research on attitudes as suggested by Herek's functional model, described in the essays of part 1 in this volume (Herek 1987). Thus, in addition to the variety of social roles and learning styles present in any collection of students, efforts to address homophobia will encounter many different types of attitudes, each of which require distinct types of intervention. Given this reality, the effectiveness of any educational program lies in part in its ability to meet the multiple needs of a diverse audience (Stevenson 1988).

Attitudinal change is also dependent on the opportunity to clarify and identify inconsistencies in one's value systems that may lead to unjust or discriminatory assumptions or beliefs about lesbians, gay men, or bisexual people (Rokeach and Ball-Rokeach 1989). By listening to the perspectives of other participants while experiencing and articulating the shifts and contradictions within their own perspectives, students are able to bring new meaning to the assumptions that form a base for their belief systems. By humanizing bisexual people, lesbians, and gay men, by exposing the myths of the heterosexist reality in which participants are submerged, and by revealing the ways in which unconscious participation in this reality results in extensive consequences for other human beings, this program promotes what Freire (1973) calls a "critical consciousness" or awareness. This awareness is one in which an individual's unconscious participation in an oppressive status quo is interrupted through educational efforts that expose problems in that status quo.

Measuring the Impact

Our discussion so far has highlighted theoretical explanations of how the structure and process of EOP workshops function to combat homophobia and heterosexism. In this section we turn to three data sources that speak directly to the impact of this program: an institutional report on the climate for gay men, bisexual people, and lesbians at the University of Michigan, a longitudinal study of the attitudes and experiences of the class of 1994, and evaluations distributed by the EOP at the conclusion of each workshop.

University of Michigan

The University of Michigan is a large public research institution located in Ann Arbor, a town of one hundred thousand people located forty miles west of Detroit. The student body of the University of Michigan includes over twenty-three thousand undergraduate students and ten thousand graduate students. It is insufficient, of course, to expect broad far-reaching social change simply by talking with three thousand University of Michigan undergraduate students a year; thus it is necessary to understand the context in which we attempt to dislodge homophobic attitudes.

In June of 1991 the study committee on the status of lesbians and gay men published a report entitled *From Invisibility to Inclusion: Opening the Doors for Lesbians and Gay Men at the University of Michigan* (Bader et al. 1991). After reviewing the various campus climate studies completed in the last few years, the report documents a climate at the University of Michigan comparable to other universities in which

> ignorance, misconceptions, and falsehoods about homosexuality and homo-
> sexuals abound. Hence, it is not surprising that discrimination against gay
> men and lesbians is widespread at the university and that many gay men and
> lesbians experience insensitivity, defamation, and harassment in one form or
> another. (4)

Or, as one faculty respondent put it, "The climate for lesbians and gay men at the U of M? It's a hell of a mess" (Bader et al. 1991:154). In the end the study committee made forty-nine recommendations, which ranged from suggesting the need for a social area for lesbian, gay, and bisexual students to developing particular benefits for domestic partners. A number of the recommendations emphasized educational strategies as a solution to the "cycle of ignorance, invisibility, and intolerance" experienced by members of the university community (ii).

Several respondents to the open-ended query made by the study committee discussed the EOP workshops as helping to create a more tolerant climate for lesbians, gay men, and bisexual people. These students and faculty described the programs as "knowledgeable," "extremely useful," "very successful," "very educational," and "a tremendous success" (Bader et al. 1991:144, 145, 151, 175, 176). In all cases those mentioning the workshops found them to be beneficial to the participants.

Looking at Attitudinal Change Over Time

A study of the undergraduate experience of the class of 1994 at the University of Michigan provides other evidence that the Educational Outreach Programs are effective at promoting more accepting attitudes among university students (*The Michigan Study* 1994).[1] This study includes surveys distributed at college entrance and three subsequent time points. Senior year data indicate that students who participated in the EOP were more than twice as likely to rate themselves as more accepting of lesbians, gay men, and bisexual people: two-thirds of seniors who participated in the EOP at some point in their four years rated themselves as more accepting after four years of college, while only one-quarter of those who did not participate rated themselves this way.

Can this increase in acceptance be attributed to the EOP, or are students who are likely to become more accepting also more likely to attend an EOP workshop? We believe both are true, as evidenced in tables 1 and 2. Students were asked at entrance whether they would be accepting and supportive of a person who was gay, lesbian, or bisexual. Table 1 represents 571 students who indicated some level of acceptance of lesbians, gay men, and bisexual people when they first entered college, while table 2 represents 471 students who were not accepting at entrance. Comparing tables 1 and 2 shows that nearly one in five students who were accepting at entrance attended EOP workshops sometime during the following four years (table 1; 16 percent), while fewer than one in twenty of those who were not accepting attended these workshops (table 2; 4 percent). More than one-third of those who were accepting at entrance rated themselves as significantly more so in their senior year (table 1; 37 percent), while less than one-fifth of those who were not accepting at entrance described themselves this way (table 2; 18 percent). Thus, those students who entered college with relatively accepting attitudes were more likely to attend the EOP and more likely to increase their acceptance, regardless of whether they attended an EOP workshop while they were at college.

However, this is only part of the picture. Further examination of the relationship between attitudes at entrance and EOP participation reveals that students who attended the EOP were consistently more likely to rate themselves as more accepting at the end of four years than those who did not attend, regardless of their incoming attitudes. This can be seen by looking at tables 1 and 2. Table 1 shows that two-thirds of students who attended the EOP rated themselves as more accepting at the end of four years, while only one-third of those who did *not* attend the EOP rated themselves as more accepting. A similar pattern can be seen in table 2: half of the students who attended the EOP rated themselves as more accepting, while less than one in five of the students who did *not* attend the EOP considered themselves more accepting by their senior year. Thus, among those students who entered college expressing some level of acceptance *and* among those students who did not enter with such acceptance, those who experienced themselves as more

TABLE 1

Senior Year Attitudes of Students Who Indicated at Entrance That They *Were* Accepting and Supportive of Lesbian, Gay, or Bisexual People

	Less accepting or no change	Somewhat more accepting	More accepting	Totals
Attended EOP	21%	12%	67%	16%
Did not attend EOP	39%	30%	32%	84%
Totals	36%	27%	37%	100%

Chi-square = 40.2, p < .001, n = 571

TABLE 2.

Senior Year Attitudes of Students Who Indicated at Entrance That They Were Not Accepting and Supportive of Lesbian, Gay, or Bisexual People

	Less accepting or no change	Somewhat more accepting	More accepting	Totals
Attended EOP	10%	37%	53%	4%
Did not attend EOP	47%	36%	17%	96%
Totals	45%	37%	18%	100%

Chi-square = 18.1, p < .001, n = 471

accepting after four years were more than twice as likely to have participated in an EOP workshop.

These results strongly indicate that the EOP promotes more accepting attitudes in general among college students. The results also provide evidence that the EOP reaches students with a range of attitudes and is effective across this range. However, this study does not provide information about the specific relationship between the EOP and attitudinal change. For this, we turn to the evaluations collected by the EOP presenters themselves.

Educational Outreach Program Evaluations

Written evaluations have been collected following each EOP presentation for at least the last decade. While these evaluations have changed over the years, they have typically included information about the general demographics of participants, ratings of specific program components, and short responses to open-ended questions. Average workshop ratings have consistently been high (between 4 and 5 on a scale of 1 to 5) throughout the years. Thus these programs are experienced as effective for the vast majority of participants.

Our analysis of these evaluations focuses on the written responses to four questions: What did you hope to gain from today's presentation? How were these expectations, needs or goals met or not met for you? What about the program was most helpful or valuable? What about the program was least helpful or valuable? We chose four points in time in the last decade and carefully examined participant responses to these four questions. Overall, we considered seventeen workshops, all of which took place during 1984, 1989, 1991, and 1993. All were led by at least one male and one female facilitator, were presented to undergraduate audiences, and were subject to some preliminary data collating. While these dates span significant differences in awareness of and attitudes toward homosexuality, bisexuality, AIDS, and related social policy, responses from these selected years are consistent and are generally representative of the kinds of feedback received by the EOP program and facilitators.

There were 512 evaluations associated with these 17 programs that we read to determine recurring themes in participant responses to the program. Thus we used a grounded theory approach in which the specifics of our understanding of the data arose from an in-depth reading of the evaluations themselves rather than from preconceived theory (Glaser and Strauss 1967). Through this examination of the evaluations, we identified three types of variation in the participant experience of the EOP: variations in expectations, process, and outcomes. We discuss and clarify each of these areas below through the inclusion of specific quotes taken from the evaluations.

Expectations   When asked what they hoped to gain from the EOP presentation, many students wanted more accurate information about this topic. Sometimes these *informational goals* were expressed very generally: "a better understanding of homosexuality," or "just to become aware of what homosexuality is all about." Other informational goals were more specific: "learn why a person is gay," "learn about the gay community," and "I wanted to hear what gays feel for each other—the distinction they make between friends and 'more than friends.'" Seeking increased information about bisexual people, lesbians, and gay men was one of the most common objectives of the program participants, however, other types of objectives were voiced as well.

Empathic goals   These stressed a desire to better understand the experience of being lesbian, gay, or bisexual. While informational goals tended to be more focused on the self as a recipient of knowledge, empathic goals were directed outward and expressed a desire to connect with people who are gay, lesbian, or bisexual: "I basically wanted a sense of sharing," "get an understanding of what a homosexual has to deal with," and "a better understanding of a gay lifestyle and how gays deal with problems such as stereotypes."

A third type of expectation expressed in the EOP evaluations extended beyond the individual level to address social issues.

Critical goals   These amplified descriptions of the experience of being gay to include a recognition of the need for social change. People who reflected these goals tended to be interested in learning strategies for confronting homophobia themselves: "I hoped to dispel some of my own homophobia," "an understanding of how to handle people who are homophobic," "a further understanding and help to relieve more biases," and "a better understanding between straights and gays."

Process   Comments about most helpful and least helpful aspects of the program provide insights into the variations in the process by which participants preferred to learn about this topic. Every set of evaluations considered mentioned all parts of the program at least once among the list of most helpful aspects. In general, there were fewer comments regarding the least helpful aspects, but here, too, participants offered an array of responses that very much reflected a variety of approaches to this experience. When asked for suggestions about improving the program, participants revealed an even wider array of possibilities. Some participants asked for smaller group discussions, while others from the same workshop suggested that discussions take place only within the group as a whole. Some participants criticized the presenters as being too impersonal, while others from the same workshop stressed how appreciative they were of the presenters' openness. While a few sets of evaluations reflected some agreement on things that had gone either particularly well or not well in that workshop, even in these cases there was no agreement on these matters.

Outcomes   While there were many outcomes participants took from these workshops, three in particular seemed to occur with frequent regularity: assured, informed, and challenged. Participants who left the workshop *assured* seemed to be contrasting their experience in the workshop with the stereotypes and myths about homosexuality they brought to the workshop. These were the students best represented by the title of this chapter, "But you seem so normal!" Other versions of this response include: "I feel like 'gays are people, too!' " "Both males seemed very ordinary, not eccentric," "It's great to feel that all people are people and there's really nothing strange or unnatural about folks who are gay," and "All of you are very nice and 'normal.' Thank you."

A number of participants indicated they had been *informed* by their participation in the workshop and commented on their increased understanding of the experiences of lesbians, gay men, and bisexual people. Comments included those such as, "My brother is gay. We get along great and I think I can understand him better now," "My theory on gayness being biological was shot to hell, but I gained a more humanistic and emotional view rather than a biological they-can't-help-it view," "It opened my eyes to what it is really like to be gay," and "I gained knowledge to help me speak up for gays, lesbians, and bisexuals in the company of ignorant people."

Finally, some students were *challenged* by their experiences during the workshop, directed either at their own behavior or their reaction to social norms on this topic. Examples of this type of outcome include, "Sometimes I feel mad because I know they are so discriminated against and sometimes I feel society doesn't let me be close to my friends," "If I were gay I'd like to be able to be public. I'm a very physical person with my boyfriend in public and I wish homosexuals could be as open. I almost feel guilty," "Hearing people's perceptions/fears/misconceptions about homosexuality was a real eye-opener for me," "It was helpful to hear about the pain experienced by gays who confront more conservative environments," and "While I consider myself open and together, I still have a lot to learn."

Variations in expectations, process, and outcomes reinforce the theoretical understanding of attitude development and of the learning process presented earlier in this chapter. They remind us that success has no single definition when it comes to addressing homophobia and heterosexism in a college environment. Rather, successful strategies are ones that recognize the scope and depth of workshop audiences by utilizing a multidimensional approach to workshop design. These variations are not exhaustive; they represent only a partial understanding of the diversity in needs, abilities, and perspectives that participants bring to these programs. This analysis also does not reflect the impact of social identities such as gender, race, ethnicity, or sexual orientation on students' expectations and experiences of these workshops. However, this study has been a first step toward articulating the need for a multidimensional approach to homophobia education. We hope that future research extends and refines these findings in order to increase our collective resources and ability to challenge these harmful attitudes.

Bisexual people, lesbians, and gay men need a host of human and civil rights issues addressed in addition to the eradication of intolerant beliefs. Homophobia and heterosexism are supported by various social institutions that result in discrimination and violence toward lesbians, gay men, and bisexual people. Individual attitudes and social behaviors work together to form an interlocking system of oppression that must be addressed at various levels and by different kinds of social change. Developing strategies for reducing homophobia on a college campus is just one solution that must be considered in concert with legislative changes, demonstrations, pride rallies, and so forth.

NOTE

1. The views expressed in this essay do not necessarily reflect the views of the Office of the Vice Provost for Academic and Multicultural Affairs.

REFERENCES

Bader, R., R. Chambers, C. Dolan-Greene, V. Gordan, P. Kahn, M. Ross, C. Summers, and J. Thorson. 1991. *From Invisibility to Inclusion: Opening the Doors for Lesbians and Gay Men at the University of Michigan.* Ann Arbor: University of Michigan, Affirmative Action Office.

Edwards, B., P. Myers, and J. Toy. 1993. "Combating Homophobia Through Education." In D. Schoem, L. Frankel, X. Zúñiga, and E. Lewis, eds., *Multicultural Teaching in the University*, pp. 249–59. Westport, Conn.: Praeger.

Freire, P. 1973. *Education for Critical Consciousness*. New York: Continuum.

Glaser, B. G., and A. L. Strauss. 1967. *The Discovery of Grounded Theory*. New York: Aldine de Gruyter.

Herek, G. M. 1987. "Can Functions Be Measured? A New Perspective on the Functional Approach to Attitudes." *Social Psychological Quarterly* 50:285–303.

hooks, b. 1984. *Feminist Theory: From Margin to Center*. Boston: South End.

—— 1989. "Toward a Revolutionary Feminist Pedagogy." *Talking Back: Thinking Feminist, Thinking Black*, pp. 49–54. Boston: South End.

Lorde, A. 1984. "Age, Race, Class, and Sex: Women Redefining Difference." *Sister Outsider: Essays and Speeches*, pp. 114–23. Trumansburg, N.Y.: Crossing.

The Michigan Study, 1990–1994: A Study of Diversity in Higher Education. 1994. Ann Arbor: University of Michigan-Ann Arbor, Office of the Vice Provost for Academic and Multicultural Affairs.

Pellegrini, A. 1992. "S(h)ifting the Terms of Hetero/sexism." In W. J. Blumenfeld, ed., *Homophobia: How We All Pay the Price* , pp. 39–56. Boston: Beacon.

Retzloff, T. 1991. "Outcast, Miscast, Recast: A Documentary History of Lesbians and Gay Men at the University of Michigan." In R. Bader, R. Chambers, C. Dolan-Greene, V. Gordan, P. Kahn, M. Ross, C. Summers, and J. Thorson, *From Invisibility to Inclusion: Opening the Doors for Lesbians and Gay Men at the University of Michigan*. Ann Arbor: University of Michigan, Affirmative Action Office.

Rokeach, M., and F. J. Ball-Rokeach. 1989. "Stability and Change in American Value Priorities, 1968–1981." *American Psychologist* 44(5):775–84.

Stevenson, M. R. 1988. "Promoting Tolerance for Homosexuality: An Evaluation of Intervention Strategies." *Journal of Sex Research* 25(4):500–11.

Thompson, B., and E. Disch. 1992. "Feminist, Anti-Racist, Anti-Oppression Teaching: Two White Women's Experiences. *Radical Teacher* 41:4–10.

Toy, J. 1991. Suggestions from Jim Toy regarding text of Retzloff. Letter (August).

Paula Alida Roy

Language in the Classroom:
Opening Conversations About
Lesbian and Gay Issues in Senior High English

In December 1992 the student newspaper at the New Jersey high school where I teach published a special issue dealing with attitudes toward homosexuality in our school. An anonymous gay student responded in a letter:

> As far "out" as I am in all other aspects of my life . . . I do not consider being out a viable option, and anxiously await getting out of [high school] and into college, where the atmosphere tends to be less cruel. The people whom I know that did come out or were found out in high school were ostracized, harassed, and physically assaulted.

While this student may be naively optimistic about the college world, his view of the high school environment verifies my observations and concerns. On the other hand, my work with young people has also convinced me that they are potentially more open to reflection about homosexuality than many adults. While I do not contend that there is a magic formula for changing attitudes, teachers can design strategies to create safe communities in which homosexuality, as a human condition, is invited into the classroom conversation.

I teach college preparatory high school English to juniors and seniors in an affluent conservative middle-class suburban community. The administrative leaders of the school district respect efforts to educate for diversity. Our geographical location not far from New York City lends a somewhat sophisticated edge of awareness to student attitudes. While these factors make my efforts easier than those of teachers working without community or administrative respect and support, I note that the very nature of public school requires thoughtful approaches to the teaching of what many regard as "values," especially when those "values" run counter to those of members of the community. While few would defend blatant racism or anti-Semitism and would expect the school to counter such prejudices, many would suggest that discussions of sexism and homophobia do not belong in school classrooms. Because we are a public school, however, I must acknowledge the ethical tension I sometimes feel between deeply held religious and family values and equally deeply held beliefs in equality and justice. I know the young people in my classes do not choose to be there and are therefore a captive audience. I also acknowledge, as a feminist teacher, the hierarchies of power that control the classroom dynamic. I worry about abusing that power if I use my position to denounce or trivialize religious beliefs or family values. I acknowledge these tensions not to suggest that they silence me but to embrace them as part of the challenge and therefore as potentially creative of respectful and innovative pedagogy. While inclusiveness, acknowledgment of diversity, and liberating student voices are hallmarks of feminist pedagogy, the power balance between teacher and students at the high school level is complicated by issues of adolescent development and expectations of supervisors, parents, and colleagues. The challenge for the feminist teacher is to find effective, honest ways to create and maintain a healthy, safe climate for learning, to honor and validate voices (and silences) of teenaged students who do not choose their classroom. I understand that as I seek to share the power of learning and discovery with my students, I risk being misunderstood as abdicating my role in the institution of school. To nurture a feminist pedagogy, my students and I must balance within the frames of hierarchical assumptions about power and authority in school.

For years I have kept informal records of student evaluations of my teaching and samples of student writings. Last year I asked students from my junior and senior classes to offer specific comments on what they noticed about my approaches to this subject. These voices add resonance to this chapter. The three strategies or approaches I describe in this chapter may be labeled: 1. classroom community 2. language and literature 3. student writing and research. These approaches are interactive, not discernibly separate from one another in the day-to-day work of the classroom.

Creating Classroom Community

I set as my main goal the creation of a safe, inclusive classroom community in which any topic can be discussed respectfully and in which topics often considered too political or sophisticated for high school students can be normalized into the discourse of the subject and the class. Anyone with a clear memory of high school will recall the pick-up-and-move rhythm of the day, with bells ringing to signal exodus from one classroom and subject and entrance a few minutes later into a new mix of students and teacher. Such an environment does little to foster a spirit of community. I spend the first days of school working consciously with students to create a community environment in which we are more to one another than talking heads. I greet my students with a handshake, taking time to "touch" them and say names. We move the desks into a circle. I devise exercises that encourage students to write about themselves, to introduce themselves and others, to ask questions about me and my teaching approaches, to reflect on their positive and negative memories of school. I collaborate with the students to develop guidelines or norms for our class. Invariably issues of respect arise, giving me the first opportunity to introduce some discussion of diversity, to mention race, class, gender, *and* sexual orientation. One of the guidelines that I suggest, if no one else does, is that we value questions over answers and that no subject should be unacceptable for respectful discussion. In my students' evaluations of my teaching, the most frequently cited aspect is the openness of discussion. As one student noted, "The classroom atmosphere just had an 'open' sense. I felt that no issue was too unacceptable to talk about." Of course, once a teacher makes a commitment to a climate that welcomes open discussion, she needs to be prepared to adjust lesson plans and assignments to accommodate student interests and concerns! The time spent creating community also helps students to form bonds and to develop a sense of OUR class as a special place. Later, when discussions heat up and young people find themselves confronting their own values and ideas in a context where others disagree, we all know one another's names and have some sense of ourselves as a community. Both hostility and indifference are difficult to maintain among people we know. The sense of community needs to be restored now and then by giving students and teacher the opportunity to reflect together. I provide frequent opportunities for students to offer feedback—at the end of marking periods and semesters, after heated discussions or problems, at the end of units.

While none of these strategies deals directly with homophobia, I consider them important steps toward creating mutual respect. They take little time and teach communication skills essential in a high school English curriculum. These strategies also challenge traditional assumptions about teacher-student relationships in the public high school setting and thus help me to expose students, many for the first time, to an alternative critique of how power and hierarchy function in the classroom. When, for example, I write with my students, sit with them as one voice among many in the discussion of classroom norms, share decision making with them, I invite an implicit (sometimes explicit) evaluation of traditional assumptions about power in school. From this base my students and I can open conversations about any subject. Conversations about homosexuality, homophobia, and heterosexism are the liveliest, the most controversial, and often the most thoughtful exchanges we share.

Language and Literature

The simplest ways I use language in the classroom feel most important to students. Over and over again they reinforced the normalizing of references to gays and lesbians in ordinary classroom discourse. Amanda noted, "My English teacher tried to make us aware of our use of language. For example, when people made certain generalizations, she would point that out, citing groups of people who may not be included." Her classmate Jen added, " I noticed it most when we would talk about a poem or something else that involved love. You [the teacher] would tell us that love did not have to be male-female. I think this is a good technique and it also helps the student to see the work in many different ways." Jill said, "Ms. Roy by doing simple little things in class helped to normalize homosexuality, bringing it closer almost to parallel heterosexuality. What I mean is, by talking about love in a novel and comparing it to the real world, she might say "two people" rather than 'a man and a woman' or even mention not only a man and a woman but also two people of the same sex." I was interested to hear this same student go on to offer a perceptive analysis of the effect of this strategy:

> She is treating them [lesbians and gays] as equal and on the same bill tossing aside the deviant or taboo sense of homosexuality. . . . Words were also an important part of the class. Correct and respectful terms, when dealing with anyone, were always used, but Roy also brought to light derogatory terms in context to reflect attitudes and experiences. By doing small things that do not disrupt the normal flow of class . . . Roy helped to make her class more sensitive to homosexuals, putting them on the same level as heterosexuals.

Early on each year I find opportunities to say the words *homosexual, lesbian, gay, homophobia* in a normal tone of voice, with no particular context. I might include them in a list of differences apparent in any group or about authors we will read during the year. I ignore the first stirrings or smirks, unless someone says something outrageous, at which early point we have a town meeting to discuss language and its power. At that time, or when appropriate, I also air the derogatory terms, maybe as part of an exercise on stereotypes or language. Before we are into the third week of school I have begun to normalize the discourse by getting the words into the classroom air and making clear that just as no one would think of saying "nigger" out loud, so "fag" or "dyke" are hurtful and unacceptable.

I also watch my pronouns, especially, as students noted, when dealing with romantic love. I avoid the exclusive he-she language. It is amusing to note the missed beat that happens in the classroom the first time I say "she-she" or "he-he" when talking about love. I also keep an eye on my nouns, as in *girl-girl, boy-boy* as well as *boy-girl*; many shorthand expressions we rely on to convey whole narratives are loaded with heterosexist assumptions. The same vigilance is necessary in language about families. After my own divorce, I realized the painful exclusionary quality of much conventional language about parents and families. I stopped talking automatically about birth parents and moms and dads. Now I try to make family references inclusive of the possibility of gay/lesbian parents as well.

An English curriculum offers its own opportunities for conversation about homosexuality, even in a public high school where there are few works dealing explicitly with gay and lesbian characters or themes. The first and most obvious strategy involves inviting authors to come out of the classroom closets where they are too often kept. I make a point of mentioning that Whitman or Cather or Baldwin was gay/lesbian and also note contested scholarship about such authors as Dickinson and Hansberry. I have been criticized by colleagues and students who ask if I talk about the heterosexuality of Hawthorne or Kesey; my response to them is that, unless stated, the assumption is that the author is "straight." These questions and challenges can provide opportunities to define and explain heterosexism and how heterosexist attitudes promote ignorance and invisibility. When students explore authors' biographies, I encourage them to share what they learn about the authors' lives. This candor dignifies the humanity of the lesbian or gay author and, in cases where facts have been suppressed or the scholarship is contested, students learn more about the craft of the biographer and the subjectivity and selectivity of scholarship—valuable lessons in any English classroom! One student who presented his research on Audre Lorde to his English class told me:

I chose the only viable option in discussing Lorde's sexuality. And that was to be frank and forthright with no sugar coating. Simply because Lorde was a Black, lesbian feminist does not mean that she was abnormal. . . . To understand her poetry you must understand her. As readers and as emerging poets we cannot closet ourselves.

From direct classroom discussion of homoeroticism in novels such as *Annie John* and *A Separate Peace* to exploring controversial critical interpretations of *My Antonia,* English teachers have many opportunities to normalize lesbian/gay themes as subjects for reflection, composition, and research. While this area seems to offer the most obvious ground for cultivation of understanding and interest, many teachers and students resist such discussion, feel embarrassed by it, or consider it inappropriate for high school. My response continues to be that the study of literature is the exploration of the much clichéd "human condition," a condition that certainly includes sexuality in all its dimensions. By keeping the discussions of homosexuality alive in the legitimate context of several themes or interpretations of literature within the curriculum, the teacher stands on solid pedagogical ground. That is not to say that in the current climate of censorship and attacks on schools teachers talking about homosexuality are immune from attack. In fact, few do address the subject openly, perhaps out of fear of reaction. I find, however, that students are interested in and open to multiple approaches to literature. As Jill noted:

> Critical and sensitive discussion of gay and lesbian issues in the high school classroom is extremely important. . . . Homosexuals are people . . . and the inclusion of their literature and ideas is not only helpful in giving them equality and confidence but they offer another point of view which is wonderful enhancing education and opening minds.

Each marking period students spend a certain number of free periods in our resource center, reading and responding to short reserve readings. Response sheets stapled to each piece encourage students to talk to one another in writing about the works they choose to read. Again, I provide a menu of choices, from critical articles about works we are studying in class to offbeat or controversial pieces from editorial pages, magazines, journals. I always include several pieces on gender issues, homophobia, and lesbian and gay lifestyles. Over the years I have noticed how often students gravitate to those pieces, even students hostile to classroom discussion of diversity. I suspect that the private space allows them to let down defenses and indulge their quite natural curiosity and interest. I have collected responses over the years. A particularly popular reading a few years ago was Anna Quindlen's "Evan's Two Moms," an essay about the adoption by two lesbians of a little boy (33). A very conservative senior responded:

> When I saw the title on this article, I rolled my eyes back and . . . gave my "what's next" sigh and allowed my hairless head three staccato shakes left and right. I threw it back on the pile of articles and looked for another. . . . Somehow, five minutes later, I had worked my way back to it. Anna Quindlen. All right, I thought, I can appreciate good editorial writing. So I read it.

He goes on to describe the effect of the reading on his own attitudes toward legalizing gay/lesbian relationships.

> What Quindlen seems to be saying is that before we even have the gall to debate private sexual behavior as a matter of social or religious aberration, we ought to make sure these kids have a nurtured, open-minded life. . . . Two gays wanting to be married doesn't promote homosexual activity, doesn't foster homosexual children.

That excerpt, one of many in response to that particular article, was read by other students in the ongoing written dialogue about the readings. The teacher voice is largely silent here, although sometimes I add my response to the sheet. This strategy is another avenue for opening conversation about gay and lesbian issues and provides students with opportunities to respond to challenging material and to one another.

Student Writing and Research

My teaching methods rely more and more on the power of writing as an instrument of thinking, student liberation, and empowerment. My students write every day, to focus their thinking, record their questions, respond to one another. They keep journals in which they are encouraged to reflect on our discussions. They work in writing groups, sharing ideas, drafts, editing. They select their own topics and approaches to papers. Just as homosexuality is a legitimate topic for discussion and reading, it is also appropriate for writing. As the year progresses, many students address the topic in opinion papers, in research papers about authors or themes, in stories and poems and plays. In the brainstorming/prewriting exercises and small and large group discussions that precede any major writing assignment, I make a point of opening the gay/lesbian subjects up as possibilities. I have had students write about gay authors, themes, issues in many forms and voices. Because we have established a classroom community, the work done by one student becomes open to others in writing groups, large group discussions, and student presentations. Obviously this influence cannot be preplanned or guaranteed to happen the same way each year. But in my experience it does happen when students are invited to write about their own lives and topics of their choice. Last year for example, I taught a student very involved in the AIDS quilt project. When she realized that she could write about her experiences, she educated us all about the project and about the homophobia she had experienced working on it. In fact, many students' lives have been touched by the AIDS epidemic in some way; while it is problematic if all discussion of homosexuality centers around AIDS, it is often the first road into open discussion, as when a student last year wrote about her gay uncle whose family was ashamed of his death from AIDS. This week five current seniors decided to build their major senior seminar papers around an exploration of growing up gay and lesbian; they will be working together and sharing their readings and research with all of us in the class.

Over the years several students have "come out" to me in journals and personal writings. Now that my students work in writing groups, I do not encourage them to share personal journals. I think it would be unfair to encourage young lesbian and gay teenagers to take unnecessary risks. While they might be "safe"in my classroom, as one student pointed out to me, "There have been occasions when in my next class I have heard fellow classmates use terms such as 'faggot' and 'dyke' right after sitting through forty-five minutes of discussion talking about how 'open-minded' and 'nonhomophobia and aware' they are. One English teacher's efforts are not enough." That comment and conversations I have had with students often make me wonder if attitudes change or if students in classes such as mine respond to teacher cues. While there is no way to answer that question definitively, I believe that positive change can be grouped into three categories: (1) the invisible gay/lesbian students have at least one period a day in which their identity is validated; (2) students already supportive of gay/lesbian rights feel additionally empowered; (3) open-minded but ignorant students have an opportunity to learn, discuss and question assumptions. Some students no doubt "play the game" according to what they perceive are my rules; I suspect that even among those students, as evidenced by the remarks in response to Quindlen's piece, there is some movement.

In conclusion, I should like to emphasize that these strategies are interactive and recursive, part of a dynamic pedagogy that is opportunistic, fluid, and student centered. The very act of organizing material and writing about it here minimizes this dynamic, renders it more static than it is in daily practice. I believe that the effect of these approaches is powerful, that effects, positive and negative, spiral out from small centers, and that a classroom community or a student organization can be such a center. Students from my classes often take leadership roles in combating homophobia in our school community and in educating others. I have seen student attitudes change in the course of a year, as evidenced by their own use of language in writing and speaking, their interest in reading about and researching gay and lesbian topics, their questions, their developing awareness and critiques of what they see and hear in the world around them. Since the work of my classroom is public, other teachers seek me out with questions or requests for material or ideas. In this way I have also built quiet coalitions with colleagues who want to take small steps toward change.

The strategies I describe here help me and my students open liberating conversations. As Jen reminds me,

> People don't want to be told they are homophobic; they want to figure it out for themselves. Our classroom was a good place for someone to do this. No, we did not talk about this issue that much. In fact some may say we did not talk about it at all. However, I think that by not actually talking about it and just mentioning it when it comes up, people will have a better time accepting it.

The distinction Jen makes here is an important one. If students are lectured to about their negative attitudes or if a teacher makes the classroom a political soapbox, conversations do not open. They clamp shut. A pedagogy that involves students and teacher in ongoing encounters with relevant topics, among them gay and lesbian issues, can generate dialogue, raise new questions, and reframe old ones for young people in public schools.

REFERENCES

Cather, W. 1918. *My Antonia*. Boston: Houghton Mifflin.
Kincaid, J. 1983. *Annie John*. New York: Penguin.
Knowles, J. 1959. *A Separate Peace*. New York: Bantam.
Quindlen, A. 1993. "Evan's Two Moms." In A. Quindlen, *Thinking Out Loud*, p. 33. New York: Random House.

Paul Van de Ven

Promoting Respect for Different Viewpoints and Ways of Living to Australian High School Students

State of New South Wales's public school system: "All public schools are expected to promote . . . [respect for] different viewpoints and ways of living which contribute to our democracy" (NSW Department of School Education 1991b:6–7). This laudable principle is repeated as part of the rationale for the education system's teaching unit to address homophobia in schools: a six-lesson module included in the curriculum document Resources for Teaching Against Violence (NSW Department of School Education 1991a). It was not just high-mindedness, though, that led to the development of the module. The catalyst was outrage expressed by various community groups and governmental agencies at increasing violence toward gays and lesbians. By 1991 up to thirty bashings per week were being reported in inner-city areas of Sydney and numerous gay-related murders had been committed within the state of New South Wales. Of particular concern to education authorities was the fact that most of the physical assaults and homicides were perpetrated by school students or recent graduates.

This essay examines the purpose, content, and teaching strategies of the module. It does so from the functional perspective that was rejuvenated, and applied to homophobia, by Herek (1986a; 1987). According to this approach, homophobic attitudes serve different purposes based on the psychological benefit derived from holding a particular belief. Herek postulated and found support for a four-function conceptual model of the dynamics of antigay and antilesbian prejudice. First, homophobia may serve an *experiential schematic* function based on past adverse contact with homosexuals. Second, homophobia may serve a *social expressive* function by helping individuals to win approval from significant others—especially peers—for the adoption of antihomosexual postures. Third, homophobia may serve a *value expressive* function by helping individuals to affirm their identity by expressing important personal values, for example, by echoing antihomosexual dogma in the case of people who subscribe to conservative religious ideologies. Fourth, homophobia may serve a *defensive* function through the characterization of gay and lesbian people as a suitable symbol to be attacked, thereby avoiding personal anxieties and insecurities associated with gender role and sexuality.

A basic tenet of the functional approach is that a different persuasive appeal, consonant with the function served by an individual's attitude, has to be presented to optimize the possibility of attitude change. For change to occur, current attitudes have to be rendered dysfunctional while target attitudes are provided with reinforcement. With experiential schematic homophobia, positive interactions with gays and lesbians under favorable conditions may result in less hostile attitudes. With social expressive homophobia, exposure to peers' positive dispositions or to pro-homosexual statements from significant role models of heterosexual masculinity and femininity may be useful. With value expressive homophobia, appeals to competing values of the target group, such as "live and let live" and "do unto others as you would have them do unto you," may result in greater empathy with homosexuals. With defensive homophobia, provision of sex education and accurate information about homosexuality, including presentation of models that demonstrate that sexual orientation is a continuum of feelings, behaviors, and preferences, may counter homophobic anxieties.

Outcomes of the module for a sample of thirteen- to sixteen-year-old high school students are also reported. The module was implemented in a ninth grade class in two coeducational schools, two boys' schools and two girls' schools, all located in the Sydney metropolitan area. Schools were selected as representative of middle Australia in terms of socioeconomic status (SES) and for reflecting the multiculturalism of Sydney. That is, each school's intake area was of average SES and each school drew students from diverse ethnic and religious backgrounds. One hundred thirty students participated and responded to a questionnaire prior to instruction (pretest), immediately after instruction (post-test), and three months later (follow-up).

Data collection consisted of individual responses to three scales that measured homophobic cognition (i.e., thinking), homophobic affects (i.e., feelings), and behavioral intentions toward homosexuals. Cognition was assessed by the Modified Attitudes Toward Homosexuality Scale (Price 1982).

Three separate affects of homophobic guilt, homophobic anger, and delight were assessed by the Affective Reactions to Homosexuality Scale (Van de Ven, Bornholt, and Bailey 1993) that was adapted from the "affective adjective checklist" developed originally by Ernulf and Innala (1987; Innala and Ernulf 1992). Homophobic guilt was a measure of discomfort associated with homosexuality and homosexuals. Homophobic anger was a measure of disgust toward gays and lesbians and contempt for their civil rights. Delight was a measure of positive feelings in relation to homosexuality and homosexuals. Behavioral intentions toward gays and lesbians were assessed by the Homophobic Behavior of Students Scale (Van de Ven, Bornholt, Bailey 1993). Each student also wrote a short story (after Bleich 1989) in which he or she described a conversation with someone on the issue of homosexuality and detailed, in particular, how attitudes toward gays and lesbians were expressed. The complete measurement instrument is described and reprinted in Van de Ven (1994).

Teachers' subjective assessments of the module were also collected. After follow-up measurement teachers provided written responses to three questions that asked about their perceptions of outcomes, whether or not they would recommend the module to colleagues, and any plans to reuse the module.

Purpose of the Module

The module is available for use with ninth through twelfth grade students. Before implementation in classes, the approval of the school principal and the consent of students' parents or guardians had to be obtained. The stated aims of the module were (1) to provide a means by which a school can address homophobia, (2) to provide a forum in which students can identify questions that they have about homosexuality and that they would like to ask of gay and lesbian people, (3) to provide information on discrimination and the law, and (4) to provide a means by which a school can minimize discrimination against gay and lesbian people.

The development of the module acknowledged that homophobia is a serious issue and that schools are an important social institution for addressing antihomosexual prejudice. Furthermore, the dissemination of the teaching resource recognized that schools had to be provided with specific antihomophobia strategies that went beyond platitudinous policy statements to meaningful teaching and learning initiatives. The individuals who developed the module appreciated that schools have a responsibility for all people, including gays and lesbians. They also understood that schools have an obligation to inform students about *all* aspects of antidiscrimination statutes and the consequences for breaching them. The focus on schools in the aims conveyed an implicit message that a whole school rather than an isolated classroom approach should be taken.

Content and Teaching Strategies

The material in the module was first presented as a one-day crime prevention workshop by officers of the NSW Police Service and community youth workers. The initial presentation was to students attending an inner-city high school. This school had been the subject of adverse publicity following the murder of one of its gay teachers and the killing of a gay man in a park adjoining the school. The former homicide remains unsolved. Eight youths—four of whom were current or previous students of the school in question—were convicted over the latter death.

The module was subsequently rewritten by the Police Service Gay/Lesbian Client Consultant and four Department of School Education employees. This version involved approximately five hours of teaching time, divided among six sessions, each of roughly fifty minutes duration. The instructional unit was designed for flexible presentation as a one-day activity or as a series of lessons over a number of weeks. The latter option was used in the evaluation of outcomes reported here.

Session 1 introduced the unit of work by defining *homosexuality* and *homophobia*. Next, each student anonymously completed a handout by marking "true," "false," or "don't know" against nine statements about homosexuality. For example, the first three statements read: "Most gay and lesbian people would change if they could," "If you have a homosexual experience it means that you are gay or lesbian," and "Lesbians and gay men rarely force their sexuality on others." Completed handouts were collected, retained, and later collated by the teacher for use in session 2.

In the next activity four large sheets of paper were pinned to bulletin boards around the room. Students added statements to each sheet of paper, which had a different unfinished sentence as its heading: (1) I've heard that gay men . . . (2) I've heard that lesbian women . . . (3) Violence against gay and lesbian people happens because . . . and (4) Violence against gays and lesbians can include. In the larger group the teacher generated discussion about students' responses to each sentence stem. Main points were drawn out by asking questions as if a naive inquirer, such as "How do you know that?" or

"Does anyone else in the group think that is true?" Toward the end of the lesson the teacher's focus was changed to one of testing the truth of students' responses and giving accurate information.

Session 2 started by providing an opportunity for students to reflect on the previous session and to identify what they had learned. Students then worked in small groups to compile a list of questions that they would like to ask of gays and lesbians. Questions were then shared with the class and recorded on large sheets of paper. Afterward, the teacher presented collated handout results (from session 1) and used prepared overhead projector transparencies to provide accurate information regarding each of the handout statements.

Session 3 involved a panel of lesbians and gays who responded to students' questions. A twenty-seven-minute audio tape of interviews with five gay men and five lesbians is included in the module. These interviewees, of various ages and occupations, respond openly to questions about their coming out, relationships, families, and work. The tape was developed for use by schools (e.g., those in isolated rural areas) that may have difficulty convening a gay and lesbian panel. The research reported here used speaker panels rather than the audio tape in this phase of the intervention. Each speaker panel comprised five or six gays and lesbians, with at least two members of either gender.

Session 4 established a link between homophobia and violence through students' reading and discussion of five prepared scenarios that related incidents of homophobia to everyday school and social events. The content of the scenarios was (1) a gay member of a school sports team is victimized, (2) a teacher witnesses one of his students assault a gay person, (3) a lesbian student is harassed at school, (4) a student is victimized because his mother is a lesbian, and (5) a talented art student, presumed to be gay, is assaulted. The vignettes encouraged participants to consider acceptable ways of relating to lesbian and gay people. In small groups, which were facilitated and monitored intermittently by the instructor, students responded to set discussion points about one or more of the scenarios. Toward the end of the session, one student from each group reported back to the whole class.

Session 5 explored the relationships between prejudice, discrimination, violence, and the law. The teacher commenced by summarizing the processes and content of previous sessions. In this summary the teacher focused on the unacceptability of violence toward *any* person, the social construction of stereotypes, and the observation (from session 3) that in most areas gays and lesbians are similar to heterosexuals. Whole class discussion was generated around the question "When people consider others as different, what might happen and why?" Students then examined and discussed an antidiscrimination Board of New South Wales brochure that listed and defined all the forms of discrimination illegal in this state. Harassment and unfair treatment of gays and lesbians in relation to employment, goods and services, accommodations, and public education are against the law in New South Wales. Since March 2, 1994, vilification of homosexuals has also been outlawed in this state. Concluding this session, students read and discussed newspaper clippings about acts of homophobic violence and the serious consequences for victims and perpetrators.

Session 6, the concluding lesson, provided students with an opportunity to reflect on and integrate their learning. In pairs students recorded on overhead projector film what they had learned through participation in the unit of work. Each pair then shared its responses with the class. In small groups students subsequently prepared an action plan of school practices that might be implemented to prevent discrimination against minority groups. In a final plenary session each group presented its plan for incorporating recognition of issues related to homophobia and methods for addressing them in school policies and practices. During the culminating activity the teacher distributed brochures that listed the names and telephone numbers of counseling and support services where gay and lesbian students could seek help.

Analysis of Content and Teaching Strategies

The module incorporated a number of sound pedagogical principles. Foremost, it handled issues that could generate strong personal responses from students, teachers, and community members in a sensitive way. Individuals' needs and feelings were acknowledged and managed sensitively within the context of the module. For example, from the outset the instructor created an environment in which the topic could be discussed openly and in which individuals could air their opinions, be they antagonistic or friendly. Hostile reactions were initially acknowledged in a nonjudgmental way and not challenged by the instructor until after the first session.

Many activities in the module involved group discussions. As part of the preparatory work the teacher and students were required to establish ground rules for the successful functioning of the group. Groups were encouraged to agree on rules that allowed only one person to speak at a time, that dealt effectively with individuals who persistently made it difficult for the group to work, that maintained confidentiality and built trust, and that fostered free expression of opinions coupled with willingness to have them challenged.

This highly structured and sequenced unit of work took students from the known (their present state of understanding) to the unknown. As it did so, previous learning was reviewed and reinforced before each new topic was introduced. Different learning styles were accommodated by incorporating a range of individual, small group, and whole class activities that utilized varied written, spoken, and visual media. Wherever possible, the module drew upon familiar school and social events that reflected students' personal experience of the world. Learners were continually challenged to explore ways to combat homophobia. Most important, the unit of work culminated in a plan for action that was generated by the group itself.

Effective pedagogy rather than specific theory for combating homophobia characterized the module. Nevertheless, various aspects of the content and teaching strategies of the intervention were consistent with an attitude function perspective. The opportunity for positive interaction with the gays and lesbians who comprised the speaker panels had the potential to undermine experiential schematic functions based on past unfavorable contact with homosexuals. Ideally, positive interactions for attitude change should be intimate and ongoing rather than superficial and momentary, should involve people who share beliefs and values, and should occur under conditions that foster cooperation rather than competition (Herek 1986b; Lance 1992; Olson and Zanna 1993). Achieving such close and sustained interaction in the course of a relatively brief teaching unit was not possible. The available evidence does indicate, however, that lesbian and gay speaker panels are beneficial when used *in conjunction with* other educational strategies rather than as a stand-alone homophobia reduction strategy (Croteau and Kusek 1992).

The module provided opportunities for students to observe some of their peers responding positively toward gays and lesbians. Although they were not planned specifically, it could reasonably be anticipated that a number of students would respond positively to the introductory checklist and to the sentence stems of session 1, during the discussion activities throughout, and during the feedback and action planning activities of session 6. Other positive responses could be anticipated in the informal discussion among participants as the work progressed. These types of encounter had the potential to reinforce pro-homosexual attitudes and censor negative attitudes. In so doing, the classmates' positive reactions would reduce negative attitudes that served a social expressive function based on peers' support for the utterance of antihomosexual attitudes.

To undermine value expressive functions based on, for example, religious dogma, the module reinforced alternative values that may be of importance to youth of today. The module emphasized nonviolence and antidiscrimination. It attempted to develop an appreciation of how it would feel to be harassed or attacked. It made explicit the fact that antihomosexual aggravation and violence are criminal offenses in New South Wales. Above all, it provided opportunities for students to affirm gay and lesbian rights and thereby assert a libertarian identity of freedom of expression and equal rights for all.

The module attempted to overcome students' defensiveness by debunking several of the myths and stereotypes surrounding homosexuality. It provided accurate information about such matters as the amount of choice in sexual orientation, the nature of homosexual behaviors, and the origins of homosexuality. Other misconceptions could be addressed as they arose incidentally during the course of instruction.

Outcomes

Outcomes of the module were assessed with 130 ninth grade students by analyzing stories they wrote and by measuring five variables on a questionnaire: homophobic cognition, homophobic guilt, homophobic anger, delight, and behavioral intentions.[1] On each of the five numerically scaled variables male students were significantly more homophobic than female students. On one of these variables, homophobic anger (measured by adjectives such as *despising* and *disgusted*), the module had the desired effect for all groups of participants. That is, levels of homophobic anger were significantly lower after intervention and remained so three months later.

On cognition (i.e., in response to statements such as "Homosexuality should be a criminal offense") the module resulted in a significant and lasting reduction in homophobia for females. While the male students' level of homophobic cognition declined immediately following the instruction, within three months their level of homophobia returned to their premodule level. These effects were similar in coeducational and single-sex schools.

On the affective variable, delight (measured by adjectives such as *accepting* and *happy*), females in single-sex schools increased significantly—the desired outcome—and remained so three months later. Males in single-sex schools increased immediately following the instruction, but after three months their score on delight trended toward their premodule level. In contrast, for both male and female students in coeducational classes the intervention had no significant effect on delight. This finding points to a difference between mixed and single gender schools in regard to the dynamics of homophobia. Students in single-sex schools are more likely to shift toward feelings of support for gay men and lesbians, possibly because, in the absence of opposite-sex peers, the pressures in these settings to maintain exclusive allegiance to heterosexuality are less severe.

On the behavioral measure students' behavioral intentions (e.g., their willingness to speak with gays and lesbians in class) were significantly less homophobic immediately after the instruction, but there was a slight trend toward more homophobic behavioral intentions three months later. The module had no significant effect on students' homophobic guilt—their feelings of dread or discomfort associated with homosexuality (measured by adjectives such as *embarrassed* and *awkward*).

Content analysis of students' short stories also demonstrated that males were more homophobic than females. For students attending coeducational high schools the percentage of short stories with "positive content only" (i.e., expressing pro-homosexual attitudes) increased after the intervention. The males' short stories rose from 17 to 33 percent positive, whereas the females' short stories rose from 41 to over 70 percent positive. For students attending single-sex schools the percentage of short stories with positive content remained fairly constant across measurement intervals. The males' short stories remained between 10 and 13 percent positive, whereas the females' short stories remained between 62 and 69 percent positive.

Statistical analysis of the entire 130 students' short story data revealed that the module resulted in a significant and lasting reduction in homophobic attitudes. However, separate statistical analyses of short story content for the different groups involved in the study produced significantly favorable results only in the case of female students in coeducational settings. This finding is at odds with the earlier inference that single-sex environments may be more benign in terms of homophobia reduction. A possible explanation is that for the females in single-sex schools a ceiling effect—characterized by an unusually high proportion of positive narratives initially—made change much less likely to occur.

Teacher Reactions

As is typically the case for selecting staff to handle sensitive issues in schools, school principals or student welfare committees expressly chose the six teachers who implemented the module. All of the teachers—two males and four females—were experienced practitioners. After the instruction they provided written feedback about the module. In response to a question about whether or not they would recommend the kit to other teachers, all stated unequivocally that they would. Asked if they planned to use the kit again, four of the teachers indicated that they intended to do so, two of whom had already commenced using it with other classes. Two teachers had not made any formal plans to reuse the module. One of these declared that she "would definitely use the kit again," while the other said that he "will probably do so next year."

Before the teachers had reviewed student evaluations, they subjectively assessed the module outcomes. Five of the teachers felt that the module had been successful and had made an impact in reducing homophobic attitudes and behaviors, at least with the majority of the students. The other teacher, from a boys' high school, commented that "the kit was good in terms of supplying information . . . [but in some] cases the desired outcomes of the kit simply could not be achieved due to students' entrenched attitudes—many of which seemed to come from home!"

Specific favorable mention was made about certain aspects of the module. The most positive features were perceived to be the clear and easy-to-follow documentation, the use of strategies that encouraged students to speak openly and honestly about their views, the way the module proceeded from general information about homosexuality to more complex value judgments about discrimination and violence, the way the module challenged students' misconceptions about homosexuality, the use of scenarios that were personally meaningful to students, the way students' attention was drawn to the actual consequences of violent behavior, and, above all, the use of a speaker panel. In summary, the teachers who implemented the module thought it was an effective teaching resource—a perception partially borne out by the objective assessment of outcomes.

Discussion

The module achieved several desirable outcomes when used with mainstream high school students. The effects were generally better and more lasting for females, with male students more obstinate and tending to relapse on some of the variables within a few months. The finding about regression, coupled with the observation that male students held more negative views about homosexuals than female students, suggests that the module may have more lasting impact on males' attitudes if it were extended to include planned revision activities. These activities could take the form of additional discussion sessions and remeeting the gay and lesbian panelists several weeks after the presentation of the module.

The impact of the module might be enhanced if lesbians and gays were more involved in its teaching. For example, the members of the speaker panel could participate, perhaps informally at the outset, in activities before and after the speaker panel activity of session 3. More sustained cooperation of this type may further undermine any negative attitudes based on past unfavorable contact (i.e., serving experiential schematic functions). In addition, to reduce the impact of hostile attitudes based on peers' support for homophobic dispositions (i.e., satisfying social expressive demands), the module may be supplemented with recorded statements by popular adolescent role models whose attitudes toward homosexuals are positive. Suitable examples may be found among musicians, actors, and sport stars. These recordings could also be used to counter negative attitudes that serve to maintain existing, antihomosexual values (i.e., serving value expressive functions). To do so, they would have to reinforce competing values of the student target group such as equality, justice, and nondiscrimination.

Teacher, Counselor, and Systemic Change

Well-designed teaching packages can reduce aspects of high school students' homophobia, but, as the literature suggests, teaching against homophobia may need to be complemented by other strategies. A useful starting point would be to attempt to overcome the ignorance, complacency, or antigay and antilesbian prejudice of many educators. It has been argued and demonstrated that most teachers are ill-prepared, in both knowledge and attitudes, to deal effectively with lesbian and gay youth (Fassinger 1993; Sears 1992). Training in sensitivity to gay and lesbian issues should help to reduce antihomosexual prejudice among school administrators, teachers, and support staff (Berrill and Herek 1990; Mason 1993). Raising the awareness of educational personnel regarding homosexuality may be achieved through informal discussion, professional workshops, invited speakers, conferences, and staff meetings, as well as through undergraduate and graduate training programs. The cornerstone of such education and training efforts, Fassinger (1993) advises, must be attitude examination rather than merely imparting knowledge.

It is equally important to ensure that all school psychologists and counselors are adequately prepared and open to handling the sexual orientation inquiries of students (Grayson 1987). All students have to deal with issues related to homosexuality (Sears 1992) and approximately 10 percent of students served by school counselors will develop gay or lesbian identities (McFarland 1993). Even so, little attention has been paid to educating school counselors about the developmental issues of gay and lesbian youth (McFarland 1993). The high degree of counselors' negativism toward homosexuals (Sears 1992) poses a significant barrier to achieving equity in support services for gay and lesbian students and to achieving understanding and acceptance of sexual diversity among students generally.

In schools homophobia and heterosexism are shaped and reinforced by interrelated processes of exclusion and inclusion; *exclusion* of positive role models and images of lesbian, gay, and bisexual people, and persistent *inclusion* of homosexuality in negative contexts such as HIV/AIDS and violence (Friend 1993). To overturn these dual processes of heterosexist silencing, schools and educational systems might work to encourage and support gay and lesbian teachers and students to come out and be visible. Only when lesbians and gays become conspicuous and valued contributors within educational organizations will their voices be heard. Only then will competent lesbian and gay adults be able to provide the sources of information and the effective role models that all students, not least gay and lesbian adolescents, deserve.

Another important strategy to reduce homophobia would be to have, for education systems and in all schools, unambiguous antidiscrimination policies and programs that treat *all* forms of discrimination—racism, sexism, heterosexism, and the like—with contempt (Fassinger 1993; Herek 1989). Formal policies may be established to prohibit antihomosexual harassment, to encourage reporting and monitoring of incidents, to support victims, and to publicize penalties for antihomosexual victimization (Berrill and Herek 1990). These policies would benefit from vocal administrative support for the place of gay and lesbian people in the educational community. Such support would help to develop a climate of affirmation of lesbians and gay males such that antihomosexual remarks among staff and students are no longer tolerated (D'Augelli and Rose 1990). In addition to the inclusion of sexual orientation in antidiscrimination policies, a supportive climate would be advanced by a requirement that gay and lesbian perspectives be incorporated across the curriculum (Fassinger 1993; Berrill and Herek 1990).

Educational interventions such as the module under consideration here may do little more than shift "surface responses" to questionnaires rather than undermine current heterosexual masculinities that are the foundation of homophobia. A long-term strategy for combating antihomosexual prejudice would be to focus on confronting sexism and deconstructing hierarchical and repressive notions of gender that give rise to homophobia. Heterosexual masculinity is socially constructed and socially imposed. It can be resisted and changed (Frank 1987). In Mason's (1993) analysis, the starting point for challenging traditional dominant masculinity is the acknowledgment that heterosexism is an ideological system that affects everyone adversely. From there it would be possible to start to dismantle assumptions of homosexual lifestyles as pathological or immoral and inherently inferior to those of the heterosexual. In particular, it will be necessary to intervene in strongly enculturated forms of masculinity and eradicate the association of maleness with masculinist concepts of competition, aggression, and violence and of exploitation and subordination of women and other men. Ultimately, when masculinity and sexuality have been redefined and people helped to understand how their lives could be enhanced without heterosexuality as the institutionalized social norm, homophobia will cease to be functional.

Each of the strategies above has the potential to significantly reduce homophobia in educational settings. The effects of these strategies, implemented in conjunction with antihomophobia teaching modules, should be a priority on the research agenda for combating heterosexism.

NOTE

I express my appreciation to Michael Bailey, Laurel Bornholt, James Sears, Ian Smith, and Walter Williams for their helpful comments and suggestions, and to the administrators, teachers, gay and lesbian panelists, and students who facilitated the research.

1. See Van de Ven, Bornholt, and Bailey, "Homophobic Attitudes and Behaviors," for details of the psychometric properties of the scales, and Van de Ven, "Effects on High School Students," for particulars of the methodology, data analysis, and results of the study. Briefly, the experiment was conducted as a repeated measures, 2 x 2 factorial design, with gender and type of school (coeducational v. single-sex) comprising the factors. Data obtained on five numerically scaled variables were evaluated by multivariate and univariate analyses of variance. Short stories were content analyzed and the results tested for significance using nonparametric statistics (sign tests).

REFERENCES

Berrill, K. T., and G. M. Herek. 1990. "Primary and Secondary Victimization in Anti-Gay Hate Crimes: Official Response and Public Policy." *Journal of Interpersonal Violence* 5:401–13.

Bleich, D. 1989. "Homophobia and Sexism as Popular Values." *Feminist Teacher* 4(2/3):21–28.

Croteau, J. M., and M. T. Kusek. 1992. "Gay and Lesbian Speaker Panels: Implementation and Research." *Journal of Counseling and Development* 70:396–401.

D'Augelli, A. R., and M. L. Rose. 1990. "Homophobia in a University Community: Attitudes and Experiences of Heterosexual Freshmen." *Journal of College Student Development* 31:484–91.

Ernulf, K. E., and S. M. Innala. 1987. "The Relationship Between Affective and Cognitive Components of Homophobic Reaction." *Archives of Sexual Behavior* 16:501–9.

Fassinger, R. E. 1993. "And Gladly Teach: Lesbian and Gay Issues in Education." In L. Diamont, ed., *Homosexual Issues in the Workplace*, pp. 119–42. Washington, D.C.: Taylor and Francis.

Frank, B. 1987. "Hegemonic Heterosexual Masculinity." *Studies in Political Economy* 24:159–70.

Friend, R. A. 1993. "Choices, Not Closets: Heterosexism and Homophobia in Schools." In L. Weis and M. Fine, eds., *Beyond Silenced Voices: Class, Race, and Gender in United States Schools*, pp. 209–35. Albany: State University of New York Press.

Grayson, D. A. 1987. "Emerging Equity Issues Related to Homosexuality in Education." *Peabody Journal of Education* 64:132–45.

Herek, G. M. 1986a. "On Heterosexual Masculinity: Some Psychical Consequences of the Social Construction of Gender and Sexuality." *American Behavioral Scientist* 29:563–77.

— 1986b. "The Social Psychology of Homophobia: Toward a Practical Theory." *Review of Law and Social Change* 14:923–34.

— 1987. "Can Functions Be Measured? A New Perspective on the Functional Approach to Attitudes." *Social Psychology Quarterly* 50:285–303.

— 1989. "Hate Crimes Against Lesbians and Gay Men: Issues for Research and Policy." *American Psychologist* 44:948–55.

Innala, S. M., and K. E. Ernulf. 1992. *The Relationship Between Affective and Cognitive Components of Homophobic Reaction: Three Cross-National Replications*. Göteborg, Sweden: University of Göteborg, Department of Psychology. Göteborg Psychological Reports, vol. 22, no. 2.

Lance, L. M. 1992. "Changes in Homophobic Views as Related to Interaction with Gay Persons: A Study in the Reduction of Tensions." *International Journal of Group Tensions* 22:291–99.

McFarland, W. P. 1993. "A Developmental Approach to Gay and Lesbian Youth." *Journal of Humanistic Education and Development* 32:17–29.

Mason, G. 1993. *Violence Against Lesbians and Gay Men*. Canberra: Australian Institute of Criminology. Report no. 2.

NSW Department of School Education. 1991a. *Resources for Teaching Against Violence*. Sydney: New South Wales Department of School Education.

—— 1991b. *The Values We Teach*. Sydney: New South Wales Department of School Education.

Olson, J. M., and M. P. Zanna. 1993. "Attitudes and Attitude Change." *Annual Review of Psychology* 44:117–54.

Price, J. H. 1982. "High School Students' Attitudes Toward Homosexuality. *Journal of School Health* 52:469–74.

Sears, J. T. 1992. "Educators, Homosexuality, and Homosexual Students: Are Personal Feelings Related to Professional Beliefs?" In K. M. Harbeck, ed., *Coming Out of the Classroom Closet*, pp. 29–70. Binghamton, N.Y.: Harrington Park.

Van de Ven, P. 1994. "Challenging Homophobia in Schools." Ph.D. thesis, University of Sydney.

—— In press. "Effects on High School Students of a Teaching Module for Reducing Homophobia." *Basic and Applied Social Psychology*.

Van de Ven, P., L. Bornholt, and M. Bailey. 1993. "Homophobic Attitudes and Behaviors: Telling Which Teaching Strategies Make a Difference." Paper presented at the annual conference of the Australian Association for Research in Education, Perth, Western Australia (November).

Sue Sattel, Melissa Keyes, and Pat Tupper

Sexual Harassment and Sexual Orientation: The Coaches' Corner

The great American sports machine is an institution that has been called savagely sexist and homophobic (Lenskyj 1986; Kane and Parks 1992). A central element of sport experience for male athletes, their coaches, and often their parents is the reproduction of power and privilege. Many athletes learn to equate manhood and masculinity with attitudes and behaviors that demean and devalue women. In such a sport culture the presence of females is problematic at best and a fundamental threat to male supremacy at worst (Kane and Snyder 1989; Theberge 1987). Occasionally, the balance in power shifts slightly, with legislation and policies, but the culture changes slowly and the problems are complex.

Federal legislation requiring equal opportunity for girls and boys in athletics (Title IX of the Education Amendments of 1972) has made it easier for a girl to be an athlete and not automatically be considered homosexual, but the legislation has done little to change the stereotype that being interested in certain sports (basketball, golf, tennis) or certain sports-related occupations (physical education, coaching) must mean she is a lesbian.[1] In some schools female athletes are expected to dress "like ladies" off the court to counteract the impression that they are too masculine.

Sex-role stereotyping and sexism, glued together by homophobia, have kept progress from being as great as it could be with this legislation. Teachers and coaches must be taught about homophobia and heterosexism and their interconnection with gender equity and sexism (Griffin and Genasci 1990). We can also learn to understand heterosexism through our understanding of the dynamics of racism and sexism (Pharr 1988). Wherever we start—as long as we start—will be OK.

In American schools gay, lesbian, and bisexual students face a barrage of scorn from their peers that results in low self-esteem, vulnerability to addiction, substance abuse, or suicide (O'Conor 1993–1994; Treadway and Yoakam 1992). The school culture actively reinforces societal prejudices, both against student athletes and against hidden gay and lesbian teachers and coaches (Woods and Harbeck 1992). The locker room, particularly the boys' locker room beginning in about junior high school, is a place where behavior that is highly gendered occurs. Mariah Burton Nelson notes that a culture develops whereby nakedness in the locker room is coupled with talk establishing heterosexuality or sexual dominance. This continues into high school, college, and professional sports as players who could speak lovingly of their wife or girlfriend instead speak of dominating women and disparagingly of gay men to prove they are not bisexual (Nelson 1994; Curry 1991).

Sexual harassment and antisexual orientation comments are on a continuum, with sexual harassment and lesbian/gay-baiting on one end of the continuum and molestation, rape, date rape, and murder on the other. Therefore, the practices in the locker room of talking of dominating women and speaking disparagingly of gay men and lesbians must be intervened upon by teachers and coaches (Sattel 1995a). Parents and family members, who reinforce heterosexism in the athletic arena by making it seem acceptable, must be educated as well.

There has been little progress in altering the perception that there are no gays who are athletes. When a boy is younger, he tends to think it is impossible to be gay and be an athlete (Messner and Sabo 1990). Thus, if he is gay, the athlete might dissociate and think of himself as *acting masculine* rather than *being masculine*. Consequently, gay men learn to pass for straight. They feel they must pass as straight to avoid suffering in potentially homophobic settings such as athletic teams and locker rooms.

Similarly, in the population as a whole many gay men and lesbians live isolated lives, out of touch with gay or lesbian culture.

> Their lives are as impoverished as those of their heterosexual colleagues in terms of access to information and research. In the absence of information to counteract the stereotypes, homophobic beliefs are internalized by lesbians and gay men, just as racist beliefs are internalized by people of color and sexist beliefs are internalized by women.   (Griffin and Genasci 1990)

Challenges are being made to this stereotypic thinking. The Gay Games IV in New York, which began with thirteen hundred athletes in 1990, drew eleven thousand competitors in thirty-one sports in 1994 (Dochterman 1994). In Minnesota in February 1995 female high school hockey players held their first tournament. The athletes depicted in the photos and game coverage of the tournament, all suited up, looked surprisingly like the boys we were used to seeing. The struggle for girls to get ice time—let alone equal ice time—had been long and bitter, but there is clearly no going back for these young women. Nor is there a going back into the closet for the gay men and lesbians who can finally integrate their athleticism and their sexual orientation in the gay games athletic events.

One important new tool to alter the harassing culture of athletics and the school is to enforce the laws and policies against sexual harassment. All schools that receive any federal money are prohibited by Title IX of the 1972 Education Amendments from discriminating on the basis of sex. Sexual harassment is a form of sex discrimination that includes verbal comments and harassing behavior between members of the same or other sex. Anti-sexual orientation comments and behaviors are beginning to be included and prohibited under Title IX and the Constitution's Equal Protection Clause (see Seventh U.S. Circuit Court of Appeals on Nabozny 1996). By law, schools must have developed a complaint procedure to handle sex discrimination cases that covers sexual harassment. Many schools include sexual orientation harassment as part of that procedure. In addition, many states have legislation that strengthens Title IX, and many school districts now have policies that specifically address sexual orientation harassment as an interference with equal educational opportunity. The challenge is to enforce these policies.

A coach can play a significant role in changing the culture of the school because he or she plays such a significant role in the life of the athlete. Coaches need to educate themselves and their athletes to a greater sensitivity to the problems of gender violence, stereotyping, and bias. There is no national certification of coaches, and they may have limited knowledge about how power can be used and abused—making education and training more critical (Nelson 1994). Coaches and school administrators need to examine and eliminate from the sport environment all sexist talk, both their own language and that of the athletes. A football coach who uses plays named *date rape, fag right,* or *fag left,* like a wrestling coach who still uses the term *Saturday night ride* for a particular hold, may be accused of violating the law in addition to contributing to a hostile environment for the athlete.

Coaches help athletes work as a team, cut back on drug use, stay out of trouble, and take school more seriously. But they also manipulate in-group/out-group tensions to ensure conformity with a follow-my-orders-and-win personal power approach to control. Some use ridicule, often tinged with homophobia and misogyny, to insure conformity. "One coach hung a bra on a player's locker to signify that the player wasn't tough enough" (Nelson 1994).

Coaches call players "pussies" or "limp wrists" and tell them to "go home and play with your sisters." If coaches are expected to monitor this, they need to realize that they are models after which athletes pattern themselves (Sabo and Panepinto 1990).

Another tangible "benefit" athletes get out of their relationship with the coach is that they may believe they can get away with anything, that "coach will take care of things" if they get caught. Community leaders, law enforcement and school officials often look the other way. Athletes are often held in such high regard that they expect and sometimes demand differential treatment for their transgressions. This causes it to appear as if there were two systems of justice: one an athletic system of justice, used mostly by male athletes, and the other for the rest of the us (Melnick 1992). That dual system can cause some athletes to feel they are invulnerable or "above the law," and perhaps was a factor in the domestic violence exposed in the O. J. Simpson and Mike Tyson trials.

In cases where the coach is a woman, a problem can result for gay and lesbian athletes as well. If the coach's sexual orientation is questioned, her coaching job is made that much more difficult. The problems women encounter as female coaches of mens' teams add to the complexity. They encounter glances and gestures from other teams or verbal references to disgrace—as in "you can't lose to a woman"—and, sometimes, unfair treatment from officials (Fields 1991; Nelson 1994).

The demands of modern living (less family time, fewer community rewards) make it increasingly important that there are coaches willing to put in the time it takes to help a student reach her or his potential. We salute the many fine coaches who are willing to take on this responsibility. We believe that some changes—conscientious changes—will make an even greater difference in the lives of all young athletes.

Models, Techniques, and Strategies

In this section we present a model from the sex equity field as the basis for addressing sexual orientation in athletics and physical education. Sex equity techniques are used because specialists in the field have more than twenty years' experience in talking about an initially unpopular subject—changing sexist behavior—and because there is a clear connection between homophobia and sexism. Homophobia is a very strong technique used to maintain limited sex roles that narrow potential contributions persons can make to society.

We base our proposed strategies on those drawn from sex equity, from sexual harassment prevention, and from antihomophobia work in education. These strategies include assessment, adoption of policies and procedures, raising awareness, inclusionary curriculum and instruction, and support for students. We base our proposed strategies on five principles:[2]

- We can make use of the current trends in education. For example, at this writing most educational institutions are involved in restructuring, which probably includes a goal that all children can learn. If data are being collected to assure that all students are learning, we need to ask questions about nonparticipation and failure in academic and extracurricular areas. Which students are not involved in sport? Why are they not more engaged in school? Is harassment on the basis of sexual orientation one reason why more students are not involved in athletics?
- We can concentrate on behaviors rather than only attitudes: if you can't change their minds, change their mouths. Most people who harass on the basis of sexual orientation can change. However, we also assume that a small percentage of people will never change their attitudes on this issue but may find it difficult to continue their homophobic behavior. We advocate that readers concentrate on those who are eager to change or are indifferent to the issue.
- We must be clear about the link between heterosexist behaviors on the part of educators and the limiting effects of sex role stereotyping. We can point out that by calling boys "sissies," "girls," or "wusses" and girls "jocks" or "dykes" we're taking part in a long continuum that touches on students' career choices, academic success, and even adult relationships.
- We recognize that all students are vulnerable to name-calling and pressure based on sexual orientation, regardless of students' actual orientation. Students who will never be lesbian, bisexual, or gay often feel compelled to act out rigid sex roles on the athletic field or are intimidated because of the subtle or overt behaviors on the part of coaches and other athletes that convey homophobia.

- We cannot assume that *all* parents and *all* coaches are heterosexual, are homophobic, hate gays and lesbians, or have as their greatest fear that their children/athletes might be gay or lesbian (Griffin 1993–1994).

The strategies that follow from these five principles are directed toward athletes of any sexual orientation as well as toward all types of educators.

Assessment of the current situation   Look around the athletic arena. What is happening that discounts, intimidates, or excludes lesbian or gay students? How do coaches, teachers, and other students intimidate any or all students through use of the fear of homosexuality? Is name-calling common? Is it clear that in order to be perceived as a "real" and valued male or female athlete, students must adhere to rigid, exaggerated, and unrealistic sex roles? How are those roles conveyed? Who is *not* a part of the athletic program? Why do some girls prefer to be cheerleaders and members of the pep club, even though they are excellent athletes in physical education class? Why are some boys openly hostile to athletes and coaches? Coaches themselves may want to make use of self-assessment instruments designed to alert coaches to boundary issues that might be interfering with their ability to work effectively with a team or athlete because of sexual harassment. The following is a sample from an assessment instrument, asking for a *yes* or *no* response to each statement.

> I often tell my personal problems to this athlete.
> There is something I like about being in the office with this athlete when no one else is around.
> I find myself making sexual jokes around this athlete (Women's Sports Foundation 1994).

Policies and procedures   Policies currently in place in public schools and postsecondary institutions usually include a statement that the school does not discriminate on the basis of sex (and other civil rights categories) in its programs or practices, as prohibited by federal law. In Massachusetts, Minnesota, and Wisconsin statutes prohibit discrimination on the basis of sexual orientation in public schools and colleges.

> Wisconsin's statutes that prohibit discrimination against students in K-12 and post-secondary educational institutions include sexual orientation as a protected category. The definition of prohibited discrimination for K-12 is "any action, policy, or practice, including bias, stereotyping, and pupil harassment, which is detrimental to a person or group of persons and differentiates or distinguishes among persons, or which limits or denies a person or groups of

persons opportunities, privileges, roles, or rewards based, in whole or in part, on ... sexual harassment ... or which perpetuates the effects of past discrimination." (WI 9.02[5], Wisconsin Administrative Code)

The definition of *harassment* "means behavior toward pupils based, in whole or in part, on ... sexual orientation ... which substantially interferes with a pupil's school performance or creates an intimidating, hostile, or offensive school environment." (WI 9.02[9], Wisconsin Administrative Code)

School districts must adopt policies and procedures, including complaint procedures, that implement the above prohibitions.

There is no reason why schools should not adopt nondiscrimination policies that include sexual orientation as a protected category; indeed many schools, such as the University of North Carolina at Chapel Hill, do state such a commitment. Los Angeles public schools have full inclusion of sexual orientation and gay and lesbian interests in the district's multicultural, human relations, counseling, and nondiscrimination policies. The typical policy statement usually includes the following language:

Make an institutional commitment to teach to all children in every school, a curriculum informed by the principles of gender-equity, multiracial and multicultural knowledge and perspectives, including but not limited to the history and experiences of women, racial, ethnic, and religious minorities, as well as lesbian and gay people and people with disabilities. (Philadelphia Schools: Multicultural-Multiracial-Gender Education Policy Implementation 4.1)

Harassment includes any physical or verbal conduct which is related to a person's gender, sexual orientation, race, color, age, religion, national origin, marital status or disability and which: has the purpose or effect of creating an intimidating, hostile or offensive school environment; has the purpose or effect of substantially or unreasonably interfering with a student's school performance; or otherwise adversely affects a student's school opportunities. (Omaha Schools: Code of Conduct)

Educators presenting a workshop on sexual or racial harassment for coaches and physical educators can include sexual orientation as one of the categories protected by school policy or can mention sexual orientation in workshop activities. School district and university officials report that policies are useful for enforcement of rules designed to prohibit harassing and discriminatory behavior. However, adoption of policies and procedures prohibiting discrimination and harassment on the basis of sexual orientation will not eliminate the problem, as policies alone do not eradicate discrimination. Such policies may exist only on paper, may never be disseminated, or may never be implemented, reviewed, or monitored. Even if no formal policies exist, coaches and physical educators support students by absolutely prohibiting verbal or physical harassment based on sex or sexual orientation during practice, at contests, or in any school-sponsored setting.

We advise school districts to adopt and implement policies that include sexual orientation as one category among others in which discrimination is prohibited, to include bias and stereotyping in the policy's definition of discrimination, to clearly illustrate the type of behavior that is prohibited, giving examples of name-calling that include sexual orientation as prohibited along with racial and other epithets.

Schools report to us that they are successful when they notify parents about school policies that prohibit discrimination and publicize policies that value the contributions of all students and parents, adopt behavior codes for both athletes and spectators that prohibit harassment on the basis of perceived or real sexual orientation and post the code in locker rooms and sports venues, include sexual orientation as a protected category with every other civil rights category (whether or not it is included in state law), and work with state and local athletic associations to make sure that sexual orientation is included in the list of categories under which students are protected in that organization's programs and practices.

> The Minnesota State High School League has adopted a policy prohibiting sexual harassment which includes sexual orientation discrimination. It states that for a first offense of sexual harassment, an athlete loses the right to play in two consecutive games in his or her sport. For a second offense, the athlete loses six consecutive games in his or her sport, and for a third offense, the athlete loses twelve consecutive games (Sexual Harassment Rules and Consequences for Students. Minnesota Statute 129.121, subdivision 6)

Officials feel that this policy is a deterrent to sexual harassment and abuse activities that can develop, such as the notorious Spur Posse in California in which high school athletes made sexual conquest a sport with no consequences to their athletic standing.

Staff awareness programs   In order to move coaches, teachers, and student athletes away from behaviors that perpetuate discrimination and harassment on the basis of sexual orientation, staff and student training programs need to provide a rationale for why behaviors must change, define what is happening that might be biased or harassing, and help people practice new behaviors that are supportive, inclusive, and affirming. Some training is better than nothing, but only long-term training designed to change teacher attitudes produces "significant" change (Keyes 1992; Granberry 1980).

The district is liable for hostile environment sexual harassment in which an official of the institution knew or reasonably should have known of the harassment's occurrence and failed to take appropriate steps to halt the conduct. The Office for Civil Rights, U.S. Department of Education, has issued Letters of Findings on same-sex harassment (such as complaint no. 01–92–1327), and several civil lawsuits are pending on this topic. Dr. Linda Delano, former director of women's athletics at Hamline University, developed and conducted presentations for school district coaching staff in her role as president of the Coalition to Promote Women in Athletic Leadership. Topics in her presentations included sexual harassment, inclusivity, treatment of boys versus girls, responsibilities and ethics, etc. An educational institution that provides staff awareness training for coaches on these topics is minimizing its risk. As with most interventions on this topic, other than anecdotal information and on-site evaluations collected following such workshops, summative evaluation about long-term effectiveness is not yet available. Districts have reported that the climate of respect in their school has improved with active enforcement of the sexual harassment policy and intervention on sexual orientation baiting. Athletes have complained about or objected to coaching abuse with positive results.

> Sharon Euerle, Athletic Director, Mankato West High School (MN), reports that the school's principal meets with each class in the fall to discuss the harassment policy which includes sexual and sexual orientation harassment prohibitions; the athletic director meets with the coaching staff and parents in pre-season meetings to discuss the guidelines and penalties; and the school plays and pepfests are reviewed to screen out cross-dressing and other activities that would make fun of an individual because of gender or sexual orientation. Minnesota statute includes sexual orientation in the string of categories protected from discrimination in educational institutions.
>
> Heidi Keppley, Dassel-Cokato (MN) Public Schools, reports that students who harass on the basis of sexual orientation are suspended using the district's sexual harassment policy just as are students who make other sexual comments as warranted.   (Sattel 1995b)

The cognitive approach is not always successful in overcoming deep-seated stereotypes and misinformation, and sometimes the culture of the school or university mitigates against attitude and behavior change (Duttweiler 1989). Negotiation theory posits that interests are what move people to take their positions in the first place (Fisher and Ury 1981), and an effective stance to take is to focus on the *interests* of the harassers, not their *positions*. Those who are harassing on the basis of sexual orientation may have differing positions but similar interests; for example, both harassers and those being harassed need to feel validated in the school environment and both may recognize that low self-esteem can cause students to disengage from the system. Both may fail to gain vocational and other life skills, be unable to get a job, and fall onto public assistance. However, the victim of harassing comments is more apt to have taken the first step on the slippery slope toward failure.

A number of training programs are available that specifically target discriminatory behavior and either include or may be modified to include behavior change techniques addressing homosexuality. Teachers and coaches have attended staff development sessions designed by the Anti-Defamation League of B'nai B'rith, called "A World of Difference," that help participants confront their own stereotypes and biases and struggle with changing negative attitudes and behaviors. These strategies are shared with students in programs to end sexual, racial, and religious harassment through multicultural education programs and at places adopting the Robbinsdale Public Schools (MN) offensive behavior correction program.

Other techniques for successful, behavior-changing, staff development include

- collecting data on gay/lesbian/bisexual issues in your school, then using the data to develop activities to inform heterosexual students and support homosexual students
- providing workshops on discrimination for coaches, trainers, athletic directors, cheerleaders, bus drivers, custodians, and anyone associated with the interscholastic or intercollegiate athletic program; including sexual orientation and homophobia as a subject in that training
- Breaking the link between athletics and sex roles; finding other reasons for boys' involvement in athletics than proof of manhood; promoting the many reasons girls should be involved in athletics: their academic achievements, maintenance or heightening of self-esteem, avoidance of early parenting, and success in adult life; not reinforcing with male ath-

letes that they are "real men" or with female athletes that being strong and assertive is "not ladylike"

Curriculum inclusion   Sex equity specialists have called for inclusion of sex equity principles in curriculum, instruction, and the educational environment or climate. The Minnesota State Board of Education requires every school to submit a plan for including multicultural, gender-fair, disability-sensitive material and resources throughout the curriculum. Some districts include sexual orientation as part of the gender fairness concept. In this state and others, equity specialists ask that persons who are gay or lesbian be included in athletic training programs and school environment programs. Plays that include gay and lesbian issues are performed to heighten sensitivity. Student athletes can learn that gays and lesbians are not limited in achievement and that success for gay or lesbian athletes would come easier without the exclusionary and harassing tactics used against them. The phenomenal success of Martina Navratilova in tennis and Greg Louganis in diving cannot be disputed even if a coach does not like gays or lesbians.

Another very successful strategy is including in the curriculum courses or units on justice, equity, and prejudice reduction. For example, students at an alternative high school in Madison, Wisconsin, are required to take a full semester that focuses on acceptance and celebration of diversity and prejudice reduction. Homosexuality is part of that school's definition of diversity, and students receive disciplinary action if they harass others on the basis of sexual orientation.

Addressing the history of sport and the sexual orientation of prominent athletes is also helpful. Psychology of sport courses include topics about sexual orientation in sport and history, literature, science, and mathematics and can include contributions of those frequently excluded from the curriculum—persons of color, women, lesbians, and gays. Phyllis Scattergood of the National Resource Center on Gay and Lesbian Youth indicates that equity specialists are finding success in talking with coaches when sexual orientation is included in a list of other groups protected from discrimination, bias, and harassment. Coaches, in turn, can be inclusive when talking about justice, fair play, and team building. Cordelia Anderson, from Sensibilities, Inc., in Minneapolis, is working with the Minnesota Amateur Sports Commission and the National Alliance for Youth in Sports to provide materials and training to reduce coach, fan, and parent abuse of young athletes. Districts are also using material on child-centered coaching and breaking barriers for entering and retaining an interest in sports. These include programs that work for parents and fans as well.

Support for students   Just as sex equity specialists advocate support for "pioneering" students in courses that are not traditional for their sex, coaches and teachers can ask guidance counselors to initiate peer or counselor-led support groups for those accused of being gay or lesbian. Many students may be interested because others have assumed that they are homosexual, not because they actually are. Others have relatives or friends who are gay, lesbian, or bisexual.

> Many school districts in the country (San Francisco, Los Angeles, St. Paul, MN) provide support groups that are counselor and/or peer led. Many educational activities are carried out in the school during commemoration of gay pride events. Additionally, sensitivity to diversity is shown in Central High School, St. Paul, MN, where students designed a button with a pink triangle that says Humans Unafraid of Gays (HUG).[3] It is distributed to students, educators, community members and state agencies.   (Smith 1994)

> In one rural school far from city programs that support lesbian or gay students, the high school guidance counselor made contact with a school psychologist from a city that had a support group for gay students. The educators were able to set up a "pen-pal" arrangement between the students in the two high schools so that the isolation of the rural students was broken and the students could communicate with others going through similar teen struggles with sexuality.   (Interview with Keyes at the Annual Conference of the Wisconsin School Counselors Association, March 1988)

Coaches should assume that any team has gay or lesbian student members. Just as coaches, spectators, and opposing players are sanctioned for name-calling based on race, let everyone involved with the program know that name-calling on the basis of sex or sexual orientation will not be tolerated.

Student athletes and coaches carry enormous prestige in our schools. While much has been written about the benefits of interscholastic and intercollegiate competition, there is a growing awareness of the equity problems associated with high school, postsecondary, and professional athletics as well. Parents, many coaches, community members, and athletes themselves are demanding fair, democratic, and respectful treatment. Those in the field of athletics and sport would do well to address these concerns immediately.

As Mariah Burton Nelson (1994) says: "We need to keep saying that no form of sexual abuse or harassment or discrimination is sporting."

NOTES

An extensive bibliography used to develop this chapter is available from Pat Tupper, Educational Resource Center, Minnesota Department of Education, 550 Cedar Street, St. Paul, MN 55101.

1. There were three hundred thousand female high school athletes in 1971 and almost two and a quarter million, duplicated count, in 1993–1994 according to the National Federation of State High School Leagues.

2. We acknowledge the excellent work that Pat Griffin has completed to lay the foundation (and even the framework) for the strategies in this chapter.

3. Write to G. Ferguson, Health Start, Inc., 640 Jackson St., St. Paul, MN 55101, for information on the Humans Unafraid of Gays (HUG) buttons .

REFERENCES

Curry, T. 1991. "Fraternal Bonding in the Locker Room: A Profeminist Analysis of Talk About Competition and Women." *Sociology of Sport Journal* 8:119–35.

Dochterman, R. 1994. "Games Without Shame: With Painful Playground Memories Still Ringing in Their Ears, Many Gays Are Coming Back to Sports—But on Their Own Terms," *Minneapolis Star Tribune,* June 29, pp. 12A.

Duttweiller, P. C. 1989. "Components of an Effective Professional Development Program." *Journal of Staff Development* 10(2):2–6.

Fields, L. R. 1991. Presentation—Minnesota Coalition to Promote Women in Athletic Leadership, September 28.

Fisher, R., and W. Ury. 1981. *Getting to Yes: Negotiating Agreement Without Giving In.* New York: Penguin.

Granberry, J. E. 1980. "The Effects of Racial and Sexual Awareness Training on the Professional Staff of a Southeastern Michigan School District." Ph.D. diss., University of Michigan.

Griffin, P. 1993–1994. "Homophobia in Sport: Addressing the Needs of Lesbian and Gay High School Athletes." *High School Journal* 77(1/2):80–87.

Griffin, P., and J. Genasci. 1990. "Addressing Homophobia in Physical Education: Responsibilities for Teachers and Researchers." In M. A. Messner and D. F. Sabo, eds., *Sport, Men, and the Gender Order: Critical Feminist Perspectives,* pp. 212. Champaign, Ill.: Human Kinetics.

Kane, M. J., and J. Parks. 1992. "The Social Construction of Gender Difference and Hierarchy in Sport Journalism—Few New Twists on Very Old Themes." *Women in Sports and Physical Activity Journal* 1(1):49–83.

Kane, M. J., and E. Snyder. 1989. "Sport Typing: The Social "Containment" of Women in Sport. *Arena Review* 13(2):77–96.

Keyes, M. 1988. Interviews, Annual Conference of the Wisconsin School Counselors Association, Stevens Point, Wisconsin, March.

—— 1992. *Measuring Changes in Educator Attitudes as a Result of Technical Assistance in Sex Equity.* Ph.D. diss., University of Wisconsin, Madison.

Lakey, D. 1990. "Sexual Harassment in Sports." *Physical Educator* 47(2):22–26.

Lenskyj, H. 1986. *Out of Bounds: Women, Sport, and Sexuality*. Toronto: Women's Press.

Letter of Finding Re: Complaint No. 01–92–1327 involving Nashoba Regional School District, Bolton, Massachusetts, Region 1, U.S. Department of Education, Office for Civil Rights, Boston.

Melnick, M. 1992. "Male Athletes and Sexual Assault," *JOPERD* 65(5):32–35.

Messner, M. A., and D. F. Sabo, eds. 1990. *Sport, Men, and the Gender Order: Critical Feminist Perspectives*. Champaign, Ill.: Human Kinetics.

Nelson, M. B. 1994. *The Stronger Women Get, the More Men Love Football: Sexism and the American Culture of Sports*. New York: Harcourt Brace.

O'Conor, A. 1993–1994. "Who Gets Called Queer in School? Lesbian, Gay, and Bisexual Teenagers, Homophobia, and High School." *High School Journal* 77(1/2):7–12.

Pharr, S. 1988. *Homophobia: A Weapon of Sexism*. Little Rock: Womens Project.

Sabo, D., and J. Panepinto. 1990. "Football Ritual and the Social Reproduction of Masculinity." In M. A. Messner and D. F. Sabo, eds., *Sport, Men, and the Gender Order: Critical Feminist Perspectives*, pp. 119–20. Champaign, Ill.: Human Kinetics.

Sattel, S. 1995a. *Sexual Harassment of Students: Prevention, Intervention, and Investigation*. Frederick, Md.: Aspen.

—— 1995b. Telephone interviews, Winter.

Smith, M. 1994. "St. Paul Schools to Give Gay Students Resources, Support." *Minneapolis Star Tribune*, March 3, p. 1B.

Theberge, N. 1987. "Sport and Women's Empowerment." *Women's Studies International Forum*, 10:387–93.

Treadway, L., and J. Yoakam. 1992. "Creating a Safer School Environment for Lesbian and Gay Students." *Journal of School Health* 62(4):352–57.

Women's Sports Foundation. 1994. *Prevention of Sexual Harassment in Athletic Settings: An Educational Resource Kit for Athletic Administrators*. East Meadow, N.Y.

Woods, S. E., and Harbeck, K. 1992. "Living in Two Worlds: The Identity Management Strategies Used by Lesbian Physical Educators." In K. M. Harbeck, ed., *Coming Out of the Classroom Closet: Gay and Lesbian Students, Teachers, and Curricula*. Birmingham, N.Y.: Harrington Park.

PART IV

Working in Professional Training Programs

Rita M. Marinoble

Elementary School Teachers:
Homophobia Reduction
in a Staff Development Context

Several months after the tragic explosion of the U.S. space shuttle *Challenger* in 1986, one of those small pin-on buttons began appearing at educational conferences around the country. The button, still treasured by many educators, displays the simple but powerful words of schoolteacher Christa McAuliffe, who lost her life in the shuttle accident. The button reads: "I touch the future. I teach."

For most elementary school students the classroom teacher becomes a strong role model, and favorite teachers from childhood are often the subjects of reminiscences in adulthood. Much of a young child's day is spent with one teacher who, at the very least, augments the care and guidance given at home and, in some cases becomes the most stable emotional support in the child's life. Given the power and breadth of their influence, elementary school teachers must be acknowledged as a key group of professionals who can play a vital role in altering the way our nation's schools respond to gay/lesbian/bisexual issues. In order for them to understand their role, however, considerable work must be done in the school setting to reduce homophobia among these teachers. Since staff development activities have become institutionalized in most school districts, this is a logical avenue through which to proceed.

Rofes (1989) suggested that substantive change in schools' approaches to gay/lesbian/bisexual persons and subject matter requires several steps. These include increasing teachers' comfort level with discussion of homosexuality, integration of lesbian/gay/bisexual topics into school curricula, and abandonment of the presumption that all students will grow up to be heterosexual. In this chapter I describe a staff development module incorporating these suggestions. I developed the presentation while working as an elementary school counselor in the San Diego Unified School District.

Setting, Set-up, and Presenter(s)

As with any staff development activity, good preparation is the first step toward success. This section outlines some preparatory information that is helpful to the success of this particular presentation.

In terms of setting, it is optimal to conduct the program at one elementary school site, drawing participants only from that school's staff. This brings an intimacy to the experience that is more difficult to achieve in a larger group or a group composed of persons from different schools who do not know one another. Such intimacy often facilitates discussion of what, for many, is a sensitive or controversial topic. Ideally, all teachers, teaching assistants, clerical personnel, and support staff (e.g., nurse, counselor, psychologist) will participate in the activity. Regarding set-up, the presentation can typically be scheduled as part of a staff development day when students are not in attendance. It is helpful to use a room or area that is spacious enough to accommodate the entire staff and also allows for breaking into smaller groups for discussion. Most of the sessions that provided data for this chapter were held on the school site, but off-site locations can be a good alternative if they are available and accessible.

Variations on these suggestions about setting and set-up certainly can be used without seriously impacting the success of the program. In terms of the presenter(s), however, it is absolutely essential to involve persons who are very comfortable with the subject matter, who have strong skills in group facilitation, and who are prepared for the controversial nature of discussion and questions that may accompany this presentation. McFarland (1993) proposed school counselors as potential presenters of information about gay or lesbian youth, but cautioned that an outside consultant would be a better choice if the counselor is not thoroughly at ease with the subject matter.

Homophobia can be deeply imbedded and highly resistant to change in many individuals. Some participants may believe that elementary schools have no reason to address this topic. Statistically, every audience will include one or more teachers or other staff members who themselves are gay, lesbian, or bisexual and who may be at any one of several points in the coming out process, which includes dealing with their own internalized homophobia. The effective presenter(s), regardless of their own sexual orientation, must be prepared for, and sensitive to, these possibilities in delivering this program. When an openly lesbian, bisexual, or gay school district employee serves as presenter, as in my own case, an increased level of credibility may sometimes be achieved. The most crucial factors, however, are that the presenter(s) be comfortable with the topic and skilled in group facilitation of controversial material.

Three-Phase Module

This staff development module, entitled "Gay/Lesbian/Bisexual Issues in the Elementary School," consists of three phases. Each phase can typically be done in one hour, making the entire module a three-hour experience. The phases are "Conceptual Framework," "Group Discussion," and "Action Strategies." This section explains in detail how I conduct each phase.

Conceptual Framework

Most elementary school teachers relate well to the notion of students at risk. This phase of the module presents a two-faceted conceptual framework that ultimately identifies the gay, lesbian, or bisexual student clearly as a student at risk. I emphasize at the outset that few elementary students fully identify themselves as gay, lesbian, or bisexual in these early years of life. But the subtle, and sometimes not so subtle, awareness of somehow being different is beginning for many of these students.

The first facet of the conceptual framework draws from the work of McCarty (1989) on self-esteem and school success. McCarty suggested a number of important experiences that must take place for a young student to develop and maintain a level of self-esteem that leads to success in school and, eventually, in adult life. These include the experiences of safety, positive identity, and connectedness. Safety involves freedom from physical, sexual, or emotional abuse as well as protection from social ridicule and stressful situations. Positive identity includes feelings of uniqueness and specialness, along with a sense of being important in a good way. Connectedness involves inclusion, acceptance, affiliation, and affection, with particular emphasis on the child's experience of unconditional love from significant adults. I share these basic concepts with participants, writing key phrases on a chalkboard or flipchart.

I then move to the second facet of the conceptual framework, briefly explaining Troiden's (1988) model of homosexual identity formation. This model includes the four stages of sensitization, identity confusion, identity assumption, and commitment. The first stage—sensitization—occurs pre-puberty and thus is the chief area of concern at the elementary school level. While the child holds the more socially acceptable self-image of heterosexuality, there is a growing sense of being somehow different than same-sex peers. For some elementary-age children, puberty begins earlier than usual, and Troiden's second stage—identity confusion—begins to unfold. The child begins to acknowledge feelings that could be homosexual. Intense confusion often results from this altered perception of self and from the stigma and misinformation the child likely has experienced regarding the subject of homosexuality. Again I write some of the key phrases on the board or chart.

After presenting both conceptual perspectives, I compare the key phrases written for each. Such a comparison graphically illustrates the potentially serious issues of self-esteem, school success, and overall life adjustment that face elementary students who begin to experience a homosexual identity. In a homophobic society the early stages of the process of homosexual identity development can significantly erode the solid ground of safety, positive identity, and connectedness that are so important to the child's success. Hence students who are in these early stages must be viewed as students at risk.

Next I solicit questions and comments from the staff regarding the conceptual framework. Since many participants are probably hearing the information about homosexual identity development for the first time, it is especially important, as time permits, to respond thoroughly to questions in this area.

Group Discussion

Following the presentation of the conceptual framework, I break the staff into small groups of four to six people. Group members are instructed to spend about thirty minutes sharing with one another their experiences and views in response to the following two questions:

1. How do you handle the lesbian/gay/bisexual topic when it comes up in your classroom?
2. Would you use (or have you used) instructional materials that incorporate gay/lesbian/bisexual persons or issues?

In terms of the first question, many teachers can recall the occasional student who is teased or taunted by peers as "faggot," "lezzie," or "queer." Sometimes students will ask directly for information about homosexuality from teachers or other school staff. Perhaps students have seen a recent television program that incorporated a gay, lesbian, or bisexual character or topic and they bring their ideas about it into the classroom. Within the small group, participants share with each other their reactions and approaches to these types of situations.

Regarding the second question, I have found that most elementary teachers are unfamiliar with instructional materials that include gay/lesbian/bisexual persons or issues. Furthermore, regardless of familiarity, few teachers are eager to use such materials because of the controversial nature of the topic. The small group portion of this phase is designed to allow teachers to express their anxieties and misgivings in this area and, in some rare instances, their successes with instructional materials. After approximately half an hour, I reconvene the entire staff. The remaining half-hour of this phase is spent in discussion format, processing what took place in the small groups. This includes sharing of participants' comfort levels in talking about the topic with their colleagues. During this time I also facilitate awareness among the participants of the important influence they have, not only in reducing the risk factors for lesbian/bisexual/gay students but also in promoting the acceptance and celebration of diversity among all students.

Action Strategies

In this closing phase of the module I share some ideas and materials, which leads to a group discussion of specific strategies teachers can use to incorporate their increased awareness about gay/lesbian/bisexual issues into the school setting.

Perhaps the most important idea to be conveyed at the elementary school level is the notion that teaching children to respect and value all types of diversity is a basic first step toward improving the way the school, and ultimately the larger society, responds to gay/lesbian/bisexual persons and subject matter. While diversity is most often associated with race and ethnicity, it also encompasses areas such as family configuration, socioeconomic level, the differently abled, and so on. If children learn that differences exist in many aspects of life, and come to view this as positive, they will be better prepared to deal with the specific diversity related to sexual orientation. Many children may not be exposed extensively to issues of sexual orientation in elementary school. Yet it is here that the foundation of values and attitudes must be built that will enable these children to accept and affirm diversity in sexual orientation, in themselves and/or others, as they proceed through adolescence into adulthood.

Next I explain a variety of instructional materials and related references that may be useful to the elementary teacher. Such materials include age-appropriate stories that affirm differences and celebrate diversity, children's books that positively portray a gay, lesbian, or bisexual character, books that inform about important historical figures who were gay, lesbian, or bisexual, and samples of curricula that address gay/lesbian/bisexual issues. It is very helpful to have actual copies of some of these materials available for participants to see.

While it is not within the scope of this essay to provide an extensive list of specific resources, there are two that offer an excellent starting point for anyone interested in gathering materials. First, the National Education Association's Human and Civil Rights Division has developed training information for school personnel entitled "Affording Equal Opportunity for Gay and Lesbian Students Through Teaching and Counseling." For information, phone (202) 822–7700. Second, Alyson Publications has a series of children's books that convey positive images of gays and lesbians, including titles such as *Heather Has Two Mommies* and *How Would You Feel If Your Dad Was Gay?* For these and others in the series, contact Alyson Publications, 6922 Hollywood Boulevard, Suite 1000, Los Angeles, CA 90028.

After sharing these ideas and materials, I work with the teachers in developing a list of action strategies they can immediately begin to use to incorporate their increased awareness about gay/lesbian/bisexual issues into their teaching process. The content of this list varies from site to site depending upon school population, characteristics of the community, level of support from school administrators, and teachers' openness to change. For instance, if a school is racially balanced, the teachers might be more able to connect the action strategies to notions of diversity. Likewise, if a community is particularly conservative, the teachers may not feel able to solicit broad-based support for the use of materials that directly address the sexual orientation issue.

The following is an example of an action strategies list that was developed at a session I conducted in San Diego:

1. Consciously and consistently affirm the inherent worth of each student in the classroom.
2. Actively support a no-tolerance policy for slurs or jokes regarding gay, lesbian, or bisexual persons that occur in the school setting. This applies to students and staff alike.

3. Identify and use instructional materials, such as books and videos, that support the acceptance of diversity.
4. Obtain sample curricula from around the state and/or nation that include the lesbian/gay/bisexual topic. Where feasible, infuse some of the ideas into the school's existing curriculum.
5. Be alert to signs of a sexual orientation issue that may appear in a student. When it seems appropriate, seek help from a qualified professional within or outside the school community in dealing with this student and his or her family.
6. Select a teacher who is interested in serving as a resource person for the school regarding gay/lesbian/bisexual issues in education. Allow this teacher to attend further training in the community and bring current information back to the school site. If possible, have this resource person establish and update an information file to be kept with other staff training materials on the school site. Such a file could include newspaper or magazine articles, school district policy statements, curriculum ideas, and so on.
7. Offer support to any positive change efforts that may be taking place at the school district's policymaking level regarding gay/lesbian/bisexual issues. Such support could take the form of letters, phone calls, oral testimony, or committee participation.

After this list of strategies is formulated, I solicit closing comments or questions from participants. Evaluation forms are then distributed, completed, and left in a designated box near the exit. The evaluation forms used for the presentations reported in this chapter do not require participants to include their names but do request that they identify themselves as "teacher" or "other staff member."

Evaluation Data

A total of 112 teacher evaluations and 48 follow-up interviews provided the data summarized in this section. Although nonteaching staff members also completed evaluations, the data obtained from teachers was compiled separately and is of primary interest within the context of this chapter. The evaluations were those collected at the conclusion of the module. The follow-up interviews were done three to six months after the teacher had participated in the module. They took place in person or by telephone.

Written Responses

A modified version of the school district's standard staff development eval-

uation form provided this feedback. These forms are designed in survey format, requesting both quantitative and qualitative information from participants. Responses in each of these two areas were generally very positive and
encouraging. Quantitatively, teachers were asked to indicate on a Likert-type
scale the extent to which the program had improved their comfort level in
discussing gay/lesbian/bisexual subject matter and to rate the anticipated
helpfulness of the program to their teaching effectiveness. In terms of comfort level, over 90 percent of the teachers indicated "Improved" or "Substantially Improved" as a response. In anticipating the helpfulness of the information to their teaching, about one-third of the teachers responded with
"Very Helpful" and over one-half with "Somewhat Helpful." Thus, only a
very small percentage of the teachers in this survey group had neutral or
negative expectations in this area.

Qualitatively, teachers were asked to share professional insights they had
gained, specific ways they intended to utilize the new information in their
classrooms, and personal reactions to their participation in the module. For
the most part, these responses were very positive, with a few scattered negative reactions. The following excerpts are representative of the many positive
comments received:

- Never thought of these kids as "at-risk" before.
- Would like more info on curriculum materials.
- Awkward at first, but I felt much more at ease by the end of the afternoon.
- Helped me with ideas about how to handle one of my sixth-graders
  whom I believe is already in touch with his homosexuality.
- Realize I've been teaching pretty much with the assumption that all my
  students are heterosexual . . . Oops!!

Some negative responses were as follows:

- There is no way we can use these materials! The parents will protest and
  our jobs will be on the line.
- Too controversial to talk about at the elementary level.
- My religious and moral beliefs conflict with teaching any of these ideas.

The negative responses helped me prepare more fully for future presentations. In one case I located a teacher who had successfully used some of the
instructional materials and had her co-present that phase of the module
with me. Since moral and religious beliefs are extremely sensitive areas, I
simply continued to encourage open-mindedness among the participants.

The preponderance of positive comments made it clear that most of the elementary teachers surveyed, while not entirely comfortable with the subject matter, were receptive to attaining greater awareness and understanding of gay/lesbian/bisexual issues. Delivery and discussion of this topic as a staff development module probably contributed to their openness, since hearing innovative and even controversial ideas in a staff development context is an established professional experience for most teachers.

Interview Responses

The follow-up interviews were conducted to get some sense of the extent to which teachers' actual behaviors and practices were consistent with the written response data obtained on the day of the program. Interviewees were selected randomly from each site where the training had been held. Among the forty-eight teachers interviewed, only three indicated they had, in fact, done little to implement what they had learned from the staff development module. Of the remaining forty-five teachers, thirty-three were able to explain various activities or materials they had incorporated into their classroom. These most often related to diversity in general rather than to homosexuality in particular. For instance, a number of teachers had developed classroom discussions or projects related to books that describe a character who is ridiculed for being somehow different.

Only eight of the thirty-three teachers actually had discussed lesbian/gay/bisexual issues in some way in the classroom setting. These teachers were mostly women, all in the first ten years of their teaching career, who had usually encountered the topic before the staff development activity and generally seemed to be innovative and open-minded in their approach to teaching. Among these eight, three were using one or more of the children's books that convey a positive image of gays or lesbians.

Twelve teachers indicated that they were in the planning stages of implementing some ideas they had gained from the staff development program. These ideas included a classroom study of family diversity that would address families formed by gays or lesbians, a current events assignment that would include lesbian, gay, and bisexual rights as a possible topic, and a discussion of television shows that positively depict a gay or lesbian character.

Two teachers had become politically involved in school district efforts to better address issues of sexual orientation. One of these teachers is openly lesbian and the other is her female colleague who began to see a need for more heterosexual voices in this arena. Several teachers mentioned in some way that they had become much more alert and sensitive to media representations of homosexuality. Others expressed an ongoing desire for more training or information on the gay/lesbian/bisexual topic.

In general, these follow-up interviews revealed that increased teacher comfort level about gay/lesbian/bisexual issues had remained constant or grown since the staff development experience. Implementation strategies, however, were occurring more slowly and with somewhat less frequency than the written evaluations had anticipated. Many teachers shared their continuing anxiety about directly discussing the topic of homosexuality with elementary school students. They indicated that while their own comfort level with the topic certainly was better, they had concerns about parental reactions, student maturity level, and so forth.

Such concerns point up the risk factor that clearly is involved here, and I have begun to incorporate some dialogue about risk taking in subsequent presentations. In addition, it has been helpful to brainstorm with teachers about specific language that can be used to appropriately introduce the gay/lesbian/bisexual topic at the elementary level.

Administrative Support

The school principal is usually the key administrator in terms of getting support for a site-based staff development activity. Although school restructuring efforts have given considerable influence to site governance teams, the principal's support is very important in setting a positive tone for implementation of this module. Higher level administrators are often important role models for principals, so their support is helpful as well. In San Diego, once sexual orientation was added to the district's nondiscrimination policy, top level administrators were required to attend a training session about lesbian/gay/bisexual issues in education. Eventually, all school principals were briefed on the new policy and were encouraged, though not required, to do some site-level education on the gay/lesbian/bisexual topic. The module presented in this chapter was first conducted at a site with strong principal support, and word then spread to other sites that the training was available and helpful.

While no method can guarantee principal support, the following suggestions are offered:

1. Set up a one-on-one meeting between a supportive teacher or other staff member and the school principal. Ask that the principal consider the equity and human relations perspectives that clearly call for schoolwide discussion of lesbian/bisexual/gay issues.

2. Identify supportive administrators in the district and work with them to get the gay/lesbian/bisexual topic on the agenda at a management meeting. Principals usually are required to attend these meetings, which are held regularly in most districts.
3. Solicit support from parents, particularly if the school has an active parent group. Granted, many parents will be far from supportive, but even a small group that is visible, vocal, and convincing can go a long way toward influencing a school principal. Most cities have a local branch of PFLAG (Parents and Friends of Lesbians and Gays) that may be helpful in gaining parent support. Some schools have used PFLAG members as guest speakers at parent meetings, frequently with positive results.
4. Videotape some successful presentations such as the one described in this chapter. Show portions of the tape to a school principal who may be reluctant, offering proof that the topic is, in fact, discussable and interesting to staff at the elementary level.
5. Many local teachers' unions have a human relations component. Urge this group to make the gay/lesbian/bisexual topic visible to principals through articles in district publications, memoranda to school site managers, and so on.
6. If the school district does not include sexual orientation in its nondiscrimination policy, work hard to get this accomplished. Once inclusion is achieved, it provides a persuasive rationale for school principals to provide their staff with information about gay/lesbian/bisexual issues. In many school districts a few supportive administrators are sufficient to get the ball rolling. These people convince others, successful programs are implemented, and word of their success spreads. In districts where administrative support is nonexistent, a module such as this one could be very difficult to conduct and other methods of reaching teachers would have to be devised.

Elementary school teachers have considerable influence in the lives of young people and, by extension, on the future fabric of society. Reduction of homophobia among these teachers is a key element in any realistic plan to overcome heterosexism. The staff development module presented in this chapter represents one strategy that seems to work well with this important group. This module can be used as presented here or adapted as needed by a school site or district. Regardless of how the module is used, it is important to evaluate each presentation and, when possible, to follow up the initial experience with interviews, surveys, or further formal sessions on gay/lesbian/bisexual issues. Ongoing dialogue about these issues, along with implementation of specific strategies at the classroom, school, and district levels, has the potential to substantially change the way our nation's schools respond to lesbian, gay, and bisexual persons and subject matter. Such change is vital in the battle against heterosexism.

REFERENCES

McCarty, H. 1989. *Self-Esteem: The Bottom Line in School Success*. Galt, Cal.: Hanoch McCarty.

McFarland, W. P. 1993. "A Developmental Approach to Gay and Lesbian Youth." *Journal of Humanistic Education and Development* 32(1):17–29.

Rofes, E. 1989. "Opening Up the Classroom Closet: Responding to the Educational Needs of Gay and Lesbian Youth." *Harvard Educational Review* 59:444–53.

Troiden, R. R. 1988. "Homosexual Identity Development." *Journal of Adolescent Health Care* 9(2):105–13.

Patricia Hulsebosch and Mari E. Koerner

You Can't Be *for* Children and *Against* Their Families: Family Diversity Workshops for Elementary School Teachers

It's May and Cora Chalmer's fourth grade class is making Mother's Day cards. They are working at tables in groups of three, and Marita and her aide are walking around the room, helping children decide what to include in their card and writing greetings. Marita comes to one table at which Joseph is making two cards. Marita sees that he's making two Mother's Day cards and asks, "Do you have a mother and a step-mother?" Joseph responds, "No! Two mothers. My mothers are lesbians." Another child, Tinisha, asks, "Ms. Chalmers, what's a lesbian?"

In recent years the need for serious discussion of homosexuality as an equity issue for education has begun to be addressed, but what should a teacher do if something like the above hypothetical situation occurs? Equity professionals and social activists (Grayson 1992; Friend 1993) remind us that "if we truly intend to eliminate oppression, heterosexism and homophobia must be addressed" (Lorde, cited in Grayson 1992:171). Most attention to homophobia and schooling has focused on adolescents; the higher incidence of dropouts, runaways, and suicides among gay and lesbian teenagers is a central issue when arguing for the urgency of a visible gay and lesbian presence in schools (Herdt 1989; Rofes 1989). Homophobia in schooling is highlighted as a significant factor in the mental health of youth who are exploring sexuality during high school years.

It is more difficult, however, to find an explicit discussion of the importance of gay and lesbian issues in the elementary school curriculum. In those instances where there have been attempts to include such discussions in the explicit curriculum of elementary schools (e.g., in the New York City Board of Education "Children of the Rainbow" diversity curriculum and through elementary picture books like *Heather Has Two Mommies*), these efforts have been resisted and/or censored. And yet incidents like the ones at the beginning of this chapter point to the need for all teachers to have an awareness of gay and lesbian members of society and to acknowledge them as part of their students' families and communities. In order to do this teachers must understand the problems created by pervasive homophobia and develop tools to combat them.

(In)Visibility, Difference, and Teacher Responses

At the national and local levels debates rage about what constitutes a "legitimate" lifestyle. These debates affect the people who live out these lifestyles and, increasingly, their children and the teachers of their children. Teachers are being asked to confront their own family values: the feelings, beliefs, and values that shape their teaching and interactions with people who influence their students beyond the classroom. Some of these beliefs are as simple, and, at the same time, as complex as what they and their students define as a "real" family. Today's elementary school teacher is fully aware (but often ignores) that the nuclear family of Dick and Jane fame is no longer typical (if it ever was). Although the changing American family has been with us for awhile, it is only in the last decade that gay and lesbian parenthood has become a visible phenomenon.

If lesbian and gay families have "captured popular imagination," as Lewin (1993) believes, then teachers may have already begun to think about the implications of having children from *openly* gay and lesbian families in their classrooms. Beginning school means moving from the world of the private to the public arena. Schools are often one of the first places in which the lives of children and their families become public and it becomes general knowledge that they or their parents are different from others: i.e., Spanish-speaking, deaf, poor, or gay. Since schools are "the strongest, most active transmitters of mainstream culture" (Martin 1993:322), children whose families don't fit the normative ideal—white, middle-class, able-bodied, heterosexual—are likely to be subjected to stigma based on their difference (racial, economic, or sexual) from that ideal. For children with lesbian or gay parents, common school events, such as making Mother's Day cards (as in the opening "critical incident"), may push them "out in the world."

The ideal school curriculum is both a window to the ideas and perspectives of other people as well as a mirror through which learners can see and understand their own experiences (McIntosh and Style 1988). The current focus on multicultural education comes, in part, from a realization that, for effective learning to take place, school must feel safe. Any place in which one's culture, communty, or parents are devalued or derided cannot be safe for children.

Family diversity workshops are rooted in a particular concept of multicultural education, one that includes not only diversity in the curriculum but also teaches students to take personal, social, and civic action (Grant and Sleeter 1988). Activism is learned through explicit teaching and implicit modeling, both in school and in day-to-day life. Some children grow up in families that teach them ways to advocate for their own experiences and beliefs as well as those of others.

> I started knowing my mother was different when I was five and I started school. A lot of people there were straight, and my mother started to talk to me about how she was different. But it wasn't until I started first grade that I really realized things.... I brought this book to first grade for my sharing day. It's called *Many Mommies.* My teacher had this whole big talk about it. She talked about it. She talked about all different kinds of families. (Serena—2d grade, cited in Rafkin 1990:19–20)

But some families and children do not know how to advocate. Our intent is to help teachers learn how they can take a proactive stance toward heterosexism, sexism, and homophobia and, in turn, teach their students to do the same.

Home-School Interactions

We have found "families," a topic familiar to elementary educators, to be particularly useful in starting a dialogue on issues related to heterosexism and homophobia. While there have long been parents who have left heterosexual for same-sex relationships in which they have then raised their children, lately there has been a surge in the gay community of people who are deciding to begin parenting with their same-sex partner (Weston 1992). "What has changed is the conviction, often reported by older gays and lesbians, that a person should get married or at least renounce gay involvements if he or she wants children" (Weston 1992:169). In the 1970s support groups for gay fathers and lesbian mothers began, and gay periodicals introduced columns that offered advice on child rearing (Weston 1992:165). Although, numerically, adopted children taken together with children from heteroalliances still account for the majority of lesbian and gay parents, during the 1980s the children of artificial insemination (AI) began to overshadow other kinds of dependents (Weston 1992:169). There are an estimated six to fourteen million children having a lesbian or gay parent, and the number will be increasing as the recent wave of babies born from AI and adoption in the gay community enter schools (Singer and Deschamps 1994).

An additional influence has been the gay rights movement of the 1970s, which has led to more gay parents who are "out" or public about their sexual orientation. For some this is a strategy to gain political power and promote self-respect (Weston 1992). Many gay and lesbian parents feel strongly about the importance of being honest about their orientation if their children are to have positive self-concepts and value difference in others. As one author says about her own experiences, "We aren't willing to spend years telling [our son] how great our family is and then say, 'Well, now you can't tell anybody else about it' " (Martin 1993:322–23). There is also more media attention to all aspects of gay and lesbian life, and there are more books on lesbian and gay youth (Herdt and Boxer 1993), children of gay and lesbian parents (Rafkin 1990), parents of gay and lesbian children (MacPike 1989), and lesbian and gay parents (Martin 1993).

Finally, and perhaps most important, there has been a growing understanding in elementary schools that learning must be rooted in the early experiences that children bring to school. More educators are realizing that if children are to grow up prepared to live in a complex multicultural society, more of the diversity represented in the lives of children in today's classrooms must become part of the overt school curriculum.

Although there was a time when teachers and parents came from the same communities and shared values, experiences, and perspectives, nowadays teachers interact with a variety of parents with whom they may have seemingly little in common. Home-school interactions are often challenging and conflictual for teachers (Lightfoot 1978). Yet teachers know that negotiating the goals and processes of schooling with family members is important to quality education. When the subject of interactions with parents comes up among teachers, the discussion frequently becomes animated—often heated—as they describe their concerns and frustrations over these "significant others" in their students' lives (Hulsebosch 1992). We have found educators eager for an opportunity to exchange stories and share ways to respond to parents who are as diverse as their students.

The Family Diversity Workshops

Family diversity workshops begin with a topic of interest to teachers: their students' parents. The workshops assume that teachers want to do what is best for students and proceed from the premise that you can't be *for* children and *against* their families. Just as all children must "see" themselves mirrored in school curriculum (McIntosh and Style 1988), their families must also be accounted for in schools. These workshops counteract heterosexist assumptions by making gay and lesbian family members of children visible in professional discussions on teaching and learning. When lesbian and gay family members become visible in schools, homophobia also becomes visible. Rather than attempting to eliminate homophobia through a workshop, our primary aim is to help teachers support children from every kind of family (including lesbian and gay families) by acknowledging, responding to, and involving all parents in a respectful way.

We have been leading family diversity workshops for the past four years. Our first workshop, a fifty-minute session early one Saturday morning, was the result of an invitation from a planner for a conference for early childhood educators who was developing an antibias strand and wanted to make sure that lesbians and gay men were represented on the program. Since then we have led the workshop for groups of preservice teacher candidates (both undergraduate and graduate), day-care teachers, inservice elementary school teachers, and teacher educators. The preservice education workshops have been held at the urban universities in which we teach as part of the required series of student teaching seminars. The inservice workshops have been at professional conferences for both teachers and teacher educators. The workshop sessions have, so far, been "one-shot," ranging from fifty minutes to five hours in length.

Regardless of whether they're preservice teachers, child-care workers, or experienced educators, the people who attend our family diversity workshops enter the room a bit timidly, not knowing what (or whom) to expect. We know from our past experiences that the participants in the workshop are likely to be a combination of the curious and concerned. Some will themselves be lesbian or gay educators or will have close gay or lesbian friends. Others will be committed to antibias work in general and will be eager to have an opportunity to focus on this, an issue that they have not talked about before in public. Still others will be drawn by the focus on families, since few teachers are at ease with parent-teacher interactions.

In preparation for the workshop we set up a table display of children's books (preschool through sixth grade) representing various configurations of family members, along with a variety of other books (on gay and lesbian educators, for example). We make certain to include fliers with phone numbers for local lesbian and gay resource centers and hotlines. We want to model ways to create an inclusive environment and give participants a sample of the kinds of materials available, at all ages, interests, and levels of background knowledge.

We open the workshop by introducing ourselves, how we came to be doing this workshop, what we plan to do, and why. Credentials and stories are an important part of these opening moments, and some of what we describe are our lives as teachers, activists, feminists, and parents: we represent both heterosexual and lesbian parenting. In describing our own experiences in relation to this work we model our belief in starting from the personal and being openly ideological in the work we do. We elaborate on the biases we bring to the workshop: our belief in the importance of teaching the "whole child" and starting from the "self," moving out to the larger world of ideas, a definition of multicultural education that includes activism, and our commitment to collaborative learning among professionals.

We next include some type of introduction/icebreaker activity. Depending on the length of the workshop, this can vary from something as simple as "Who you are, where you teach, and why you came," to more elaborate exercises like "Concentric Circles" (Blumenfeld 1992:284) in which participants form two circles facing one another. Each person has two minutes to answer first one question, then another, then another. We've used questions such as "What brought me to this workshop?" (if it was a choice); "What do I know about gay/lesbian families?"; "One question I have about gay/lesbian parents." Before continuing, we discuss ground rules that make explicit the need for confidentiality, respect, and speaking from the first person.

We introduce terms commonly used by asking participants to brainstorm the meanings of *gay, lesbian, bisexual, heterosexual, homophobia, heterosexism, coming out, ally, oppression,* and *prejudice.* We use this as an opportunity to begin dialogue about how each of us understands these words and the origins of our understandings. We follow this up with a five-to-ten-minute minilecture on the history of the use of the terms *heterosexual, gay, lesbian,* and *bisexual* to define people and the ways in which all identities are socially constructed (see Katz 1995; Blumenfeld and Raymond 1988).

Critical Incidents

The introductory elements of the workshop are important in laying groundwork and creating a climate of openness and respect. However, at the heart of the workshop are *critical incidents,* which portray issues related to hetero-sexism, sexism, and homophobia.

Critical incidents are brief vignettes (one to three paragraphs) used to illustrate provocative situations or dilemmas. The vignettes are designed to be realistic and down-to-earth so that educators who read them can imagine these situations in their own schools. Although critical incidents lack the rich contextual information of case studies, their brevity and open-endedness enable the readers to fill in details that match their own context and experiences. Often, in the discussions, participants will alter the incidents to match their own experiences. In doing so a context is created in which they can work with colleagues to strategize meaningful solutions to provocative scenarios.

Some of critical incidents tell the story of a child of gay or lesbian parents who, in some way, comes out for the family. Others describe homophobic reactions among school personnel or parents: e.g., in a staffing on a student in which the identity of the students' parents as gay is labeled as part of the problem. Still another tells of a gay father who talks to a teacher about his concerns about being out in school events. In other critical incidents common events that link homophobia and sexism are brought into stark relief. In one incident a boy is told he throws like a "sissy," and in another a student's mother is labeled a "dyke" because she is wearing clothes typically thought of as masculine. Through these stories teachers become aware of a bias to which they had often given little prior thought. For example, one critical incident describes a child who brings in a photo of his two gay fathers as part of an assignment of a unit on families. Some teachers had never considered this as a possibility and had then to decide their responses.

When using the incidents, we sort participants into groups of four to five, aiming for variation among members in gender, experience, and teaching setting. Each group is given two incidents, culminating with questions such as "What do you say?" What do you do?" "What issues does this incident raise?" Groups are given thirty to forty-five minutes to read them over, then problem-solve possible responses. Allowing an adequate amount of time is critical, because many participants are not used to discussing issues of sexual orientation with colleagues, and the groups are often slow to get started. During the small group time we act as facilitators by circulating around the room and sitting in briefly with each group. We sometimes ask focusing questions ("Anyone ever have any experience like this in your classroom?"

"What did you/would you do?") and work hard not to lead the group. However, having consciously "set the stage," we often find that after the "ice" has broken participants are willing to talk openly and honestly about themselves: their own biases ("Honestly, I'm a little nervous talking about this subject"), their past experiences ("There was a father who was transsexual among my day-care parents and I've never had anyone I could talk to about how to discuss it with the children"; "I have a tough time knowing how to deal with parents"), and their sexual orientation ("I am a gay teacher who has been very much in the closet"). In these discussions with colleagues teachers begin to look critically at classroom taken-for-granteds (e.g., that parents are heterosexual) and the ways in which they support homophobia. In the process they become more conscious of what they consider to be normal and how their norms may unfavorably position the children with whom they are engaged in their classrooms. Together they develop alternative strategies that parallel their responses to other forms of bias, strategies such as reading books that depict a wide range of family contexts, talking about characteristics along a continuum rather than one way or another, refusing to accept name-calling of any kind in the school, and encouraging children (and their families) to share and compare their actual experiences.

After the allotted time we ask the groups to come back to debrief their responses. During the whole-group debriefing we freely use chart paper to highlight the issues and concerns that arise: "If I let him put up his picture of his lesbian moms, I'm afraid I'll get in trouble with the principal." "What if other parents notice and say something?" "How often is this likely to come up?" "But would that be considered a real family?" Don't I need to get permission first?" "Isn't first grade (or sixth or eight) too young to discuss these issues?" "I worry that my colleagues will think I'm condoning this kind of lifestyle."

These and similar questions reflect two intertwined concerns that typically arise in connection with the open inclusion of gay and lesbian families in the classroom: "Why is this important?" and "How do I justify including gay and lesbian families in the curriculum, first to myself, and then to the people to whom I am accountable: parents, administrators and colleagues?" The debriefing provides an opportunity for us to emphasize and clarify key issues: the assumption of heterosexuality in students, families, and colleagues, the fear and hatred of sexual minorities in some people, the links between sexism and homophobia, and the price everyone pays for the oppression of any group.

One of the most important ideas to come out of the discussion groups and into the debriefing are the underlying principles that provide guidance for teachers during difficult discussions of provocative topics. What follows are some of the principles participants have talked about relying on:

- It's not possible to be for children and against their families.
- Part of being a professional teacher is to put aside your opinion in the best interest of the child.
- In this classroom we respect people.
- It's OK for different people to value different things, but the overarching value in this classroom is to be inclusive.
- My classroom will be an environment that includes information and resources for all children and their families.
- In order to be inclusive and affirm children, teachers also need to affirm themselves; often this means coming out as a gay or lesbian teacher and/or resisting homophobic actions (like name-calling) or talking honestly and openly about one's value dilemmas.

Remembered Commitments

Not all teachers are committed to eliminating antigay bias at the start of the workshop, and we wouldn't expect that any bias could be eradicated in two—or even twenty—hours. But most teachers are committed to creating a classroom in which all children feel welcome and are thus able to learn to their full potential. Critical incidents present nonthreatening situations that challenge teachers' assumptions, structures in which to discuss the event with colleagues, and means to reaffirm professional ethics by returning to core principles of caring and respect.

If a teacher has a clear rationale for her decisions about classroom practice, she is less likely to feel vulnerable to attack for supporting alternative lifestyles. By asking herself what the effect of her practice is on a child, she has a clearer sense of the right and wrong of common problems like homophobic jokes and name-calling and feels a stronger mandate to name these as hurtful. Teachers participating in the family diversity workshops say the principles they generate in these professional discussions are strong enough to give them courage (and tools) to combat heterosexism and homophobia in their schools.

In a recent discussion on gay and lesbian families in a summer institute a classroom teacher asked, "How often do gay and lesbian issues really come up in a classroom?" The answer might be, "Seldom—unless you see them."

Although biases are often difficult for the biased to discern, we're reminded of the particular invisibility of lesbians and gay men. By introducing gay and lesbian families and creating a place in which teachers can "out" their own struggles to discuss their misconceptions, misinformation and heterosexism, we enlarge the boundaries of who and what is included in elementary education. The result is seeing the whole student in a way that we might not have done before.

Many elementary school educators have within them the starting places needed to be able to combat homophobia in their classrooms. First they must be able to see the homophobia and heterosexism. They must also be able to see the connection between antihomophobia and their professional ethics and guiding principles. Finally, educators need the tools and strategies to be activists in changing their environments. In family diversity workshops educators remind one another of the priorities, concerns, and commitments that brought them into teaching. And, as teachers recommit to these first principles, they realize that they can't be *for* their students without also being *for* their parents (Ayers 1994).

REFERENCES

Ayers, W. 1994. *To Teach.* New York: Teachers College Press.
Barrett, R., and B. Robinson. 1990. *Gay Fathers.* Lexington, Mass.: Lexington.
Blumenfeld, W. J. 1992. *Homophobia: How We All Pay the Price.* Boston: Beacon.
Blumenfeld, W. J., and D. Raymond. 1988. *Looking at Gay and Lesbian Life.* New York: Philosophical Library.
Bowen, A. 1990. *Children in Our Lives: Another View of Lesbians Choosing Children.* Brookline, Mass.: Profile.
Fine, M. 1993. "Sexuality, Schooling, and Adolescent Females: The Missing Discourse of Desire." In L. Weis and M. Fine, eds., *Beyond Silenced Voices,* pp. 75–100. Albany: State University of New York Press.
Friend, R. A. 1993. "Choices, Not Closets: Heterosexism and Homophobia in Schools." In L. Weis and M. Fine, eds., *Beyond Silenced Voices,* pp. 209–35. Albany: State University of New York Press.
Gantz, J. 1983. *Whose Child Cries: Children of Gay Parents Talk About Their Lives.* Rolling Hills Estates, Cal.: Jalmar.
Grant, C., and C. Sleeter. 1988. *Making Choices for Multicultural Education: Five Approaches to Race, Class, and Gender.* New York: Merrill.
Grayson, D. A. 1992. "Emerging Equity Issues Related to Homosexuality in Education." In S. S. Klein, ed., *Sex Equity and Sexuality in Education,* pp. 171–90. Albany: State University of New York Press.
Henderson, J. 1991. *Becoming an Inquiring Teacher: A Caring Approach to Problem-Solving in the Classroom.* New York: Macmillan.

Herdt, G. L., ed. 1989. *Gay and Lesbian Youth.* New York: Harrington Park.

Herdt, G. L., and A. Boxer. 1993. *Children of Horizons.* Boston: Beacon.

Hulsebosch, P. L. 1992. "Significant Others: Teachers' Perspectives on Relationships with Parents." In W. Schubert and W. Ayers, *Teacher Lore.* New York: Longman.

Katz, J. N. 1995. *The Invention of Heterosexuality.* New York: Dutton.

Lewin, E. 1993. *Lesbian Mothers.* Ithaca: Cornell University Press.

Lightfoot, S. 1978. *Worlds Apart: Relationships Between Families and Schools.* New York: Basic Books.

McIntosh, P. and E. Style. 1988. "Curriculum as Window and Mirror." In *Listening for All Voices.* Oakknoll School Monograph.

MacPike, L., ed. 1989. *There's Something I've Been Meaning to Tell You.* Tallahassee, Fla.: Naiad.

Martin, A. 1993. *The Lesbian and Gay Parenting Handbook.* New York: Harper Perennial.

Miller, J. 1990. *Creating Spaces and Finding Voices.* Albany: State University of New York Press.

Noddings, N. 1984. *Caring.* Los Angeles: University of California Press.

Parker, P. 1987. "Gay Parenting, or, Look Out Anita." In S. Pollack and J. Clausen, eds., *Politics of the Heart*, pp. 97–99. Ithaca: Firebrand.

Pharr, S. 1988. *Homophobia: A Weapon of Sexism.* Little Rock: Womens Project.

Pollack, S., and J. Vaughn, eds. 1987. *Politics of the Heart.* Ithaca: Firebrand.

Rafkin, L. 1990. *In Different Mothers.* Pittsburgh: Cleis.

Rofes, E. 1989. "Opening Up the Classroom Closet: Responding to the Educational Needs of Gay and Lesbian Youth." *Harvard Education Review* 59:444–53.

Singer, B. L., and D. Deschamps. 1994. *Gay and Lesbian Stats.* New York: New Press.

Weston, K. 1992. "The Politics of Gay Families." In B. Thorne and M. Yalom, eds., *Rethinking the Family*, pp. 119–39. Boston: Northeastern University Press.

Toby Emert and Lynne Milburn

Sensitive Supervisors, Prepared Practicum, and "Queer" Clients: A Training Model for Beginning Counselors

In this chapter we discuss a specific component, "Counseling with Queer Clients," of the counselor training program currently in place at the Career Center at the University of Texas at Austin. Built into the philosophy of this training is the conviction that queer clients present a diverse and unique range of therapeutic concerns that require specialized skills and sensitivities on the part of counselors (Woodman and Lenna 1980; Hetherington, Hillerbrand, and Etringer 1989). Consequently, with the goal of educating our interns in ways that increase their confidence in working with queer clients and their knowledge about the gay, lesbian, and bisexual subculture, we have designed training sessions that examine four topical areas: sensitivity assessment, the process of sexual identity development, specific counseling concerns for queer clients, and the creation of safe counseling environments.

General Description of the Practicum Program

The program is designed for counseling students who, as part of their graduate degree requirements, must complete a supervised practical experience in a professional counseling setting. We typically select two to four counselor-trainees each semester and provide structured orientation to our facility and general preparation for working with our clients (typically traditionally aged college students). This training, in the form of workshops and discussions, is concentrated in the first three weeks of each semester and includes the "Counseling with Queer Clients" segment. In addition to workshop sessions, we provide weekly individual supervision and monthly conferences during which our staff meets to discuss client cases.

Evaluating Heterosexist Assumptions

Like most students of counseling (Buhrke and Douce 1991), our trainees have frequently had little coursework or practical experience specific to working with queer clients. As a result, they are often anxious about addressing issues related to sexual identity and have subtle (and sometimes not so subtle) heterosexist biases. Through several experiential sensitivity assessment exercises, incorporated into the first week of training, we seek to challenge our trainees' internalized homophobic attitudes.

Activity 1:
Self-Rating on the Kinsey Continuum of Sexual Identity

As a preface to this activity, which highlights one of the seminal studies of sexuality and asks trainees to assess their socialized perceptions concerning sexual identities, we discuss the discomfort most people experience when they talk seriously about sexuality. We then give each participant a copy of the Kinsey Continuum of Sexual Identity, a chart adapted from an illustrative graph in *Sexual Behavior in the Human Male* (See Kinsey, Pomeroy, Martin 1948:638) suggesting that sexual identity ranges from exclusively heterosexual (0) to exclusively homosexual (6), with four gradations in between. We ask trainees to place themselves on the continuum, considering fantasies, dreams, thoughts, frequency of sexual activity, and emotions/feelings.

Processing the Activity   For many of our trainees this experience marks the first time they have considered that sexual identity exists on a continuum. Some find this idea disturbing or threatening—specifically, in our experience, those whose religious views dictate heterosexuality as the only acceptable model of sexual affectation. When this response arises we ask trainees to consider the implications of this reaction for their work with questioning or self-identified queer clients. Several gay and lesbian trainees have used this exercise as a means for coming out to our staff and their peers.

Activity 2:
Neutral Gender Description

To increase the empathy of our trainees to the experience of expending great amounts of energy concealing sexual identity from homophobic acquaintances, we use an activity that asks them to describe a recent "date" without revealing the gender of the person they "dated." We divide the group (usually no more than six people) into dyads; then each partner of the dyad tells a date story employing only gender-neutral language. The listener is given permission to ask probing questions that tempt the speaker to reveal the gender of her or his date. This dialogue continues for approximately five minutes.

Processing the Activity   Most of our trainees express frustration resulting from this activity and surprise at the difficulty they had in using completely gender-neutral terminology. Additionally, most express a newfound appreciation for the difficulties of concealing sexual identity. Many are able, as a result of this exercise, to recognize the significance of listening closely for the ways in which their clients employ gender-related language.

Activity 3:
Guided Imagery

We occasionally ask practicum students, within the context of guided imagery, to imagine themselves waking up one morning as a queer person. In the course of the exercise we explore situations that may be unique: an incident of overt discrimination, interacting in a social setting, how family members may respond to their being out, etc. We may have participants imagine fears that arise as a result of "discovering" themselves to be queer and satisfactions that may exist in that discovery as well. Depending on the sensitivity and maturity of our trainees, we may also include a segment that asks them to imagine a same-sex attraction: what that person may look like, how he or she may respond, what it would be like to have a sexual relationship with that person.

Processing the Activity   This activity presupposes emerging empathy and sensitivity; therefore, we often use it near the completion of training. By the time we introduce it, our trainees have usually begun to integrate some of the ideas they have encountered in earlier activities. Even so, it often engenders complicated responses. Our trainees seem to have the most difficulty in talking about the idea of experiencing same-sex attraction. For many this subject has been regarded as unapproachable for most of their lives. This exercise has evoked thoughtful and provocative discussions without exception each time we have used it.

Providing a Model of Sexual Identity Development

As a follow-up activity to the sensitivity exercises, we incorporate a two-hour session into the second week of training during which we examine Troiden's

Model of Sexual Identity Development (1989). We use this model as a basis of referral throughout the practicum experience and have found that providing a framework for reference lessens the anxiety of beginning counselors as they learn to work with queer clients. As we discuss each stage in the model, we offer sample client situations illustrating specific issues that may be developmentally generated. We offer the introduction to this model in a one-hour lecture and discussion format and then allow a second hour for further questions and reactions.

Troiden's Model of Sexual Identity Development

Troiden proposes that sexual identity development can be viewed as a series of interlocking stages that have identifiable characteristics. Though the linearity of his model may be somewhat problematic, we find that when working with trainees who are mostly unfamiliar with sexual identity development as a process, Troiden's theorized stages are easy to understand and to refer to. (As they expand their knowledge of sexual identity development and their repertoire of effective interventions, however, trainees may be introduced to other theorists' ideas as part of their ongoing individual supervision.)

In what Troiden has termed the sensitization stage, homosexual people begin the process of coming out. At this developmental point, often during prepuberty, children report that they "feel different." Frequently they exhibit stereotypic cross-gender behaviors (gay males may play with dolls, dress up in their mothers' clothes, dislike sports; lesbians may be "tomboyish," like sports, wear boys' clothes, and exhibit more competitive spirit than nonlesbian peers). These unique behaviors often garner criticism from other children and adults, which commonly results in reduced self-esteem, self-hatred, or depression. Most queer children attempt to hide their natural "difference" and adopt more traditional gender behaviors.

To illustrate counseling issues that may be triggered in this stage, we introduce trainees to the scenario of Mark, a gay client whose identity development was likely affected in the sensitization stage.

> As a child, Mark loved to sing and play the piano. When other boys he knew played baseball at school, he sat on the sidelines humming. Though he felt inadequate at sports and did not want to play baseball, he was repeatedly disappointed when he wasn't chosen to play. His lack of athletic skill or interest caused his male peers to tease him. Consequently, he began to withdraw emo-

tionally and to isolate himself. Seven years later, when he entered counseling, he was severely depressed and actively suicidal.

Troiden posits that people move from the sensitization stage to the identity confusion stage, which he suggests usually occurs during late adolescence. In this stage, queer teenagers begin to experience their difference in sexual ways rather than simply as other-gender affiliation. Due to societal messages that their attraction to members of their own gender is abnormal, queer adolescents often attempt to hide their natural feelings to pursue same-sex romantic involvement and try to "blend in" to the heterosexual community. To avoid discrimination, they dissociate from their homosexual feelings and alter their behaviors to appear more "normal" (i.e., heterosexual). This sublimation of the natural self frequently results in anxiety and confusion and internalized homophobia. People in the identity confusion stage often recognize the war going on inside them and usually respond in one of the four following ways.

1. *Denial:* "putting off" dealing with sexual identity confusion. Clients may "lose" themselves in work, academic pursuits, sports, or, possibly worse, indulge in drug or alcohol abuse.
2. *Avoidance:* avoiding interactions with others who are more open about their sexual identity or avoiding contact with individuals who arouse a sexual response.
3. *Repair:* seeking ways to "change." Clients may desperately believe that they are able to become heterosexual with treatment.
4. *Acceptance:* accepting sexual identity. Clients actively seek ways to feel more at peace about their homosexuality.

To illustrate how the characteristics of the identity confusion stage may manifest themselves in a counseling situation, we discuss the case of Alicia, a woman clearly trying to "repair" her sexual identity.

Alicia, a Mexican-American, was raised in a strict, religious home and has the internalized belief that homosexual attraction is sinful. Since she feels a strong attraction to other women, she believes there is "something wrong with her" and she must "change"; otherwise, she believes herself condemned to hell. She enters therapy to "have these 'gay' feelings taken away."

Troiden suggests that in early adulthood (usually early twenties), many homosexual people enter the identity assumption stage, characterized by a tendency to seek connections with others in their subculture. Because of the societal and, frequently, familial taboos associated with same-sex relationships, the initiation into the identity assumption stage, while exciting, is also often terrifying. People usually respond in one of the following ways.

1. *Capitulation*: surrendering to the negative societal view of being "queer."
2. *Minstralization*: adopting stereotypic gay and lesbian behaviors and frequently exaggerating them.
3. *Passing*: attempting to pass for straight in some social circles while acknowledging one's homosexuality to a limited number of people.
4. *Group Alignment*: immersing oneself in the queer community, usually to the exclusion of most heterosexual contacts.

The following case study presents David, a man who has progressed through several levels of development but is still having difficulty assuming his sexual identity.

> David, a twenty-three-year-old, is very active in the gay/lesbian political arena. He also spends most of his free time at gay bars. He has frequent sexual encounters. He has lost contact with his former (straight) friends and, because he "came out to them," he feels disconnected from his family. He enters counseling after having been arrested twice for drinking and driving.

Troiden theorizes that people transition from the identity assumption stage to the commitment stage. At this point people, typically in their mid-twenties, begin to integrate sexual identity into their broader definition of self. Frequently they are in a committed relationship and self-identify as lesbian or gay to nongay/lesbian people. Other issues surface, however: for example, dual career couple dilemmas (frequently both partners in a same-sex relationship work full-time), learned patterns of competition (especially for gay men), issues around children and family, coming out at work, etc.

The situation of Annie and Kris, as described below, illustrates an issue that may appear in the commitment stage.

> Annie and Kris have been in a relationship for seven years and have recently been struggling with the idea of having a baby. Annie is sure she wants a child and is willing to carry the baby; Kris is still uncertain. She has reservations about the societal bias against lesbians having children and is also concerned about choosing a father. The two enter couples' counseling to resolve this issue.

Reactions to the Model   For most of our trainees—regardless of age, gender, or ethnicity—our introduction of Troiden's theory marks the first time they have been offered a developmental model of sexual identity development.

Reactions have been consistently favorable; many of our trainees find Troiden's ideas valuable as they begin to conceptualize sexual identity as a process. For instance, after our discussion of this model, most are able to recognize that if in an initial counseling session a client says he or she does not want to be gay or lesbian, the client may be "stuck" at a particular developmental point and is asking for help in addressing the coming out process. In our discussions of this model gay and lesbian trainees have acknowledged the validity of the experiences suggested by Troiden's stages and shared anecdotes describing difficulties in transitioning from one stage to the next.

Identifying Unique Counseling Issues for Queer Clients

The third element of our training program involves educating our practicum students about some of the specific counseling concerns of gay, lesbian, and bisexual clients. On a surface inspection the guise of the queer client's presenting issues may appear similar to issues any client could present (dissatisfaction with love/intimate relationships, career difficulties, self-esteem problems, for example). The underlying issues (e.g., same-sex romantic compatibility, being "out" in the workplace, sexual identity crises), however, are often highly charged and unique.

To illustrate some of these issues we have developed the following chart. We incorporate a one-hour session, usually during the third week of training, to present this chart to our students and allow them to respond to the content. We emphasize that this chart represents an abbreviated list of critical counseling concerns for queer clients and discuss ambiguities that surround each of the issues outlined. For example, client responses to therapeutic interventions vary tremendously and the list of suggestions we offer is in no way meant to be comprehensive. On the other hand, though each issue cited deserves detailed discussion, this chart provides our trainees specific and valuable information in a succinct manner and offers a place from which we can begin to examine together some of the unique needs of gay, lesbian, and bisexual clients.

Reactions to the Chart   Our trainees usually register initial delight when we present them with the Identifying Unique Concerns of Queer Clients Chart; they like its conciseness and specificity. However, as we discuss the ambiguities that surround each of the issues, they occasionally feel overwhelmed by the amount of information they assume they need in order to

---

FIGURE 1

Identifying Unique Concerns of Queer Clients

Issue/Concern	Developmental Stage	Specific Information for Counselors	Counseling Suggestions
Feelings of shame about gay or lesbian sex	Although lesbians, gay men, and bisexuals may continue to wrestle with feelings of shame about sex throughout their lives, this issue may be especially problematic for clients who are in the sensitization and identity confusion stages.	It is important for counselors to have examined their own attitudes toward gay and lesbian sex and to have thoroughly considered their own sexual identity issues.	Help clients normalize their feelings about sex—to abandon negative messages they have received and replace them with positive, accepting messages. Group work may be especially useful.
Concerns about developing and maintaining monogamous relationships	The struggle with the idea of a monogamous relationship often appears in the identity assumption stage. In this stage lesbians and gays are beginning to connect with other members of the subculture and relationships begin to develop. Many gay men and lesbians continue to struggle with the idea of monogamy throughout their lives.	There may be a cultural bias on the part of many counselors toward strict monogamy, often a strong value in the heterosexual community. Counselors should be aware that in some of the homosexual community this value may not be mirrored.	Assist clients in identifying what they want and need from relationships in terms of monogamy. Explore the kinds of messages clients may have previously learned about monogamy and nonmonogamy.
Desire differences within couple and desire deterioration	Later in the commitment stage—often in primary relationships—homosexual people, like heterosexuals, may begin to notice differences in their level of sexual desire.	Counselors should be aware that gay men, especially, may have difficulty admitting a reduction in sexual desire. Lesbians may need to explore unexpressed anger and issues related to relationship boundaries.	A common error for counselors just beginning to work with queer clients is to deemphasize sex because they (the counselors) are uncomfortable talking about it. Ask clients about sex—what they believe about it and what their experiences have been. Assist clients in identifying what they need and want from relationships and help them learn to ask for that.

FIGURE 1 *(continued)*

Identifying Unique Concerns of Queer Clients

Issue/Concern	Developmental Stage	Specific Information for Counselors	Counseling Suggestions
Career decision making	Although career issues often surface in the identity assumption stage, they may be affected by sexual identity in any developmental stage.	Counselors should acknowledge that certain fields are openly hostile to gays and lesbians and that, especially in the identity assumption stage, clients may disregard their interests, values, and skills and focus on a career field that appears accepting of their sexual identity.	Explore career options, discuss loss issues, address the importance clients place on being out in the workplace. Discuss genuine interests, values, and skills and the impact sexual identity may have on career decisions.
Coming out in the workplace	Probably most evident in the commitment stage, possibly also in the identity assumption stage.	Counselors must have examined their own beliefs about the importance of being out in the workplace to avoid influencing clients' choices.	Help clients identify issues they may have around coming out to supervisors and work colleagues, addressing fears and assisting clients to make an informed decision about their course of action.
Dual career couple issues	Probably appear most in the later stages of identity formation, like the commitment stage.	For gay men, dual career couple issues are often compounded because both men in the couple have likely been socialized to believe that each of their careers should take precedence. Lesbian couples may have difficulty deciding whose career should be predominant because they both feel disempowered about asking for what they need.	Couples therapy may be especially helpful. Address issues of empowerment and entitlement. Consider suggesting group work, specifically a "career couples" group.

FIGURE 1 *(continued)*

Identifying Unique Concerns of Queer Clients

Issue/Concern	Developmental Stage	Specific Information for Counselors	Counseling Suggestions
Coming out to family	Often surfaces as an issue in the identity assumption stage, but may appear at any time in the client's life. Some people never come out to their families.	Counselors must assess the possibility of a bias on their part that clients should come out to their families. There are reasons not to come out to family, and clients need a safe and neutral place in counseling to explore those reasons.	Sensitively explore when/if clients should come out. Role-playing the specific dialogue that might ensue with the family member(s) may be especially useful. Assess family history of responding to crises, e.g., violent reactions, detachment.
AIDS	The issue of AIDS is not, of course, exclusive to homosexual clients, but it is certainly an issue that may appear in all stages. Clients may have excessive fears about AIDS, may have friends or acquaintances who are HIV-positive, or may, in fact, be HIV-positive themselves.	Counselors should, of course, educate themselves about this topic and must take an inventory of their feelings about HIV. It is necessary that counselors working with gay, lesbian, and bisexual clients not harbor false information about this disease, and they should know about community resources and agencies for referral.	Clients in the early stages of coming out and just beginning to have sexual encounters need to be informed about the risks, and clients in later stages will likely have strong reactions to the AIDS dilemma. Like talking about homosexual sex, discussing "safer sex" with clients may be difficult, but if the client does not initiate the topic, the counselor probably should.
Religious Cynicism	May appear in any stage.	Many homosexual people suffer from guilt about their same-sex attraction. This guilt is almost universally related to religious ideologies. Those queer clients who consider themselves religious may feel abandoned by their religion and feel anger at the oppression that comes at them from "religious" people.	Help clients explore their ideas about spirituality and assist them in coming to greater levels of acceptance within themselves. When appropriate, refer clients to religious/spiritual groups who are open in their celebration of homosexuality (for example, the Metropolitan Community Church).

work with someone who is dealing with sexual identity issues. To reassure them, in our discussion of the chart, we pause frequently to clarify, explain, and enhance, and we reiterate that the chart is meant to be a concrete source of referral. We also emphasize that they will not be expected to know or understand all the information presented by the chart immediately, that, like "coming out," learning to work effectively with queer clients is a developmental process.

Creating a Safe Therapeutic Environment for Queer Clients

After practicum students begin to assimilate the information we have offered them about counseling with queer clients, we often employ role-playing techniques as a method of allowing them to practice the skills they are acquiring and to evaluate the progress they are making toward becoming nonheterosexist practitioners. We emphasize that role-playing is about skill building, not critical evaluation. We do not want our trainees to be intimidated; rather, we want them to feel comfortable to experiment and react freely.

In the role-play situations, we, as supervisors, first model an appropriate line of questioning and then allow our trainees to imitate the model. For example, the supervisor initially plays the role of the counselor in the scenario while the trainee plays the client; then the roles are reversed. This modeling allows the practicum student to observe a suitable line of questioning that she or he may then adapt in playing the role of counselor.

The following scenarios illustrate difficult situations that may arise in therapy with queer clients. We discuss each of these scenarios with our students and then role-play appropriate counseling responses. These scripted transactions are based in part on actual client situations and depict dialogues that imply safety, empathy, and openness on the part of the counselor.

Scenario 1:
The Client Admits That He or She Is Gay/Lesbian
in the Counseling Session

If the counselor has been successful in establishing a trusting environment, it is possible that a queer client will bring up the issue of his or her sexuality. When this occurs, we suggest a script similar to the following one.

CLIENT: *I feel like I need to tell you something. It's pretty important in our work together, but I feel uncomfortable saying it to you.*

COUNSELOR: *There's something you'd like me to know about you, but you are a little afraid to tell me.*

CLIENT: *Yep. That's it.*

COUNSELOR: *I'd like for you to be able to say things to me that you think are important to our work. Am I doing something that's making you feel uncomfortable about this issue you want to bring up?*

CLIENT: *No, I feel very safe talking to you. This is such a hard issue for me to talk about with anyone.*

COUNSELOR: *Some things are hard to say—even to ourselves.*

CLIENT: *I think maybe that's it. I'm having a hard time admitting to myself that . . .*

COUNSELOR: *That what?*

CLIENT: *That . . . I'm a lesbian.*

COUNSELOR: *That was really difficult for you to get out wasn't it?*

CLIENT: *Yes.*

COUNSELOR: *Well, I appreciate your telling me. It feels good that you trust our relationship enough to let me know about this issue that's obviously a tough one for you. I want to say that I don't feel any different toward you now than I did before you told me. In fact, I feel that our relationship just got stronger and more honest. How does it feel for you to have said that to me?*

Scenario 2:
The Client Admits He or She Is Probably Homosexual,
But Wants to Change to Become Heterosexual

For some people who are coming out to themselves, it is not unusual to want to "change"—to become heterosexual. Although there are many avenues counselors could pursue in this situation, the following scenario illustrates one line of questioning.

CLIENT: *But I don't want to be gay.*

COUNSELOR: *What leads you to believe you are gay?*

CLIENT: *Well, ever since I can remember I've been fighting this urge to love men. And I hate it.*

COUNSELOR: *How strong is this "urge" for you?*

CLIENT: *Very strong sometimes.*

COUNSELOR: *How strong is it today?*

CLIENT: *On the very strong side. It has been for several months now. That's* what made me finally decide to come to talk with you. Because I don't seem to be able to control it anymore. And there's a part of me that doesn't want to.

COUNSELOR: And a part of you that does? Tell me about that part.

CLIENT: Well, it seems like if I let myself follow these urges and adopt a "gay lifestyle," I'll be giving up everything I ever thought I'd have later in my life—like a wife and children, I mean. My parents and my brother may hate me if they ever find out. Nothing in my future life will look like what I had planned for it to; that scares me. How could I give all that up?

COUNSELOR: It seems like some of your discomfort with the idea that you might be gay is connected to letting go of this dream you've had for what your life would be like.

CLIENT: Yeah, because I'm not just giving it away; I'm also taking it away from my family and friends. They've always had the same ideas as me—that I'd grow up, have a good job, get married, have children—the typical stuff that happens to people. And if I'm gay and none of that happens . . .

COUNSELOR: Let's play for a few minutes with the idea that you are not gay—that you are heterosexual—how would your life be then?

CLIENT: Easier. If I'm gay, it feels like I'm going to be working all my life to help people understand why I am the way I am. I don't want to do that. It'd be so much easier to be straight.

COUNSELOR: Let's open a different door here. What would be some of the good things about letting yourself follow these "urges" to love men you've talked about?

CLIENT: I'd feel relieved, and it'd be exciting.

COUNSELOR: Let's pretend that everyone in the world accepts you as a gay man and you are free to pursue your sexual attraction to men, how might your life look five years from now?

CLIENT: I'd be in a relationship where the man I was in the relationship with was sensitive and caring and adored me.

COUNSELOR: How does it feel to be thinking and talking about those ideas of what your life could be like?

CLIENT: It feels good to be thinking about it, but it all seems unattainable.

COUNSELOR: Let's pretend that today you decide to deny these feelings and live your life as a heterosexual. What would your life be like five years from now?

CLIENT: Rotten. I'd feel trapped, and I don't think I could ever have a satisfying relationship with a woman.

COUNSELOR: That reaction is pretty strong. I need to let you know that, as a counselor, I cannot change your sexuality. Lots of studies have been conducted on the possibilities of changing someone from a homosexual person to a heterosexual one, and, although it's not conclusive, the research indi-

*cates that behavior can change, but the "urges," as you've described them—
the feelings—don't. Just like some people are born left-handed and others
right-handed, some people are born gay or lesbian and others straight.
What's your reaction to that?*

CLIENT: *I think in my heart I know I'm one of those people who was born gay.
I can't be heterosexual, but it sure would be easier.*

COUNSELOR: *I understand how you would feel that way. In our culture it
might be "easier," but not necessarily better.*

CLIENT: *Yeah.*

Reactions to Role-Playing Exercises   In the initial phases of training most of
our practicum students express performance anxiety when asked to role-
play counseling situations. To counter these fears we verbally assure our
trainees that our interest in role-playing exercises is grounded in a belief that
it is a highly effective tool for exploring and practicing new techniques and
rehearsing familiar ones. Additionally, in staff development sessions, in case
conferences, and in supervision our trainees observe our professional staff
role-play with each other, which significantly decreases their anxiety. Many
of our practicum students progress in their comfort level to the point where
they ask to incorporate role-play situations as a routine element of their
weekly supervision sessions.

The activities described in this model of training are usually perceived by
our practicum students to be nonthreatening and frequently engender gen-
uine discussions of heterosexist bias and strategies for addressing the bias.
We find that presenting practicum students with this training provides them
with a theoretical framework on which they can begin to build their knowledge of homosexual identity development and a pragmatic repertoire of
appropriate counseling interventions that increases confidence in their ability to work with queer clients. Coupling the ideas presented in this chapter
with attentive ongoing supervision often allows our trainees to overcome
some of their previous anxieties and to join us in the sensitive fight against
our culture's legacy of heterosexism.

REFERENCES

Buhrke, R. A., and L. A. Douce. 1991. "Training Issues for Counseling Psychologists in Working with Lesbian Women and Gay Men." *Counseling Psychologist*
19(2):216–38.
Hetherington, C., E. Hillerbrand, and B. D. Etringer. 1989. "Career Counseling

with Gay Men: A Developmental Perspective." *Journal of Counseling and Development* 66:144–46.

Kinsey, A. C., W. B. Pomeroy, and C. E. Martin. 1948. *Sexual Behavior in the Human Male.* Philadelphia: Saunders.

Troiden, R. R. 1989. "The Formation of Homosexual Identities." *Journal of Homosexuality* 17(1/2):43–73.

Woodman, N.J. and H. R. Lenna. 1980. *Counseling with Gay Men and Women.* San Francisco: Jossey-Bass.

Elizabeth P. Cramer

Strategies for Reducing
Social Work Students' Homophobia

I would then express my beliefs about homosexual behavior and give her the option of seeking other social workers. . . . I believe homosexuality is a perversion and a deviant behavior.
Graduate social work student

They [lesbians and gay men] have the same problems in their relationships as heterosexual couples do. [I want] to be more understanding to their feelings. [I want] to learn to be more accepting.
Student in undergraduate social work course

The first quotation clearly demonstrates negative attitudes toward lesbians and gay men. The second quotation indicates that the student intends to be more understanding and accepting of lesbians and gay men. The second quote is consistent with social work values and ethics. The first is inconsistent with social work values and ethics, yet there are social work students and professionals who hold these beliefs and behave professionally in a manner that fails to meet the service needs of lesbians and gay men.

In this essay I will describe levels of homophobia among social work students and professionals. In addition, I will discuss inclusion of lesbian/gay content in the social work curriculum as well as strategies to reduce homophobia among social work students. I will recommend methods for addressing lesbian/gay content in social work education. Throughout this essay I utilize case examples from my teaching experience and data I have gathered from undergraduate and graduate students in social work courses.

Homophobia Among Students in
Social Work Courses and Professionals

The nondiscrimination statement in the National Association of Social Workers' *Code of Ethics* (1993) includes sexual orientation, yet social workers continue to practice, condone, facilitate, and collaborate with discrimination on the basis of sexual orientation. Discriminatory behavior on the part of social workers includes refusal to provide services and judgmental responses to clients' disclosures of their sexual orientation.

Few empirical studies have been conducted that assess social workers' homophobia. These studies have resulted in conflicting data, as evidenced by the differences in percentage distributions found in table 1. The four studies depicted in table 1 measured homophobia among social work student and professional populations using the Index of Homophobia (IHP) (Hudson and Ricketts 1980).

TABLE 1

Percentage Distributions of IHP Scores

Studies	0–25	26–50	51–75	76–100	N	Mean
Hudson & Ricketts (1980)[a]	0.04	0.41	0.48	0.07	300	53
Wisniewski & Toomey (1987)[b]	0.04	0.65	0.25	0.06	77	48
Cramer (1993)[c]	0.01	0.08	0.39	0.54	80	74
Oles, Black, & Moore (1995)[d]	.16	38	.30	.07	240[e]	45

Notes:
[a] = Undergraduate students in departments of social work, sociology, and psychology at University of Hawaii at Manoa.
[b] = Master of Social Work professionals in Ohio.
[c] = Multidisciplinary undergraduate students in an introductory social work practice course at University of South Carolina.
[d] = Multidisciplinary undergraduate students in an introduction to social work practice and human behavior course at Texas Christian University and Florida International University and a graduate level human behavior course at Flordia International University.
[e] = 9 percent missing data.

The discrepancies in the mean scores in the studies noted above may be due to such factors as the characteristics of the sample (Cramer's sample was mostly criminal justice majors) and the geographic region of the study (Cramer's study was the only one exclusively in the Southeast). Studies that compare social workers or social work students to other helping professionals or students in similar disciplines show that social work students and professionals are among the most homophobic (DeCrescenzo 1984; Smoot 1991).

There are several reasons why social work students and professionals are homophobic. There is a paucity of content concerning lesbian/gay issues in social work education, with a notable lack of social work-focused literature concerning practice with lesbians and gay men. Social work students and professionals experience societal pressures to be homophobic and/or they feel anxieties about their own sexual orientation. Furthermore, there are few openly lesbian and gay social workers who can be role models and/or sources of support for students and professionals (Dulaney and Kelly 1982).

Inclusion of Content on Lesbians and Gay Men in the Social Work Curriculum

There has been little content regarding gay men and lesbians in social work programs (Humphreys 1983; Newman 1989). Presently, the Council on Social Work Education's accreditation standards require social work programs to include sexual orientation in their nondiscrimination statements and its curriculum policy statement mandates inclusion of content concerning lesbians and gay men (Council on Social Work Education 1992).

Education about gay male and lesbian clients is necessary because students who enter public or private practice are likely to work with lesbian and gay clients (Kahn 1991; Modrcin and Wyers 1990) and are unlikely to have received adequate information about this population before entering social work courses (Newman 1989). Social workers may also have professional relationships with colleagues who are lesbians or gay men.

Educational Strategies in a Southeast University

I have employed several educational strategies to reduce social work students' homophobia, including educational units, course assignments, instructor self-disclosure, and speakers' panels. These strategies have had varying degrees of success. The nature of these educational techniques will be described in this section of the essay and their outcomes will be discussed in the next section.

Educational Units

I designed and implemented a study to determine the effects of a short-term educational unit about lesbian identity development and disclosure in a social work methods course (Cramer 1995a). The sample was six sections of sowk 705, "Foundations of Social Work Practice," at the College of Social

Work, University of South Carolina. This is the first graduate level methods course taken by social work students after they enter the program.

The typical student in this sample of 107 persons was a white, female, southeasterner, thirty-one years of age. Most of the students had no previous human services experience. Over three-quarters of the students were either Baptist, other Protestant, or Catholic, and on average they attended religious services twenty-three times within the past twelve months. Most of the students were raised in working-class or middle-class homes. Their parents, in general, were rated as having low levels of acceptance of lesbians. Over two-thirds and nearly three-quarters of the students definitely know acquaintances who are lesbian and gay men respectively. One-quarter of the sample definitely have close friends who are lesbians; six have lesbian family members. A higher number of students definitely have close friends and family members who are gay men or think they may have acquaintances, close friends, or family members who are lesbians or gay men.

The study measured whether the educational unit influenced students' attitudes toward gay men and lesbians, their knowledge about lesbian identity development and disclosure, and their anticipated professional behavior with lesbian clients. Students' attitudes toward lesbians and gay men were measured by Herek's Attitudes Toward Lesbians and Gay Men Scale (1988). I developed a ten-item multiple choice test, the Lesbian Identity Development Knowledge Measure, to assess knowledge about lesbian identity development and disclosure. Additionally, I developed an instrument (four short case vignettes) to measure students' anticipated professional behavior with lesbian clients—the Anticipated Professional Behavior Measure (Cramer 1995a). The study also examined whether instructor disclosure as lesbian versus instructor disclosure as heterosexual influenced students' attitudes, knowledge, or anticipated professional behavior.

Four class sections (two groups) received a three-hour educational unit. Two classes (the comparison group) were pre- and post-tested and did not receive the educational unit. The educational unit was divided into three main parts: (1) descriptive information about lesbians and gay men using hypothetical stories, (2) models of lesbian identity development and disclosure and their applicability to social work with lesbian clients, and (3) a case vignette discussed in small groups followed by group presentations to the class along with a discussion of the practice skills necessary to work with lesbian clients.

Course Assignments

I have offered assignments that provide students with the opportunity to research and conduct a class presentation concerning group work with lesbians/gay men or a subgroup of lesbian/gay persons (e.g., groups for abused lesbians). In addition, I provide an assignment in an advanced clinical practice course with families, which offers a group of students the opportunity to experience themselves as a hypothetical family with a lesbian/gay member.

Instructor Self-Disclosure

I have disclosed my lesbian identity to students in graduate social work classes that I have taught. Usually the disclosure occurs during a unit on lesbian/gay issues. I wait until trust and rapport has been built with the students and after they know me as an instructor and for the person who I am. I avoid disclosure for the sole purpose of meeting my own personal needs. Before the class session ends I ask the students about their experience with my disclosure and I discuss what it was like for me.

Speakers' Panels

I organized a fifty-minute lesbian/gay speakers' panel in an introductory undergraduate social work course for nonmajors (Cramer 1993). I was both the instructor for the course and the data collector. About one-third of the class members were African American and most of the class grew up in the South. During the class session prior to the panel, eighty students completed the IHP (see table 1).

A diverse group of five lesbians and gay men were recruited for the panel. Two gay men in a couple relationship participated on the panel; one was Hispanic and a professional social worker, the other was African American and worked in a program with youth. There was a lesbian couple on the panel; one was white and an undergraduate student at the university, the other was African American and employed in media services. The fifth panelist was the instructor's former partner (the author did not come out to this class), an African American woman employed as a computer operator at a bank. The panelists were in their twenties and thirties. Three of the panelists had previous experience with being on a lesbian/gay speakers' panel.

Outcomes of Educational Strategies to
Reduce Social Work Students' Homophobia

Previous studies have demonstrated the positive effects of education in reducing students' and professionals' homophobia. This section will describe the outcomes of these studies including those that I conducted.

Teaching Techniques and Educational Units

Generally, education and media have the possibility of impacting students' attitudes toward homosexuality. In a path analysis of heterosexual students' attitudes toward lesbians, educational and media influences were found to be a direct predictor of positive attitudes toward lesbians (Newman 1987). As noted in the introductory chapter, an increase in positive attitudes toward gay men and lesbians by students in human sexuality courses and in training for mental health professionals has been demonstrated (Rudolph 1989; Schneider and Tremble 1986; Serdahely and Ziemba 1984). None of these studies, however, examined the effects of an educational unit on social work students' attitudes toward lesbians and gay men, their knowledge about lesbian identity development and disclosure, and their anticipated professional behavior with lesbian clients.

Results of my research on graduate social work students demonstrated that an educational unit positively influenced students' attitudes toward gay men for those students who received the educational unit from a lesbian instructor. Attitudes toward lesbians were not significantly better among students who received the educational unit as compared to students who did not receive the unit. The improvement in attitudes toward gay men and not toward lesbians may be in part due to the fact that students' pretest attitudes toward gay men were significantly more negative than their pretest attitudes toward lesbians, creating more room for improvement in their attitudes toward gay men. Students who were in the classes who received the educational unit from the lesbian instructor and the heterosexual female instructor showed a higher level of knowledge about lesbian identity development and disclosure than the students who did not receive the educational unit. Perhaps knowledge is the least threatening dimension of the three areas examined. It does not require the student to change deep-seated values or beliefs. Anticipated professional behavior with lesbian clients improved among students in all three groups but was not significantly better among the students who received the educational unit.

The limited effectiveness of this educational unit may be related to the influence of such factors as religiosity, religious affiliation, socioeconomic status, and level of familiarity with lesbians, which were related to students' attitudes. Religion, familiarity with lesbians, region of childhood home, and childhood household income were several of the variables related to anticipated professional behavior. These variables may have a stronger influence on students' attitudes and anticipated professional behavior than the professions' code of ethics.

Course Assignments

Ethnographic research has been one strategy that has been shown to contribute to a reduction in homophobia among social work students (Garrett and Thornton 1994). Ethnographic research involves in-depth, open-ended interviews for the purpose of understanding the person and her or his worldview, direct observations of persons to learn about them in the context of their environment, and analysis of written documents that include literature written by members of that community. Garrett and Thornton have successfully incorporated ethnographic research course assignments in social work practice courses and human behavior and the social environment courses.

Written and spontaneous comments by students involved in course assignments from classes I taught indicate that the combined experiential-didactic format was beneficial and resulted in a unique and profound learning experience.

Instructor Coming Out

There are several benefits to instructor disclosure of lesbian/gay identity, including increasing the visibility of lesbians/gays on campus, connecting with /gay/lesbian students, and dispelling heterosexuals' misconceptions about lesbians and gay men. Instructor's disclosure of gay or lesbian identity is another strategy shown to reduce students' homophobia. Instructor self-disclosure as a lesbian in an advanced social work practice course was evaluated by students as a positive experience (Cramer 1995b). A typical student response to the question "How do you feel about the instructor's level of self-disclosure?" follows: "I was very impressed. She was honest without being unaware of boundaries. She disclosed appropriately after trust and respect were developed. Her disclosures also offered the opportunity for us to grow and learn rather than meeting her personal needs."

The results of instructor self-disclosure as a lesbian lend support to the empirical evidence indicating that students' homophobia can be reduced through interaction with lesbians and gay persons (Croteau and Kusek 1992).

Speakers' Panels

Although studies have shown that speakers' panels have been effective in reducing homophobia (see a review of studies in Croteau and Kusek 1992), there have been methodological limitations to those studies that make it difficult to isolate the effects of the speakers' panel from other educational activities. Detailed descriptions of the actual speakers' panel are rare. Also, most of the studies employed one outcome measure, attitude scales. Croteau and Kusek pose an important question: "What makes a panel effective, for what outcomes, and for which individuals?" (400).

There was an interesting and perplexing dynamic during the panel that I organized. A few of the African American students aggressively challenged the comments made by one of the African American panelists who stated that being black and being a lesbian felt like a similar experience for her and that being black is natural, or who she is, and so is being gay. The class members who challenged this statement felt that being black is natural but being lesbian/gay is not. Some of the white students also agreed, and there was a short, heated exchange in which some of the white students and African American students crossed racial lines to unite in homophobia.

Fifty-nine students completed a postpanel evaluation. About one-half of the students indicated that the panel neither positively influenced their personal nor professional attitudes toward lesbians and gay men. Students' comments about what they learned fell into three categories—positive (57 percent), negative (24 percent), and not anything (19 percent). There were six general themes in the positive category. One of the themes was that lesbians and gay men are normal: "Homosexuals aren't complete weirdos!" Another complimented speakers: "Seem like normal people. They didn't let questions get to them. They were very honest people." Several of the students commented on behavior of fellow classmates that they considered to be rude and disrespectful.

Themes from the negative category centered around religious opinion/argumentation and hostility toward panel members. An example of a typical negative student response was "I am a Christian and do not pretend that I do not commit [sins]. But being gay is a sin, and these people are committing it. I say hate the sin, not the sinner. But I will never say that homosexuality is either right or natural. You are not brainwashed if you are heterosexual. You are natural."

Summary of Educational Strategies

Results of educational units in courses have shown mixed effects on students' attitudes toward gay men and lesbians. Educational units and workshops have been found to improve participants' knowledge about the lesbian/gay population. Appropriate professional behavior with lesbian/gay clients has not been as extensively studied and the results are mixed. This is an area where further research is warranted.

Course assignments, particularly ethnographic research and combined experiential-didactic assignments, have been found to reduce social work students' homophobia. Additionally, instructor self-disclosure as lesbian/gay, within the context of an ongoing relationship in which trust and respect has developed, has been effective in the reduction of homophobia. Instructor disclosure as heterosexual, particularly in the context of a discussion of heterosexual privilege and the instructor's own process of coming to understand and accept lesbians and gay men is an area of further study in which the author is engaged.

Speakers' panels alone have limited effectiveness in reducing students' homophobia. Perhaps this is due to their brief, anonymous nature as opposed to the relationship context of instructor self-disclosure as lesbian/gay. Speakers' panels in combination with the strategies listed above, however, may be more effective.

Students hold different motivations for their homophobia (such as a defensive function, general prejudicial attitudes); therefore, a multimethod educational approach is necessary (Herek 1990). The most powerful educational approach, however, may be positive interpersonal contact with lesbians and gay men (Herek 1990).

The following are several recommendations for educating social work students about lesbians and gay men and reducing their homophobia. This type of effort needs to be broad and inclusive rather than an exceptional occurrence in one or a few courses.

Assessment of homophobia among social work students should occur before their entrance into the social work program through such techniques as face-to-face interview questions and essay questions on entrance applications. Social work programs should consider assessment of such character-istics as authoritarianism and dogmatism as indicators of incompatibility with the ethical guidelines of the profession. Although the profession includes sexual orientation in its nondiscrimination statement, no clear pol-icy has emerged regarding whether colleges/schools can prohibit students' entrance into social work programs based on homophobic attitudes or dis-miss a student from a program because of homophobia. Measurement of students' homophobia should continue while they are in the program and upon graduation.

Measurement of outcomes of educational units that cover lesbian/gay content is essential so that the profession learns what is effective in reducing homophobia and increasing knowledge about gay men/lesbians and skills in working with this population. Attitude scales in and of themselves are not sufficient for such measurement outcomes. Instruments to measure skill acquisition need to be developed as well as additional instruments that mea-sure knowledge about lesbians and gay men and anticipated professional behavior with gay/lesbian clients. The profession may want to consider shift-ing its focus from attitude change to professional behavior since social work students may be resistant to change their attitudes about this population. An educational unit should combine cognitive, affective, and behavioral con-tent and use a multimethod teaching style including experiential exercises, speakers' panels (or instructor disclosure), case studies, discussion, and small group activities.

Finally, this is heartfelt work. Those who are working to reduce homo-phobia need to recognize the psychic and physical energy that is required to educate students. This includes developing the necessary support system to process homophobia reduction efforts. I was recently told that the one expe-rience that changes a person's attitudes toward whaling is when she or he actually touches a whale. Perhaps if social work students could "touch" les-bians and gay men, to experience their undeniable humanness, they would have difficulty hating, fearing, and avoiding them.

REFERENCES

Council on Social Work Education. 1992. *Curriculum Policy Statement: Hand-book of Accreditation Standards and Procedures.* Alexandria: Commission on Accreditation, Council on Social Work Education.
Cramer, E. P. 1993. "Pre- and Postdata on Lesbian and Gay Speakers' Panel."
—— 1995a. "Effects of a Short-Term Educational Unit About Lesbian Identity

Development and Disclosure in a Social Work Methods Course." Ph.D. diss., University of South Carolina, Columbia.

—— 1995b. "Feminist Pedagogy and Teaching Social Work Practice with Groups: A Case Study." *Journal of Teaching in Social Work* 11(1/2):193–215.

Croteau, J. M., and M. T. Kusek. 1992. "Gay and Lesbian Speaker Panels: Implementation and Research." *Journal of Counseling and Development* 70(3): 396–401.

DeCrescenzo, T. 1984. "Homophobia: A Study of the Attitudes of Mental Health Professionals Toward Homosexuality." In R. Shoenberg and R. Goldberg, eds., *Homosexuality and Social Work,* pp. 115–36. New York: Haworth.

Dulaney, D. D., and J. Kelly. 1982. "Improving Services to Gay and Lesbian Clients." *Social Work* 27(2):178–83.

Garrett, K. J., and S. Thornton. 1994. "Helping Social Work Students Overcome Homophobia Attitudes." Paper presented at the Annual Program Meeting of the Council on Social Work Education, Atlanta, March.

Herek, G. M. 1988. "Heterosexuals' Attitudes Toward Lesbians and Gay Men: Correlates and Gender Differences." *Journal of Sex Research* 25(4):451–77.

—— 1990. "Homophobia." In W. R. Dynes, ed., *Encyclopedia of Homosexuality,* pp. 552–55. New York: Garland.

Hudson, W. W., and W. A. Ricketts. 1980. "A Strategy for the Measurement of Homophobia." *Journal of Homosexuality* 5(4):357–72.

Humphreys, G. 1983. "Inclusion of Content on Homosexuality in the Social Work Curriculum." *Journal of Social Work Education* 19(1):55–60.

Kahn, M. J. 1991. "Factors Affecting the Coming Out Process for Lesbians." *Journal of Homosexuality* 21(3):47–70.

Modrcin, M. J., and N. L. Wyers. 1990. "Lesbian and Gay Couples: Where They Turn When Help Is Needed." *Journal of Gay and Lesbian Psychotherapy* 1(3):89–104.

National Association of Social Workers. 1993. *Code of Ethics.* Rev. ed. Silver Spring: National Association of Social Workers.

Newman, B. S. 1987. *Development of Heterosexuals' Attitudes Toward Lesbians.* National Symposium on Doctoral Research and Social Work Practice. Ohio State University, College of Social Work.

—— 1989. "Including Curriculum Content on Lesbian and Gay Issues." *Journal of Social Work Education* 25(3):202–11.

Oles, T. P., B. Black, and L. Moore. 1995. "Acknowledging and Confronting Homophobia Among Social Work Students." Paper presented at the Annual Program Meeting of the Council on Social Work Education, San Diego, March.

Rudolph, J. 1989. "Effects of a Workshop on Mental Health Practitioners' Attitudes Toward Homosexuality and Counseling Effectiveness." *Journal of Counseling and Development* 68(1):81–85.

Schneider, M. S., and B. Tremble. 1986. "Training Service Providers to Work with Gay or Lesbian Adolescents: A Workshop." *Journal of Counseling and Development* 65(2):98–99.

Serdahely, W. J., and G. J. Ziemba. 1985. "Changing Homophobic Attitudes Through College Sexuality Education. In J. P. DeCecco, ed., *Bashers, Baiters, and Bigots: Homophobia in American society,* pp. 109–16. New York: Harrington Park.

Smoot, L. R. 1991. "Homophobia Among College Students Majoring in Engineering, Physical Education, Psychology, and Social Work." Master's thesis, California State University, Long Beach.

Wisniewski, J. J., and B. G. Toomey. 1987. "Are Social Workers Homophobic?" *Social Work* 32:454–55.

Mollie M. Wallick and Mark H. Townsend

Gay and Lesbian Issues in
U.S. Medical Schools: Climate and Curriculum

In June 1993 the American Medical Association (AMA) added the words *sexual orientation* to the group's nondiscrimination bylaws, thereby banning discrimination against lesbian, gay, and bisexual (LGB) doctors in its membership. The resolution had been considered—without a favorable vote—on four prior occasions. What is the current climate for LGBs in *undergraduate* medical education, using official nondiscrimination as a barometer?

In this chapter we explore the climate in U.S. medical schools and continue with a report of available support services, curricular treatment of homosexuality at our school and throughout the United States, and students' affective responses toward gay men and lesbians. We conclude the chapter with a discussion of ways to address antigay bias in academic medicine.

To determine how frequently sexual orientation is included as a protected category, we surveyed deans of U.S. medical schools in early 1994 (Wallick, Townsend, and Cambre 1995), asking whether or not specific categories were afforded protection in an institutional statement. Of 126 schools accredited by the Liaison Committee on Medical Education (LCME), representatives of 97 schools (76.9 percent) returned a completed questionnaire. While 95 percent or more of the schools included race, handicap, color, national origin, age, and religion in their list of protected categories, about two-thirds included veteran's status and sexual orientation (only one-half included marital status).

Large schools were somewhat more likely than small schools to ban antigay discrimination in a formal statement. (For purposes of comparison, the designation of school size was based on the criterion used in a prior survey [Townsend, Wallick, and Cambre, 1991].) A stronger trend was noted in private schools, which were more likely than public schools to have a nondiscrimination policy. By region, protected inclusion was most likely in the Northeast and North Central region.

Support Services for Gay and Lesbian Students

In our earliest research in the area of LGB issues in U.S. academic medicine (Townsend, Wallick, and Cambre 1991), we assessed supportive programs by surveying self-identified LGB students at the 1990 annual meeting of the American Medical Student Association (AMSA), through its standing committee on Lesbian, Gay, and Bisexual People in Medicine (LGBPM).

Respondents were anonymous, except for their gender, medical class level, and school; of seventy-two students, thirty-one were female. Responses were from thirty-one states and the District of Columbia, representing sixty-one of the sixty-eight U.S. schools with LGBPM chapters.

As was true at private schools regarding sexual orientation as a protected category, LGB groups, too, were found most often in private institutions, reflecting more support of the administration perceived by their students. Also reported more frequently by private school students were access to a gay group in the community and availability of faculty to discuss LGB issues. Similarly, there is an apparent relationship between supportive programs and nondiscrimination policies based on school size: a large school (with more students than the mean of the sample's class size, 136.6) was more likely to have an LGB group, and students in a large school were more likely to have access to a group in the community.

Access to support groups—both in the community and institutionally based—was more likely in the Northeast and West; LGB groups were more often official in the North Central region and in the Northeast. Within the school setting support groups were either student- or university-organized and included students from a single school or several area schools. Some groups were affiliated with national organizations, for example, LGBPM or the American Association of Physicians for Human Rights, the multispecialty organization for LGB physicians and their supporters that changed its name on National Coming Out Day to the 1994 Gay and Lesbian Medical Association. The typical function of a student group was described as socialization and discussion. All LGB respondents expressed a desire for a support group at their schools, if none existed, with men more likely than women to value the group's official recognition. "Fear of being openly gay" was indicated most often as the reason for a support group's nonexistence.

Faculty with whom to discuss LGB issues were more available in the Northeast. Students were informed of such faculty members most often by word of mouth, with only 7 percent of faculty having an official title related to this role. With one exception (a man), the students without an LGB student-faculty liaison expressed a desire for an identified liaison.

Only 6 percent of the students considered the programs at their schools already adequate. Of those responding, most believed that their undergraduate medical experience would be improved if the school provided social and support groups and if there were openly gay and lesbian faculty. Others asked for an official nondiscrimination policy and the imposition of negative sanctions for homophobic comments or acts.

Homosexuality: Academic Treatment in the United States

Among the areas assessed in our survey of support services (Townsend, Wallick, and Cambre 1991) was the way in which the institution addressed the subject of homosexuality. Most students cited lectures in human sexuality as the method most frequently used; they indicated their preference that gay issues be addressed within all courses, along with their desire for meetings with LGB physicians and patients. Results of our initial study stimulated further exploration of how *faculty* responsible for presenting information on homosexuality view the topic's academic treatment (Wallick, Cambre, and Townsend 1992). While students at different levels of training are necessarily limited in their perspective of the entire curriculum, we thought it likely that faculty would have a more inclusive view.

In June 1991 we distributed a questionnaire at the annual meeting of the Association of Directors of Medical Student Education in Psychiatry (based on the conventional wisdom that the topic is most often included first in behavioral sciences and later in the psychiatry clerkship). Each director was asked whether another department presented information on homosexuality and, if so, to identify the appropriate contact person(s) for follow-up.

Of 126 LCME-accredited medical schools, representatives of 82 (65 percent) completed the questionnaire, with responses received from 38 states and the District of Columbia. While large schools (137 or more students) and small schools were almost equally represented, more responses came from public than from private schools.

No significant differences were found on the basis of class size or the public-private dichotomy. However, schools with sexual orientation as a protected category and those located in the West devoted nearly twice as many hours in addressing LGB issues than those located in other regions of the country or without a nondiscrimination policy. (Geography was apparently independent of category status, since protected inclusion of sexual orientation was *less* likely in the West than in the Northeast and North Central region.)

Consistent with the earlier student survey, the most frequently reported instructional strategy was lecturing in human sexuality, once again followed distantly by panel presentations and meetings with LGBs, both health care providers and others. Faculty were asked to specify other methods used in presenting information on homosexuality; eleven directors cited small-group discussion. Only one person reported gay and lesbian issues as integral to most current teaching (the preference expressed earlier by the students). Eight respondents indicated the subject's total absence in the curriculum, a disturbing finding, identical in percentage to the students' prior report. One director stated that homosexuality was addressed only in the context of illness related to human immunodeficiency virus (HIV); in all, twelve respondents indicated the topic's treatment in discussion of HIV.

We invited the respondents to propose other ways in which the topic might be addressed. Several stated that, in general, LGB issues should be discussed more widely. Some suggested the use of case material involving LGB patients throughout the curriculum. Others asked that LGB patient care be taught in each clinical rotation, including ways to perform sensitive histories and physicals. Two directors expressed their desire to reduce antigay prejudice but did not offer a specific method to accomplish this.

We were able to match students' responses (from our earlier study) with those of faculty at the same school in thirty-nine instances; response agreement between the two groups was 70 percent across all teaching strategies. In cases in which a director's report of a utilized strategy contradicted the corresponding student's report (19 percent), it is likely that the student had not yet been exposed to the method but would be, later in his or her training. More difficult to explain were the infrequent cases (11 percent) in which a student indicated a particular strategy's use—e.g., case vignettes in medicine rotation—in contradiction to a negative report by a faculty member. Perhaps such occurrences represented the latter's lack of knowledge concerning the subject's academic treatment by another department; this possible lack of knowledge was one limitation of the study, since we surveyed only psychiatric faculty, unless directed elsewhere.

Homosexuality:
Curricular Treatment at Louisiana State University
School of Medicine–New Orleans (LSUSM-NO)

For the past decade at LSUSM-NO, three hours of the first-year behavioral sciences course have been devoted to the topic of homosexuality. During the first two hours a brief lecture is followed by a panel presentation by lesbian and gay physicians who are available later to answer questions posed by class members. Additionally, invited parents of lesbians and gay men—members of the local chapter of Parents, Friends, and Families of Lesbians and Gays (PFLAG)—are introduced so that questions may also be addressed to them. The final hour is a small-group discussion (eight to nine students with a group leader) to deal further with the topic in "safer" surroundings.

The opening lecture on biological foundations of sexuality is given by a neurophysiologist; the presentation includes neurohormonal theories of sexuality, along with evidence of genetic and anatomical contributions to homosexuality. The panelists are introduced immediately after this brief lecture, and their presentations are divided into two forty-five minute segments. In the first the panelists relate personal information about themselves; in the second round they discuss how they treat LGB patients. An often highly spirited question-and-answer session concludes the two-hour classroom portion.

The content of the panelists' remarks varies from year to year, as do the panelists themselves. Usually, the physicians describe their own coming out process, which may include how their families reacted to news of their homosexuality and how the LGB physicians reconciled their sexuality with their religious faith. One presenter relates how his grown children dealt with his homosexuality acknowledged in mid-life. Another describes feelings of isolation she experienced as one of the few women students at her medical school: she assumed there were no other lesbians in medicine. Still another panelist reports her perceived need to be circumspect about her orientation during residency and shares her feelings upon overhearing antigay remarks. Customarily, during this first hour, one of the panelists informs the audience of local resources available to LGB students, including support groups and social organizations.

The second half of the presentation varies with the panelists' medical specialties but always includes taking a comprehensive nonjudgmental sexual history, along with organized psychiatry's changing views on homosexuality over the years. The panelists often use this time to present issues in lesbian and gay health, such as the higher rates of suicide in LGB adolescents and of breast cancer in lesbians and the relationship between homophobia and sub-stance abuse in lesbians and gay men.

The question-and-answer portion of the class, too, has varied in content from year to year. Students often have questions about the biological data in the opening remarks; this may be the easiest material for them to discuss, especially in a large classroom setting. Perhaps it is not surprising that stu-dents at a deep southern medical school are disturbed at times by the pan-elists' reference to religion, either to reports of their church's unfavorable reaction to their sexuality or, conversely, to a panelist's continued and enthusiastic church membership. Over the years many emotionally laden questions have been raised regarding such remarks by panelists. Additional discussion, often sparked by questions of fellow students, occurs in the sub-sequent small groups.

As the class is leaving for small group seminar rooms at the conclusion of the two-hour session, panelists are frequently surrounded by students with additional questions. At times lesbian and gay students use this opportunity to introduce themselves and to initiate mentoring relationships. Some LGB students have acknowledged the panel as the catalyst in their decision to come out in medical school. Occasionally students approach panelists with pejorative comments; such rare negative remarks are usually couched in guarded terms, such as "I'll pray for you."

The more intensive working through of feelings that arises when students are confronted with LGB colleagues or patients occurs in the highly interac-tive small groups, facilitated by a departmental faculty member or resident. The group leaders have reported a wide range of experiences in this third hour, from confrontational discussions regarding the normality of homo-sexuality to groups in which LGB students disclosed their sexuality and were open to questions from other students.

Group Affective Response Toward
Homosexuality at LSUSM-NO

Recognizing that attitudes affect not only the quality of health care but patients' and physicians' comfort as well, we explored the group affective response toward homosexuality of the 1991 entering class at LSUSM-NO on three occasions during the students' first year (Wallick, Cambre, and Townsend 1993) and once again during their junior year (Wallick, Cambre, and Townsend 1995). Of interest was the possibility of group attitude change following exposure in the middle of the first year to the panel and small group discussion described in the previous section and, later, following the clinical experiences afforded by third-year clerkships.

Males represented 66 percent of the 186 matriculants, all Louisiana residents, who ranged in age from eighteen to forty-two years, with a mean age of twenty-two and a half years. The class was comprised of 146 Caucasians, 18 African Americans, 14 Asian/Pacific Islanders, 7 Hispanics, and one American Indian. The majority of the students attended Louisiana schools as undergraduates; there were two students with Ph.D.s and one with a master's degree. While no information as to students' religion was available, the Roman Catholic Church has extensive influence in south Louisiana and Baptist denominations predominate in the northern part of the state.

We asked the students to complete the Index of Attitudes Toward Homosexuals (IAH) (Hudson and Ricketts 1980) on the first day of the behavioral sciences course at the beginning of the school year, at the end of the first semester (two weeks after the panel on homosexuality), at the end of the academic year, and during the required third-year psychiatry clerkship. Because their responses were anonymous, students could choose not to participate or could withdraw from the study with impunity at any time.

Of 186 first-year students, 180 completed the IAH at the beginning of the academic year. Participation dropped only minimally at mid-year, but more precipitously at year's end; 185 students completed the IAH during their third year. We attributed the attrition in class participation at the end of the first year to the gradual decline in class attendance frequently lamented by medical educators. Resistance to continuation in the study could not account for the lower attendance, since the students were unaware of when the IAH would be administered. It was somewhat reassuring that the person proctoring the questionnaire reported her impression of full participation of students on all occasions.

Table 1 demonstrates a decrease in group homophobic attitude over time, with the reduced mean score at mid-year continuing its downward trend at the end of the academic year, though rebounding somewhat by junior year. By combining the upper two categories in table 1, a 10.4 percent decrease in the number of students rated homophobic can be seen from the beginning to the end of the freshman year; the overall junior year decrease, when measured from the initial administration of the index, was 6.9 percent. However, in spite of noted declines, the group mean score remained in the "low grade homophobic" category throughout the three-year study.

TABLE 1

Attitudes of Medical Students Toward Homosexuality Before, After, and Following 1991 Panel Discussion and at Conclusion of Psychiatry Clerkship

| | First Year | | | Third Year | | | |
| IAH Category | Before | | 2 weeks After | | 5-month Follow-up | | Conclusion of Clerkship |
	% N		% N		% N		% N
High homophobic	27.2	49	23.2	39	17.5	20	20.5 38
	74.4				64.0		67.5
Low homophobic	47.2	85	45.2	76	46.5	53	47.0 87
Low nonhomophobic	21.7	39	25.0	42	29.0	33	27.6 60
	25.6				36.0		32.5
High nonhomophobic	3.9	7	6.6	11	7.0	8	4.9 9
Class participation (N = 186)	96.8	180	90.3	168	61.3	114	99.5 185
Mean score on IAH	62.2	58.8	56.8		58.3		

All but two of the twenty-five IAH items showed varying degrees of decline in homophobic attitude over the course of the first year. After two years all but two item means remained lower than the initial measurement. Many of the IAH items that changed significantly following baseline appear to reflect the content of the panel presentation itself and offer strong support for this educational method.

Addressing Anti-Gay Bias in Academic Medicine

Although an official policy adopted by almost two-thirds of responding schools suggests that academic medicine is beginning to address antigay bias, we consider this merely an appropriate starting point. Students also need assured access to sensitive advocates, faculty mentors, and official support groups.

At LSUSM-NO one successful way to ensure students' awareness of support services has been the appointment of an official Faculty-Student Liaison for Gay and Lesbian Issues (MMW); the students are informed of the liaison and of community groups in their matriculation packet. Although such liaisons exist at only a handful of schools, they may be of great assistance to gay students, providing counseling and reassurance and directing them both to potential faculty mentors and to peer and community support. At our school, for example, the liaison's role has included working with students toward the goal of self-acceptance, dealing with the dilemma of selectively revealing or concealing sexual identity, residency selection, relationship issues, a forced outing to the dean, and HIV status. At other schools some LGB students indicated their preference for a gay student-faculty liaison, but more important in their judgment is that the liaison is readily accessible, that confidentiality is assured, and that students cannot be identified as gay merely by waiting outside the liaison's office.

At some schools LGB students, too, provide support to their peers and also educate their heterosexual counterparts concerning homosexuality. For example, members of LGBPM at Temple University, along with faculty and administrators, wrote "A Community of Equals: A Resource Guide to the Gay and Lesbian Community," which is distributed to all students, residents, and faculty (Office of Student Affairs, Temple University School of Medicine). The guide book describes LGB services throughout the region and instructs students in providing more sensitive healthcare; it has been adapted for use by several other medical schools. Some gay students—at Temple and elsewhere—participate in panel presentations in an attempt to increase awareness of LGB issues.

But, more often, gay students remain closeted throughout their training. The pressure to conceal their sexual identity in medical school can be intense, most often beginning with the application process itself: applicants are often unwilling to reveal their orientation, fearing that homosexuality may diminish their chance of acceptance. Once enrolled, LGB students find themselves in a milieu that discourages individual expression (Knight 1981)—a milieu in which the students' solidifying sexual identity may come into conflict with a professional socialization process emphasizing conformity. As a result, many LGB students do *not* come out and, instead, remain isolated and alone, concealing not only their identity but significant relationships, activities, and accomplishments as well.

The fact that gay students are discouraged from revealing their sexual identity imposes many barriers to their full inclusion in the medical school culture. One of the most potent is that LGBs are often presumed not to be present. This heterosexist presumption can change only if gay students make themselves known—a daunting task, considering that medical students often depend solely on their peers for companionship and support. Coming out is made even more difficult by the circumscribed way in which LGB healthcare is treated in undergraduate medical training. In U.S. schools patients in case studies are rarely identified as lesbian or gay; if a patient's sexual orientation is mentioned, it is most often in the context of AIDS. By the same token, specific health care needs of LGB patients are seldom noted.

The implication of this omission in undergraduate training is that gay students' existence is unimportant and their concerns irrelevant. Does this oversight nurture a sense of alienation among LGB medical students? Recently, Tjia (1993) surveyed students at a national medical meeting and found that LGBs were more likely to have used mental health services and to have performed less well academically during the school year; while perhaps not true of all LGB students, the results are nonetheless disturbing. Other studies (Mosbacher 1993; Schatz and O'Hanlan 1994) suggest that being either closeted or openly gay while in medical school may exact an emotional price.

Discussion

In our curricular surveys of LGB issues in academic medicine faculty and students agreed that the topic of homosexuality was taught essentially through lecturing in human sexuality, followed only distantly by panel presentations and meetings with gay men or lesbians. One faculty respondent proposed the need for "an acceptable, less threatening way to teach (the topic)." We speculate that this apparent discomfort in discussing LGB issues may be due to lingering association of homosexuality with deviance and psychopathology. Alternatively, it may be related to its frequent inclusion in instruction regarding HIV, thus linking gay identity—and not high-risk behavior irrespective of orientation—with a frightening pandemic illness.

We consider it likely that the marginalization in the curriculum reported in our surveys trivializes the topic's importance in the minds of both faculty and students. (It is unfortunate that, at our medical school as well, LGB patient care—other than in the case of HIV—is mentioned rarely outside of our course.) A bold innovative approach is needed, perhaps implementation of a curriculum that focuses exclusively on homosexuality, such as one proposed by Stein (1988), representing the American Psychiatric Association Committee on Gay, Lesbian, and Bisexual Issues. Included are objectives, suggested topics and content, instructional approaches, strategies to stimulate further teaching, and selected references. Clearly stated is the committee's philosophy that instruction *not* be restricted to sexuality:

> Such isolation of content tends to reinforce stereotypes about gay men and lesbians as hypersexual and diminishes the importance of other aspects of gay male and lesbian identities and lifestyles. When teaching about homosexuality does occur in the context of courses on sexuality, it should be presented as a normal variation of sexual behavior (5).

The curriculum suggests the inclusion of specific topics in regularly scheduled seminars and lectures on homosexuality and the presentation of gay
men and lesbians "as visible patient and faculty models in order to confront
stereotypes and overcome prejudice" (5).

In evaluating our study of students' attitudes toward homosexuality, we
acknowledge that attitudinal change is multifactorial: it occurs throughout
medical school, as a consequence of maturation, acculturation, and a multi-
tude of environmental and educational influences. A further limitation of
our attitudinal research is its lack of generalizability to other schools, especially those in other regions of the country. (A reevaluation at Columbia
University [McGrory, McDowell, and Muskin 1990] of an earlier study at the
University of Mississippi of medical students' attitudes toward AIDS and
homosexual patients [Kelly et al. 1987] effectively documents the impossibil-
ity of generalization. Based on differences in the students' demographic
characteristics and in their interaction with LGBS, the New York City
researchers' predictions of markedly contrasting attitudes at the two schools
was proven accurate.) But in spite of inability to attribute causation and to
generalize results, we were nonetheless encouraged by our findings. While
we expected a decline in the students' mean score on the IAH shortly after the
panel and small group discussion, we were pleased that the diminution not
only maintained but continued to decline throughout the first year. We
interpret the rebound effect demonstrated during the third year as an indication that much more curricular emphasis on diversity is needed each year
for the diminution in homophobia to continue over time—and, indeed, to
maintain at a reduced level.

We have opened the closet door on sexual orientation in academic medicine
by exploring issues of climate and curriculum as viewed in the 1990s by medical students and faculty throughout the United States. Based on our
research and on our own experience, we propose that *all* medical schools
ban antigay discrimination in a formal statement and that *all* schools
approve both an LGB student-faculty liaison and an official support group.
Further, we recommend that students' interaction with lesbians and gay men
be assured, along with frequent small-group discussion focused on LGB
issues. Finally, we endorse the recommendation of students in our initial
research (shared by three faculty members in our subsequent study) that
teaching about the care of gay and lesbian patients be wholly integrated
throughout the curriculum, from the basic sciences and introductory clini-

cal courses through the full range of clinical experiences. Only when faculty members' and students' sensitivity and comfort with LGB issues are enhanced will future physicians' stereotypical attitudes regarding sexual orientation be further attenuated.

REFERENCES

Hudson, W. W., and W. A. Ricketts. 1980. "A Strategy for the Measurement of Homophobia." *Journal of Homosexuality* 5:357–72.

Kelly, J. A., J. S. St. Lawrence, S. Smith, H. V. Hood, and D. J. Cook. 1987. "Medical Students' Attitudes Toward AIDS and Homosexual Patients." *Journal of Medical Education* 62:549–56.

Knight, J. A. 1981. *Doctor-to-Be: Coping with Trials and Triumphs of Medical School*, pp. 39–56. New York: Appleton-Century-Crofts.

McGrory, B. J., D. M. McDowell, and P. R. Muskin. 1990. "Medical Students' Attitudes Toward AIDS, Homosexual, and Intravenous Drug-Abusing Patients: A Reevaluation in New York City." *Psychosomatics* 31:426–33.

Mosbacher, D. 1993. "Alcohol and Other Drug Use in Female Medical Students: A Comparison of Lesbians and Heterosexuals." *Journal of Gay and Lesbian Psychotherapy* 2:37–48.

Schatz, B., and K. O'Hanlan. 1994. *Anti-Gay Discrimination in Medicine*, p. 21. San Francisco: Report of the American Association of Physicians for Human Rights.

Stein, T. S. 1988. "A Curriculum for Learning About Homosexuality, Gay Men, and Lesbians in Psychiatric Residencies and Medical Schools." Paper presented at the annual meeting of the American Psychiatric Association, Montreal, Quebec, June.

Tjia, J. 1993. "Assessment of the Effects of Sexual Identity Confusion on Academic Performance." Paper presented at the annual meeting of the American Association of Physicians for Human Rights, Portland, August.

Townsend, M. H., M. M. Wallick, and K. M. Cambre. 1991. "Support Services for Homosexual Students at U.S. Medical Schools." *Academic Medicine* 66:361–63.

Wallick, M. M., K. M. Cambre, and M. H. Townsend. 1992. "How the Topic of Homosexuality Is Taught at U.S. Medical Schools." *Academic Medicine* 67: 601–3.

—— 1993. "Freshman Students' Attitudes Toward Homosexuality." *Academic Medicine* 68:357–58.

—— 1995. "Influence of a Freshman-year Panel Presentation on Medical Students' Attitudes Toward Homosexuality." *Academic Medicine* 70:839–41.

Wallick, M. M., M. H. Townsend, and K. M. Cambre. 1995. "Sexual Orientation and Nondiscrimination Policies." *Academic Medicine* 70:2–3.

Suzanne Iasenza

Educating Criminal Justice College Students About Sexual Orientation, Homophobia, and Heterosexism

Racism and homophobia are real conditions of all of our lives in this place and time. I urge each of us here to reach down into that deep place of knowledge inside [him]herself and touch that terror and loathing of any difference that lives there. See whose face it wears.
Audre Lorde, "The Master's Tools Will Never Dismantle the Master's House"

Teaching college students about diversity is a challenging and necessary business in this place and time. Homophobia and heterosexism are categorical newcomers and, for some, inappropriate additions, to definitions of diversity. Despite reports of increasing violence toward persons perceived to be lesbian or gay and the numbers of our youth who contemplate suicide because of societal mistreatment of sexual minorities, many educators abdicate their responsibility to raise these issues in the classroom. If only we may idealistically rely upon our educators, as Sears (1992) suggests, to reduce heterosexual (and race, gender, and class) hegemony.

College students preparing for careers in criminal justice may especially benefit from education about sexual orientation, homophobia, and heterosexism. Knowledge of the history and nature of harassment of lesbian and gay people by police provides students with a context within which to understand the wary or hostile attitudes of some lesbian and gay citizens toward law enforcement officers. Corrections officers are faced daily with managing rising numbers of prisoners with AIDS and HIV, some of whom are homosexually active. Forensic psychologists and social workers in our hospitals and courts need to know how to work therapeutically with lesbian and gay youth, couples, and families who come to them in crisis. Lawyers may well be engaged by lesbian and gay people for help with wills, adoption of children, child custody, or incidents of discrimination. As in some other large urban areas, the criminal justice professions are becoming more openly integrated with heterosexual and homosexual personnel, and in some instances, as in the case of the New York City Police Department, lesbian and gay people are actively recruited. This calls for increased knowledge, understanding, and acceptance among people of various sexualities.

In this chapter I will describe the cognitive and experiential materials and strategies I have used over an eight-year period teaching about sexual orientation, homophobia, and heterosexism to undergraduate students preparing for careers in criminal justice. The curricular strategies mentioned here are cumulative, having changed and developed over the eight years I have developed personally and professionally in relation to the subject matter and in response to student feedback. I also have included, where appropriate, additional strategies used by colleagues that have proven to be useful.

Description of Student Population and the Course

The students who I teach reflect the diversity of the student population at the college and within the New York City area, where most of the students reside. Over half of the students are female. About one-third of the students are African American, another one-third are Latino, about one-quarter are white, with the remainder being Asian. Most of the students come from lower-income families and are the first generation in their families to attend college.

We have a broad age range of students, with a third of the students twenty-five years or older. John Jay College has one of the largest and most active programs for students with disabilities, including services for people with learning, physical, and emotional disabilities. One-fourth of our students are criminal justice professionals who are returning to college to advance their careers.

As I will describe later, I have planned the curriculum of the course to utilize the perspectives that a multicultural group can offer. The course described in this essay is the first part of a two-semester course that provides peer counseling training and practicum experience to students. The course has attracted a diversity of students—part-time criminal justice professionals as well as full-time students—who are interested in learning interpersonal skills to help with human problems. Students must apply for entrance into the course, have at least a 3.0 grade point average and thirty college credits, submit a recommendation from a professor, and attend an interview. Each class begins with eighteen students. Over the past eight years approximately 140 students have completed the course.

The general objectives of the course are twofold. First, I strive to give the students the necessary knowledge and skills to provide academic and personal counseling to their peers. Second, my aim is to help students become aware of and to develop "the person" who is the counselor, striking a balance between the "doing" and "being" of the counseling endeavor. More specifically, in relation to diversity issues, my aim is to help students develop critical thinking skills, nonjudgmental self-awareness and analysis, and an appreciation for differences in people's histories, identities, and subjective realities of race, ethnicity, gender, class, religion, sexual orientation, and degree of able-bodiedness.

Creating the Context

In his paper on antihomosexual attitudes Gregory Herek (1994) describes the choice of the majority of lesbian and gay activists to shift from liberationist strategies to reformist strategies in an effort to change public opinion about homosexuality over the past twenty years. People tend to be more responsive to the notion of lesbian and gay people's rights as a minority group (reformist position) than to the need for surpassing gender and sexual restrictions and achieving our inherent bisexual potentials (liberationist position).

I, too, have found the reformist position the most useful in reaching the students I teach, especially considering the strong religious beliefs of many of the students. For students who have been raised predominantly within strict Muslim, Catholic, or Baptist family traditions, accepting lesbian and gay people as anything other than sinners is more likely possible if viewed as a human rights issue (i.e., loving thy neighbor) than a sexual rights issue (the prohibitions against most things sexual within these traditions are universally known).

A second reason why a reformist position is more useful is because of the racial diversity of my students and the emphasis on multicultural perspectives in curricula at the college and across the nation at this point in history. By the time students enter my course, most have taken the required race and ethnicity course that is part of the core requirements and/or have encountered race and ethnicity content in other coursework. Many know of the importance, even if reluctant, of examining the existence and effects of racial and ethnic inequalities in American society. Most of the students of color in the class are knowledgeable and articulate about the struggle for social justice for nonwhite people around the world and are quick to quote Malcolm X, the most popular of the civil rights leaders for many of them. The reformist position, that of basic civil rights for a minority group, is familiar to them and a struggle with which they can identify. Although some students of color express resentment toward any analogy that is made between black civil rights and gay/lesbian civil rights, the discrimination they have suffered often creates an openness to the pain of other oppressed people.

Finally, the reformist position that I present in the course compliments the theoretical underpinnings of client-centered counseling theory that is presented in the course. The theory emphasizes the need for authenticity, unconditional positive regard for the client, and the belief that the client possesses the necessary inner wisdom and resources with which to work through problems and achieve self-actualization. This stance as it is applied to working with lesbian and gay clients forces students to confront assumptions and judgments about sexual orientation that may hinder the therapeutic alliance.

It is within this context of a racially and culturally diverse group of students who have chosen to take a course that is about helping people that the topics of sexual orientation, homophobia, and heterosexism are presented. They are interwoven with issues of counseling and multicultural experience, emerging as natural parts of the fabric of living. Throughout many years of teaching about sexual orientation I have found it most impactful when the topics are made personally and professionally relevant, finding the unique entry points for a particular group considering the historical and cultural context.

Creating the Classroom Environment

It is essential to create a safe classroom environment when teaching course content that is especially sensitive and emotionally evocative. Class begins with an icebreaker that permits the professor and students to share some information about themselves. People sit in a circle throughout the semester to foster interaction and an atmosphere of intimacy. We discuss ground rules, which include speaking one at a time, respecting different perspectives, confidentiality, and attendance and punctuality. I also introduce the process of "going around the circle," in which every person is invited to say something on a particular topic. This encourages equal participation. Students are free to pass their turn to speak if so desired. The general expectation is that students and the professor are committed to fostering an environment where people may self-disclose and share opinions without judgment or attack. Students are reminded of this commitment as needed throughout the course.

Having created both a viable context and a safe environment, the work of teaching about sexual orientation, homophobia, and heterosexism may begin. In the next sections I will describe the ways that I integrate sexual orientation into the coursework through written assignments, group discussions, small group exercises, role plays, and creating opportunities for personal contact with lesbian and gay people.

Written Assignments and Group Discussion

One of the requirements of the course is to read articles on various topics related to counseling and mental health issues and to write a two- to three-page reaction paper in which students express their thoughts and feelings about the topic. Students read one article and write one reaction paper per week. After students have handed in their papers, a class discussion is conducted on the material. The papers in the first few months of class are about counseling various groups of people (i.e., "Counseling African Americans," "Counseling Latinos," "Counseling Lesbians and Gays," etc.). These papers serve as the springboards to examining students' feelings and experiences about similarity and difference, stereotypes, and prejudice.

Cannon (1990) argues for the need to develop specific ground rules for class discussions about race, gender, sexual identity, and class. Through trial and error I have come to appreciate the importance of providing a conceptual framework that facilitates students' ability to grapple with these very complex and emotionally demanding topics in a constructive way. The writings of Katz (1985), McIntoch (1989), and Lorde (1977) have been found to be particularly useful for this purpose.

These articles provide some basic working premises that facilitate class discussion (Iasenza and Troutt 1992).

1. Prejudices are learned and are embedded in institutional structures and processes   This involves discussing the origins of prejudice, how families, media, and other structures in society develop and perpetuate false images and beliefs about members of our own groups and those of others, and how we internalize and project those beliefs. We explore how "the other" gets constructed, by whom, and for what purposes. For example, I discuss how the construction of the notion of a homosexual minority who threatens family values allows the heterosexual majority to position itself as superior. Students must agree to neither blame the victims of oppression nor to blame themselves for the inaccuracies about people that result from these systems of oppression. We discuss who benefits from prejudice, exploring the notion of privilege and how denial of prejudice or passivity about everyday injustices perpetuates inequality.

2. Prejudicial beliefs, attitudes, and behaviors can be modified through self-examination and experiences with others   It is important for students to identify the experiences in their lives that have created certain assumptions and stereotypes as well as to feel that there are concrete and personal ways to diminish their own prejudices and those of others.

I introduce the notion of racial identity development (Helms 1990) to help students appreciate the process and characteristics associated with different stages of identity development and expand it to include sexual identity development. I do this by first writing Helms's stages of black racial identity development and white racial identity development on the blackboard. As we review the stages of racial identity development, including stages of denial of one's blackness or whiteness, denigration of one group or the other, overidentification with one group or the other, ending with an appreciation of all racial groups, I give examples from my own life of when I had experienced different feelings about black people and my being white. I then ask students to consider what stages they have experienced, how different stages felt to them, and how they would feel dealing with persons who are in different stages of development. Helms's work is most helpful in normalizing feelings associated with race and dismantling the dichotomous thinking that one is either prejudiced or not. It allows students to appreciate the process of working on one's prejudices rather than having to deny them. After examining Helms's model, I introduce Cass's (1979) model on sexual identity development to present the notions of stages and process as they relate to sexual orientation.

3. Prejudices are interrelated. People who are prejudiced toward one group tend to be prejudiced toward other groups.   We discuss the experience of majority-minority group membership, the difficulties of belonging to more than one minority group, the degrees of prejudice we may feel toward one group or another, how we justify prejudice toward one group more than another group, and the tendency to make hierarchies of oppression (the can-you-top-this competition between groups about who has been more oppressed).

4. Prejudice limits the experience of those who hold them.   We are all hurt by prejudice in society. We explore the personal and professional losses involved in maintaining our prejudices and not challenging those of others—how personal relationships are limited and professional competency is compromised. I ask students, some of whom are already employed in criminal justice professions, to recall job incidents that they felt involved prejudice and how these affected them.

One police officer discussed an incident in which fellow heterosexual officers made jokes about a gay officer in their unit. He stood by and listened, laughing along with them. He didn't feel guilty about his behavior until several months later when he learned that some of the officers in the unit went too far with their antihomosexual sentiments by turning off their walkie-talkies when the gay police officer was on the streets, an act of harassment that put the officer's life in jeopardy. He felt that such prejudice not only affected the gay officer but endangered the morale and cohesiveness of the whole unit.

No matter what particular subspecialty students major in within criminal justice, law, police science, forensic psychology, or corrections, they tend to be career-oriented, concerned with issues of justice, and anticipate dealing with diverse collegial and client populations. They know that public service careers like those in criminal justice require highly developed human relations skills and that alleviating intergroup tensions will often be part of their work.

I find that students with these career interests respond best to techniques and interventions that connect the class material to on-the-job situations. For example, when we discuss an article on counseling gay men, I ask students to identify what parts of the article would be helpful in working with gay counselees, gay prisoners, a gay-bashing incident, or a domestic dispute between gay male partners. Providing a career focus motivates them to explore and discuss difficult issues that ordinarily most would avoid.

Group discussions of these premises are lively and generate a variety of feelings including anxiety, defensiveness, sadness, anger, confusion, guilt, as well as a variety of psychological defenses such as denial, projection, avoidance, and minimization. Many students share personal stories of rejection and pain due to prejudice. Some share their remorse and shame about participating in cruel or unfair behaviors. Most students pay attention to racial or ethnic issues, ignoring issues of sexual orientation. This is most obvious in the way that students write and speak about the 1977 Lorde article, one in which she discusses the challenges of being a black person, a woman, and a lesbian. This article is read and discussed along with the McIntoch article. Most students discuss McIntoch to the exclusion of Lorde. Those who do discuss Lorde focus more on her race or gender than on her sexual orientation.

Lorde's article is useful in helping black students examine resentment they may have about analogies sometimes made between the struggle for black rights and the struggle for gay rights. Black student resentment often stems from two sources: (1) the belief that skin color is an essential part of identity whereas sexual orientation is a choice and (2) the fact that skin color as opposed to sexual orientation is obvious. Gay people can pass as heterosexuals whereas black people have no defense against discrimination. I encourage students to identify the different challenges and privileges associated with skin color and sexual orientation. It is important to acknowledge differences between race and sexual orientation while challenging students to consider Lorde's basic premise that there are no hierarchies of oppression as well as having them consider Lorde's dilemma of managing both a black and a lesbian identity where she experiences race and sexual orientation as equally important aspects of her identity.

It is easy to collude with students in avoiding the topic of sexual orientation, a topic that often creates anxiety or hostility. However, the use of articles that are read, responded to in writing, reviewed by the professor, and then discussed in class provides many entry points for raising the issue. Sometimes I will begin a class discussion by sharing my reactions to their papers. So, for example, I may wonder out loud why so many students did not write about Lorde's challenges as a lesbian. Or, when an article doesn't address sexual orientation directly but may be applied to it, I expand its usefulness. For example, after students read, write about, and discuss McIntoch's article, which deals exclusively with privilege based on race, I give them an assignment to make a list of examples of other types of privilege, including heterosexual privilege. Finally, I spend time making comments and asking questions on students' written assignments. Some students use the writing assignment to express feelings that they do not want to share in class. These usually include extensive negative feelings about homosexuality or their own experiences with same-sex relationships.

Student's Questions About Homosexuality

In-depth discussion about sexual orientation occurs after students read and write their reactions to two articles, one on counseling lesbian women (Browning, Reynolds, and Dworkin 1991) and one on counseling gay men (Shannon and Woods 1991). Students usually have many questions and issues about homosexuality and, though anxious, welcome the opportunity to discuss them. Below are the most common questions that arise from group discussion.

Are people born gay or influenced by some (negative) experience?
Do people become gay (especially lesbians) because they have been rejected or hurt by the other sex?
How does someone know if he/she is gay?
Can people become gay because of exposure to gay culture?
How can I accept homosexuality and not lose God?
How can homosexuality be OK when my family is so negative about it?
How can homosexuality be normal when only a man and a woman can have children? How do gay people have children?
Why do gay people have to flaunt their sexuality (by coming out)?
If it's a choice, why would someone choose to be gay? What could possibly be good about being gay?
How can I provide good counseling with a gay or lesbian person if I do not believe that homosexuality is right?

Over the years group discussion of these questions has differed greatly, depending on the amount and type of experience students have had with gay and lesbian people. Those who have gay and lesbian friends or who are openly lesbian/gay have often grappled with many of these issues and serve as coeducators with the professor. I utilize these students as coeducators by asking them to share their experiences about having gay and lesbian friends or being gay/lesbian themselves. Those who have lesbian or gay friends often share touching stories about how they had to give up their stereotypes about gay people, ultimately realizing that their gay/lesbian friends are no different than their heterosexual friends. Openly lesbian and gay students often share their life stories, providing their classmates with a real-life individual with whom to converse about homosexuality. These conversations normalize homosexuality and raise consciousness about the presence of lesbian and gay people in the classroom and in people's lives.

I will often intersperse discussion with some didactic presentation on sexual orientation such as Kinsey's (Kinsey, Pomeroy, Martin 1948) notion of the sexual orientation continuum (including the notions of bisexuality and whether sexual orientation is a choice) and more recent thinking on different aspects of sexual orientation (Klein, Sepekoff, Wolf 1985). I provide working definitions of homophobia and heterosexism. Students are more familiar with the former than the latter. We critically examine the term *homophobia*, prejudice due to the fear and loathing of homosexuals, for its accuracy and its usefulness in understanding people's negative reactions to gays and lesbians. We also discuss the professional responsibility to challenge our prejudices and the possibility of separating them out of our professional lives. As one career police officer stated, "I take off my prejudices when I put on the blue (uniform)."

Open discussion of homosexuality often acts as the catalyst for students to express confusion and struggles about other topics such as sexuality in general, the role of religious beliefs in their lives, their need to conform to parental/societal expectations, fear of being too different, and personal experiences of having been stigmatized in some way. The depth of self-disclosure and of identification with the struggles of gay and lesbian people vary greatly among students, depending upon how defended they are against exploring the topic and how limited their contact is with gay and lesbian people. For some, reading and discussion keeps sexual orientation at an abstract level. Experiential strategies make the issue more personal.

Small Group Exercise and Role Plays

Two experiential exercises have been useful in raising the issues of sexual orientation and homophobia on the personal level. The first is a cultural exploration exercise that is conducted in small groups. Students come to class having written down their responses to a set of questions about their cultural backgrounds. The questions include What is your cultural background? What types of rituals, traditions, and food/clothing, etc., do you associate with your culture? Who is in your family? How are boys and girls treated in your family? Who makes the decisions in your family? What do you like most/least about your culture/family? What other cultural group do you feel you most identify with and why?

When I present the assignment I review the questions and spend some time going over definitions of family, using inclusive language (i.e., *spouse, partner, lover*). Students share their responses to these questions in small groups of six. Afterward we discuss the exercise in the large group. Many gay and lesbian students who have come out in class do so during this exercise.

They have expressed feeling supported by the language and definition of family I present. They preferred sharing about their sexual orientation within the context of family/cultural life (rather than within the context of a discussion on sexuality) and they felt safer sharing in a small rather than a large group. When students come out in class, the issues of sexual orientation become much less abstract and nongay students are faced with deeper levels of their feelings about homosexuality.

A second exercise that often reveals covert homophobia is a role play that students do in pairs to practice setting professional boundaries in the counseling relationship. Students take turns playing the client and counselor in a scenario in which the client relentlessly asks the counselor for a date and the counselor practices setting limits. Students are randomly paired off for this exercise.

I first became aware of the opportunity to explore homophobia using this exercise when some male students experienced so much discomfort expressing or receiving sexual interest with another male that they had difficulty completing the role play (some females in same-sex pairs have expressed discomfort, but the intensity is considerably lower than for the males). In these instances I have taken time out of our discussion of professional boundaries to explore students' feelings about their own homosexual feelings and those of others, their attractions and repulsions toward members of the same sex, gender differences about these feelings, and how these feelings may affect the counseling relationship.

Contact Experiences with Gay and Lesbian People

Research has shown that increased positive interpersonal contact with gay and lesbian people reduces negative attitudes about homosexuality (Herek 1994). Many of my students declare in class that they have never met or known a gay or lesbian person. Some say that they have "heard" about some neighbor or distant relative "being that way." Students report either having been taught nothing or been taught negative messages about homosexuality. Personal contact with gay and lesbian people provides a positive experience, shifting the issue from the theoretical to the personal.

Contact may be achieved in various ways. Outside gay and lesbian speakers may be invited to visit the class. Often gay and lesbian student groups at colleges are willing to speak to classes. Students are usually more deeply affected by a visit from their peers than by speakers from the gay and lesbian community. The New York City Police Department uses gay and lesbian officers to conduct sensitivity training about homosexuality in the academy. They believe that the impact is much stronger because they are fellow officers. Likewise, I have found that students are most affected by speaking to gay people whom they know and can identify with. My first choice is to utilize lesbian and gay students who are in the class. I would next use past lesbian and gay peer counseling students or students who are members of our lesbian and gay student organization. As a last resort I would invite members of the gay and lesbian community in New York. The most important criteria for student speakers is that they can articulate their experiences and be receptive to the variety of questions and responses they are likely to receive.

Whether there are gay or lesbian students in the class, we may continually educate students about sexual orientation by using inclusive language and using gay and lesbian examples when illustrating a point. This kind of context supports self-disclosure on the part of gay and lesbian students, if they are so inclined. The impact of self-disclosure of the professor's sexual orientation on classroom dynamics is usually quite powerful and, as some have suggested, requires thoughtful timing and presentation (Adams and Emery 1994; Beck 1983).

Gay and lesbian students in my class have come out over the years, and recently I have discussed my lesbian identity with students in the classroom. The genesis of and factors contributing to my decision to self-disclose are too complex to discuss here, but the initial purpose for disclosure had to do with applying equal standards of integrity and honesty for myself that I have asked from my students. I disclose my sexual identity toward the middle of the semester, after a relationship has been established with the students and when issues of sexual orientation have begun to be explored.

Students' reactions to self-disclosure by other students or the professor are varied. Most express being shocked, surprised, or confused because the person doesn't look or act like the stereotypical lesbian/gay person. They then feel ashamed at having that reaction. The opportunity for a deeper level of self-examination of misconceptions about gay/lesbian people becomes possible.

The professor's disclosure elicits additional reactions. Students are surprised that a professor would disclose this information. Most admire it or feel that the disclosure suggests trust and closeness on the part of the professor. Some question whether the professor can still be a role model, others believe that he or she makes a better role model, one who believes in him or herself and lives life according to personal rather than societal standards. My students are amazed at the extent to which they project heterosexual assumptions, and they appreciate my willingness to act as a resource person about sexual orientation issues.

Effectiveness of Strategies

In written evaluations of the course students report having learned vital counseling skills but, more important, learning about themselves in new ways. They are grateful for the discussions on sexual orientation, which gives them an opportunity to hear diverse perspectives and to learn about their assumptions, myths, stereotypes, prejudices, and judgments within a safe environment. Many report feeling that the experiences in class increased their empathy toward gay and lesbian people, making them better people— more open and self-aware. The self-disclosure of gay and lesbian students and of the professor in class is experienced as "being more helpful than reading hundreds of articles on homosexuality." One student commented that he was glad to know a lesbian on a deeper level.

Experiential strategies—role-playing, discussions with fellow lesbian and gay students, discussion with a lesbian/gay faculty member, the small group cultural sensitivity exercise—were the most effective in changing student attitudes and behaviors. Students felt that these experiences prepared them for their careers, helping them to deal with difficult or sensitive issues on the job. Many felt that they now would be more comfortable dealing with domestic disputes between gay and lesbian people, intervening in harassment of gay/lesbian people, providing counseling, and educating others about homophobia and heterosexism.

I continue to see behavioral changes in students after they have completed the course. Some heterosexual students become interested in learning more about lesbian and gay issues. They have asked me for reading lists and guidance about topics that are relevant to gay and lesbian people that they might use for subsequent courses. Others have consulted with me about how to be supportive to gay and lesbian friends or family members with whom they have close relationships. Some lesbian and gay students become more involved in the college gay and lesbian organization, write papers about lesbian/gay issues for other classes, and reveal their sexual identities to other professors and classmates.

There is no doubt in my mind that students leave this course different people than when they entered it. They are more knowledgeable and skilled as helpers as well as more sensitive about how race, ethnicity, gender, and sexuality affect their lives and those of others. For many, the course had been the first opportunity to discuss homosexuality in an in-depth way. Even though the assignments and discussions were uncomfortable, and often difficult, students felt the increased skills and self-enlightenment that resulted made the process well worth it. As their teacher, I wholeheartedly agree.

NOTE

I would like to thank Professors Robert DeLucia and Carolyn Tricomi for their unending support of the development of this course. I am also indebted to the members of the City University of New York Faculty Development Seminar on Race, Gender, and Class where many of my initial ideas were nurtured.

REFERENCES

Adams, K., and K. Emery, 1994. "Classroom Coming Out Stories: Practical Strategies for Productive Self-Disclosure." In L. Garber, ed., *Tilting the Tower: Lesbians Teaching Queer Subjects*, pp. 25–34. New York: Routledge.

Beck, E. T. 1983. "Self-Disclosure and the Commitment to Social Change." In C. Bunch and S. Pollack, eds., *Learning Our Way: Essays in Feminist Education*, pp. 285–91. Trumansburg, N.Y.: Crossing.

Browning, C., A. L. Reynolds, and S. H. Dworkin. 1991. "Affirmative Psychotherapy for Lesbian Women." *Counseling Psychologist* 19:177–96.

Cannon, L. W. 1990. "Fostering Positive Race, Class, and Gender Dynamics in the Classroom." *Women's Studies Quarterly* 18:126–34.

Cass, V. C. 1979. "Homosexual Identity Formation: A Theoretical Model." *Journal of Homosexuality* 4:219–35.

Helms, J. E. 1990. *Black and White Racial Identity: Theory, Research, and Practice.* New York: Greenwood.

Herek, G. M. 1994. "Assessing Heterosexuals' Attitudes Toward Lesbians and Gay Men: A Review of Empirical Research with the ATLG Scale." In B. Greene and G. M. Herek, eds., *Lesbian and Gay Psychology: Theory, Research, and Clinical Applications,* pp. 206–28. Thousand Oaks, Cal.: Sage.

Iasenza, S., and B. V. Troutt. 1992. "Appreciating Differences." In R. Delucia, ed., *Transitions: The Urban College Student's First Year Experience,* pp. 193–208. Needham Heights, Mass.: Ginn.

Katz, J. H. 1985. The Socio-Political Nature of Counseling. *The Counseling Psychologist* 13:615–24.

Kinsey, A. C., W. B. Pomeroy, and C. E. Martin. 1948. *Sexual Behavior in the Human Male.* Philadelphia: Saunders.

Klein, F., B. Sepekoff, and T. J. Wolf. 1985. "Sexual Orientation: A Multi-Variable Dynamic Process." In F. Klein and T. J. Wolf, eds., *Two Lives to Lead: Bisexuality in Men and Women,* pp. 35–49. New York: Harrington Park.

Lorde, A. 1977. "There is No Hierarchy of Oppressions." *Interracial Books for Children Bulletin* 2:9.

—— 1984. "The Master's Tools Will Never Dismantle the Master's House." In A. Lorde, ed., *Sister Outsider: Essays and Speeches*, pp. 113. Trumansburg, N.Y.: Crossing.

McIntoch, P. 1989. "White Privilege: Unpacking the Invisible Knapsack." *Peace and Freedom* (July/August), pp. 10–12.

Sears, J. T. 1992. "Educators, Homosexuality, and Homosexual Students: Are Personal Feelings Related to Professional Beliefs?" In K. M. Harbek, ed., *Coming Out of the Classroom Closet: Gay and Lesbian Students, Teachers, and Curriculum*, pp. 29–79. New York: Harrington Park.

Shannon, J. W., and W. J. Woods. 1991. "Affirmative Psychotherapy for Gay Men." *Counseling Psychologist* 19:197–215.

Chuck Stewart

Sexual Orientation Training
in Law Enforcement Agencies:
A Preliminary Review of What Works

From the 1950s and 1960s public opposition to the developing lesbian and gay liberation movement quite often took the form of police violence and legal harassment. Law enforcement has historically been associated with heterosexist oppression and the 1969 uprising at New York City's Stonewall Bar was an attack against the police in response to years of oppression. Given this historical reality, improving relations between law enforcement agencies and the lesbian and gay community should be a high priority in the effort to reduce heterosexism (D'Emilio 1983).

Sexual orientation training within law enforcement is a fairly new endeavor and one that often causes great controversy. Virtually every law enforcement agency in the United States performs some type of social sensitivity education. These programs—referred to as cultural awareness, diversity, sensitivity, or human relations education or training—are usually presented as a separate course or workshop. In the only national survey of police cultural awareness programs, the American Correctional Association and Police Executive Research Forum (ACA and PERF 1992) found that most police training programs do not address the individual differences of minorities or the special needs of gays and lesbians. Many police cultural awareness trainings "come right off a training shelf, indicating that the material covered in the program must be broad enough to relate to a number of training audiences, and thus making the programs generic and not relevant to the participants" (St. George 1991:12). Furthermore there is great inconsistency in the ways that agencies implement cultural awareness training. "The amount of training ranged from short roll-call training sessions to 16-hour plus blocks provided to agency employees" (ACA and PERF 1992:23) and the "materials used for training for police agencies varied greatly . . . [as well as] training approaches" (ACA and PERF 1992:24).

There is a strong belief that cultural awareness is essential for modern police agencies and that training is an important element for developing cultural awareness (ACA and PERF 1992:7). But what are the characteristics of "effective" cultural awareness programs and the elements of "effective" cultural awareness training? Unfortunately, there are no published reports by any police agency or training institution on the assessment of program and/or training effectiveness. That is not to say that police researchers do not claim to know what makes for program and training effectiveness. Many authors have outlined elements of "effective" multicultural or sensitivity programs (ACA and PERF 1992:24; Cizon and Smith 1970; Siegal and Senna 1991). Even critics of sensitivity training programs often make their own suggestions on how to improve training effectiveness (St. George 1991). However, none of these claims are substantiated by empirical research nor are the ethnographic methods used discussed.

Besides the general lack of research, there is much confusion as to what the goals of cultural awareness training programs for police should be. Confusion exists not only regarding the appropriate goals of such programs but also regarding what constitutes "cultural awareness" (Martin 1993). For example, in California the enabling legislation for police training on cultural awareness (SB 2680 and AB 401) states that the goal of cultural awareness training is to provide "adequate instruction on racial and cultural diversity in order to foster mutual respect and cooperation between law enforcement and members of all racial and cultural groups . . . [and that] 'cultural diversity' include, but are not limited to, gender and sexual orientation issues." As interpreted by the California Commission of Peace Officer Standards and Training (POST), their *Guidelines for Law Enforcement's Design of Cultural Awareness Training Programs* (1992:ii) states, "The purpose of cultural awareness training is to focus on principles that hold promise for moving California law enforcement to a higher level of understanding, acceptance, and appreciation for our diversity." A review of other state cultural awareness programs (ACA and PERF 1992) reveals a similar wide range of goals that are either ambiguous or unrealistic. Phrases such as "heighten sensitivity of officers," "increase awareness," or "know how to treat each member of the community" are used to state the goals of the program. "Often the goals are broad, sociologically based, and unmeasurable" (St. George 1991:8).

The question of effectiveness is a major problem for cultural awareness training programs in police agencies. Conservatives might classify cultural awareness training programs effective if the number of citizen complaints and lawsuits against police actions were reduced, whereas liberals might consider programs to be effective if the incidence of police brutality was reduced. But are either of these measures directly related to the effectiveness of the cultural awareness training program? Not necessarily. The reporting of hate crimes against gays and lesbians is a prime example of the manner in which the explosion of reported incidents could be related to citizen knowledge of the law and police efforts to make reports rather than a real increase in such crime. Previously, homophobic violence was seldom reported. Further clouding the issue of effectiveness are researchers who estimate that 90 percent of what is taught in the academy has no relationship to the actual demands of the job and that no single educational experience has a direct relationship to police performance (Shelden 1982).

Police agencies have engaged in cultural "sensitivity training" for more than twenty years. Because of the delicate nature of the subject, the programs have rarely been scrutinized by trainers or supervisors (Stewart 1993). Yet officers informally criticize the trainings and those who are responsible for implementing the programs often do not take the subject seriously. Why is there such a negative backlash and resistance from the officers?

> For many officers, the "sensitivity" title of the training alone sends a message that they are viewed as insensitive. The notion that police are insensitive is repugnant to many officers who have been involved in pulling victims from car crashes, talking people out of suicide, and helping to deliver babies."
>
> (St. George 1991:8).

Lee Brown (1973) identified four additional reasons why police cultural awareness training programs are often derided by officers: "(1) Many were hastily established because it was 'fashionable' to have one; (2) many were created exclusively to 'prevent riots'; (3) often the programs became the dumping grounds for misfit officers; and (4) because of the historical context in which they were formed (1960s), the programs were looked upon as programs geared specifically for Blacks" (22). Thus, a continuing problem with cultural awareness training programs within police agencies is the ways they are perceived by the officers. Instead of viewing trainings as opportunities for officers to learn about different cultures and personal biases, they are often perceived to be forms of punishment imposed upon them through outside political pressures.

This psychological resistance by police officers to cultural awareness training reveals a basic conflict between the goals of policing and the goals of cultural awareness training. Police officers have historically been drawn from the minority immigrant groups being policed, which has led to "problems of corruption, discrimination, political favoritism and personal prejudices" (Barlow 1992:7). The professional model was implemented and thought to overcome these problems by focusing on creating police officers who are legalistic, emotionally detached, and apolitical (Goldstein 1990). This is very different from the professional model exhibited by the professions of teaching, social work, and counseling, where the focus has been on the client. The police professional model attempted to remove emotions and personal prejudices from police officers (Walker 1980; Richardson 1980). This entailed removing any sense of loyalty to one's own social group or to the people in the community. A primary conflict with the establishment of cultural awareness training programs is that, by design, the trainings are meant to make police officers aware of the needs of the many differing constituents in the community with which officers serve—in direct contrast to police professional detachment.

Another source of resistance to cultural awareness training emanates from the police stereotype that characterizes police as being hypermasculine (Yarmey 1990; Rokeach, Miller, and Snyder 1971), authoritarian (Blach 1972; Coleman and Gorman 1982), prejudiced and bigoted (Bayley and Mendelsohn 1968; Rafkey 1973, 1979), needing to be in control (Gudjonsson and Adlam 1983), and cynical by nature (Lester and Brink 1985). Although these stereotypes have been shown to be false and the reality is that police reflect the values of the community in which they live (Adlam 1982; Atwater, Bernhart, and Thompson 1980; McNamara 1967; Bent 1974), these stereotypes are believed by the community and ascribed to by police recruits and even many police veterans. Cultural awareness training is the anathema of the police stereotype.

To summarize, gays and lesbians and the issues of sexual orientation have unique needs in relationship to police subculture. Sexual orientation training within law enforcement must address the issues of goal clarification, the police subcultural norms that disdain sensitivity training, conflict between professional detachment and sensitivity to community needs, and the hypermasculine/authoritarian/bigoted/cynical police stereotype's influence on identity formation.

Theoretical Model

Relying on psycholinguist research on learning (e.g., Chomsky 1957, 1965; Krashen 1982; Smith 1988; Vygotsky 1986), the model used in my research assessing effectiveness of police sexual orientation training posits four elements of effective learning:

1. Comprehensible   Comprehensible input needs to start with the student's understanding of gender, sex, and police work and be extended toward the program's goal of reducing heterosexism. For example, trying to explain sexual orientation variance using the Shively and De Cecco (1993) *tri-continua model* based upon gender identity, social sex role, and sexual orientation to police officers who find Kinsey's bipolar model unbelievable would not be the best starting place. Instead, a discussion of police work needs to emphasize that people of differing genders, sexual orientations, and sex roles are equally effective as officers.

2. Meaningful   When designing gay and lesbian training programs, meaning is the most overlooked element of the program. Programs typically grow out of political considerations and are often taught by gay rights advocates who have a personal stake in the program. The program may have meaning for the teacher, but this does not automatically imply that the program will have meaning for students. For a program of sexual orientation to have meaning for police officers, it must be relevant to police subculture.

3. Modeled   Teachers of multiculturalism are often viewed as being outside police subculture, and not "real cops." Effective teachers need to be the kind of persons students want to emulate and those who demonstrate acceptance of gays and lesbians.

4. Authentic   Within the classroom context the instructor needs to continually relate sexual orientation issues to police work and engage students in activities that have direct application to their identities and job. Treating sexual orientation in a one-time workshop reinforces the belief that it is not related to police work, is politically motivated, and must be endured.

In this study I solicited the participation of California police agencies. Seven agencies and academies from northern, central, and southern California participated. At each locale I observed sexual orientation training classes and, sometimes, the entire cultural awareness program. A six-part assessment instrument composed of the (Modified) Attitude Toward Homosexuality Scale (MATHS) (Price 1982; MacDonald et al. 1973), Index of Homophobia (IHP) (Hudson and Rickets 1980), Homosexuality Knowledge Index (HKI) (Sears 1992), Gender Identity, Sexual Identity, Emotional Identity (Stewart 1995), 4-Item F Scale (Lane 1955), and Police Behavioral Scenarios on Homosexuality (PBSH; Stewart 1995), was given to the participants before and after the training module. All told, 438 students were observed, 167 completed pre-/post-testing, and 6 participated in interview. One- to two-hour interviews were conducted with participating students, instructors, program administrators, agency/academy administrators, and representatives of the local gay and lesbian community. Interviewees were asked questions about levels of homophobia within the police agency, appropriate behaviors between police and gay and lesbian workers and community contacts, and suggestions for improving the acceptance of gays and lesbians. All interviewees were also asked to complete the assessment instrument so as to measure the culture of the organization and community with respect to homophobia. Approximately half of the fifty nonstudent interviewees completed the assessment instrument. I also participated in agency ride-along within the local gay and lesbian sectors. Often, riding with police officers while on duty for a number of hours allowed them to relax enough to really open up about the homophobia in their agency. The findings presented here are based on partial data collection and analysis. For more complete conclusions, see Stewart (1995).

Preliminary Findings

Sexual orientation training must be assessed within context of the environment in which it is conducted. The preliminary findings of this research vividly demonstrate the interplay of police culture, program structure, teaching methodologies, and course content. Police culture in California agencies are extremely heterosexist. Interviews revealed great disparity in most agencies between the perception held by high-ranking administrators and the gay and lesbian officers concerning the agencies' acceptance of homosexuals and/or the discussion of homosexuality. Administrators usually claimed that homosexuality was "not an issue" and that officers were judged solely on merit; yet gay and lesbian officers were well aware how dangerous it was to be an open homosexual. Only in those agencies that made a point of publicly recognizing the achievements of open gay and lesbian officers (such as award banquets, press releases) and that included daily conversations recognizing the personal relationships in which the gay and lesbian officers were engaged (such as "How is your wife or girlfriend?" to the lesbian officers) was the cultural norm less heterosexist. On the MATH and IH "sworn" heterosexual police personnel rated higher levels of homophobia than civilian or gay police personnel, and recruits rated even higher (see table 1).

TABLE 1

Comparison of Homophobia Levels for Law Enforcement Personnel

	MATH Scores	Index of Homophobia Scores	N
Heterosexual recruits (in gay-negative police environments)	53, 53, 55, 59	37, 36, 36, 44 34, 28, 28, 55	
Heterosexual recruits (in gay-friendly environments)	78	61	6
Homosexual recruits (in gay-negative environments)	64	49	2
Homosexual recruits (in gay-friendly environments)	92, 87	94, 90	1, 1
Heterosexual administrators (in gay-negative police environments)	46	29	2
Heterosexual administrators (in gay-friendly environments)	89, 81	66, 67	1, 2
Heterosexual administrator and instructor (with gay son)	95	99	1
Homosexual police officers (including instructors of sexual orientation training)	92, 96, 92	91, 93, 90	4, 2, 2
Heterosexual community members (either with gay children or who helped develop sexual orientation training curriculum)	75, 89	69, 91	2, 1
Homosexual community members (who were instructors or helped develop sexual orientation training curriculum)	89, 90, 95	93, 96, 98	3, 1, 4

NOTE: Scoring is on the scale 0 = gay-negative and 100 = gay-positive.

Furthermore, empirical testing revealed that if an overall agency was gay-affirming then both administrators and their recruits would score more gay-positive than in a gay-negative environment and vice versa (see table 1). This suggests that recruits reflect their academy administrators and administrators select students who reflect their own values. When respondents were asked to write statements of feelings and/or beliefs they had toward homosexuals or about homosexuality, 55–70 percent of recruits reported negative beliefs, with 27–59 percent believing that homosexuals are "sick" and "unnatural and a sin." Police administrators were less antigay, with approximately 41 percent making negative statements of which only 27 percent reported that they believed homosexuality to be a sickness or sin. More important, almost one-fourth of police administrators believed that homosexuals are just like "regular" people and should have equal rights, compared to the only 15 percent of recruits who expressed this pro-right view.

Most California law enforcement agencies and academies are still evolving their cultural awareness programs. Sexual orientation is highly controversial and most agencies feel ill-prepared to deal with the subject. Many programs simply structured sexual orientation as part of a laundry list of protected classes with no specific information or intervention attempted. One common approach was to bring in a panel of lesbians and gays for approximately two hours to share their personal experiences with students and to answer questions as they came up—which they rarely did. This required very little preparation or understanding by the agency, was low cost, and content was haphazardly covered. Because of the lack of open gay or lesbian officers at most agencies, the panelists were primarily nonpolice community activists and were not well received. A few agencies attempted to convey information through direct teaching by a trained instructor or expert. Some used trained police officers, while others used college academics—usually gay or lesbian themselves. The more structured trainings included lecture, class discussion, group and/or individual activities, handouts, and sometimes video presentation. In all but one of the observed trainings the students had no responsibility other than to sit in class and perhaps participate in discussion. One instructor did attempt to have students complete a written home assignment, but this was fought by the students and caused concern from the contracting agency. The open gay or lesbian trainers who were police officers took an essentialist perspective, claiming that their homosexuality was an inborn orientation for which they were not "at fault." Having gay and lesbian officers as instructors, along with an essentialist approach, garnered the most respect from the students.

Recruits seemed most interested in hearing about how gay persons came to recognize their feelings and identity formation—they very much wanted to hear personal stories. The "causes" of homosexuality and the family response to having a homosexual child were also important questions for recruits. With police administrators, a much broader range of questions was asked; still, the most common questions concerned the supposed causes of homosexuality. In every class observation a significant core of self-identified Christian fundamentalists would make their negative views known. Particularly when evidence was presented showing that homosexuality is not a disease, very common, and "natural," the fundamentalists would attempt to smear the evidence as being "tainted" and biased since the research was assumed to have been conducted exclusively by homosexuals. One instructor attempted to address this issue by bringing along books written by open heterosexual researchers and holding them up to the class when the biased research attacks started.

Summary of Findings—What Works!

Training on sexual orientation is but one strategy in the fight against homophobia and heterosexism. More than anything, this research revealed the deep interplay of police culture to effective training. To make a law enforcement agency less heterosexist and more accepting of gays and lesbians it is important to bring visibility to gay and lesbian officers and to validate their relationships. Sexual orientation issues must become part of the daily routine and conversation. Homosexual behaviors and relationships need to be shared in everyday conversations and around the "watercooler" Monday mornings just as heterosexual ones are now shared. Official recognition of meritorious performance needs to include the sexual orientation of the individual. Special effort needs to be made to assist recruits away from their anti-gay feelings and beliefs toward greater tolerance and acceptance.

It is essential that law enforcement leaders model attitudes and behaviors that are nonhomophobic and embracing of sexual diversity. Using open gay or lesbian police personnel or police personnel who have a gay or lesbian child on the training panel or as instructors provided the strongest role model for the students and was better accepted by program administrators. However, their essentialist deficit perspective reinforced the myth that homosexuality is both rare and abnormal. Attempts by academic instructors to broaden student understanding of the social constructions of sexual, affectional, and gender multidimensions seemed to confuse more than achieve a reduction in homophobic feelings and heterosexist beliefs.

Course content needs to address the issues students want to know. Much of the recent research and literature on sexual orientation is based on advanced feminist theory and many of the concepts are foreign to all but an educated elite. Similarly, a deep analysis of the biological component of sexual orientation is possible only with persons familiar with genetics, testing theory, and biological brain research. Instead, this research project's findings suggest that it is best to start with the student's own feelings and experiences. Homosexuality is stigmatized in our society and fear and negative stereotypes form a basis of common knowledge. The teacher needs to start at what is known and felt (both negative and frightening), then assist students to a greater understanding of the roots of homophobia and heterosexism. Although there are some similarities between recruits and administrators, each setting requires course content aimed at their specific needs. Effectiveness in training necessitates that a small core of information be presented in an open manner, allowing students to guide the direction in which the course content evolves. Christian fundamentalists may try to capture the training, it is therefore important for the panelists or instructors to be prepared to address and limit this issue. Instructors often limit religious objections by stating that religious beliefs will not be discussed and remind police students that they have a responsibility to uphold the law—and in California that includes the protection of gays and lesbians from discrimination and physical violence. The issue of biased research could be addressed through presentation of gay research that has been conducted by open heterosexuals (although gays and lesbians may be offended that they need "validation" from heterosexuals). Very little actual information seems to be absorbed by students during a short training, suggesting that the trainings should emphasize personal feelings and students' interface with their job.

An off-the-shelf "Homo 101" course has little relevance for police officers. A few of the observed instructors created more relevance by discussing specific police scenarios in which sexual orientation had a potential impact on the situation. The students seemed to work well in small groups finding solutions to the problems. From these very real situations basic questions about sexuality and sexual identity emerged.

The trainings are often perceived as a couple of hours students have to endure with no involvement or commitment. Having students engaged in activities that are related to police work brings an authenticity that has been lacking hereto. For example, having students develop a nondiscrimination policy for their agency or develop their own course on sexual orientation training or write a procedural manual for field situations (such as investigating a gay bashing or alcohol and beverage control violation) in which sexual orientation is an important element will improve the effectiveness of the training.

This essay is a preliminary report on the first empirical and ethnographic research to be conducted on sexual orientation training in law enforcement, a complex phenomenon involving the interplay of police subculture, gay and lesbian subculture, politics, and education methodology. Because homosexuality is "hidden knowledge," the antithesis of police subculture, and known primarily by its negative stereotypes, the future of sexual orientation training in law enforcement is volatile. Hopefully, training programs will stop taking the easy way out by using guest speakers from the local gay and lesbian community service center and instead develop highly structured, goal-oriented programs that include "effective" strategies (see Stewart 1995 for complete research on this topic). Sexual orientation training, combined with strong administrative support, provides strategies that work toward overcoming homophobia and heterosexism within law enforcement agencies.

REFERENCES

American Correctional Association (ACA) and Police Executive Research Forum (PERF). 1992. *Preliminary Report on Training in Cultural Difference for Law Enforcement/Juvenile Justice Officials.*

Adlam, K. R. C. 1982. "The Police Personality: Psychological Consequences of Being a Police Officer." *Journal of Police Science and Administration* 10:344–49.

Atwater, E., B. Bernhart, and S. Thompson. 1980. "The Authoritarian Cop: An Outdated Stereotype? *Police Chief* (January) 47:58–59.

Barlow, D. E. 1992. "Cultural Sensitivity Training: Rediscovered." Paper presented at the Academy of Criminal Justice Sciences Meetings, Pittsburgh, March.

Bayley, D., and H. Mendelsohn. 1968. *Minorities and the Police.* New York: Free.

Bent, A. 1974. *The Politics of Law Enforcement.* Toronto: Lexington.

Blach, R. W. 1972. "The Police Personality: Fact or Fiction? *Journal of Criminal Law, Criminology, and Police Science* 63:106–19.

Brown, L. P. 1973. *The Death of Police Community Relations.* Washington, D.C.: Institute for Urban Affairs and Research.

California Commission of Peace Officer Standards and Training (POST). 1992. *Guidelines for Law Enforcement's Design of Cultural Awareness Training Programs* (February), p. ii.

Chomsky, N. 1957. *Syntactic Structures.* The Hague: Mouton.

— 1965. *Aspects of the Theory of Syntax.* Cambridge: MIT Press.

Cizon, F. A., and W. H. T. Smith. 1970. *Some Guidelines for Successful Police-Community Relations Training Programs.* Washington, D.C.: U.S. Government Printing Office.

Coleman, A., and L. Gorman. 1982. "Conservatism, Dogmatism, and Authoritarianism in British Police Officers." *Sociology* 16(1):1.

D'Emilio, J. 1983. *Sexual Politics, Sexual Communities: The Making of a Homosexual Minority in the United States, 1940–1970.* Chicago: University of Chicago Press.

Goldstein, H. 1990. *Problem-Oriented Policing.* New York: McGraw-Hill.

Gudjonsson, G. H., and K. R. C. Adlam. 1983. "Personality Patterns of British Police Officers." *Personality and Individual Differences* 4:507–12.

Hudson, W., and Ricketts, W. 1980. "A Strategy for the Measurement of Homophobia. *Journal of Homosexuality* 5(4):357–72.

Krashen, S. 1982. *Principles and Practice of Second Language Acquisition.* Oxford: Pergamon.

Lane, R. 1955. "Four Item F Scale in 'Political Personality and Electoral Choice.'" *American Political Science Review* 49:173–90.

Lester, D., and W. T. Brink. 1985. "Police Solidarity and Tolerance for Police Misbehavior." *Psychological Reports* 57:326.

MacDonald, A. P., Jr., J. Huggins, S. Young, and R. A. Swanson. 1973. "Attitudes Toward Homosexuality: Preservation of Sex Morality or the Double Standard?" *Journal of Consulting and Clinical Psychology* 40(1):161.

McNamara, J. 1967. "Uncertainties in Police Work." In D. Bordua, ed., *The Police.* New York: Wiley.

Martin, S. 1993. "The Problem of Multicultural Education: Background, Definitions and Future Agenda." *Multicultural Education Journal* 11(1):9–20.

Price, J. 1982. "High School Students' Attitudes Toward Homosexuality." *Journal of School Health* 52(8):469–74.

Rafkey, D. M. 1973. "Police Race Attitudes and Labeling." *Journal of Police Science and Administration* 1:65–86.

—— 1979. "The Cognitive Gap Between the Police and the Policed: An Exploratory Study in Attitude Organization." *Law and Human Behavior* 1:63–79.

Richardson, J. F. 1980. "Police in America: Functions and Control." In J. A. Inciardi and C. E. Faupel, eds., *History and Crime: Implications for Criminal Justice Police.* Beverly Hills: Sage.

Rokeach, M., M. G. Miller, and J. A. Snyder. 1971. "The Value Gap Between Police and Policed." *Journal of Social Issues* 27:155–77.

St. George, J. 1991. "Sensitivity Training Needs Rethinking." *Law Enforcement News* (November 30) 17:347.

Sears, J. 1992. "Educators, Homosexuality, and Homosexual Students: Are Personal Feelings Related to Professional Beliefs?" In K. M. Harbeck, ed., *Coming Out of the Classroom Closet: Gay and Lesbian Students, Teachers, and Curricula,* pp. 29–80. New York: Harrington Park.

Shelden, R. 1982. *Criminal Justice in America: A Sociological Approach.* Boston: Little, Brown.

Shively, M. G., and J. P. De Cecco. 1993. "Components of Sexual Identity." In L. D.

Garnets and D. C. Kimmel, eds., *Psychological Perspectives on Lesbian and Gay Male Experiences*, pp. 80–88. New York: Columbia University Press.

Siegal, L. J., and J. J. Senna. 1991. *Juvenile Delinquency: Theory Practice and Law.* St. Paul: West.

Smith, F. 1988. *Joining the Literacy Club: Further Essays Into Education.* New Hampshire: Heinemann.

Stewart, C. K. 1993. "POST Cultural Awareness Survey." Paper presented at the Comparative and International Education Society, Los Angeles, October 4.

—— 1995. *The Efficacy of Sexual Orientation Training in Law Enforcement Agencies.* Ph.D. diss., University of Southern California.

Vygotsky, L. S. 1986. *Thought and Language.* Trans. A. Kozulin. Cambridge: MIT Press.

Walker, S. 1980. *Popular Justice: A History of American Criminal Justice.* New York: Oxford University Press.

Yarmey, A. D. 1990. *Understanding Police and Police Work: Psychosocial Issues.* New York: New York University Press.

PART V

Working Within Institutions

Louie Crew

Changing the Church:
Lessons Learned in the Struggle to Reduce
Institutional Heterosexism in the Episcopal Church

In the 1950s and 1960s the Episcopal Church was at the forefront of social change, as many of its priests became activists in the civil rights movement for racial justice. In similar fashion, for the last twenty-five years the Episcopal Church has received widespread media attention as it has grappled with the ordination of women as priests and with lesbian and gay issues. Just as in other Christian churches, where women and lesbigays have organized to promote a more egalitarian and inclusive spirituality, the radical right has mounted a regressive reaction. In some cases, especially in the Southern Baptist Convention and in more fundamentalist denominations, the right seems to have gained a stranglehold, even controlling the denomination's seminaries and universities.

The Episcopal Church, in contrast, has manifested substantial progress, both for women and for lesbians and gays. Issues of gender and sexual orientation are closely related in recent Episcopal history. This essay will suggest what lessons can be learned from this effort in institutional change.

In the Episcopal Church our theology reveres scripture as but one of three sources of authority, coequal with reason and tradition. We have always required clergy to be educated, and most of our seminaries have been open to historical and critical scholarship. Few priests believe that the Bible is inspired literally word for word. As a result, few Episcopal parishes require you to hang up your mind when you enter—and few require doctrinal purity tests. Many Episcopalians look at faith analytically; we are not beholden to a confessional statement or to a magisterium's conclusions.

Episcopal polity, therefore, allows much air in which lesbigays may breathe our living witness. Having the freedom to think does not ensure that thinkers will support lesbians and gays, nor does it do away with the struggle or stigma gays and lesbians must endure: but a church free to think is a church free to allow God to act in a new way. The Episcopal Church is at once more democratic than many church structures and more centralized than many. *Episcopal* means "overseen by bishops." Bishops and all others are accountable to the General Convention, a bicameral legislature that meets triennially. During the interim the Presiding Bishop and Executive Council provide oversight at the national level. One principal bishop oversees each of the over one hundred domestic dioceses of the Episcopal Church, with much choice left to each diocese in terms of its liturgical and theological preferences, including choice of candidates for ordination.

General Convention governs the Church through constitution and canons, and it advises the Church through resolutions. Until the 1994 General Convention, when the canons were amended to ensure nondiscrimination in access to ordination on the basis of sexual orientation, the Church had never addressed lesbian and gay issues through its canons, and hence it may be said that the Church has never officially proscribed lesbian and gay behavior on the part of priests or laity, though, in fact, it has often manifested the prejudices of any age. I founded Integrity in October 1974 out of tiny Fort Valley, Georgia, as a newsletter, *Integrity: Gay Episcopal Forum*. Almost immediately, two called from Chicago, one a priest named Tyndale, the other a lay person named Wickliff (historic names in the British Anglican Church). I introduced these two to each other and to others who had written from Chicago. About a dozen met in Wickliff's apartment in December and formed the first chapter.

Chicago as the site was likely not an accident. A joke popular in the Episcopal Church at that time asked: "How many straight priests in the diocese of Chicago does it take to put in a light bulb? Answer: Both of them." Whatever the joke lacks in scientific accuracy, it makes up for by identifying a place known to have accumulated gay clergy, in this case, a critical mass ready to nurture a movement, a group with strategies for organizing.

Also in 1974 three bishops ordained the "Philadelphia Eleven," the first women priests in the Episcopal Church. These ordinations were declared "irregular," since the General Convention had frequently considered but not yet voted to approve the ordination of women. The ordinations were not declared invalid, only irregular. People inside and outside the Anglican Communion frequently describe how we "muddle through" with distinctions such as these. Almost never in our history have we had the luxury of expecting a high degree of conformity in doctrine or liturgical practice. To avoid extinction, frequently individual Anglicans and even groups of us have needed to back off from actions with which we disapprove and allow them still to happen, preferably "somewhere else."

It was not new that lesbian and gay Episcopalians got together in 1974: for at least a century earlier certain parishes and cathedrals were rumored to be relatively gay friendly. What was new in 1974 was our organizing and our announcing it to the world. That scared even many of the gay priests of the diocese of Chicago.

Within only six months Integrity held its first national convention at the Cathedral of St. James in Chicago—a product of good strategies by leaders well connected in the diocese. Many of the members of the Chicago chapter were close to the suffragan bishop Quintin Primo, one of the first African American bishops, who presided over the main Eucharist. The dean of the cathedral was extremely supportive. Several clergy members were close to prominent theologian Norman Pittenger, and they persuaded him to be the principal speaker. Dr. Pittenger, after retirement as a professor at the General Theological Seminary in New York, had identified himself as gay in a statement widely published in England, where he lived at Cambridge University. Dr. Pittenger's decision to take this risk led many of his former students to join us.

Ellen Barrett and James Wickliff served as Integrity's first copresidents. Before we had a national meeting I drafted Integrity's first constitution, to assure that we moved toward gender justice by including women and men equally at all levels. Ellen was then a candidate for priesthood in New York City.

More irregular ordinations of women took place in Washington, D.C., in September 1975, after our convention. In Washington at the time, on a missionary journey to our new chapters in the east, Jim Wickliff and I yielded to the counsel of friends who advised that our visibility at the ordination might put in jeopardy lesbians among all early ordinands.

In 1976 General Convention passed a resolution: "Homosexual persons are children of God who have a full and equal claim with all other persons upon the love, acceptance, and pastoral concern and care of the Church." Integrity members had proposed this specific wording a year earlier when we met with the Standing Commission on Human Affairs. Bishop George Murray, chair of the commission, was not known for liberalism: he was one of the clergy persons whom Dr. Martin Luther King, Jr., scolded by name in his "Letter from the Birmingham Jail." Yet Bishop Murray had grown through that earlier confrontation. We got to meet with the commission because I wrote to him as my former bishop while I was a professor at the University of Alabama (1966–1970). Others wrote to those whom they knew on the commission. Constantly we knocked on doors, wrote letters, and made our presence known as lesbigay.

That same 1976 General Convention changed the canons to permit the ordination of women. At the same time it declared homosexual persons "children of God," it "regularized" the earlier ordinations in Philadelphia and Washington. The 1976 convention passed (and reaffirmed in 1979, 1983, and 1994) resolutions supporting the civil rights of lesbians and gays.

In January of 1977 the first month women could be "legally" ordained, the Rt. Rev. Paul Moore, Jr., Bishop of New York, ordained to the priesthood Ellen Marie Barrett, who had served as Integrity's first copresident. Other lesbians had been among the Philadelphia Eleven; thousands of gay men had been ordained over centuries, but they were not out to the world; most were not out to anyone. Ellen Barrett was ordained while already out to her bishop, out to her supporting congregation, out to other diocesan review bodies, and, on the day of her ordination, out to anyone in the world who could read a newspaper. "Ordaining them" was no longer theoretical.

Reaction was swift and volatile. For months Episcopal newspapers and magazines fulminated. Meeting in Port St. Lucie nine months later, the House of Bishops said ordinations of gays and lesbians should not happen. They passed a strong resolution condemning homosexuality as unbiblical. They asserted that the Church "is right to confine its nuptial blessing exclusively to heterosexual marriage." No one sought dialogue with lesbigays this time.

Yet, at Port St. Lucie, the bishops tabled a measure to censure Bishop Moore. With glorious irony some of the bishops most annoyed by the ordination of Ellen Barrett still needed to protect dissent, namely, their own. Since the canon law now made it legal to ordain women, bishops who felt women should not be priests did not want to be forced to ordain them. At Port St. Lucie the House of Bishops adopted a "conscience clause" permitting bishops to refuse to ordain women. During the 1980s at first a few, then a few more bishops began to quietly ordain gays and lesbians who were out to them, protected by that same notion of conscience.

At the 1979 General Convention the Commission on Human Affairs, now chaired by the Rt. Rev. Robert Spears, Bishop of Rochester, presented an extremely positive report that called for the ordination of qualified lesbians and gays and was favorable to blessing same-sex unions. On Sunday at the beginning of the convention in 1979, one of our strong local leaders in Denver, a priest named Ric Kerr, was host to the Presiding Bishop John Allin, who came to see the marvelous work that Ric and his parish had done to reclaim a depressed neighborhood and create a multicultural congregation. Along with Bishop Allin came a large entourage to witness this success story. In his sermon Ric came out, gently claiming gays' place at God's table. At the reception Bishop Allin, with whom I had met several times earlier, said, "I knew you'd be here for this. You're everywhere!" The convention itself was affected by the Port St. Lucie statement (which as a statement by the bishops alone was not enforceable). Convention approved a negative resolution, but one milder than that approved by the House of Bishops. In a compromise, both houses of convention said it was "not appropriate" to ordain anyone sexually active outside the bonds of heterosexual marriage. Integrity members behind the scenes helped to convey our anguish and rally support. Over three dozen bishops plus scores of lay and clerical deputies signed a dissent document stating that as an act of conscience they could not abide by that resolution. Among the original dissenters was the Most Rev. Edmond Browning, while he was still Bishop of Hawaii. He was elected Presiding Bishop in 1985. Around 1980 the Rev. Carter Heyward, one of the Philadelphia Eleven, a theologian serving as professor at the Episcopal Divinity School, came out as lesbian, as have scores of others.

Throughout the period from 1979 onward many bishops have more actively ordained lesbians and gays who are open throughout the ordination process—to their sponsoring congregations, to diocesan commissions on ministry, to diocesan standing committees, and to their ordaining bishops. Few of these ordinations come to the attention of the press, nor do those in the process seek to publicize them as such. Integrity leaders now cite over one hundred such ordinations, most of whom are members of Integrity.

In another gesture of inclusion, the Diocese of California began the Parsonage as a peer counseling center in the Castro, a lesbian and gay neighborhood of San Francisco. The Rt. Rev. William Swing, Bishop of California, passionately told a meeting of the House of Bishops in 1987 that their unlove sent far too many lesbigay clergy to San Francisco and New York and reminded us that we as a Church are interconnected and must grow into that realization. Integrity has grown unevenly. In 1984, after ten years, we had about twelve hundred members, the same number we had by our second anniversary in

1976. However, in our second ten years we doubled our numbers. We began 1995 with seventy-five chapters and about twenty-five hundred members. Each group must have at least ten members to become a chapter; the New York City chapter sometimes has over three hundred members. Chapters currently average thirty members and meet at least once a month, some once a week, for a service (usually a Eucharist) and for educational/social time. Most chapters meet in local parishes. The goal has never been for Integrity to replace one's parish but, instead, for Integrity to refuel members to go back into their own parishes empowered to incarnate a loving lesbigay presence there. The secondary, but always present, goal is to affect the preaching and teaching of the Episcopal Church on the parish, diocesan, and national levels. In this Integrity is probably unique among lesbigay ministries. For example, many members of Dignity, the organization of lesbigay Catholics, use the Dignity mass as their only church attendance. Dignity, too, has had little or no influence on the policies of the Roman Catholic Church, nor are they likely to have much chance to do so in a nondemocratic environment. On the other hand, most of the Protestant groups (Affirmation, Presbyterians for Lesbians and Gay Concerns, etc.) work as hard on the "political" front as the environment of their denominations permit, but they rarely have regular worship services outside a parish environment.

In 1995 Integrity membership is larger than that of all the Protestant lesbigay caucuses combined, despite the Episcopal Church's being a relatively small denomination. Why? Some feel that our structure may be essential: Integrity is structured to remain active in the parish, diocese, and denomination, but also protected from being co-opted by priorities of the hosts. Others suggest that our numbers merely reflect a higher percentage of lesbigays in the Episcopal Church.

Most Integrity chapters have been formed by and are led by lay leadership. Some dioceses, however, have included Integrity in their diocesan budgets and the bishop appoints a chaplain for Integrity. In one of the more unusual cases, Bishop Spears, together with the Roman Catholic Bishop of Rochester, called for and funded a joint Integrity/Dignity chapter in that city. That group, with the bishops' permission, began blessing lesbian and gay relationships in 1976. Chapters sometimes have a small core of priests who serve as chaplains. More often, chapters call upon a wide network of clergy to come and preach and preside at Eucharist. These occasions have changed many a visitor. No congregation has ever had an Integrity chapter meeting there without being changed by our presence.

From the beginning Integrity has been blessed with numerous leaders who know how the Episcopal Church works, persons willing to invest the enormous amount of time and effort to connect. One of the reasons gays and lesbians have succeeded in the Episcopal Church is that we spend time learning how it operates, and then we teach one another. Almost every one of our leaders knows who's who in the Church in her diocese, in her parish, and in the Episcopal Church Center. We know how to serve these people.

Episcopalians are blessed with an open political process. Many of the same persons who shaped the Constitution of the United States shaped the constitution of the Episcopal Church. In our Church it is OK to respect political processes. Episcopalians believe in the Holy Spirit not as an icon chiseled into stone at Pentecost and allowed to say no new word, but as God's living presence among us. We believe that God expects us both to listen and to think.

It seems to me that 1979 was the high water mark of homophobia: "You shouldn't do it!" General Convention told the bishops. But the tide almost immediately started to ebb. "We will do it anyway," three dozen conscientious bishops said in reply. The house knew it could not muster enough votes to prevent the dissent. Lesbians and gays and many straights who recognized our spiritual gifts then took risks to try to ensure the tide never again turned against us.

Gains of the 1980s were most noticeable at the parish and diocesan level. The decade manifested homophobia, to be sure. In 1982, for example, the Bishop of Louisiana denied Integrity permission to use any Episcopal Church during General Convention in New Orleans. However, four years later, the Most Rev. Edmond L. Browning, at his installation as Presiding Bishop, promised that "this church of ours is open to all. There will be no outcasts." This was to become the most profound commitment of his twelve-year term, 1986–1997. Six months after his installation though, when the bishop summoned "every group in the Episcopal Church" to report what it had learned in a "listening process," Integrity alone was omitted. Our board complained and thereafter began a regular process of meeting with the Presiding Bishop. The board always brought a list of specific actions and asked him to connect board members personally to the persons at the Church Center responsible for actions of each type we brought.

Those opposed to us were badly divided in their other priorities. Some wanted mainly to preserve a male priesthood. Some wanted mainly to preserve a liturgical style. Others wanted mainly to preserve a morality they called biblical, though the morality they described was no more biblical than kids dressed in bathrobes for a Christmas pageant. They talked about families, but these families sounded more like families on TV in the 1950s than like anything in the Bible. Many longed for the days when Episcopalians held the keys if not to the Kingdom of Heaven at least to the country club. The one common ingredient to many disparate agendas was that all agreed homosexuality was an abomination. Around this one certainty many began to organize. The clearest way to persuade people that the Church was going to the dogs was to point out the growing support for homosexuals.

In 1984 a group of conservative bishops met in January to pursue ways to "revitalize" the Episcopal Church. Two of the key players were the Rt. Rev. William Frey, Bishop of Colorado (a candidate for the office of Presiding Bishop in 1985), and the Rt. Rev. Michael Marshall, a British transplant (publicly outed in the English press in 1994). A year later this group became Episcopalians United for Revelation, Renewal, and Reformation (EURRR). From the beginning the group aggressively opposed the ordination of gays and lesbians and the blessing of our relationships. They have attacked Integrity in nearly every issue of their publications.

General Convention in 1985 called for three years of dialogue on the homosexual issue. Integrity made the mistake of believing the promise, but the dialogue promised in 1985 did not occur. "You issued a check and it has bounced," we said at the hearing sponsored by the Commission on Health and Human Affairs at General Convention in 1988. As a compromise, Convention again swept everything under the rug by calling for three "more" years of dialogue, but this time Integrity launched an effort to encourage dialogue on the local level. Materials were developed, and many parishes had excellent programs, though this was not widespread.

Integrity began to wield real influence at the 1988 General Convention. Friends and foes alike credited us as having the best network at the convention, designed by Kim Byham, a brilliant New York attorney who served as our president at that time. He has coordinated our presence at all subsequent conventions and he has also been extremely effective in getting Integrity's message to the media.

For General Conventions since 1988 we have selected approximately forty persons to represent Integrity from a pool of eighty or so volunteers. Integrity spends about forty thousand dollars, which goes to housing for the volunteers (transportation and food are not paid), a booth, a nerve center, a hospitality suite, publications, and other expenses. We divide the volunteers into a variety of task forces. Legislative volunteers, for example, monitor sessions of each house. Committee meetings begin at 7 A.M. Volunteers then report to our nerve center on the progress of all legislation, noting the dates of hearings at which our volunteers might testify. With computers we generate reports far more accurately and faster than most official avenues of information. We do not limit our interests narrowly to lesbigay legislation but put our people into the full range of venues where they may share expertise. For example, at all conventions women of Integrity have served on the women's caucus, as did its first male member, Integrity legislative leader Pat Waddell from California.

In the same year as the Detroit General Convention the Diocese of Massachusetts elected as suffragan the first female bishop in Anglican history, the Rt. Rev. Barbara Harris. Harris had directed the Consultation, an umbrella progressive group of which Integrity was a founding member, along with Union of Black Episcopalians, the Episcopal Peace Fellowship, the Episcopal Women's Caucus, the Urban Bishops' Coalition, and others.

It would be impossible to overestimate the importance of these many friendships and the importance of alliances we have forged across diverse struggles. For example, in the earliest days many gay male Episcopalians were Anglocatholic opponents of women's ordination. The Diocese of Chicago, which hosted our first convention, was one of the later dioceses to ordain women. Nevertheless, Integrity's leadership steadfastly supported women's ordination from the beginning.

In 1989 EURRR launched an even more strident attack on any bishops supportive of lesbians and gays. In December the Rt. Rev. John Spong, Bishop of Newark, in a highly publicized event, ordained the Rev. Robert Williams and commissioned him as the chief missioner for the Oasis, a diocesan ministry with gays and lesbians. An endless attack, primarily as a fund-raiser, was opened by EURRR. If other bishops ordain lesbians and gays, as Spong has, the Church is surely in apostasy, EURRR relentlessly argued. As an official ministry of a diocese, the Oasis gave weight to EURRR's scare tactics that sin was overtaking the Episcopal Church. At General Convention in 1991 those opposed to ordaining lesbians and gays presented a resolution: "All members of the clergy of this church . . . shall be under the obligation to abstain from sexual relations outside holy matrimony." The resolution failed! Although the resolution did not name gays and lesbians, members of both the House of Bishops and the House of Deputies identified the catch-22 and voted accordingly. Instead, the convention passed a resolution reaffirming heterosexual marriage as the tradition of the Episcopal Church but acknowledged that many faithful Episcopalians are living in discontinuity with this tradition. Opponents of gays and lesbians left the convention howling that they had lost and that the Episcopal Church was moving toward heresy. For the first time, openly gay and lesbian Integrity members serving as deputies identified themselves as such on the floor of the House of Deputies. The House of Deputies elected its first woman ever to serve as its president.

In 1991 about three thousand people attended an evening hearing. To speak on behalf of gay and lesbian issues Integrity selected the Bishop of Los Angeles (the Rt. Rev. Frederick Borsch, the leading theologian in the House), an openly gay priest (the Rev. Walter Szymanski of Rochester, who had been leading the blessing effort since 1976), and an openly lesbian priest (the Rev. Stina Pope of Atlanta). On departure from the hearing hundreds joined in a circle to sing "We are a gentle, angry people."

In 1991 General Convention faced up to the fact that the Church had not actually had the dialogue promised for the last six years and called for a structure to ensure dialogue for the next three, with a mechanism to report the results from parish to diocese to national church. It stressed that it wanted dialogue, not argumentation. Two historic visits poignantly symbolized the dialogue. In 1992 Presiding Bishop Edmond Browning spoke at the Integrity national convention in Houston, spurned by the Bishop of Texas and scorned by EURRR. In 1993 President Pamela Chinnis of the House of Deputies spoke at the Integrity national convention in San Diego, spurned by the Bishop of San Diego. She came out as the mother of a gay son and pledged to use her appointment powers to put lesbian and gay deputies on committees of General Convention. During the 1991–1994 triennium eighteen thousand ordinary Episcopalians evaluated their parish dialogue about human sexuality—the largest response to a sexuality survey ever recorded by a Christian denomination. The committee overseeing the dialogue reported, "We estimate from the sale of dialogue guide materials that nearly 30,000 persons were actually involved in some way in this dialogue process—as many as 1,128 congregations and slightly more than seventy-seven per cent of the dioceses."

Integrity members actively participated in dialogue in our own parishes, some as leaders. Integrity, Inc. sought no official participation: we wanted the Church to own this process. As we expected, many who began the dialogue to find out more about "those people," ended by finding out much about themselves as well.

This dialogue must be credited with the radical difference of General Convention in 1994. Deputies arrived knowing that of those who had actively studied the issue "seventy percent indicate that being sexually active as a gay or lesbian person is not contrary to being a faithful Christian." In 1991 lesbigays had been at the lonely fringe: the House of Bishops had disassociated itself from the actions of the Bishop of Newark, the Rt. Rev. John S. Spong, for the Williams ordination and, at the 1991 convention, the Bishop of Washington and the Assistant Bishop of Newark averted censure for ordaining other openly lesbigays as priests. But by the 1994 General Convention at least a dozen other bishops had openly, albeit most of them quietly, ordained openly lesbigay people.

In the fall of 1993, just before the Panama meeting of the House of Bishops, the Rt. Rev. Otis Charles, retired Bishop of Utah and former dean of the Episcopal Divinity School, came out to the house and to the world as a gay man, the Episcopal Church's first openly gay bishop. It was clear to friends and foes that the center of opposition to lesbians and gays was not holding.

In an effort to block lesbians and gays, most of the bishops in the Southwest initiated a strong statement opposing ordination and blessings of lesbigay couples. They obtained the signatures of 106 bishops. Troubled by this step backward, the Bishop of Newark drafted a statement of conscience that affirmed lesbigay sexuality and spirituality and stated that he would continue to ordain lesbigays. Seventy-two bishops have now signed Bishop Spong's "Statement of Koinonia."

At first a score of 106 bishops against us versus 72 for us sounds more like defeat than victory, but not all bishops wield power equally. Diocesan bishops control diocesan policy; retired bishops do not, nor do assistant bishops. Active diocesans who signed Bishop Spong's "Statement of Koinonia" oversee 862,000 communicants compared with the 646,000 (25 percent fewer) communicants overseen by active diocesans who signed the negative document. It seems that we have won the war, even though it may take several more conventions before the opposition concedes.

The 1994 General Convention was noticeable for its inclusiveness. Lesbian and gay deputies led floor debates that resulted in significant legislation. General Convention called on the Standing Liturgical Commission to study what form the blessing of lesbigay relationships might take. Convention called upon the Church's official lobbyists in Washington to work for all legislation supportive of gays and lesbians. Convention called on the Episcopal Church Center to prepare materials to educate parents of teenagers to the issues of lesbigay and other teen suicides.

Episcopalians United for Revelation, Renewal, and Reformation came to General Convention with a one million dollar budget, but clearly they lost the day.

More church leaders began to speak out in favor of lesbians and gays. The Rt. Rev. Bennett Sims, Bishop of Atlanta, who had been a chief architect of the 1979 resolution inhibiting the ordination of lesbians and gays, explained in a 1991 open letter to the Church: "When I wrote that Pastoral Statement in 1977, I knew only one homosexual person up close. He scared me to death with his penetrating challenge that he was as complete a human being as I was." I was that person. In 1977 Bishop Sims had summoned me for discipline through the world press, yet at the 1995 General Convention Bishop Sims was the chief celebrant at a service in honor of the twentieth anniversary of the ordination of women and the twentieth anniversary of Integrity. He explained that he changed his mind when he began to know gays and lesbians as persons, as sister and brother Christians, not just as issues.

In a last desperate effort to stop the ordination of lesbians and gays, in 1995, 25 percent (76) of all living bishops took the extraordinary step of signing consents to try as a heretic Bishop Walter Righter. This was only the second heresy trial in the entire history of the Episcopal Church. Bishop Righter was attacked for ordaining the Rev. Barry Stopfel, an openly gay and noncelibate man who is in his second decade of a committed relationship with the Rev. Will Leckie, a minister in the United Church of Christ. The Court for the Trial of a Bishop met in open session three times and on May 15, 1996, read its decision. By a vote of seven to one the court ruled that the Episcopal Church has no doctrine that forbids the ordination of lesbians and gays. Those who brought the charges against Bishop Righter later announced that they would not appeal this decision. After twenty years of struggle, with many tears and prayers, a great moral victory had been won.

I realize that for many I am giving merely a political report, but politics has not driven my work in the Church, nor, I believe, has politics driven the work of most lesbians and gays in the Church. Why should it? The Church is not a significant political force today. The Church that codified heteroprivilege and heterocentric morality for the United States no longer exists as that powerful an institution. In the Church, however, lesbigays are driven instead by the Gospel imperative, the profound faith that God loves absolutely everybody. Our ministry is less about who we are than Whose we are. I attribute any success that we have to the authenticity of this calling. I believe that God is present in our world with a marvelous sense of humor, using gays and lesbians to evangelize the Church and bring it back to its first principle, namely, the boundless love of God and its absolute inclusiveness.

When the Integrity movement started we sometimes made the mistake of thinking that we were asking in. We began to discover, however, a marvelous mystery, that we lesbians and gays already are the Church, "that neither death, nor life, nor angels, nor rulers, nor things present, nor things to come, nor powers, nor height, nor depth, nor anything else in all creation, will be able to separate us from the love of God" (Romans 8:38–39).

Robert Nugent

Homophobia and the
U.S. Roman Catholic Clergy

There are approximately fifty thousand Roman Catholic priests in the United States. Two-thirds of these priests work directly under a bishop, mostly in parishes in a particular geographical area called a diocese, and are called Diocesan priests. The remainder belong to various religious orders, work in a variety of jobs under the supervision of their superiors, and are called Religious priests. This chapter will discuss only male priests, both Diocesan and Religious.

There are countless impressions, anecdotes, and personal experiences about homosexuality in the Roman Catholic priesthood, but few scientific or even serious studies available (Sipe 1990; Stuart 1993; Wagner 1981; Wolf 1989). The popular belief that a substantial number of Catholic priests are homosexually oriented seems well founded. This is especially true if we include in this figure not only those priests who are self-identified, comfortable with their homosexual orientation, and functioning at high levels of success and self-satisfaction but also those who are still in the processes of discovery, denial, or suppression.

Due to the lack of hard scientific data it is difficult, if not impossible, to substantiate the claim that homophobia is more prevalent in this population because of the official teachings of the Catholic Church on homosexuality. It is equally difficult to document the actual degree of homophobia among Roman Catholic clergy. Given the variables of this particular group, including age, educational levels, socioeconomic and ethnic backgrounds, ministerial experiences, theological orientations, and personal psychosexual histories, it is quite impossible to predict with any accuracy either types or depths of homophobia for any individual member. Despite the fact that the Catholic Church, and by extension its clerical representatives, is perceived in some quarters as a powerful, influential, and confirmed homophobic institution, it cannot be accurately concluded that each and every priest representing that institution is homophobic to the same degree. Some distinctions need to be made and recognized if we are to have an accurate understanding of the nature and extent of homophobia among Catholic clergy.

In order to describe the kinds of homophobia present among U.S. Catholic priests and to suggest some remedies to combat homophobia, we must distinguish between three major groups: heterosexual priests, homosexual priests, and gay priests.[1] This delineation employs a commonly used distinction in self-awareness and self-affirmation that has been drawn between *homosexual* and *gay*.

In this discussion the homosexual priest is one who is extremely closeted for professional or personal reasons and has reached a certain level of comfort or, in some cases, a more problematic resignation in his attitude toward his homosexuality. It also includes the priest who is more actively conflicted about his same-sex impulses and who is more likely to attempt to deny, suppress, or camouflage his homosexuality.

The gay priest values his homosexual orientation as a positive part of his personality and is generally more open and public about disclosing it in varying degrees. This category includes both the priest who identifies himself in very limited or wider personal circles as gay and the priest who is more open and public about his orientation. He might be active in ministry with gay and lesbian people, publicly supportive of gay and lesbian issues like civil rights, or involved in HIV-AIDS projects.

Heterosexual Priests and Homophobia

Homophobia exists in self-identified heterosexual priests for many of the same reasons it does among the general heterosexual population including psychological, sociological, and religious factors discussed in the growing literature on homophobia.

Among Catholic clergy, however, in all three categories, there are additional relevant factors that influence the variety of stances any individual heterosexual priest may take on homosexuality. Among the most significant components, especially for older priests, are a more traditional theological training, a mistrust or fear of sexuality and emotions, a need to conform closely to the expectations of an institution they represent in a public and official way, and their own affective experiences of sexuality.

Older Heterosexual Clergy

The vast majority of older heterosexual priests in their late forties, fifties, and sixties have limited personal experience with gay and lesbian persons. Their attitudes and behaviors in this area were shaped by more traditional theological and pastoral principles, which they learned as students. Sexual sins are to be judged with special understanding, because a habit stemming from the sexual drive often reduces or eliminates a person's full freedom to act and the person should be counseled not to give in to discouragement about overcoming such a habit.

General silence about homosexuality prevailed in the Catholic community until the mid-seventies. In 1975, partly as a response to the growing impact on society and churches of the gay liberation movement stemming from the Stonewall incident in 1969 and in response to the tentative probing of post-Vatican II Roman Catholic moral theologians about same-sex expression, the first major statement on homosexuality came from the Vatican (Sacred Congregation for the Doctrine of the Faith 1975.) Before this time priests of earlier generations rarely had any occasion to talk openly or seriously with peers about homosexuality, even on a counseling level, much less explore their own personal or theological viewpoints about homosexuality. The stigma or labeling attached to any manifested interest in the subject coupled with personal anxieties and lack of knowledge accounts for their present discomfort with the reality.

Despite their lack of familiarity with sound scientific information about homosexuality and their personal hesitancy to devote much time to study or reading in this area, many of these priests have had occasions to encounter gay and lesbian individuals throughout their years of ministry. For many of them, however, homosexuality remains a "mystery" or a "puzzle," but their own pastoral instincts tell them to treat people with kindness and care. Their information often comes primarily from the popular media, with its own myths and stereotypes, and from more informal anecdotal data not always free from a certain uneasiness with sexuality often found among traditional clergy. Yet some of them are still able to remedy earlier deficits in interpersonal relating and this also affects their postures toward homosexuality.

In this first category of older, more traditional heterosexual priests it is often their own level of psychosexual maturity that plays a major role in determining a certain variety of attitudes toward homosexuality. These attitudes can range anywhere from avoidance of the issue to trying to be sympathetic and understanding as illustrated by responses by priests of past generations to a question about how they deal with homosexuality in their pastoral work (Bowman 1994). Most of them are products of a closed seminary system that frowned on close personal friendships because of the suspicion of homosexuality. As a result, many of the priests trained in that era have been crippled in their ability to experience warm, loving friendships with either women or men. The whole issue of emotional intimacy was simply avoided as a danger to the vow of celibacy, which itself was seen primarily as not engaging in sexual intercourse. While a certain intimacy among the "jocks" engaged in athletic events was tolerated, any hint of sentimental relationships or feminine attitudes was strongly discouraged. With the advent of renewal programs designed for priests, workshops on human sexual development, celibacy, and intimacy, and groundbreaking books such as *The Sexual Celibate* (Goergen 1974) many of the priests in this group have grown in their appreciation of their own sexuality and that of others. This personal awareness of their own sexual feelings and needs has favorably influenced their interactions with gay and lesbian people. Some of them are aware of the controversy in the Church about homosexuality, and a few might be represented in the polls of Catholic clergy that indicate less than full agreement with the Church's moral judgment of homogenital expression (Keeler 1994)

This group also includes those who question on pastoral grounds the feasibility of a demand for total sexual abstinence as the only possible advice for homosexual Catholics. They evidence strong allegiance to the Church's teachings on sexuality, marriage, and family in the public forum and would not support gay marriage. But their pastoral experience has led them to respect a decision that a gay or lesbian individual might make based on life experience and a decision of conscience made in good faith.

Heterosexual Homophobic Clergy

Among heterosexual clergy, both older and some more conservative younger priests, there is also a small minority who are vocal and public about their homophobic attitudes. Some of these undertake personal campaigns to fight the influence of what they call the "homosexual agenda" in the Church (Rueda 1982.) While it is not accurate to claim that every priest who actively opposes homosexuality is a "closet case," this is undoubtedly true in some instances of older priests not reconciled with their sexuality. The rabid obsession of some of these priests with homosexuality as an evil requiring constant vigilance coupled with their intemperate language and signs of paranoia seem to evidence classic indications of the psychological mechanism called projection or reaction formation.

Younger, Knowledgeable Heterosexual Clergy

Another subgroup of heterosexual priests found in many of the younger and more educated clergy are those who are fairly knowledgeable about the topic but are also sincerely convinced, both intellectually and emotionally, of the fundamental rightness of Catholic teaching on human sexuality as found in current Church documents. Their position on homosexuality and the intellectual foundations upon which it is based is best exemplified by Cardinal Joseph Bernardin and the U.S. Catholic bishops (United States Catholic Conference 1990). In a very sensitive and pastoral way they attempt to ground this teaching intellectually and apply it when dealing with gay and lesbian individuals both publicly and privately. This group is generally more familiar with current theological questions about homosexuality and better equipped to participate in a thoughtful dialogue with gay and lesbian individuals about issues like moral decision making, challenges to Church teaching, the scriptural underpinning for Church teaching, and data from the sciences.

Chaplains and Priests in Social Justice Ministries

A final subgroup of heterosexual clergy are priests engaged in social justice ministries (racial equality, peace and nonviolence, human rights, liberation theology, etc.) and university and college chaplains. These priests are exceptional for their openness to and support of gay and lesbian individuals and projects related to their civil rights and human dignity. These are also clergy who as individuals have worked seriously to reduce homophobia both personally and institutionally. For those engaged in ministries around issues of justice and equality, the social, economic, and political relationships among the different kinds of systemic oppression are especially clear. They easily make the connections between homophobia, heterosexism, and misogyny. They are also most likely to participate in workshops and seminars on homophobia and be familiar with some of the basics of heterosexism through reading and study. Many of them are very effective in their professional and interpersonal relationships with gay and lesbian individuals. They are also the ones most likely to actively support civil rights for lesbian and gay people, either by endorsing public statements on their behalf or by testifying openly as Catholic clergy before legislative groups on behalf of gay rights legislation.

Reducing Homophobia in Heterosexual Priests

Having described, somewhat broadly, four subgroups of heterosexual priests, I would like to briefly comment on some effective means to address the different manifestations of homophobia in each of these categories.

The group of older clergy with little academic knowledge of homosexuality but often a rich experience of human nature are in many instances open to personal interaction with gay or lesbian individuals. Very often gay and lesbian family members or relatives can be the most effective means to help them reexamine their beliefs and feelings about homosexuality. Parents of gay and lesbian Catholics who encounter these priests can be very effective in passing on reading material and helping these priests establish some form of personal contact with their children. Rarely will they go out of their way to participate in an educational program. Personal friendships and social interaction are the most effective antidotes to low-level homophobia in this group of priests.[2]

There is probably no appropriate or adequate response to the second group of heterosexual priests; their homophobia is so deeply entrenched that no amount of dialogue, reasoning, or even interpersonal contacts will substantially modify their position. Fortunately, in the Catholic community their audience is mostly a small group of like-minded people who read their diatribes. Their lack of logic, their pathological dislike, and their verbal disdain of gay and lesbian people (despite disclaimers to the contrary) are more than obvious to an intelligent observer. Sometimes letters to the editor of publications in which they air their irresponsible claims can help counteract the damage of their assault. At times a stronger and more formal complaint to the priest's bishop or superior in the form of a personal meeting can also be effective, especially when the concern comes from a group such as parishioners or parents.

Among heterosexual clergy a combination of the third and fourth subgroups comprise by far the largest number of heterosexual priests for whom the label *homophobic* would not be fully accurate if understood to mean a fear or hatred of homosexual people. Homophobia, like sexuality, can also be charted on a continuum, ranging from strong emotional homophobia (gay bashing) at one extreme, to more rational homonegative responses (qualified acceptance), to a homopositive response (full acceptance) at the other. Priests whom I have described as younger and knowledgeable or as involved in social justice and chaplaincy ministries can be generally characterized as homonegative. This simply means that while they neither hate nor fear gay and lesbian people, they are neither ready to acknowledge a fundamental equality between homosexuality and heterosexuality. From their theological and biblical studies and their own lived experience of human sexuality they believe that heterosexuality is "normative" from both religious and anthropological perspectives. Usually their position rests on the centrality of the biological procreative dimension of sexuality, on the male-female complementarity concept, and on the physiobiological genital differentiation.

Their fear of homosexuality—if it can be accurately described as fear—manifests itself in an unwillingness to recognize a complete equality between homosexuality and heterosexuality or to accord same-sex marriages equal recognition and standing in the Church and society. For them, homosexuality represents a non-normative expression of human sexuality because of some perceived lack (physical procreation, biological and psychospiritual complementarity, etc.) that makes it not sinful, immoral, evil, or sick but simply something less than the ideal or fully human expression of sexuality. Catholic theologians like James Hanigan who argue for some qualified recognition of homosexuality best articulate this position (Hanigan 1988).

In terms of continuing dialogue and public discourse in Church circles about homosexuality, I believe it is both more helpful and more accurate to describe this group as homonegative or heterocentrist rather than homophobic. Likewise, the response suggested in this case would not be to homophobia but to heterosexism or heterocentrism. *Heterocentrism*, in probably the most benign definition of the term, is the belief or conviction that heterosexuality (and all the social structures that support and enforce it) is normative for human sexuality both theologically and philosophically. No matter how accepting of homosexuality this last group of priests are, they nevertheless place a negative value judgment on homosexuality both as orientation and activity. Theirs is the language at least academically of "lack," "less than," "not as good as," and "non-normative."

There are some few Catholic theologians who reject heterocentrism (McNeill 1995; Maguire 1983; Farley 1983; Guindon 1983). Most mainstream Catholic moral theologians—such as Charles Curran, who best represents this heterocentrist approach—acknowledge that the theological community must remain open to new data and new experiences that could challenge the heterosexual norm. All of them are willing to make exceptions to the norm in the case of stable and faithful committed relationships (Curran 1972).

Heterosexual priests who are heterocentrist rather than homophobic do not need an approach based on responding to homophobia as commonly understood. They cannot be called homopositive because they are unwilling to evaluate homosexuality positively. They are not willing to concede a full equality between homosexuality and heterosexuality as two possible and valid forms of human sexual development. They are, however, willing to engage in ongoing discussions, research, and reflections on homosexuality, which helps them clarify and refine their own positions and consider the merits of alternative approaches. This approach, however, requires disciplined study of academic and technical information and many individuals have neither the time nor the resources for engaging in such a demanding project. The groundwork for responding to heterocentrism has been laid in a clear and detailed exposition of its major tenets, which includes five operative models and suggested challenges (Jung and Smith 1993.)

A related and perhaps equally effective response to a heterocentrist position is personal interaction with gay and lesbian people. Catholic theologians who hold a heterocentrist position also view human experience as an important source of data for ethical and moral evaluation. They are open to dialogue with individuals who experience their homosexuality not as a human deficit but as a blessing and part of God's created order. This honest and respectful interchange can be a call to the priest who holds to a heterocentrist view of normativity. An important task and responsibility for gay and lesbian people is to articulate their experiences to enrich the theological endeavor.

The theological heterocentrist's stance on evaluating homosexuality invariably rests on an explanation that views homosexuality as a departure from some original divine plan or intent. While the scientific evidence of some genetic basis for the homosexual orientation is relevant to this discussion, it is not necessarily convincing for this heterocentrist position. Although a biological basis for homosexuality might offer a reason for the phenomenon, it ultimately does not resolve the moral or ethical issue as to whether or not this phenomenon is humanly desirable, since other biologically or genetically based realities such as alcoholism or diabetes are not considered beneficial for the human person or society. The biological basis for the heterocentrist natural law reasoning is not immune from criticism (Pronk 1993.)

Heterocentrism also includes personal, institutional, and cultural expressions. Heterosexism is defined *theologically* as the biblically or theologically based belief or conviction that heterosexuality is the normative model for all human sexuality. If one accepts this normativity as the fundamental anthropological truth about human sexuality, then logically one must put a negative judgment on homosexuality. Heterocentrism logically requires that one evaluate homosexuality negatively, no matter how benignly. In contrast, newer cross-cultural studies indicate that same-sex relationships have been accepted by many if not most cultures and religions in human history (Conner 1993; Bullough 1976; Swidler 1993; Williams 1986).

Priests who hold a heterocentrist position claim it does not necessarily mean that homosexuality must necessarily be denigrated or that gay and lesbian people need be treated with any less dignity and respect than others. For some, it does not necessarily entail opposition to the legal and social recognition of same-sex committed relationships as valuable both for individuals and the larger human society (Hanigan 1988).

It is not possible to say how many Catholic priests embrace this heterocentrist position, but as the official position of the Church it has the support of the large majority of both older and younger Catholic clergy today. All the Church's statements on homosexuality, including the recent papal rejection of the concept and legal support of same-sex marriage, find their underpinning in this theological position.

Homophobia and "Homosexual" Priests

Homophobia among homosexual priests is similar to internalized homophobia, which is widely discussed in the literature. There is, however, the added and often exacerbated tension of a public commitment to a celibate lifestyle and the expectations accompanying that commitment. Celibacy, rightly understood, can be and is for many priests both a psychologically healthy and a spiritually energizing experience. But it always requires an honest evaluation and a mature acceptance of one's sexuality. This kind of integration is especially crucial for a priest who comes to the realization of his own homosexual orientation in a church and culture that consistently promotes heterosexuality as natural and good, with the implication or the outright claim that other forms of sexual development are inferior, if not a form of psychological sickness or moral evil. The homosexual priest who has not come to even minimal understanding or acceptance of his homosexuality or is attempting to suppress same-sex impulses because of a fear of facing the implications of acknowledging them—even in a limited way—will inevitably manifest signs of homophobia directed at others or at himself. This can take many forms including avoidance and silence, a "super-orthodox" and rigid stand, subtle hostility toward gay and lesbian individuals, and even opposition to those working in gay ministry.

In more than twenty years of working with Catholic clergy I have at times met with active opposition from other priests to my ministry. These include attempts to block my workshops or seminars from Catholic facilities in various parts of the country. Invariably these are priests whom others know to be closeted homosexuals, priests often sexually active in furtive ways or emotionally and physically seductive of other males. Sometimes they hold influential positions in the power structure of the local Church.

For other sexually conflicted homosexual priests the coping mechanism takes the form of alcohol abuse, lust for power, materialistic lifestyles, and inappropriate sexual relationships with adolescent or preadolescent males. The much publicized cases of pedophile and ephebophile priests have precipitated a profound crisis of credibility for the Catholic Church and a great deal of pain and anger for victims and families. In the majority of cases the issue is not clinical pedophilia but an inability of the priests to face their own affective homosexual impulses and to relate to other adult males maturely rather than fostering dependency among younger and more vulnerable males (Sennot 1992).

Undoubtedly, part of the problem of those clergy in trouble because of their same-sex attractions has to do with the neglect of mature sexual development in seminary training and the lack of an atmosphere where the homosexual student could comfortably face issues about sexuality and celibacy. In some religious orders support groups and specialized retreats are available for students who are facing sexuality issues. Official Church guidelines for priestly formation mandate education in human sexuality that includes an acceptance and direction of their own sexuality and the expectation that they will relate warmly, easily, and joyfully with men and women alike within the boundaries of celibacy (National Conference of Catholic Bishops 1981.)

In the past fifteen years positive steps have been taken in many seminaries and religious orders both in screening processes and formation programs to help the significant number of homosexual candidates address issues of sexuality. These changes bode well for the Church's ability to reduce the number of homosexual homophobic students being ordained in the coming years (Nugent 1989).

Yet, at the same time, it must be acknowledged that there is still significant discomfort in some Church circles about the numbers of gay applicants for priesthood and religious life. Part of this stems from a continuing confusion between adult homosexuality and pedophilia. Part comes from the theological homophobia that views homosexual orientation as, in and of itself and apart from any behavior, an automatic bar to priesthood regardless of one's commitment to and ability to live a celibate lifestyle (Nugent 1989). Unrealistic and unjust policies of denial and repression concerning homosexuality either by Church authorities or students themselves in seminaries and religious communities will have disastrous repercussions. Healthy, self-affirming, and integrated ego-syntonic students who evaluate their homosexuality in a positive light might face more external social problems in an atmosphere that fosters pretense and rewards dishonesty. Self-rejecting, conflicted, and ego-dystonic homosexual candidates who evaluate their homosexuality negatively will have less external social problems but will eventually be forced, perhaps even unwillingly, to acknowledge their own internal struggles.

The issue of outing arises in these latter cases of closeted homosexual and homophobic priests, especially those who are in positions of power or authority and publicly vocal and active in their antihomosexual beliefs and behaviors. This is a difficult and emotional issue and the tactics utilized by radical gay groups who out public figures will probably not be effective when dealing with Church leadership. For some clergy, such an accusation, especially where there is insufficient proof, will only serve to reinforce a sense of righteousness and martyrdom; for the supporters of such clergy, the outing tactic will only serve to validate their belief that the priest's public, organized opposition to homosexuality is morally right and good.

The *public* disclosure of a priest's homosexuality or sexual activity as a way to counter his homophobic behavior can be counterproductive. It could even gain sympathy for the individual and serve to reinforce a misguided campaign against gay and lesbian people. In the most tragic case it could precipitate self-destructive behaviors, which have occurred when the names of prominent individuals arrested for illegal sexual activity are published in local newspapers—a practice that gay activists have strenuously opposed.

A far more effective tactic is to contact the priest's immediate superior or bishop and arrange for a personal meeting to discuss the situation. In most cases, though not always, the appropriate action will be taken and the harmful behavior of the priest will be addressed with professional or administrative remedies. If the situation is ignored or defended, then the effectiveness of outing becomes at least a viable question. Adequate discussion with responsible Church authorities, serious and mutual efforts to resolve the situation, and reasonable forewarning are essential to this process.

For those other cases of self-hating or self-denying homosexual priests whose homophobia is more inner than outward directed, professional help is far more likely to effect a positive change than hostile or angry confrontations with groups or individuals over issues of homosexuality or lesbian and gay rights. Frequently the priest's behavior comes to the attention of his superiors and he is remanded to a rehabilitation program to help him deal with his sexuality. At other times the intervention of another priest or even an empathetic gay or lesbian friend or colleague who can directly but compassionately speak with the priest about behavioral problems and apparent conflicts that might be related to unresolved sexual issues.

Homophobia and "Gay Priests"

Among Catholic priests today there is a substantial number of priests who are not only accepting and affirming of their homosexual orientation but also comfortable disclosing it to others in more or less public ways. They are for the most part successful in their work, happy in their social and personal lives, and less stressed about their homosexual identity and associations (Nash 1990.) In many parts of the country, and in a number of religious orders, there exist support groups for gay priests that have been helpful in combating internalized homophobia and in integrating priests' sexuality into a healthy commitment to celibacy. For more than fifteen years a national support group, Communications Ministry, Inc., has provided support groups, retreats, and a monthly newsletter for gay clergy and religious. Some gay priests have spoken openly about their sexuality and their struggles before groups of priests, seminarians, or other limited public forums or have written about themselves in anthologies on homosexuality and the priesthood (Gramick 1990.)

Included in this group of self-affirming and integrated priests are those who find no need to be public in any way about their homosexuality but who at the same time have successfully dealt with internalized homophobia. Some of these priests work quietly behind the scenes to better the situation for lesbian and gay people in the Church. They do not miss an opportunity to speak or act in a positive way about homosexuality without calling attention to their own situations. They are supportive of various forms of min-

istry for gay and lesbian Catholics and not hesitant to criticize Church policies or documents that cause pain for lesbian and gay people.

At the same time, they feel no real need to identify themselves as gay men
to more than a few close friends and some others—most of whom would
never suspect their sexual orientation. Some of them have risen to powerful and influential positions in the Church hierarchy. They are willing to
work for change within the parameters of current Church teaching and
practice to push the envelope on this subject. While they are most effective
behind the scenes and work quietly for the betterment of the lives of gay
and lesbian people and for a deeper understanding of the reality and experience of homosexuality, they are unwilling to adopt a public or more confrontational stance.

A second group of gay priests are those who feel a need to make known
their sexual orientation in a more public manner, even if only within their
own religious orders or dioceses. Some also feel called upon to educate the
public about homosexuality, to minister to the gay and lesbian community
through Dignity, the national organization for gay and lesbian Catholics,
through other forms of ministry, or to take an active role in HIV-AIDS work.

While the level of internalized homophobia among these last two groups
of priests is not high, there are some areas where homophobia can become
an issue. The struggle of these priests, in my experience, has been the challenge to live as a public minister of a Church that condemns homosexual acts
in strong language while attempting to speak compassionately about homosexual people. There is considerable inner dissonance generated when a person in this position is asked to articulate views that he does not accept and
that he is at times powerless to publicly oppose or reject.

For many of these individuals the stress becomes unbearable and they
decide to abandon their ministry in order to live out their sexuality more
openly (Fleishacker 1993; Monette 1993–1994). Others seem to find ways to
be self-accepting, self-affirming, and even public to some degree about their
sexual orientation. At the same time, they take steps to lessen as far as possible the conflicts arising between their professional positions and personal
lives. Priests in rural areas who are peripheral to the gay culture find support
in friends who are not necessarily gay themselves (Nash 1990). Urban clergy
generally utilize some of the social and ministerial resources of the local gay
community. Many priests find that being open about their sexuality with a
bishop or superior helps them function in a more relaxed way. Some gay
clergy, even in diocesan offices, often serve as referral resources for other

priests because they are quietly perceived not only as gay but as responsible and effective priests. Support organizations like Communication Ministry, Inc., individual or group therapy, spiritual direction from a gay-positive director, nongay supportive friends, and affirmation from other gay individuals are all important elements in a healthy resolution. There is no doubt that these priests can and do successfully resolve many of the conflicts and tensions, but doing so also requires an ongoing sensitivity that can require a good deal of psychic energy. From time to time changes in their own personal situations or in the climate of the larger Church (as when officials issue documents perceived as hostile to gay people) generate renewed stress.

Ironically, another source of tension can come from the gay community itself. Some members can be less than supportive or understanding of the choice these priests have made to balance their own personal sexual integrity with service to an institution that publicly devalues homosexuality. The question is often asked of the gay priest: "How can you continue to represent an institution that condemns homosexuality and demeans what you yourself are?" The incredulity with which the question is asked is especially strong coming from Catholics who have rejected the Church in favor of their own sexuality and do not believe there is any possibility of choosing both (Nugent 1992). What is often at work in this situation is the unexamined assumption that the only choice available for these priests is between being completely out or suffering from crippling internalized homophobia. The gay priest who is active in HIV-AIDS ministry or with gay and lesbian Catholics most often faces this attitude. He needs support from gay and lesbian friends who appreciate the reasons and the values associated with this choice and who can provide both challenge and encouragement.

Like any other profession, the Catholic priesthood includes a wide variety of attitudes toward homosexuality. Far from being a group controlled by a monolithic structure in what they believe, think, and say, Catholic priests, despite their affiliations with the institution, probably differ very little from other segments of the population in their attitudes toward homosexuality and gay and lesbian people. The common assumption that they are always and necessarily more homophobic because of their identity as priests with close ties to official Church teaching does not stand under close scrutiny. The homophobia present in the ranks of the priesthood is certainly colored by issues of mandatory celibacy, a history of a theology distorted by sex-negative thinking, and a patriarchal power system. There is no one form of homophobia that can be easily or simply analyzed in the Catholic priesthood.

Studies have shown that educational programs are successful in reducing homophobia. However, for U.S. priests, affective and interpersonal aspects are essential for combating clerical homophobia. The centrality of the Church's long history of social justice for oppressed groups, the example of Jesus, who associated with social outcasts, and the work of reconciliation that is crucial to ministry today are all additional incentives to help priests reduce or eliminate homophobia both personally and institutionally. As influential leaders in many communities and fields of endeavor they can be effective antidotes to homophobia. How they choose to do this depends on many factors. But the time and energy spent by individuals and groups in helping them overcome homophobia will have positive and lasting impact on their own lives as priests and on the lives of gay and lesbian people far into the future.

NOTES

1. The author is well aware that the unnuanced homosexual/heterosexual dichotomy is inadequate for contemporary discussions on sexuality, given the positions and insights of both essentialists and social constructionists. On the more popular level these terms are still utilized by most authors with an understanding that serves the purpose of a general discussion. Only a small percentage of Catholic priests identify themselves as bisexual.

2. This group of clergy would respond positively to the statement of the U.S. Catholic bishops who "call on all Christians and citizens of good will to confront their own fears about homosexuality and to curb the humor and discrimination that offend homosexual persons. We understand that having a homosexual orientation brings with it enough anxiety, pain and issues related to self-acceptance without society adding additional prejudicial treatment" (United States Catholic Conference, *Human Sexuality*, p. 55) and the claim of the Catholic bishops of Washington state that "prejudice against homosexuals is a greater infringement of the norm of Christian morality than is homosexual orientation or activity" (Washington State Catholic Conference, *The Prejudice Against Homosexuals and the Ministry of the Church*, Seattle: Washington State Catholic Conference, 1983, p. 4).

REFERENCES

Bowman, J. 1994. *Bending the Rules: What American Priests Tell American Catholics*. New York: Crossroad.

Bullough, V. 1976. *Sexual Variance in Society and History.* Chicago: University of Chicago Press.

Curran, C. 1972. "Dialogue with the Homophile Movement: The Morality of Homosexuality." In C. Curran, *Catholic Moral Theology in Dialogue.* Notre Dame: University of Notre Dame Press.

Conner, R. 1993. *Blossom of Bone: Reclaiming the Connection Between Homo-eroticism and the Sacred.* San Francisco: Harper.

Farley, M. 1983. "An Ethic for Same-Sex Relations." In R. Nugent, ed., *A Challenge to Love: Gay and Lesbian Catholics in the Church*, pp. 93–106. New York: Crossroad.

Fleischhacker, M. 1993. "Why I Left the Priesthood: A Letter from the Heart." *White Crane Newsletter: Journal for the Exploration of Gay Men's Spirituality* 19:13–14.

Goergen, D. 1974. *The Sexual Celibate.* New York: Seabury.

Gramick, J. 1990. *Homosexuality in the Priesthood and Religious Life*, New York: Crossroad.

Guindon, A. 1983. "Homosexual Acts or Gay Speech." In J. Gramick and R. Nugent, eds., *The Vatican and Homosexuality*, pp. 208–15. New York: Crossroad.

Hanigan, J. 1988. *Homosexuality: The Test Case for Christian Sexual Ethics.* New York: Paulist Press.

Jung, P. B., and R. F. Smith. 1993. *Heterosexism: An Ethical Challenge.* Albany: State University of New York Press.

Keeler, R. 1984. "Can a Good Catholic Be Gay?" *Newsday*, August 10, p. B5.

McNeill, J. J. 1995. *Freedom, Glorious Freedom: The Spiritual Journey to the Fullness of Life for Gays, Lesbians, and Everybody Else*, Boston: Beacon.

Maguire, D. 1983. "The Morality of Homosexual Marriage." In R. Nugent, ed., *A Challenge to Love: Gay and Lesbian Catholics in the Church*, pp. 118–34. New York: Crossroad.

Monette, M. 1993–1994. " Gay, Married and Priest Forever." *Bondings* (Fall/Winter) 16(1):5.

Nash, J. 1990. *Stress, Ego Management, and Disclosure of Homosexual Orientation Among Mid-Life Transition Male Roman Catholic Religious Professionals.* Menlo Park: Pacific School of Religion.

National Conference of Catholic Bishops. 1981. *The Program of Priestly Formation.* 3d ed. Washington, D.C.: National Conference of Catholic Bishops,

Nugent, R. 1989. "Some Issues of Homosexual Applicants." *Horizon* (Winter) 14(2):156–67.

—— 1992a. "Catholicism: On the Compatibility of Sexuality and Faith." In B. Berzon, ed., *Positively Gay: New Approaches to Gay and Lesbian Life*, pp. 156–67. Berkeley: Celestial Arts.

—— 1992b. "Seminary and Religious Candidates." In R. Nugent and J. Gramick, eds., *Building Bridges: Gay and Lesbian Reality and the Catholic Church*, pp. 105–20. Mystic, Conn.: Twenty-Third.

Pronk, P. 1993. *Against Nature: Types of Moral Argumentation Regarding Homosexuality.* Grand Rapids: Eeerdmans.

Rueda, E. 1982. *The Homosexual Network*, Old Greenwich, Conn.: Devin Adair.

Sacred Congregation for the Doctrine of the Faith. 1975. *Declaration on Certain Questions Concerning Sexual Ethics*. Rome: Sacred Congregation for the Doctrine of the Faith.

Sennot, C. R. 1992. *Broken Covenant: The Secret Life of Bruce Ritter*. New York: Pinnacle.

Sipe, R. 1990. *A Secret World: Sexuality and the Search for Celibacy*. New York: Brunner/Mazel.

Stuart, E. 1993. *Chosen: Gay Catholic Priests Tell Their Stories*. London: Geoffrey Chapman.

Swidler, A., ed. 1993. *Homosexuality and World Religions*. Valley Forge, Pa.: Trinity.

United States Catholic Conference. 1990. *Human Sexuality: A Catholic Perspective for Education and Lifelong Learning*. Washington, D.C.: United States Catholic Conference.

Wagner, R. 1981. *Gay Catholic Priests: A Study of Cognitive and Affective Dissonance*. San Francisco: Specific.

Williams, W. L. 1986. *The Spirit and the Flesh: Sexual Diversity in American Indian Culture*. Boston: Beacon.

Wolf, J. G., ed. 1989. *Gay Priests*. New York: Harper and Row.

J Craig Fong

Building Alliances:
The Case of the Japanese American
Citizens League Endorsement of Same-Sex Marriage

In May 1994 the nation's largest Asian Pacific Islander civil rights group, the Japanese American Citizens League, passed a resolution supporting same-sex marriage, thus allying itself with the gay and lesbian community on one of the most controversial human rights issues faced in the United States. The twenty-five-thousand-member JACL has had some history of self-initiated support for queer issues. In 1988, for example, JACL amended its constitution to include sexual orientation in its nondiscrimination philosophy. It also passed a national resolution supporting the right of gay men and lesbians to serve in the U.S. armed forces.

Although the National Gay and Lesbian Task Force supported JACL's efforts to secure financial redress for Japanese-Americans who were interned by the U.S. government during World War II, lesbian and gay civil rights groups have not historically supported issues important to people of color. In fact, the gay and lesbian community has often ignored people of color until such support was deemed to be necessary or desirable by the national queer leadership. The two groups found each other through the efforts of a handful of heterosexual JACL leaders and Asian Pacific queer advocates acting as go-betweens.

The Same-Sex Marriage Issue

While the nation's attention was riveted in early 1993 on the Pentagon and the question of allowing gay men and lesbians to serve in the U.S. armed forces, the Supreme Court of Hawai'i was making a ruling six thousand miles away regarding the right of persons of the same sex to marry. In the

historic case of *Baehr v. Lewin* (852 P.2d 44 [Haw. 1993]), the Hawai'i
Supreme Court ruled on May 5, 1993, that the denial of marriage licenses to
same-sex couples violated the equal protection clause of the Hawai'i constitution, which prohibits sex-based as well as other forms of discrmination.
The Supreme Court remanded the case to a trial court for further consideration. In 1996 the trial court considered whether the state has a "compelling"
interest justifying its discriminatory policy, subject to "strict scrutiny," the
highest standard of judicial review (852 P.2d 44, 67 [Haw. 1993]).

Most legal experts believe that Hawai'i *will* ultimately legalize marriage
for same-sex couples. When couples from the other forty-nine states then go
to Hawai'i, marry, and return to their homes, they will be legally married,
and recognized as married, in Hawai'i. The question will arise: will their
marriages be recognized by the federal government, by their home states, by
departments of motor vehicles, by credit card companies, by employee benefit plans, or by the health club's family plan? In many states the radical right
has already targeted this issue by proposing legislation denying recognition
to future legal same-sex marriages.

So although the litigants and the lawyers proceed apace in the Hawai'i
courts, a battle is shaping up in the other states. In that battle the gay and lesbian community will need every friend and advocate it can muster.

As the radical right continues to manipulate the American electorate, gay
and lesbian advocates have no choice but to create effective bridges to other
civil rights groups, especially groups dedicated to first amendment and
Equal Protection Clause freedoms. Such groups can understand, support,
and stand in solidarity with queer concerns. To create these linkages, the
queer community must look to those of its members who have natural
entrée to and credibility with such groups. Unfortunately, most major gay
and lesbian organizations in the country do not have people of color in
meaningful positions of visible political leadership. These groups must
assiduously cultivate, and not marginalize, leaders of color if future queer
civil rights initiatives are to enjoy broad-based support.

Support from the
Japanese American Citizens League

Ironically, JACL's first steps toward supporting same-sex marriage were taken
by heterosexuals. In 1993 *Baehr v. Lewin* lead counsel Dan Foley contacted
William Kaneko, then president of the JACL's Hawai'i chapter, encouraging
Kaneko to help him forestall an attempt in the Hawai'i legislature to block

same-sex marriage. Kaneko was also JACL national vice president for public affairs, a position that enabled him to raise the same-sex marriage issue with the national organization. Given JACL's history, Foley's request to Kaneko was not that unusual.

Hawai'i's JACL chapter had a history of taking bold stands on broadly based issues. The chapter supported financial redress for Japanese-Americans who had been relocated as well as those who had been interned. It was also vigorous in its support for a controversial discrimination case brought by Japanese-American Bruce Yamashita against the United States Marine Corps.

Kaneko brought Foley's request before the Hawai'i chapter's membership, and a resolution of support was introduced to the Hawai'i chapter in November 1993. It was debated and, although the discussion was heated, the resolution was passed, and JACL's Hawaii chapter became the first JACL entity to support same-sex marriage. In February 1994 Kaneko brought the resolution to JACL's national board of directors. A number of board members recognized the broader civil rights implications of the marriage question; however, resistance was strong from board members who were reluctant to get involved in issues "that have nothing to do with us." They voted to table the motion.

The national board of JACL directed the eight district governors to poll or evaluate the sentiments of their constituent chapters. Board member Trisha Murakawa, a former JACL national vice president, and Kaneko prepared packets of information about the issue, sent them to all chapters, and began to lobby the district governors and chapter members for support. The resolution was again presented to the national board in May 1994, where it was approved.

Kaneko and Murakawa thought their victory was secure until a JACL chapter from Utah introduced a resolution to rescind the board's approval. Such a resolution needed to be voted upon by all individual chapters and so was to be argued and decided at JACL's convention, to be held, coincidentally, in Salt Lake City in August 1994. They were then faced with the more difficult logistical task of lobbying 115 chapters and their delegates rather than talking person-to-person with the eight district governors. Both Murakawa and Kaneko expected a bruising and unpleasant battle and did not have enough information about gay and lesbian issues to carry the fight alone.

Homophobic letters opposing same-sex marriage began appearing in the *Pacific Citizen*, JACL's official newspaper. It appeared that same-sex marriage could lose JACL's support. A handful of queer JACL members, most of whom had not been previously active in gay issues, read the letters with growing alarm. Their own family, JACL—which had always been largely neutral about gays and lesbians—was on the verge of doing something hateful, homophobic, and wrong. Murakawa and Kaneko began to contact queer Asian Pacific Islander friends and advocates to help them win JACL's support. Only at this point, in mid-summer 1994, did lesbians and gay men become seriously involved in the JACL campaign.

Building the Bridge

The queer community and JACL clearly needed more information about each other; they needed a way to meet one another and create a relationship. In many ways this is parallel to the needs of those involved in traditional Japanese arranged marriages. Even today, marriage in Japan is often arranged through the *o-miai*, meetings between prospective partners who may have never met one another. Such arranged marriages are misunderstood by many Westerners. The pragmatic among us question the longevity of such manufactured matches, while the more romantic cannot imagine how two people, paired without love, could ever get along. Americans would do well to remember the long tradition of arranged marriages in many European countries.

Central to the *o-miai* tradition is the *nakohdo*, the go-between through whom the couple meets and becomes acquainted with each other. The *nakohdo* makes the initial approach to the individuals and their families, helps to acquaint each individual with the other, and oversees the first few meetings. At this stage the *nakohdo*'s familiarity with both parties makes it possible for the *nakohdo* to facilitate the finding of common ground, help smooth misunderstandings, and allow the relationship to deepen naturally. The *nakohdo* makes possible a joining of two parties who might not have come together on their own.

What was needed in 1994 was a *nakohdo*, a go-between to help the two groups better understand each other. In order to do so, the *nakohdo* had to have credibility with and knowledge of both groups, explaining the differences and commonalities and dispelling the fears and uncertainties. This was not an easy role and certainly not one for mainstream gay and lesbian leaders to arrogantly reserve to themselves.

Asian Pacific Islander queer activists from San Francisco and Los Angeles—most of whom were not previously active in JACL issues and many of whom had never before worked with one another—rallied to the call from their brothers and sisters, and a *nakohdo* was born. The ad hoc group formed to (1) write, produce, and distribute information about lesbians and gay men, (2) work with the JACL insiders, primarily Kaneko and Murakawa, who were lobbying chapter delegates from the inside, (3) locate a gay or lesbian Asian Pacific leader with a national profile who could address the convention with force and credibility, and (4) organize a task force of queer Asian Pacific Islanders to participate in the educate-and-lobby effort at the Salt Lake City convention.

The ad hoc committee, with keen knowledge and experience of both communities, performed spectacularly. They created brochures that explained the economic benefits of marriage, a question-and-answer handout that dispelled particular Asian myths about queers, and even produced a series of one-sheet comics depicting the difficulties in the coming out process particular to Japanese-Americans. Two members of the ad hoc committee had been JACL members and worked closely with Kaneko and Murakawa to coordinate the committee's activities with their own. The committee also contacted this writer, asking me to address the convention in my capacity as director of the western office of Lambda Legal Defense and Education Fund, Inc. New York–based Lambda is co-counsel in the *Baehr v. Lewin* case, providing expertise on gay and lesbian issues to lead counsel Dan Foley of Honolulu. Finally, the committee organized a cadre of about one dozen pan-Asian queers that went to Salt Lake City, set up an information booth, and lobbied JACL members.

I addressed the convention on Friday, August 5. I highlighted the civil rights connection between queer issues and those confronting Japanese-Americans. I reminded the assembled members that in 1942 the unconstitutional relocation and imprisonment of Japanese-Americans was accomplished because of racism and xenophobia and justified by inflated national security concerns. Similarly, at the beginning of the AIDS pandemic attempts were made to institutionalize people with HIV because of ignorance and homophobia and justified by trumped up public health concerns. I pointed out mainstream America's long history of dehumanizing people of color by dictating who can and cannot be included in their families—that slaves were forbidden to marry, that slave families could be torn asunder, and that, as recently as 1967, interracial couples were illegal in sixteen states. The prohibition against same-sex marriage is, I said, another example of the government telling people what their families should look like. As I spoke, I could see eyebrows furrowing and heads nodding as, at least for some delegates, the connection was made. For them it was no longer about sex; it was about family. Now some of them understood that it was not a special right but a civil right.

Final debate of the issue on Saturday, August 6, was acrimonious. Although I felt my own presentation had gone well the afternoon before, I was not convinced that enough minds had been changed.

Then U.S. congressman Norm Mineta, a Japanese-American with a long respected history in JACL, rose and asked to address the convention. Mineta's remarks clearly framed the issue: JACL's credibility as a civil rights organization was at stake.

> I believe it would be disastrous if this Convention were to repudiate the action of our National Board in this matter. There are those who have argued that gay rights issues are not Japanese-American issues.
>
> I cannot think of any more dangerous precedent for this organization to set than to take a position on an issue of principle based solely on how it directly affects Americans of Japanese ancestry.
>
> When we fought our decade-long battle for redress [for World War II internees] , we won. We could not have done so if we had stood alone in that fight. Where would we be today if the NAACP, or the National Council of La Raza, or the National Gay and Lesbian Task Force had taken the position that redress was a Japanese American issue—and had nothing to do with African Americans, Hispanic Americans, or gay and lesbian Americans? Those organizations, and their members, joined us because they understood and believed in our argument that a threat to the civil rights of one American is a threat to the rights of all Americans. They acted based on that principle—and not on a narrow evaluation of how redress affected their own communities.
>
> How can we as an organization turn around today and say that the civil rights of other Americans have nothing to do with us?

Mineta also scolded the delegates, reminding then that without the support of Massachusetts representative Barney Frank, redress for Japanese-American internees might not have happened. Frank, a gay congressman with a tiny Japanese-American constituency, was instrumental in reporting the redress bill out of the House Administrative Law Subcommittee, where it had been stuck for many years.

The convention floor fell silent. I could physically feel the last opposition weaken and melt away. The vote was called, and the national convention voted overwhelmingly to continue its endorsement of same-sex marriage. The members of the ad hoc committee embraced one another and cried for close to one-half hour. It is difficult to remember much after that.

The fear that legions of conservative JACL members would bolt the organization did not materialize. Only a few members resigned. Further, JACL found new members, as the ad hoc committee swelled to become one of its newest chapters, the Asian Pacific Islander-Lambda chapter. And the gay and lesbian community gained a new ally—an ally with over twenty-five thousand members nationally. We will not always see eye to eye, nor will we always stand together on every issue, yet JACL and the queer community will almost certainly work together again as the political climate becomes more exclusionary.

Stopping the Marginalization

The success was a group effort. Kaneko and Murakawa could not have done it alone. The ad hoc committee was simply a group of queer Asian Pacific Islanders who realized that there was a job to do, though none was an acknowledged, high-profile leader of the national queer community.

Why are such leaders of color not more evident in the ranks of queer national leadership? The white gay and lesbian community neglects communities of color. The queer movement's white leaders have often marginalized people of color and their concerns, only turning affirmatively to communities of color when mainstream queers need support. Not only do few of the major queer national organizations have persons of color in significant influential positions of political leadership, but recent personnel changes in these groups worsen the ability of the gay and lesbian movement to build effective bridges to other communities.

One national organization was urged in 1994 by one of its regional workers to reach out for fund-raising purposes to communities of color, that the effort would pay off in financial and political support for the organization, and that it would give people of color some "ownership" in the group. Instead, the organization's director of development refused the idea, asserting, "Don't bother. They don't have enough money to make it worth our time." The group's executive director agreed. During the debate over gay men and lesbians serving in the United States armed forces many groups of color protested that they were not included in the political decision making by the queer leaders orchestrating the campaign. Only when queer leaders discovered that they needed broad-based support from many groups did they finally turn to people of color who could bridge the gap between the mainstream queer movement and other communities.

It is not insignificant, then, that JACL's interest and support of the same-sex marriage issue began with the efforts of heterosexuals. When the issue was to be fought and decided at the JACL's convention in Salt Lake City in August 1994, Asian Pacific Islander queers realized that campaigning for JACL's support was up to them. They contacted one another, created the materials and presentations, and organized the campaign that resulted in success in Salt Lake City.

Queers and people of color alike must recognize that homophobia, racism, sexism, anti-Semitism, discrimination based on physical ability, anti-immigrant xenophobia, and other discriminatory isms all have the same roots. The same social dynamic created them all: the mainstream population's ability to isolate particular groups and characterize them as unequal, apart, and unworthy.

The radical right has also been successful in dividing us at a time when we should be standing together. Documented immigrants and many people of color lined up against undocumented immigrants in the campaign over California's anti-immigrant Proposition 187. There were people of color who believed that immigrants were taking jobs that "belonged" to Americans, and they supported Congress's cutback on immigration quotas that allow immigrant families to reunite in the United States. Some AIDS activists, believing that immigrants were consuming resources that would better be made available to people with AIDS, campaigned against documented immigrants, as Congress sought in 1995 to deprive even legal permanent residents of public benefits and already earned social security benefits. Queers are ambivalent about the relevance to them of affirmative action, as California faces a vote in a referendum to repeal the state's affirmative action programs.

Immigrants, legal and undocumented, have now been successfully targeted by the radical right. Women and people of color are the targets of the antiaffirmative action campaign. Which group will next be in the radical right's gunsights? The social dynamic is the same. Only the targets change. And we allow this to continue.

Where are the *nakohdos*? How can the queer community expect to make connections with other groups without effective go-betweens? Bridges must be built between groups. The success of many lesbian and gay efforts in the coming years, including the continuing work to be done in each state related to recognition of same-sex marriages, depends on cross-group and cross-organizational support. And the go-betweens, with experience between communities, can win that support.

Although figures vary wildly, queers are probably no more than 10 percent of the population and, quoting one African American lesbian, "Ten per cent never won anything." If we as a movement do not find the wherewithal to approach, work with, ally with, and maintain meaningful contact with other groups, we have little hope to create the environment needed to secure our liberties and our place at the political table.

The process will not be easy. We will discover our own sad state of preparedness to reach out. Hurtful things will be said. Doors will probably be figuratively slammed in some faces. However, we cannot be deterred. We must keep the dialogue open. At stake is not only *our* freedom as queers, but the freedom of all people who can be singled out by a vicious, mean-spirited majority. If we cannot understand this and stand united against the tide, I despair of winning the liberty so cherished by us all.

M. V. Lee Badgett

Thinking Homo/Economically

As is true of most people, a lesbian, gay, or bisexual person cannot escape his or her role as *homo economicus*, or economic human. Economic decisions and actions take up an important part of every day. Going to work, stopping off at the grocery store, preparing dinner, or helping the kids with their homework all include economic dimensions to one degree or another.

The idea that economic decisions made by gay people will be influenced by their sexual orientation is not a new one. In the 1950s, in Buffalo, lesbians may have chosen particular occupations that allowed them to dress as they chose (Kennedy and Davis 1993). The "commercialization of desire" was based on and promoted gay men's patronage of bathhouses (Altman 1982). Workplace discrimination has created and remains an ongoing issue related to economic security for many gay men and lesbians.

As the public visibility of lesbian and gay people and the movement for civil rights hit the 1990s, however, economic images and collective economic action have become increasingly important and conspicuous. A 1991 *Wall Street Journal* article called gay people "A Dream Market," citing marketing survey data that showed the average income of gay households as $55,430, $23,000 a year more than the average U.S. household (Rigdon 1991). Local newspapers cover the efforts of gay and lesbian employee groups that have organized within many U.S. workplaces and have successfully lobbied for nondiscrimination policies and inclusive benefits policies.

But our awakening consciousness of economic roles comes at a time when other forces outside the gay and lesbian communities have their own agendas for developing lesbian and gay Americans' economic image, whether they are businesses hoping to make money by marketing to an affluent subgroup or are right wing religious zealots anxious to portray gay people in an unpopular way. This essay is an economist's look at some basic economic categories and the public images they represent to ask an important strategic question for lesbian and gay people: *How should we define ourselves economically?* Like most people in our economy, we play many market roles—as producers, consumers, and investors—but when it comes to using those economic roles to promote political change, we have some choices to make about which ones are more useful and relevant. In thinking about this question, I am particularly concerned with how particular economic identities (1) fit into our political interests and goals, such as reducing homophobia and heterosexism, and (2) help our gay, lesbian, and bisexual communities build coalitions with other progressive groups and bridges to individuals and communities that think of themselves as being very different from the gay community. In this essay I conclude that producer and investor roles best fulfill those criteria and I argue that wielding consumer power does not require us to further develop an already dangerous tendency to see gay and lesbian people primarily as consumers.

Lesbian, Gay, and Bisexual People as Producers

A focus on being a producer (or worker or employee) has long been a source of class identity and politics. For centuries workers have organized themselves into unions and other kinds of groups to exert their collective influence to force changes in the workplace or in the political realm. Workplace organizing obviously fits into political goals related to the workplace, such as nondiscrimination or domestic partner policies. In survey after survey lesbian and gay people report experiences of employment discrimination (Badgett, Donnelly, and Kibbe 1992). In my own research I have found evidence that discrimination against lesbian, gay, and bisexual people reduces their incomes relative to heterosexuals with the same education, experience, and other important characteristics (Badgett 1995). Within individual workplaces even the discrimination institutionalized in benefits policies has proven vulnerable to reasoned and well-organized appeals by gay and lesbian employee groups. Workplace groups—both formal and informal— have achieved some notable successes. Private employers (such as Lotus, Levi Strauss, and Ivy League universities) and public employers (including the cities of New York, Seattle, San Francisco, and Berkeley and the Universities of Iowa, Vermont, and Minnesota) have begun to offer health care and other benefits to domestic partners of gay employees.

As the organizing process continues within individual workplaces, at some point the workplace successes will contribute to the push for a broader public policy, such as a federal nondiscrimination law. Here economic reasoning will be used on both sides of the debate. Some economists will argue that the government should let the competitive labor market erode discrimination in employment, wages, and benefits: if a firm does not hire the best workers available, then discrimination will hurt that firm's competitive position, eventually driving the discriminating firm out of business. Similarly, if a firm sees a competitive advantage in offering domestic partner benefits to attract productive workers, then that firm will do so and does not need government interference. Economic counterarguments exist, of course, particularly in skepticism that markets will erode discrimination on their own (think about the persistence of discrimination against black or female workers, for instance). In the case of domestic partner policies one could argue that individuals, employers, and society must bear large "transaction costs" in registering partnerships in many different places and ways, suggesting that one big state registry would be much more efficient.

In addition to fitting into our broad political goals, workplace activism is also an effective means of building bridges and coalitions with individuals and groups. First and foremost, workplace activism has the potential for tremendous transformations in the attitudes of heterosexual co-workers. We spend a huge part of our lives at work, and work naturally becomes a social activity as well as an economically productive one. Being in the closet diminishes the quality and quantity of social interactions with straight co-workers, but coming out opens up many new possibilities, both personal and political (Woods 1993). Discussing gay issues at work or coming out to a boss or co-worker makes gay issues much less abstract and can educate heterosexuals about many related topics that can have far-reaching effects. Heterosexual people who know gay people tend to have more pro-gay opinions (Herek and Glunt 1993), which can be useful in campaigns to defeat antigay amendments or to pass gay civil rights laws. For example, several years of work by Microsoft employees who had formed Gay, Lesbian, and Bisexual Employees at Microsoft (GLEAM) paid off in 1992 when they were able to convince the company to write letters in opposition to antigay referenda in Oregon and Colorado.

Universities have been the site of enormous gains in the effort to get domestic partner benefits and are good examples of the power of gay workplace activism to educate heterosexual people about the truth of lesbian and gay people's lives (Badgett 1994). During the effort on my own campus we were able to turn a potentially cumbersome political process into a highly successful educational opportunity. Public hearings on a proposal to provide campus-level benefits to domestic partners (such as library cards and access to child care facilities) brought many lesbians and gay men out to tell the stories of their families, stories that many heterosexual co-workers had never imagined. After listening to these experiences of gay and lesbian co-workers, many heterosexuals told us that they had learned something important and had, in many cases, changed their initially negative opinions to support the proposal. Many of those folks became important political allies in our efforts.

A second important opportunity contained within workplaces is the potential for building coalitions with other groups fighting for fair treatment, such as unions or employee groups for women and/or for people of color. Working with other groups in coalitions might mean taking on some issues not commonly thought of as related to sexual orientation, but I would argue that coalitions improve the chances of *all* groups' goals being reached. At Microsoft GLEAM formed a diversity coalition with groups of African American, Hispanic, Jewish, Native American, and deaf and hard of hearing employees ("Corporate Focus" 1993). The coalition's efforts within the company led to the empowerment of a diversity manager who was able to start moving on several important diversity policies.

Finally, even in a modern market economy, work is a virtuous activity and is an important part of our political and cultural foundations as well as of our economic foundation. By portraying ourselves as workers and producers to the more general public outside our workplaces, we are promoting a positive image.

Lesbians, Gay, and Bisexual People as Consumers

Of course, like all people, gay people are also consumers as well as producers. In the current market environment, however, our interests as consumers are quite complicated. Several possible relationships between consumption and political goals invite analysis: (1) creating and promoting our public identities as "queer consumers" in the U.S. marketplace, (2) targeting our consumption choices to influence corporate policies and media images of gay people (through boycotts, for example), and (3) developing separate lesbian/gay/bisexual markets, or "queer capitalism."

(1) The connection between consumption and social status and opinion is, on the face of it, a clear one. As economist Thorstein Veblen (1934) wrote at the end of the last century, "The basis on which good repute in any highly

organised industrial community ultimately rests is pecuniary strength; and the means of showing pecuniary strength, and so of gaining or retaining a good name, are leisure and a conspicuous consumption of goods" (84). But is conspicuous consumption—and the attendant development of a queer consumer identity—a useful strategy for gay, lesbian, and bisexual people? Thanks in part to the efforts of marketers who portray us as an attractive and affluent group of consumers, there is a growing consciousness among lesbian and gay people of being "gay consumers," and, thanks to the right wing, this image has spread widely outside the lesbian, gay, and bisexual communities. But while in other circumstances this economic role could contribute to the broad political goal of "gaining or retaining a good name," consciously establishing a gay consumer identity per se is not likely to be a good strategy for building coalitions and bridges.

First, some of the assumptions behind the interest in marketing to gay people are wrong. In particular, some marketers (in inadvertent collusion with the radical right wing) portray gay people as being well-educated and having high incomes (for example, Rigdon 1991). But this image comes from surveys of gay magazine and newspaper readers or from people attending gay events. Such samples of gay people are *biased* toward people with high incomes. Surveys of other magazines or newspapers also typically find higher than average incomes for readers, and travel and admission costs for events make it unlikely that people at gay events are economically representative of all gay people.

Other more reliable and representative surveys give a very different picture of the economic status of lesbian and gay people. Data from the Yankelovich Monitor, a random sample of U.S. households, show that self-identified gay people's household incomes are virtually the same as heterosexuals' (Elliott 1994). My own study of data from the General Social Survey at the University of Chicago makes a more detailed comparison of people with the same education, experience, occupation, and location, and I find that gay and bisexual people (who are defined by behavior) actually earn *less* than straight people (Badgett 1995).

Second, building a consumer movement based on an inaccurate portrayal of our economic clout is not only dishonest but it may actually alienate potential allies as well. In this era of growing economic inequality cries of injustice coming from a supposedly prosperous group are likely to fall on resentful ears. The radical right has seized upon this image to divide and conquer a potential progressive coalition. Literature in the Colorado

Amendment 2 campaign reveals this strategy at work: "Are homosexuals a disadvantaged minority? You decide!" A table below that headline compares (the biased) gay income figures from marketing surveys to the much lower incomes of African Americans.

(2) We do not have to develop a consumption-based identity to wield consumer power, however. The gay, lesbian, and bisexual communities have used consumer boycotts of Coors, Cracker Barrel, and Colorado, for instance, to exert economic pressure to reverse homophobic employment practices and laws. The economic effectiveness of boycotts is difficult to measure, since so many other factors influence companies' sales revenues and can hide the impact of even a well-organized boycott (certainly a difficult feat considering the national markets for most products). But regardless of whether companies are more concerned about the economic or the public relations impact of boycotts, boycotts clearly contribute to changes in policies (see Snyder 1991; or Putnam 1993).

Given the proliferation of boycotts in the 1990s, coalition opportunities abound. Environmentalists, in particular, have skillfully used consumer action, and many other groups concerned about employment fairness, animal rights, and reproductive rights include consumer action in their arsenals. Coalitions could take the form of mutual support of boycotts directed at different companies or of combined forces in targeting one company. And those alliances are likely to continue outside the workplace in the electoral arena, such as when gay participation in the Coors boycott in the 1970s gained the Teamsters' support for Harvey Milk's election as the first gay supervisor in San Francisco (Shilts 1982).

Although both consumers and workers can form coalitions with other groups, I would argue that consumer action works very differently than worker action when it comes to bridge building. Media campaigns, which are an integral part of many boycott strategies, are likely to increase the visibility of lesbian, gay, and bisexual people and the realities of their lives. In much gay consumer action the image of gay people is the very issue, as in the controversy surrounding the movie *Basic Instinct*, which led to a boycott and the Catherine-did-it media campaign. The impersonality of consumption and of media images distinguish workplace action from consumer action, however. A character who comes out in a television series might remind a viewer of a workplace friend, but a real co-worker who comes out can engage her colleagues in a conversation (or struggle) about a variety of complex issues over a period of time. But this qualitative distinction is not made to denigrate the importance of gay visibility. The television character might create a natural topic for a real workplace discussion, and positive media images of gay people might make it easier for gay employees to come out at work.

Consumer action may also involve difficult choices for activists. An economically successful boycott is designed to hurt a company's management or shareholders; that means the company's workers will be hurt as well. This creates the possibility of conflicting loyalties, as it would for a lesbian union member who is asked to boycott products made by members of her union, for example. Some gay employee groups have discouraged outsiders from putting direct pressure on the group's employer, preferring to work through internal political processes first.

These drawbacks to consumer activism argue for a careful selection of targets, focusing on companies that can make direct improvements in the lives of gay, lesbian, and bisexual people rather than boycotts to punish a company's failure to denounce somebody else's policy or a company's consorting with one of our enemies. For instance, the Cracker Barrel Old Country Stores Inc. boycott targets a company that has openly fired lesbian and gay workers simply because of their sexual orientation. Successfully directing pressure against Cracker Barrel's policy of discrimination would clearly improve the lives of the fired workers and the remaining gay employees at Cracker Barrel. The more direct an attack a boycott makes on egregiously unfair behavior, the more likely gay *and* straight people are to participate and to create change.

(3) The first two relationships between consumption and political goals are more related to "homo economics" than to a "homo economy." Capitalism plus concentrations of gay people in large urban areas have made a queer economy possible in gay enclaves. Should gay people come together as producers *and* consumers to create a queer capitalism? A completely separate economy is difficult to imagine, but we have long had explicitly gay-and-lesbian-owned businesses around, such as bookstores, bars, cafés, magazines, and newspapers, providing much needed social and cultural bases for gay lives and organizing. In the last few years, though, a new breed of entrepreneurs (both gay and straight) have begun to market products to lesbian, gay, and bisexual people that we could already buy in their mainstream forms, such as beer, credit cards, and long-distance telephone service. Do we owe either generation of gay businesses our economic loyalties in a positive reversal of consumer action via boycott?

Using the criteria set out earlier, the first question is whether queer capitalism promotes our political goals. The early generation of gay and/or lesbian businesses had some direct and indirect political potential. Those businesses created meeting places that facilitated political organization and the spread of important ideas, news, and information to gay people, making the further development of gay, lesbian, and bisexual culture and politics possible. Many of the newer businesses' products are more economically than culturally based, but some companies offer to donate part of their profits to gay organizations, creating a positive potential financial impact for political efforts. (Without more research it is difficult to tell how gay community-centered the new gay businesses are compared to the standard profit-seeking company, particularly in term of developing an ethic of philanthropy and of more socially responsible employment practices.)

Given that they all, in at least some way, contribute to the furthering of our political goals, why not sit back and let a thousand flowers bloom? In a market economy, of course, that will happen. But the marketplace is dynamic, and successful gay businesses and products will attract the attention of mainstream capitalists, who are always looking for profit-making opportunities. We have seen this happen in both the retail and publishing end of the book business, for example, as the mainstream spills over into the tributaries nurtured by small lesbian and gay presses and bookstores: large publishers offer sizable advances for books targeted at gay communities, and chain bookstores have developed large lesbian and gay sections in stores located in gay neighborhoods. Even if this competition is fair, would we want to protect gay-owned or targeted businesses from cutthroat competitors, since "our" businesses support our political activities, or should we just shop at the cheapest bookstore and find the cheapest credit card available and then donate our savings ourselves (the economically "rational" decision)?

Before directly answering that question, consider the implications for promoting queer capitalism with respect to the other criteria. By definition, a separatist economy is not well-suited to coalition or bridge building. Even worse, an overemphasis on developing a gay economy would be internally divisive, placing lesbian, gay, and bisexual people with competing economic loyalties, such as those based on race, ethnicity, or gender, in a tricky position. Furthermore, access to capital and credit to start a new business varies significantly by race, wealth, and gender. A queer economy is thus likely to reproduce racial, gender, and class inequality.

Given that risk, it might seem that the sink-or-swim approach is best suited to gay businesses. But, at this point, distinctions between products offered by gay-centered businesses become important, and the difference involves whether markets, without concerted economic action by gay people, would provide the kinds of goods and services that we need in the quantities we desire. Ideally, markets are supposed to supply the goods and services that consumers want, otherwise businesses have a profit-making opportunity available. If the rate of profit is not high enough, though, mainstream companies might not shift into a gay market, as when Time Inc. canceled plans for a magazine targeted at gays and lesbians, citing a lower than expected profit potential as the reason (Carmody 1994). But other publishers of gay magazines and newspapers, presumably lesbian, gay, or bisexual themselves, have accepted losses as well as profit rates far lower than the return that Time Inc. expected from its investment. In other words, some gay-targeted products and retail establishments (e.g., bars, bookstores, and publications) constitute a basic community infrastructure that might be worth protecting because they provide and preserve something better than what other mainstream companies could supply.

Lesbian, Gay, and Bisexual People as Investors

Another way of thinking about a decision to support some lesbian and gay businesses is as an investment in the economy and the community. In economic terms investments involve giving up something now for some future return, and investors play an important role in any economy. Gay people also make economic investments in the financial sense, particularly through retirement and pension funds. That kind of investment was used effectively as a political tool in the anti-apartheid movement, and at least one gay and lesbian group, the Wall Street Project, is trying to use the collective shareholder clout of gay people and their allies to influence corporate policies, starting with Cracker Barrel (Patron 1991). Investment advisors provide information on the gay-friendliness of corporations to allow socially conscious investors to screen out companies with poor records on policies related to lesbian and gay employees (Sullivan 1993; "Investing in Change" 1993).

Lesbian, gay, and bisexual people make many other decisions that could also be thought of as investments: having children, coming out, joining political groups, renovating homes, or creating families, to name a few of the bigger decisions. In a way those decisions are both means to facilitate larger goals about how we want to live as well as the actual achievement of goals. Along with heterosexuals we share the goal of a better future, whether it is for our kids or for future gay, lesbian, and bisexual people. This gives us numerous opportunities for building bridges and coalitions on a wide variety of concerns, from the quality of education to crime and violence in our country. Two mothers or two fathers going to a PTA meeting can create a revolution in the attitudes of straight parents. Perhaps the best example comes from openly lesbian or gay elected officials who must represent all of their constituents, regardless of sexual orientation. Both in their campaigns and in office those officials build links across issues and communities, bringing lesbian, gay, bisexual, and heterosexual people together on a very basic human level.

All of the economic roles seen in a basic description of a market obviously fit together more tightly than their separate presentations in this overview. And, just as obviously, we do not have the power to completely define our economic identity on our own: too many others want to do it for us, whether they are profit-seeking companies, the media, or the right wing. We control the political strategies that we pursue, however, and we must use economics wisely. Promoting ourselves as producers and community investors is likely to result in the perception that we are more virtuous and socially upstanding than if we collaborate in a portrayal of ourselves as hedonistic consumers. Those identities as producers and investors provide us with potential ties to other groups and promote more human contact with heterosexuals. We can mobilize our power as consumers without taking on all the economic and cultural baggage that goes along with being identified primarily as consumers. We should use our economic power in whatever way is necessary, leveraging it in coalition with other groups and using it to reach out to others who must learn to see us as fully human. Our economic clout, broadly construed, goes far beyond the money in our pockets, and we can turn our economic power into political change.

NOTES

An earlier version of this essay was presented at "Homo/Economics: Market and Community in Lesbian and Gay Life," Center for Lesbian and Gay Studies, The Graduate School, City University of New York, May 7, 1994. I thank Anne Habiby, Walter Williams, Lisa Moore, and Patricia Connelly for useful conversations.

REFERENCES

Altman, D. 1982. *The Homosexualization of America*. New York: St. Martin's.

Badgett, M. V. L. 1994. "Equal Pay for Equal Families." *Academe* (May/June) 11:26–30.

—— 1995. "The Wage Effects of Sexual Orientation Discrimination." *Industrial and Labor Relations Review* 48(4):726–39.

Badgett, M. V. L., C. Donnelly, and J. Kibbe. 1992. "Pervasive Patterns of Discrimination Against Lesbians and Gay Men: Evidence from Surveys Across the United States." Washington, D.C.: National Gay and Lesbian Policy Institute.

Carmody, D. 1994. "Time Inc. Shelves a Gay Magazine." *New York Times*, June 6, p. C7.

"Corporate Focus: Making Microsoft's Meritocracy Work." 1993. *TheGay/Lesbian/Bisexual Corporate Letter* 2(1):3–6.

Elliott, S. 1994. "A Sharper View of Gay Consumers." *New York Times,* June 9, p. D1.

Herek, G. M., and E. K. Glunt. 1993. "Interpersonal Contact and Heterosexuals' Attitudes Toward Gay Men: Results from a National Survey." *Journal of Sex Research* 30(3):239–44.

"Investing in Change: New Investment Advisory Letter Targets Gay-Friendly Growth Stocks." 1993. *G/L/B Corporate Letter* 2(2):4.

Kennedy, E. L., and M. D. Davis. 1993. *Boots of Leather, Slippers of Gold: The History of a Lesbian Community*. New York: Routledge.

Patron, E. J. 1991. "Using Money to Make Change." *Advocate*, December 17, pp. 70–71.

Putnam, T. 1993. "Boycotts Are Busting Out All Over." *Business and Society Review*, no. 85, pp. 47–51.

Rigdon, J. E. 1991. "Overcoming a Deep-Rooted Reluctance, More Firms Advertise to Gay Community." *Wall Street Journal*, July 18, B1.

Shilts, R. 1982. *The Mayor of Castro Street*. New York: St. Martin's.

Snyder, A. 1991. "Do Boycotts Work?" *Adweek's Marketing Week* (April 8) 32(15):16.

Sullivan, K. 1993. "Firms Rated on Sexual Politics: Policies Toward Gay, Lesbian Employees Logged in Database." *San Francisco Examiner*, Sept. 9, pp. 1, 3.

Veblen, T. 1934. *The Theory of the Leisure Class*. New York: Modern Library.

Woods, J. D. 1993. *The Corporate Closet: The Professional Lives of Gay Men in America*. New York: Free.

James M. Andre

Economic Power as a Means of Reducing Heterosexism: Personal Financial Planning Strategies

One of the keys to the success of the gay and lesbian movement has been the selective channeling of money and resources to the many worthy people and organizations working for the benefit of the community. Because there is a strong correlation between economic power and political change, it is critical to continue to support these efforts to eliminate heterosexism. We can support those who support us through our spending and investing. Consider spending with lesbian and gay businesses and professionals who are active in supporting community organizations through contributions of time and money. Through socially responsible investing we can seek out companies with policies matching our concerns. There are also companies we may want to avoid when spending or investing.

This essay presents some suggestions for building financial success and security, with the goal of raising the economic status of members of the community. The image of a financially responsible community, which helps its less fortunate members and contributes positively to society as a whole, will in and of itself help reduce antigay prejudice. This chapter will suggest ways of reaching a level of financial security that will enable committed individuals to increase their own wealth and, at the same time, help support the organizations working to help the community and reduce heterosexism. The focus is on practical steps to accomplish these goals.

Sources of Income

The three major sources of personal income are employment, investment, and charity. *Employment* is the primary source of income for most individuals and takes the form of a regular paycheck. Matching your passion, talent, and abilities with the kind of work that is appropriate will maximize your satisfaction and hopefully your earning capacity. *Investment* is a key element leading to financial security. The goal is to move from having to work for your money to having your money work for you. Making this adjustment requires self-discipline and a knowledge of how to save and invest. *Charity* is an all-encompassing term meant to include all the other sources adding to your wealth. Some examples include gifts, inheritance, marriage, and winning the lottery.

Financial planning involves deciding what to do with these three sources of income. Most people are just a conduit for the money they obtain. It is spent on housing, automobiles, insurance, food, clothes, entertainment, travel, and a variety of other expenses. In order to build personal wealth, income must be saved and invested. This will allow us to be financially secure in the future. In addition to consumption and investment, the remaining major use of funds by most individuals is related to charity and estate planning. We will be able to support organizations doing important work through charitable contributions and the disposition of our estate.

Getting Started

Pay Yourself   First A little bit of what you earn should be yours to keep. The primary rule of financial planning is to start saving and investing immediately. Do not wait until you have paid off your car or your credit cards.

I recommend that you set a goal of saving a minimum of 10 percent of your gross pay each paycheck. If possible, you should increase that amount to 15 or 20 percent. The most painless way of doing this is to have your employer withhold the designated amount from your paycheck and invest it in a savings or retirement program. Many employers offer excellent plans for saving and investing as part of their benefits package. These plans generally reduce your taxes, which are deferred until you withdraw the funds. This means that if your top combined federal and state tax rate is 33 percent, your out-of-pocket cost for contributing six hundred dollars is only four hundred dollars.

It is also possible to make a deposit in your savings account each pay period and invest the money on a regular basis. Just write a check to yourself on payday and deposit it in a savings account. Some individuals choose mutual funds in which to invest and mail their checks directly to the mutual fund manager each period. Do not disdain saving small amounts since they add up to staggering amounts over time because of the power of compounding. You will be amazed at how quickly this money will grow if you invest early and reinvest.

It takes discipline and sacrifice to accomplish this critical step in financial planning. You might have to reduce your housing expenses, avoid buying a new car, or delay taking an expensive vacation. However, it is absolutely imperative to make these sacrifices early in order to reap the rewards of being financially secure in the future. It is also reassuring to know that you have a substantial amount of resources in savings and investments.

Time Is Your Greatest Ally   The earlier you start a regular saving and investing program the greater the benefit. If you save four hundred dollars at the end of each month, beginning at age twenty-five, and you invest these savings at an annual rate of return of 8 percent in a mutual fund, you will have $1.4 million when you turn sixty-five. If the rate is 12 percent your investment will be worth $4.7 million. Obviously, time and a good rate of return are your greatest allies.

Investing for Success

Investing Your Money   It is advisable to review your investment portfolio on a regular basis in order to make adjustments when necessary. Generally, younger investors are less risk averse and willing to take some chances in higher return investments. Older investors tend to be more conservative and invest in lower risk investments. Younger investors (aggressive) have time to recoup losses while older investors (conservative) want to minimize any chance of loss. If you have a potentially terminal illness you may want to be more conservative in your decisions in order to minimize the possibility of losses.

Mutual Funds   In choosing investments, I recommend beginning with mutual funds since it is a simple way to hire professionals to manage your money. You will be able to have a diversified portfolio with a minimal amount of money. You can select from a variety of types of funds as well. There are growth funds, growth and income funds, bond funds, global funds, select funds, value funds, index funds, and a variety of others. Using resources such as *Money Magazine, Money Guide, Consumer Reports*, newspapers, and other publications or newsletters will allow you to choose appropriate funds. If necessary, you may want to work with a competent financial planner, investment counselor, or broker.

Building a Portfolio   While mutual funds are an easy first step in your saving and investment program, over time you will be able to diversify your own portfolio of investments. You can do this by buying a home and making other investments. When you are young, about 20 percent of your investments can be in higher risk categories such as single stocks or new business ventures. Your home and other real estate investments might account for 30 percent to 40 percent of your portfolio and mutual funds will be 40 percent to 60 percent of the total.

These are very general guidelines; your personal investment portfolio will depend on a variety of factors that include your tolerance for risk. It is important to remember that there is a correlation between risk and reward. The greater the chance of a high return, the greater the risk of losing your money. Don't forget, if it sounds too good to be true it probably is too good to be true.

Socially Responsible Investing   Some people today are voting with their dollars by practicing socially responsible investing (SRI). This approach has had an impact on ending apartheid in South Africa and encouraging companies to adopt positive social and environmental policies. You can practice SRI through *avoidance investing*—the exclusion of investments that conflict with your social values—and *supportive investing*—seeking out companies whose corporate policies match your values. The best approach may be to retain your investment and conduct a letter-writing campaign with those companies to lobby them to adopt nondiscrimination policies and domestic partner benefits programs. It is always important to remember that an investment should be financially sound before it is socially responsible.

There are a number of major companies that have been supportive of gay issues, including AT&T, Microsoft, Levi Strauss, and Apple. These companies deserve our support both as consumers and as investors. There are also many gay-owned businesses and professionals that are supportive of community organizations and we should try to do business with them. This does not mean, however, that you should settle for high prices or inferior service or quality.

Managing Your Credit

Avoid High Interest Debt   It is unacceptable to have any credit card debt if you want to get ahead. You are undoubtedly paying an extremely high rate of interest (from 14 percent to 22 percent). Pretty soon it is difficult to pay more than just the interest charges on the debt. If your current income does not allow you to make headway in paying off this debt, I suggest you consider getting an additional part-time job until the debt is repaid.

I recommend canceling and cutting up all your credit cards if you cannot pay them off every month. Operate on a cash basis to avoid a recurrence of this problem. You should keep one major credit card (Visa or Mastercard) to use for emergencies. By the way, Diners Club seems to have the best insurance program for car rental coverage. It also requires you to pay off the balance every month. Most cards now allow you to earn mileage or points or discounts. This is fine as long as you pay off the card every month.

Using Debt   Some types of debt are acceptable, including student loans and mortgages. You may need to borrow to purchase an automobile, but it might be better to pay cash for a cheaper used car than to borrow for a new car. I generally recommend buying versus leasing.

If you are already deep in debt but own a house, consider consolidating your debt in a lower-rate home equity loan. This will reduce your finance charges and boost your tax deductions since mortgage interest is deductible (subject to certain requirements). If you do not own a home, you may still be able to get a debt consolidation loan from your bank or credit union. Just remember to destroy the credit cards that caused the problem.

Controlling Expenses

Live Within Your Means   The temptation to spend money is an ever present danger. J. Grady Cash, author of *Conquer the Seven Deadly Money Mistakes: The No-Math, No-Nonsense Way to Reach Your Financial Dreams* (1995), determined that all money mistakes fall into one of seven patterns, or "spending personalities." The following spending personality self-test will determine your behavior. It is possible to have tendencies toward more than one behavior. Assign a number to each item below that most closely corresponds to your behavior.

> *1—Never; 2—Seldom; 3—Once in a while; 4—Frequently;*
> *5—Almost Always*

FANATICAL —Do you shop for weeks for the best price?
IMPULSIVE —Do you tend to make unplanned impulsive purchases?
PASSIVE —Do you procrastinate before making a needed purchase or
      avoid asking questions when talking to salespeople?
AVOIDANCE —Do you use shopping as an escape from the pressures of life,
      to get back at your partner, or do you buy gifts out of guilt?

ESTEEM —Do you prefer to buy in prestigious stores, avoiding discount
chains like Wal-Mart or Kmart?

OVERDONE —Do you have a collection, hobby, or activity for which an
outside observer would consider your spending excessive?

HOT POTATO —Do you buy suddenly, after putting off a significant purchase for days or weeks?

A score of 3 or above for any item indicates a tendency toward a specific
spending personality, with higher scores of 4 or 5 indicating a greater potential for problems. If you scored 2 or less on all questions, congratulations.
You are a smart shopper.

Some money-saving tips recommended by Cash are listed below:

Spend by choice. Make a conscious decision to buy rather than impulsively
making a purchase. Ask yourself if this is a priority item you really need
and want.

Leave the presence of the item before buying. This is especially true when
making sizable purchases. In spite of what the salesperson may say, you
will probably not miss out on an incredible buy.

Investigate before buying. Check consumer magazines and compare prices
at other locations and make sure that the item being purchased will fit
your needs.

Avoid buying on credit. Do not spend income you have yet to earn.

Search for creative ways to fill your need. Can you borrow or rent the item
you need or buy it used? Are there other ways to meet your need?

Ask for a discount. For example, if you are a member of AAA auto club, you
are entitled to substantial savings on hotels and car rentals.

A great deal of self-discipline and restraint is required to build your
wealth. Everyone wants your money. You are inundated on a constant basis
by advertising and marketing programs. Buy the best quality you can
afford at the best price you can find. It is absolutely critical to be able to say,
"I cannot afford this." Remember that some of what you earn should be
yours to keep.

Planning and Budgeting   In order to get ahead it is important to do some
planning. For most individuals the largest monthly outflows are for housing
and transportation, so it is imperative to be very careful when buying or leasing your home or automobile. Some general guidelines suggest that housing
should cost between 20 percent and 35 percent of your take-home pay. Your
other debt payments (loans, credit cards, etc.) should amount to no more
than 20 percent of your paycheck. Savings should be about 10 percent to 20

percent of your gross pay. It is advisable to consider spending less than you think you can afford. In other words, don't buy or rent more house or more car than you can afford.

Here is a simple way to find out where your money is spent. Using your checkbook, list all of your income and expenditures for the past four months. Set up a column on the left for a description and label each column by month. You can use this as a basis to plan out your expenses for the next twelve months. Sometimes it helps to budget your outflows as if you make about 10 percent to 15 percent less than you actually earn. Be sure to include a line for savings and investment. You can now set some goals for the future. Computer money management programs such as Quicken can be very helpful in this analysis. You can write your checks on computer and track all your income and expenses.

The most serious financial problems arise as a result of the poor management of monthly payments. If you do not carefully budget your income, you will spend more than is available and end up running up your credit cards or other debt. It is not the down payments on purchases that cause the biggest problems. It is the total of the monthly payments that causes financial distress. Do not let your fixed expenses make it impossible for you to save.

Buying a Home

Home Ownership   One of the benefits of a regular savings program is that many people can eventually have enough cash for a down payment on a home. Perhaps relatives can chip in to help. Owning a home is a forced savings plan because you will pay off the loan over time. In fifteen to thirty years you will own your home free and clear, whereas if you rent you will be burdened paying ever increasing rent. By being a homeowner you also get the advantage of a tax shield, since the interest portion of the house payments and your property taxes are deductible, resulting in lower taxes. Paying your home loan off early is advisable only if you cannot earn as much on investments as you are paying for your mortgage.

It is important to know the real estate market because it is possible to lose money if you pay too much for your home. If your rent is extremely low or you do not plan to stay in the area for long, it may not make sense to buy. There are many factors to consider in making the decision to buy a home, and it may not be the best for everyone. You may want to work with gay or lesbian professionals in the real estate brokerage and lending fields. It is important that you choose someone who is qualified and experienced in the area in which you want to buy or sell.

It is also advisable to err on the side of caution when buying. Instead of buying the most expensive property you can afford, you may want to subtract about 10 to 20 percent from the maximum price for which you qualify. You might also wish to rent out a room or two in your house to bring in extra income. This will allow you to continue saving and investing and not have all your income going to house payments and maintenance. In a few years, when you have built up some equity, you can trade up to a more expensive property.

Choosing a Loan   Choosing between an adjustable rate versus a fixed rate home loan depends on the market and your personal situation. If rates are low and you are intending to occupy the property for a long time, it may be wise to get a fixed rate loan. On the other hand, if you intend to trade up in about five years, an adjustable rate may be a better choice. There are so many programs and options it is impossible to say that one type is always preferable. Your realtor or lender can help you choose the best alternative. Also, when interest rates are low it is often wise to refinance your home to reduce your expenses or shorten the term of your loan. However, increasing the amount you owe and the dollars you'll spend in interest is detrimental to savings.

Building Your Balance Sheet

Capital Preservation   One of the most important principles in financial planning is the preservation and growth of your capital. You want to cultivate and grow your investments. Gifts, inheritances, lottery winnings, or other unexpected lump sums should be invested. If necessary, use the interest and dividends generated by the investments for monthly expenses. Large sums of money are hard to come by and it is wise to invest them to build your financial security rather than frittering them away on consumption.

Starting a Business   Do not be limited by your present resources. If you have a great idea for a business, get out and sell it to people. Write a business plan and raise the money. If you have a good idea, you will attract the money and the people you need to build the organization. There are books available on starting businesses and developing business plans. It is wise, however, not to tie up all your assets in the business. You must continue saving and investing even while going into business.

Keep in mind that having a business can be risky and sometimes results in problems. One of the biggest mistakes made by individuals in business is continuing to pour good money after bad in trying to prop up a failing concern. I have watched individuals use up their life savings and the equity in their homes only to end up eventually closing the business anyway. Give your best shot to save the business but set up a drop dead amount of capital that you are willing to invest. Try to avoid signing personal guarantees. If you have a business that is closing down, be sure to satisfy the government for any amounts of taxes you owe to avoid having your future wages garnished or your assets seized.

Insurance

Insurance and Other Benefits   It is extremely important to carry adequate insurance on your health, life, home, automobile, and other assets. Your life insurance proceeds will become part of your estate, which can be left to worthy individuals and organizations. Disability and liability insurance are also recommended. Your employer may supply some of these items as benefits, but it is wise to look into maintaining separate policies of life and disability insurance in the event that you change jobs or careers. If you work for a large organization, it is important to take advantage of the benefits offered, since they are generally at a very good price with no prescreening required. You may be entitled to additional life insurance and long-term care benefits as well. While domestic partner benefits are attractive, there may be substantial costs and tax consequences.

Viatical Settlements   Life insurance has also been important in supplying income for the terminally ill through viatical settlements. Many individuals with AIDS have benefited by being able to tap into their life insurance proceeds while they are still living. They sell their insurance policy at a discount to a company that continues to pay the premiums and is the beneficiary of the proceeds upon the death of the insured. This has become a popular alternative for many individuals and it is advisable to get quotes from different companies and seek professional help if necessary. The proceeds should be invested to generate the income needed for monthly expenses.

Community Support

Charitable Giving   As members of the lesbian and gay community, we have endured some very difficult times. The outpouring of community support for various AIDS organizations and political causes has been gratifying. Since we are responsible for the community in which we live, it is critical to continue supporting the causes in which we believe. This includes, besides AIDS charities and political groups, other deserving organizations like ONE Institute International Gay and Lesbian Archives, local community centers, the Gay and Lesbian Alliance Against Defamation, and various scholarship funds.

Estate Planning   One of the most critical aspects of financial planning is preparing for possible disability and death. You should have a will and/or a trust and a durable power of attorney to be used in the event of illness. The power of attorney appoints individuals to make decisions about your welfare if you should be incapacitated. You can choose beforehand what measures should be taken to keep you alive. Be sure to give a copy to your doctor. Many individuals specify that no unusual efforts are to be made to keep them alive if the quality of their life will deteriorate substantially.

Setting Up a Trust   If you have a sizable estate, it may be advisable to set up a trust to avoid probate and other costs involved in settling your estate. You can save a substantial amount in taxes and expenses by doing some planning. Find a qualified lesbian or gay attorney who is experienced in doing estate planning to get the best service. You will put your property in trust, with you as the trustee, and you can specify successor trustees to manage the trust assets.

Establishing a Foundation   Another alternative to consider in the disposition of your estate is the possibility of setting up a foundation that will support community research, organizations, and activities you want to encourage. This can be done while you are still living. There are many foundations that have as their major objective to support gay and lesbian groups and projects. The foundation is managed by you or your choice of successors. This is an excellent way of leaving a lasting legacy.

Remember, *the best way to get rich quick is to get rich slow.* By practicing the principles and ideas in this essay, you will become financially secure. This will allow you greater freedom in making financial choices in the future. The keys to success are to begin early and save regularly. You will be amazed at the growth of your investments and the feeling of security you will gain. For some individuals, the steps in this chapter are easy and sensible. Others will have difficulty in practicing these principles. You must make a commitment to practice these principles at all times.

Our goal is to help develop a financially responsible community that will take care of its own and contribute to the well-being of society. Your personal success will spill over to the community in the form of volunteerism and monetary support. The result will help improve the credibility and image of the lesbian and gay community. Along with improving your own standard of living, you will be able to support those individuals and organizations that are making a difference in fighting heterosexism.

Although you can take most of the above steps yourself, it is important to get expert advice when necessary. Some of the previous suggestions may require competent and capable advice from a financial planner, broker, attorney, or an accountant. There are many capable and experienced gay and lesbian professionals in these fields. The most important step is to get started now.

REFERENCES

Cash, J. G. 1995. *Conquer the Seven Deadly Money Mistakes: The No-Math, No-Nonsense Way to Reach Your Financial Dreams.* Hampton, Va.: Center for Financial Well-Being.

Colvin, T. 1994. "Money That Pays: How To Create a Small Fortune in Mutual Funds." *Business Today* (Spring) 22:14–17.

Farber, W. 1994a. "Socially Conscious Investments." *Genre* (April) 17:82.

—— 1994b. "Risky Business." *Genre* (June) 19:98.

Feine, D. 1993. "Investment Tips: How to Make Money Grow." *Genre* (November) 14:84, 110.

Hugar, J. H. 1994. "Selecting the Right Mutual Fund: Evaluating the Evaluations." *Supplement to Los Angeles Business Journal,* January 17, pp. 33A, 36A.

Kapoor, J. R., L. R. Dlabay, and R. J. Hughes. 1994. *Personal Finance.* Burr Ridge, Ill.: Irwin.

Kochis, T. 1994. "Time to Review the Basics and Some Non-Basics of Personal Finance." *Supplement to Los Angeles Business Journal,* January 17, pp. 32A, 34A.

Lake, A. 1994. "Buyer Beware." *Sky* (May) 9:114–28.

Mickens, E. 1994. "Waging War on Wall Street." *Advocate,* April 19, pp. 40–45.

Nelson, B. 1992. "Gay Money: Who's Got It? Who Wants It?" *Genre* (October) 8:20–25, 64, 69, 76, 78–79, 88–89.

Rowland, M. 1994. "Waking Up Your Savings Plan at Work." *New York Times,* June 25, p. 37.

Brian McNaught

Making Allies of Co-Workers: Educating the Corporate World

"Help! I just got a question I can't answer." The telephone message request came from a gay employee about to lead his first in-house workshop for colleagues on the issue of homophobia in the workplace.

"We asked for questions in advance," he said. "One person cited a Masters and Johnson study and a Kinsey Institute study that allegedly reports you can change your orientation. I know you can't change, but how do I prove it? Did Masters and Johnson say that?"

No, they didn't. I recognized the quotes from a packet of materials assembled and distributed nationally by a group that opposes civil rights for gay people. Those same misrepresentations had popped up verbatim in my workshops from time to time. My advice to the gay employee was to acknowledge up front he was not a sexuality educator, to speak from his heart as a gay person, and to stay focused on workplace issues. He did so and called to say proudly that the workshop was a success.

I would like to have been there to help correct the misrepresentation of the Masters and Johnson study and the Kinsey Institute research because such inaccuracies perpetuate ignorance. Providing accurate information helps create understanding and a tolerance of difference. But it isn't always possible or practical for a company to have a trained homophobia educator present. Nevertheless, companies themselves can design effective education about homophobia, particularly when the sessions involve input from gay, lesbian, and bisexual employees.

The suggestions offered here for designing and implementing a workshop on homophobia or on lesbian and gay issues in the workplace are based upon my own work and reflect my bias about effective education.

Having a clear set of goals, I believe, is the most important first step. What is the company trying to accomplish and why? If the company is clear about why it is making the effort, it won't get sidetracked by nonissues, such as what the Bible does or doesn't say. This is of interest to some people but ultimately not essential to the discussion.

The company's overall goal for diversity training is generally the creation of a more productive work environment for all employees. More specifically, the company's goals for the workshop might be (1) establishing the company's commitment to nondiscrimination against gay, lesbian, and bisexual employees, (2) providing information on the extent of homophobia and its impact on all employees, and (3) building allies in the effort to eliminate homophobia. Having clear goals decreases the likelihood that confused employees will ask, "Why are we here? Is the company trying to dictate our moral beliefs?"

The stated goals for my workshop, formulated in collaboration with my corporate clients, are:

1. Employees will understand the corporate commitment to and policy on nondiscrimination (where applicable).

Sometimes employees are unaware that management has taken a formal stand on this issue. Learning of such a commitment is an important first step in securing the employees' openness to addressing gay issues in the workplace. If the company does not have a nondiscrimination policy, an educational effort for policymakers would be a wise starting point.

2. Employees will explore and articulate thoughts and feelings on homophobia and homosexuality.

This is the core issue of the workshop. Provided with a supportive atmosphere, participants need to be encouraged to ask questions and appropriately express feelings. If education, and not merely dictating company policy, is the goal, it is essential to ensure that all questions and comments are welcome. I tell participants that I want them to feel free to raise their hands at any point to comment on what I have said. "If we disagree, we'll acknowledge that we have a difference of opinion and move on," I add.

There is a distinction between dialogue and debate. Dialogue is important to answering questions many people have. Debate bogs down the process, often bores the other participants, and takes valuable time away from other topics of concern. Offering to meet during the break or at the end of the workshop with anyone who wishes to further discuss an issue is a nice way of ending a protracted single-issue debate.

3. Employees will replace myths about homosexuality with accurate information.

Ignorance is the enemy. Lack of exposure to a subject such as homosexuality generally creates anxiety. Many people are misinformed about lesbian, gay, and bisexual people. Replacing myths ("Gay people choose to be gay") with accurate information ("People don't choose their sexual feelings, only whether or not they will act on them") helps lower anxiety. In my "Homophobia in the Workplace" workshop, I provide the most current information about homosexuality, but I always encourage the participants to do their own reading on the topic.

Gay, lesbian, and bisexual speakers can also be very effective in dispelling common myths. Ideally, these speakers should be employees of the company.

4. Employees will explore the effects of homophobia on all employees.

Even people who hold strong negative beliefs about homosexuality are often shocked to discover the impact jokes and offensive comments have on their colleagues. Once fair-minded individuals fully understand the effects of homophobia, they are less inclined to tolerate inappropriate behaviors in the workplace.

5. Employees will strategize means of eliminating destructive behaviors from the workplace.

People can agree that inappropriate behaviors ought to be stopped but not know how to do it. I ask the participants, "What happens if you are at the lunchroom table and your office mate starts to tell an AIDS joke or makes an antigay comment? How do you step in? Is there a comfortable way to change the subject?"

What follows is a description of the workshop for corporate clients that I conduct either alone or with a colleague. It is offered here as a model of effective training on gay issues in the workplace. Feel free to borrow, copy, revise, or ignore.

No two workshops I conduct are exactly the same. They are made different by the unique quality of each audience, by my variability, and by the variability of my co-facilitator. Any workshop will reflect the personality, experience, and priorities of the presenter(s) and participants.

That said, I believe it is important to have the workshop begin with a strong statement of support from a person in management. He or she can set the stage by underscoring how seriously they take the issue and how glad they are to provide this opportunity for everyone to explore the subject. If it is a department meeting, it ought to be the department head who introduces the workshop. If the workshop is sponsored by the company's diversity management office, a representative of that office should open the session by discussing the company's commitment to creating a safe, productive work environment.

Employees who feel anxious or confused about the subject often take their lead from their supervisors. Two examples of how managers can affect the atmosphere of a workshop on gay issues come quickly to mind.

The manager of one department showed up halfway through my workshop for his employees. No one introduced me or the topic to the group. I introduced myself and spent a considerable amount of time making the case for why this subject was a work-related issue. It was at this workshop that an angry young engineer pleaded with his colleagues, "I don't care what the company policy says. Homosexuality is a sin. The future of civilization is at stake."

The manager of another department attended my workshop in advance of inviting me to speak to his group. He then called each of his employees and told them why he had invited me and why he wanted them to attend the workshop. On the day of the event he introduced the subject by explaining his own understanding of how bias can take a terrible toll. As a high school student, he said, he was part of a gang of boys who taunted a young man who was gay. He explained how horrible he felt when the gay student committed suicide. He set the tone for our time together. His employees were serious, attentive, and asked sensitive questions about how productivity is affected by homophobia.

In my experience, management almost always sets the tone, for good or for bad.

I also believe strongly that there should be some gay or lesbian presence in the workshop. If the facilitator is a heterosexual person, lesbian, gay, and bisexual people should be brought in to talk about how homophobia and heterosexism have affected their lives. If there are not gay employees who are available or feel safe enough to speak to the group, most cities have gay speaker's bureaus. If that is impractical, there are audiovisual aids that can be used.

Having gay people speak about their lives allows some heterosexual people their first opportunity to put all they have heard about homosexual men and women into perspective. Providing a human being who challenges the myths, the jokes, and snide comments is a very effective means of raising awareness. More than any facts I offer, my presence as a happy, self-affirmed gay man is the most powerful tool I have to combat ignorance on this issue. In this instance, the messenger becomes the message.

When I arrange for lesbian and gay guest speakers, I always request a man and a woman. If only one can come, I ask that it be a lesbian woman so that the audience doesn't see and hear the issue from only my perspective as a white male.

My co-facilitator is most often my friend Pamela Wilson. In addition to being a nationally known, highly skilled sexuality educator and trainer, author, and editor, she is an African American heterosexual woman. I love the black-white, female-male, straight-gay balance our collaboration provides. Such diversity allows a great number of participants to connect or identify with our life experiences and perspectives.

Following the introduction by the department head or representative of the diversity management office, I present the goals of the workshop and the premises of our time together. It is here that I outline how homosexuality, homophobia, and heterosexism are work-related issues.

The premises are:

1. The corporation is making an effort to create a safe, productive work environment for all employees.
2. Gay people and people who care about them work among you.
3. Heterosexism and homophobia are present in the workplace, manifested in negative comments, jokes, or assumptions of heterosexuality (heterosexism).
4. Homophobia and heterosexism take a toll on people's ability to be productive in the workplace.
5. Homophobic behavior results from misinformation, fear, and a lack of exposure to gay people. Education reduces the chance that people will engage in or tolerate homophobic behavior.
6. Employees are entitled to their own belief systems. Tolerance does not equal acceptance. It is inappropriate behavior, not beliefs or values, we seek to change.

While stating and building a strong case for each premise, I attempt to learn more about the audience. I will ask, for instance, how many people, by show of hands, know someone who is gay. Usually at least half to three-quarters of the participants raise their hands, depending upon where in the country the workshop is taking place. The geographical location also influences the response when I inquire, "How many of you know someone who is HIV-positive?"

When building the case for the effect of ignorance on the anxiety we feel over this issue, I report George Gallup's findings that only 15 percent of Americans feel they had good sex education at home and only 10 percent had good sex education in high school. Again, I ask group members to raise their hands if they believe they received good sexuality education at home or school. Typically, only one or two people put their hands up, indicating their parents did a decent job of talking to them about sex. Likewise, on the second question I'll see only a few hands—and those raised hesitatingly—to indicate that they had a good sex-education program in high school.

"In our house, we didn't talk about sex," I offer. "And in my all-boys Catholic high school, taught by the Christian Brothers of Ireland, we got only a half-hour film from the Navy on gonorrhea. Most people my age learned about sex by laughing at jokes we didn't get. We would pretend we understood but had to go home and try to figure it out for ourselves. We didn't have Phil and Oprah to explain things to us." People laugh and nod in recognition.

I also remind them that none of us had books at home or in school that explained homosexuality. "Where were we to look if we wanted to find out about these people we called 'queer'?" I ask. "What was the source of our factual information about homosexuality? Given this, how can we be expected to be comfortable with something we've never had the chance to learn about or discuss?"

My style of education is very personal. I believe that in building one-to-one relationships, I can break through the them-versus-us mentality that often separates homosexual people from heterosexual people. My attitude toward my audience is that most of the women and men sitting in the room want to know more than they do. Most of the participants have had very little opportunity to ask questions about this issue. Most feel anxiety about the time we are going to spend together and most are pretty nice people who don't want to feel fear. Many of them are now seeing a gay person up close for the first time. Most do not have strong religious beliefs on this issue, but some do. Most of them are used to being made to feel guilty about their racism, sexism, and anti-Semitism (among other prejudices) in diversity classes, and they expect that that is my intent. I also believe that most of them need to feel safe, need to feel understood, before they will be willing to share.

Pam is very good about establishing ground rules that help people feel safe. Before introducing the first exercise, which has as its goal surfacing the feelings of the participants, she reminds them that we are talking about two difficult issues: sexuality and difference. She also acknowledges how hard it can be to speak up in an environment of peers where you are expected to know and parrot company policy. "We are sometimes afraid of saying stupid things, aren't we?" she says. "Well, let's agree that the only stupid question is the one we don't ask. And let's agree that we will keep an open mind today. Sometimes we find ourselves disagreeing with a comment before someone finishes the sentence. Let's let everyone finish before we judge the comment. And let's avoid put-downs like, 'Boy, is that dumb.' We're all here to learn and we're entitled to our feelings."

The first exercise we offer is a "continuum choice" exercise. Four easels are generously spaced at the front of the room. A flip chart is on each. Pam poses three questions, one at a time, and, in response to each she asks the participants to stand in front of the flip chart that best answers the question from their perspective. We remind the participants there are no wrong answers.

Exercises such as this help us achieve the goal of providing the participants with an opportunity to discuss and learn more about the issues. With the continuum choice exercise, any set of questions can be created. Ours are:

1. How would you describe the atmosphere for gay, lesbian, and bisexual employees in your workplace? Would you say it is very hostile, somewhat hostile, somewhat accepting, or very accepting?

2. If a new employee came to you and confided that he or she was gay, what would you think was the best thing for him or her to do, given your assessment of the workplace: stay in the closet, come out to only a few close friends, come out to a supervisor, or come out to everyone?

3. There is going to be an office picnic on Friday. Every employee is invited to bring family members. An openly gay employee plans to come. Would you be most comfortable if he or she would come with a date of the other sex, come alone, come with a same-sex date but refrain from engaging in any displays of affection, or come with a same-sex date and feel as free as heterosexual co-workers do in engaging in displays of affection? (We explain here that we are talking about *appropriate* indications that the two are a couple.)

Once participants have placed themselves along the continuum, we ask a few volunteers to talk about why they chose to stand where they did. Lively discussion among the employees generally results from the exchange. We encourage participants to make up a fifth option if none of the options we provided suits them or to feel free to move from easel to easel if they change their mind at any point during the discussion.

The value of beginning with such an exercise, time permitting, is that it encourages reflection about the conditions of the office and about personal feelings. It also almost always guarantees that the myths that will later be addressed are raised by the participants themselves. These include I don't tell my colleagues my personal business. Why do I need to know that someone is gay? If people choose a homosexual lifestyle, that's their business, but why is it a work-related issue? I wouldn't want them coming to the picnic with a date because I am afraid it would influence my children's development.

It's best for the facilitator not to argue with statements made by the participants in this exercise. The purpose of this segment is to get people to think and to express their thoughts and feelings. Often these thoughts and feelings are based upon misinformation. If Pam or I hear a myth, we interject, "Some people believe that. We'll talk more about that later."

Following this exercise, the program proceeds to an important presentation on sexuality. The introduction to this section includes the acknowledgment that scientists are still in the process of studying and understanding the full dimensions of human sexuality and that we have much more to learn. It also includes the encouragement that everyone read for themselves current literature on the subject.

Our presentation on human sexuality provides the important distinctions between biological sex, gender identity, gender role, and sexual orientation. Workshop participants also learn about Alfred Kinsey's research into American sexual behaviors and about how sexual orientation is different than sexual behavior and sexual orientation identity.

It is this section of the workshop that lays the important groundwork for understanding how homophobia is like racism and sexism. It is here we address the issues that often make this topic most confusing for some people. Of particular importance to many of the participants is hearing that people don't choose their sexual orientation. The other distinction that helps clarify the issue for some people is that homosexuality is not defined by behavior but rather by feelings, whether or not those feelings are acted upon.

At this time a facilitator should expect the most questions and the most debate. The questions often come from parents who want to learn more about the sexual development of their children. They appreciate the opportunity to clarify the issues of gender identity, gender role, and sexual orientation.

If there is debate, as sometimes happens, it often comes from people who feel that much of the information being presented is biased. These individuals will generally insist that homosexuals choose to be gay and can change their sexual orientation.

Pam and I have found that the factual information on sexuality and sexual orientation changes the way many people see these issues. Most participants are amazed by what they did not know. If disagreements arise from this factual presentation, facilitators should prevent debates by agreeing to disagree and moving on.

If it is not possible to offer a component on sexuality in the workshop, companies should, at the very least, provide written resources for the participants. These may include recommended readings and/or a list of the materials available in the company's library or human resource office.

As I mentioned earlier, gay, lesbian, and bisexual employees should, if possible, be asked to participate in diversity workshops as speakers. This provides a wonderful opportunity for heterosexual co-workers to ask questions and to learn firsthand how homophobia and heterosexism can impact a person's life. In the process some people will let go of old stereotypes and biases. Having a gay employee speak also provides the closeted homosexual person in the audience a positive role model. Watching the other members of the audience respond to the gay speaker with respect, and often with support, likewise presents the closeted employee with a vision of what is possible for her- or himself.

These lesbian, gay, and bisexual employees or volunteers from outside the company should be provided sufficient time to talk about their lives and about their work. I believe that it is particularly helpful if the gay people offer enough personal information about themselves to enable a heterosexual colleague to connect person to person. An example might be:

> Hello. My name is Patrick Mooney. I'm thirty-eight years old. I've worked at this company for twelve years in the public relations office. I'm the middle child of five Irish Catholics. I'm out to my parents and siblings and recently told my office mate that I am gay. I came out at work because I was tired of lying and hiding and I was sick of hearing AIDS and fag jokes. I've been in a relationship for eleven years. I have to admit to being a little nervous about being here because I see some people in the audience that I know but who didn't know that I am gay. I am going to stop talking now so that Kathleen can tell you about herself. But if you have any questions for me, I hope you'll feel comfortable asking.

Ample time should also be allowed for questions. It is here that hetero-sexual employees have the best opportunity to bridge the gaps that separate them from their gay colleagues. They can do so by asking for information that will help them better understand the issues. Appropriate questions include How long have you known you were gay? How did your parents respond? How did your office mate respond? Does your boss know? Are you afraid that coming out at work will affect your career? Why do I need to know you are gay? How has coming out affected your attitude about work? What do you want from the company? How can I be supportive?

Questions that I would consider inappropriate would be those that seem hostile, too personal, or call for opinions the gay volunteer isn't qualified to offer. Examples of such questions would be Do you believe you are living in sin? Have you tried to change? What do you do sexually? Do you have AIDS? Is the singer Madonna a bisexual?

I also think that gay, lesbian, and bisexual employees who volunteer to speak ought not to be expected to present the latest scientific research on the frequency of homosexuality among identical twins, to explain the Salk Institute study on brain differences in gay and heterosexual men, or to provide a thorough explanation of how domestic partner benefits are set up in corpo-rations like Levi Strauss. These men and women are experts in their particular professions. They also happen to be gay and have volunteered to talk about their lives. Being lesbian, gay, or bisexual, as they well know, doesn't make them an authority on homosexuality. They are best used as resources of how it feels to be a gay employee of the company. And what a great resource they are!

The next exercise we introduce helps the participants surface, discuss, and learn more about the myths about homosexuality. The employees are asked to provide us with the words our culture uses to describe gay people. "Pretend you are all from another planet. We have sent you out with pen and paper to report on how homosexual people are perceived. Let's start with the names we have for homosexual men and women. Please just call them out and we will record them on the flip charts at the front of the room."

The words we get include *gay, lesbian, homosexual, he-she, fag, dyke, bulldagger, butch, homo, queer, queen, sissy, pansy, fairy, fruit, lezzie, punk, shim, mariposa,* and *poof,* among others.

"What images did you hear about?" we'll ask. "What mannerisms were discussed?"

We record *limp wrist, lisp, light in the loafers, swishy* (for men), and *manly* (for women).

Under "professions" we get *hairdresser* for men and *truck driver* for women, among others.

When we ask for any other words that come to mind, we hear *promiscuous*, AIDS, *child molesters, transvestite, transsexual.*

Once we have surfaced these words, I explain their origins and meanings. I challenge the myths by citing current studies, such as the ones that show that most sexual abuse of children involves a young girl with an adult male in her family. I also point out that all the slang terms for gay men are feminine or "soft" words (*sissy, pansy, fairy*) and all the slang terms for lesbian women are masculine or "hard" words (*butch, bulldagger, dyke*). This underscores how many people confuse homosexuality with gender role and gender identity. One of the common eroneous beliefs about homosexuality is that gay boys and gay girls are confused about and uncomfortable with their gender.

It is also at this time that I offer my perspective on the close link between sexism, homophobia, and heterosexism.

The advantage of this popular exercise is that it surfaces the stereotypes people have of homosexuals and provides an opportunity to discuss the myths, it creates a snapshot of the world in which gay, lesbian, and bisexual people are forced to live, and it presents the case for appropriate use of language.

With the backdrop of these offensive words and images, I then dramatize the destructive power of homophobia by describing what it is like to grow up as a gay person. I do this in two ways. First, I lead the group through a "guided fantasy" that makes real the isolation and pain of having a secret you don't understand and are afraid to share with anyone for fear that they won't love or respect you anymore. The role reversal helps heterosexual employees understand why a gay colleague might need to come out and to understand what the person means when he or she says, "I'm gay."

The other way I bring home the powerful negative impact of homophobia and heterosexism is by telling my story of growing up as a gay man. It is a sometimes humorous but generally painful description of fear, denial, struggle, despair, and ultimately self-acceptance and love. By the vote of nearly every postworkshop evaluation ever completed for my workshop, the telling of my story is the most powerful tool in communicating the seriousness of the issue of homophobia.

The truth is, it could be any gay person's story. What happens when homosexual men and women tell their story is that heterosexual people are able to imagine us as vulnerable children, confused and frightened by our feelings. It is then that they are best able to understand the difference between sexual orientation and sexual behavior. It is for that reason that I stress once again that these workshops must provide participants with the opportunity to meet and talk honestly with a self-affirmed lesbian woman, gay man, or bisexual person on a personal level.

The last exercise of our day-long workshop helps the employees strategize the means of eliminating destructive homophobic, heterosexist, and AIDs-phobic behaviors from the workplace. We ask six people from the audience to participate in a scripted role play that depicts a conversation full of bias against homosexual employees.

The scenario has six employees sitting at the lunchroom table discussing the assignment of a new person to their work area.

> PAT: *Have you met the new guy who has been assigned to our area? He seems nice enough. Whose office is he going to share?*
>
> CAROL: *He does seem nice enough, but there's a rumor flying around about him. Someone from his other location called to report that he's gay.*
>
> TERRY: *You're kidding. Well, he's not going to share my office. I mean it. I'll quit first.*
>
> PAT: *What are you so worked up about?*
>
> TERRY: *Would you want to share an office with a fag? What if he has AIDS? What are people going to think of me? There's an opening in my office, but he's not going to be in it.*
>
> CAROL: *Maybe he should work with Bill. Rumors fly about him, too. Have you ever seen him at an office function with a woman?*
>
> TERRY: *That's a perfect solution. The new guy can work with Bill. That way we can confine the germs to one area. And who knows, maybe romance will bloom.*
>
> TED: *I'm real uncomfortable with this conversation.*
>
> CAROL: *Oh, come on, Ted. Terry has a right to his opinion.*

Following the reading of the scenario, we ask the participants as a group, "Do you think this conversation could happen in your work environment?" Generally the answer is yes. We then ask the employees to break into groups of four and answer the following three questions:

> 1. How would you feel if you were a gay person sitting at that table, and how might it affect your work?

2. What examples of homophobia and heterosexism can you identify in the conversation?
3. What steps could you take to address the homophobia and heterosexism present in the conversation?

When the group reconvenes, we process their responses to questions 1 and 2 and record on flip charts their interventions for question 3. Their interventions are listed under two headings: *Reactive* and *Proactive.* The reactive measures that are often suggested include using humor to derail the conversation, refusing to laugh at antigay humor, educating colleagues about AIDS, heterosexist assumptions, and homosexuality, citing company policy about nondiscrimination, pulling Terry aside to confront him with the effects of his behavior, leaving the table, reporting the conversation to a supervisor, personalizing the issue by saying, "I know gay people and I'm offended by this conversation," or saying, "The new guy can share my office."

As we help the participants explore which response feels most comfortable for them, we also ask, "Is Carol correct? Does Terry have a right to express his opinion?" A lively, thoughtful discussion generally follows. Most people agree that if it is appropriate to express opinions on controversial topics at work, a person should use noninflammatory language. Even then, they say, they wish the company would provide clear guidelines on when, where, and if such discussions should take place.

Under the proactive heading, we list "personal" measures and "corporate" measures that can be taken in a preventive manner to create an environment that is free of homophobia. The personal measures include attending a workshop on homophobia in the workplace, displaying a pro-gay symbol or book in your office, talking positively to colleagues about the issue, and using inclusive language (*partner* rather than *spouse*). The corporate measures include, among others, having a nondiscrimination policy, offering training on the issue, providing domestic partner benefits, and supporting gay employee groups.

At the end of our workshop participants meet and interact with representatives of the company's gay, lesbian, and bisexual employee support group. These representatives, usually a woman and a man, sometimes a heterosexual and a homosexual person, talk briefly about themselves, their work, and why they are involved in the support group. They also explain the group's goals, provide resources, and explain how to participate in the group's activities. They then answer questions from the workshop participants.

Before leaving the workshop, employees are asked to fill out an evaluation. Each company provides its own form, but typical questions include (rating from 1—very positive—to 5—very negative):

1. In general, how did you feel about the workshop?
2. How meaningful was the workshop to you as a member of this company's working environment?
3. How meaningful was the meeting to you as an individual?
4. How would you rate the effectiveness of the consultants?
5. How would you rate the effectiveness of the workshop as a whole?
6. If you have attended other affirmative action workshops, how did this session compare?

The results of these postworkshop evaluations and questionnaires can assist the company enormously in determining the success of the training, in redesigning the training, and in assessing employee support.

In-house diversity trainers and lesbian and gay employee speakers have an abundance of resources available to them for designing and presenting workshops on gay issues in the workplace. Among these materials are books that explain current research on homosexuality and describe useful training exercises. Also available are audiovisual aids that effectively communicate the personal and professional dynamics of the issue.

Robert L. Barret

Creating Change:
Making an Impact in the Local News Media

The gay experience in the South suffers from the kind of negative stereo-typing that limits the perception of gay, lesbian, bisexual, and transgendered persons across the country. Many believe that to be gay in the southern states is to be constantly faced with an immovable oppression that stifles both individual and collective identity. Certainly, like other small cities, the gay communities in the South remain largely closeted. But, in cities like Atlanta and Miami, there are visible and active communities that have become acknowledged and valued parts of their cities' life. It is possible to be more out in the South, and there is no time like the present when the national media is filled with various expressions of homosexuality. This chapter will present a case study of my effort in a medium-sized Southern city and will include a model for gaining access to the media that may be useful for others.

Accessing the media in the South poses a unique challenge. First, there is generally an absence of more liberal, so-called left-wing, groups to push these primarily conservative communities toward more inclusive positions. Until recently the influx of population groups from outside the region has been limited. However, with the rise in popularity of the sun belt states and increased participation in national business opportunities, it is common to find many residents who grew up in more diverse and tolerant cities. Still, the close connection between church and elected officials exercises a some-what rigid strain of conservatism, especially when it comes to homosexual-ity. Strategizing to gain access to the media requires careful planning and the creation of specific requests.

Charlotte, North Carolina, has been my home for most of my professional life. I have worked in business, as a high school teacher, and finally as a university professor as this business-dominated city has grown from 100,000 to over 450,000. As I began to come out, I realized that I needed to be in a more positive environment, so I sent myself to "gay boot camp" in San Francisco. As a psychologist, finding work in California was a challenge, but ultimately I was successful in working in a heavily HIV-oriented private practice and served on the staff of the Behavioral Medicine Unit at the University of California San Francisco Medical School. As stimulating as the work and the city were, I determined that I would not be secure in my gay identity until I returned to my hometown and came out publicly. Accordingly, after two years I returned to my present academic position as professor in a graduate program in counseling.

When I returned to Charlotte I was determined to live as an openly gay man. Because I had come out after many years of heterosexual marriage and had been somewhat visible as an HIV activist, I felt great apprehension about how I might be received. My initial impression was one of dismay as I read the consistently negative stories about homosexuality in our local newspaper, the *Charlotte Observer*. These accounts focused on arrests in public parks and highway rest stops and implications in cases where youth leaders had been arrested for sexual molestation. There was not a single instance where a positive image was presented.

To be fair, this newspaper is the largest and most liberal in the state. The editorial staff has provided courageous leadership in school desegregation and takes editorial positions that are generally against the right-wing policies of our senior senator, Jesse Helms. However, the paper described sexual orientation as sexual preference and pretty much presented the issue in moral terms. For example, when a gay rights issue did come up, typically reporters would turn to religious leaders to comment. Little or no effort was made to locate a spokesperson from the gay community. While adopting personnel policies that protected employees from discrimination based on sexual orientation and keeping on their payroll the sole "out" gay activist, the newspaper staff failed to understand the need for stories that would help the reader understand the complexity and diversity within the gay community.

And the gay community was of little help in promoting a more positive view. Mirroring the larger city, gay men and lesbians are conservative when it comes to gay rights, and there is no radical presence that could push for more fair presentation. To its credit, the community supported a gay switchboard, several lesbian social groups, a political organization that suffered from a lack of vision and timid leadership, and was in the process of starting a gay youth support group. There was also the more visible AIDS service organization, which had become mired in a somewhat public controversy between its board and executive director over positioning itself as a leader in the gay rights movement. There was an absence of public gay leadership that articulated a progressive gay agenda.

Getting Started

My first effort was to gather together a group of leaders in the gay community for informal meetings that assessed where we were versus where we wanted to be. These men and women represented some of the gay and lesbian organizations but gathered to discuss one primary question, "What needs to happen next in this city in order for our community to be more effective?" We met irregularly and without any stated intention to do anything other than talk. Individuals suggested projects and followed through, but the group never acted as a body. Discussions were held with other groups in the gay community and we also had a meeting with the mayor, a conservative Republican, in an effort to get him to see who we were and how we lived. While he takes public positions that oppose our presence, he was willing to meet with us for dialogue. Frankly, some of this conversation included damage control created by the distribution of our local gay newspaper, *Q-Notes*, which featured explicit sex ads. The staff of this newspaper had decided to send copies to elected officials, and we were concerned that the ads promoted a negative and untrue stereotype that did more harm than good. The mayor's response was generally negative, and he even said, "We don't want Charlotte to become another San Francisco." It was clear that we could not expect support from him, although he did encourage us to meet with other city council members.

We were keenly aware that there was an opportunity to promote change on several fronts. So little had been done that almost any effort would produce at least some positive gain. Even our meeting with the mayor was viewed as a success. It was the first time he had been face to face with lesbians, gay men, and bisexuals who wanted to just talk about issues. Still, deciding where to focus our energy was a challenge. The gay community was invisible, so virtually any intervention would be groundbreaking. For me, though, the image in the press continued to be threatening and created major hurdles in my goal of being more public about my sexual orientation. So, independently, I decided to approach the press.

Taking Action: Targeting the Press

My initial effort was to write a letter to the publisher of the newspaper, the *Charlotte Observer,* owned by Knight-Ridder. In my letter I mentioned that I had been living in San Francisco and that I had returned to Charlotte to resume my work at the university and in my psychology practice. I stated that my reason for writing was the negative image the paper promoted about what it means to be lesbian or gay, and I made specific references to stories that had appeared since my return. I closed by offering to bring some people from the gay community down to talk with the editors so that they might be more informed about who we are. I mailed the letter with much apprehension, for the risk seemed great.

The university had adopted a protection clause that included homosexuality in its employment code, but there were no out gay or lesbian faculty or staff. I came out to my dean and provost following a meeting with the GLB student group where I heard loud and clear, "We can't be the only ones on this campus who are visible. Where are the adults who can help us?" But I worried that the clients in my practice would disappear or that publicity would place me at personal risk. However, I recognized that the editors were unlikely to write about us as individuals without prior consent unless we created news. Three days after I mailed my letter I received the publisher's response. Basically he said, "Good Idea. You will be hearing from the editor shortly to schedule the meeting."

The next step was to gather six persons who were willing to participate in this discussion. Actually that was easier than I had anticipated, although a few were worried about exposure and possible career damage, and there were no African Americans willing to attend. The final group was composed of a CPA in private practice who chaired the AIDS service organization board, a small business owner, a lesbian who had recently opened a gay and lesbian bookstore, and two other lesbians who were working on the gay youth project. We agreed to coordinate what we were doing with lesbian and gay employees at the paper. As I met with them I retrieved copies of stories that had been done in other southern newspapers. I also contacted the National Gay and Lesbian Task Force for assistance and received copies of surveys that included a list of employers who had gay-positive personnel policies. My intention was to go to the press with samples of the ways similar communities had dealt with this issue and with specific requests and ideas for stories.

Before our meeting at the newspaper the panel assembled and discussed how we would present ourselves, who would say what, possible questions and credible answers, and potential consequences. We identified the ideal outcome and what we thought was reasonable, and we spoke about our personal fears and how we would protect ourselves. Each was supported in her or his right to withdraw at any time. We agreed that we would introduce ourselves in terms of our family background, education, and work, to show our lives in the fullest dimension. We also decided to keep the tone of the meeting on a positive note. This would be accomplished by acknowledging the difficulty the press has in keeping abreast of the news in the gay community, the role the paper has set in adopting positive personnel policies, and the supportive stance taken in previous editorials. We were going to strive to make an alliance with the editors and to educate them about our agenda.

With a mix of high hopes and apprehensions we met as a group and drove to the newspaper armed with our handouts and suggestions. We were escorted into the editor's office, where he had assembled a group of other editors and reporters. As we began to introduce ourselves, we talked about our families, how we came to Charlotte, our hopes for the community at large, and how it felt to be living as gay people in this time and place. The editors and reporters listened very attentively, and we could see that they were opening to us and even liking us. It was a charged moment in which all of us knew something important was happening. We could see attitudes changing and stereotypes falling away. One editor stopped us and stammered, "Wait a minute. Now I get it! This is a civil rights issue, not a moral issue." Another was challenged when he used the term *sexual preference* by explaining to him the implications of that term. His response was that a conservative minister had told him that was the correct term to use and he had never given it much thought. (The day after we left that editor sent a notice to all reporters that henceforth the term *sexual orientation* was to be used when describing homosexuality.)

The tension in the room was creative and charged with excitement. Our conversation covered many topics but generally addressed ways the newspaper could present a more balanced view of who we were. We gave good suggestions and continually affirmed the positive efforts they had made to be more inclusive. We did not sculpt them as the oppressor, rather our attitude was one of helping people of goodwill become more enlightened. We gave them copies of stories that had run in Louisville, Atlanta, and New Orleans newspapers and, as we left them with a list of suggested stories and people in the gay community who had volunteered to serve as press contacts, we praised them for their efforts in the past and took responsibility for the fact that we had been invisible. We sensitized them to our fear of exposure and agreed with them that they could not carry a story unless individuals were willing to be identified.

As our discussion came to a close, it was obvious that the meeting had been a success. There was a sense of mutual understanding and appreciation for what had occurred. We asked to continue the dialogue on a semi-annual basis, and, after agreeing, they asked if we would come back and make a similar presentation to their reporters. We left without any commitments other than to continue our conversation. We did not know what they would do, but we did know that some fundamental change had been made. The excitement we felt was enormous. Our sense of pride in who we were expanded, and we realized that we have a story to tell that is interesting and important. We knew that we could expect support from some nongay leaders in Charlotte.

Meeting with Reporters: Going Public

Two months later we anxiously returned for our meeting with the reporters. For several reasons the group was new. A couple of people were unable to attend, and we were told to limit the number to four. Once again we had met as a panel before going to the press. We recapped what had worked before, made plans about who would talk about what issues, and reaffirmed our stance as wanting to be helpful rather than to condemn. Our emotions rose when we saw posted throughout the building signs proclaiming, "Gay Readers Panel, 2–3 P.M., Room 2."

We had been warned that the audience might be small because of a current news crisis and were surprised to find the room filled with over fifty men and women who seemed as tense as we were. Once again we led with introductions that showed us as family members and community activists. And once again the dialogue became intense quickly. There were antagonistic questions from some that we were able to field without attacking. But the overall reception was extraordinary—really far beyond our hopes. Sports writers asked questions about when an athlete's sexual orientation should be reported. Others wanted to know who they could contact for particular stories. A few challenged us and were obviously homophobic. We responded to each question and challenge respectfully and carefully. We did not want to raise their defenses by attacking them for what they had done in the past. Our objective was to educate them about who we are in the belief that if they could understand they would report on us more favorably. At the conclusion of this exchange one of the senior editors came up and said, "This was magnificent. You folks have created a major change at this newspaper today. You are going to be amazed at what is about to happen."

As I was leaving the room, a woman approached and said that she would like to do a story about me. I offered to get a group together to meet with her, but she was firm. "No," she said, "I want to write about you." I mumbled that I would see if I could get my daughters to come up so we could talk to her together. "No. I want to write about you," she said more firmly. I finally said that I needed to think about it before saying yes.

In the following days I spent a lot of time worrying about letting her do the story and not letting her do it. I finally realized that this was part of why I had returned and that going public was one of the best ways to let my friends and associates over the past twenty-five years know that I am gay. I did tell my ex-wife and daughters that I was going to do this and hoped they would understand.

We did the interview, and I waited anxiously for the Sunday paper a couple of weeks later. There I was, on the front page of the local section, telling the story of coming out, leaving my family, going to San Francisco, and returning to the university. Almost before I had finished reading it, the phone rang. A woman's voice said, "Is this the Dr. Barret whose picture is in the paper today?" When I replied, Yes," she said, "Well, let me tell you what you need to do." I cut her off with, "What I need to do is to not listen to what you have to say. Thanks for calling." And I hung up the phone. Every other call was positive, and throughout the week I received letters and comments from strangers that were universally positive and supportive. Old friends across the South wrote encouraging words. People would stop me in the grocery or the gym and tell me that they were glad that I was here and to keep up the good work. I was stunned by the enormous support I received. The university was largely silent. I had a couple of encouraging notes from faculty members I did not know. My colleagues in my department said nothing. One gay man in another department approached me and said, "Bob, it is not safe to be out on this campus."

Two weeks later my apprehensions rose when an employee of the newspaper called to tell me that I would be mentioned in the publisher's weekly column on Sunday's op-ed page. On that morning I was excited to find an article headed, "Gays Deserve Equal Rights" (Neill 1992).

Elsewhere in that same day's paper was an article on the gay youth group, an article on gay rights in the political process, and a review of a book by a gay author. We jokingly said that they had enough news on our community to create a separate section, "section Q." That day was also the kickoff event in the gay community for the Clinton/Gore campaign. Over five hundred jubilant people turned out to hear local politicians encourage us to participate in the electoral process, to dance, and to give money to the political effort. For many this was the first time that politics seemed relevant.

In the weeks that followed we kept in touch with the people at the newspaper. We called them when there was news and did not complain when they did not cover our stories. One call advised them about the gay pride celebrations taking place throughout the country in June and suggested that they run a picture that represented some of the more serious gay organizations rather than one that promoted a stereotype. They asked the Associated Press for such a picture and let us know that it was used in newspapers all over the country.

Follow Through Meetings

We have initiated a continuing dialogue with the newspaper staff. There have been other stories about individuals and activities in the gay community. And there have been editorials that support our cause. When the city council was considering an extension of civil rights protection to lesbians and gay men, the newspaper supported the change. When the state legislature was considering amending the crime against nature laws, the *Observer* editorialized in favor of the change. Although both of these changes were defeated, many have come to understand and support some of our issues.

Of course, there is still work to do. We were advised that the paper was going to begin including gay commitment notices along with heterosexual marriages. However, there was a change of the managing editor, and that policy change was deferred indefinitely. The new editor seems sympathetic, but she is not as assertive when it comes to taking the kind of risks that reporting on the gay community entails. Still, during our local gay pride week the paper included stories on a daily basis that told what was going on in a positive tone. And there have been several pieces on the op-ed page written by various members of the gay community.

There has also been a backlash from those who oppose us. Prejudicial comments are common in the letters to the editor section of the paper. And pastors of the more conservative congregations have upped their rhetoric against us. Still, our state gay pride march, held in Charlotte for the first time in June 1994, drew only a handful of Bible-thumpers, over four thousand marchers, and included a worship service sponsored by the local clergy association.

Similar efforts with the visual media have not been as successful. We met with the management of the two major television stations and left feeling we had accomplished little. However, we did give them a list of contact persons for specific issues, and they have followed through, expanding the range of people who participate in local news stories.

Assessing the Change

This change has not occurred without some resistance from the gay community. I was approached on two occasions by gay men who threatened to burn my house down. They did not want news covering the gay community because their co-workers would be talking about it and they did not know what to say. Any publicity threatened to expose them. The silence of many is difficult to understand. Closets become comfortable after a period of time, and I suspect that positive presentations of lesbians and gay men challenge us all to be more out. There will never be universal agreement about what kind of coverage is appropriate, and we knew that some would criticize us for what we were doing.

Assessing the impact of this effort is complex. We live in a time when the gay rights movement is making progress on many fronts. There are more people totally out in Charlotte than before. There is a routineness to reporting on gay activities that presents another kind of challenge: How to get the press to quit focusing on us because of our difference and begin to see us in terms of our likeness? The energy in our community has mushroomed, and now there are lots of activities and even financial pressures as we try to support all that we want to accomplish. Our gay youth group is well established and now has a yearly prom that is covered in all media and draws no protesters. We have a presence in the local political process so that now politicians court us for our support and include us in candidate education panels. There are more people out at work, more people out to their families, more people who are willing to be public, more who are pressing for change.

The model we used worked. It was successful in part because the time was right. But it also created change because it was developed thoughtfully and thoroughly. None of us who participated have had our homes destroyed or been hassled by phone or even seriously threatened. And none of those who have followed us into the public eye has been harassed or exposed to discrimination. For me personally, my psychology practice flourishes with a mixture of straight and gay clients. There are now seven of us out at the university, and we have a gay, lesbian, and bisexual professional group that meets monthly. My students have not disappeared, and there are now five very out students in the program in which I teach. The steps outlined below detail our approach and will be of use in a number of situations.

- Make your initial approach at the top. If the person in charge supports the effort, those below will be more confident. Be sure the tone of your letter/conversation is not overly challenging and accusatory.
- Create a panel that is representative of the diversity in the gay community and be up front in stating that the panel does not represent all points of view.
- Have the panel meet and carefully strategize before meeting with the media. *Careful planning of content and tone is critical.*
- Prepare handouts that show what other press has done, suggested stories, and names of key people in the lesbian, gay, and bisexual community who have agreed to serve as press contacts.
- Acknowledge the difficulty in covering the gay community and help reporters understand the fear many experience as they come out in the press.
- Follow up the meeting with letters of appreciation and initiate future meetings.
- Follow up with individuals who have been in the press to be sure they are having a successful experience.
- Be patient but assertive. Point out insensitive stories and continue to press for fair coverage

The work does not end with one or two meetings. A story on a lesbian and gay studies course was headlined, "Gay Studies Course Offered Without Protest." We called the paper on the negative slant on the story by pointing out that a more accurate and positive headline would have been something like, "Gay Studies Course Offered Is Fully Enrolled." We have pointed out stories that have not been covered and constantly encouraged reporting that is more informed. For example, when the local MCC church was having its services interrupted by neighbors surrounding the property with chain saws and lawn mowers, no story appeared until we had complained. Helping the media understand what is news is an obligation we must take on. We also have to work in the lesbian and gay community to build support for the advantages of stories about our activities. The sponsors of an annual party that raises a significant amount of money for the local AIDS service organization still refuse to allow coverage, but the paper continues to approach them each year.

Certainly not every effort will be as successful as ours. What is important is that the press be invited to meet gay, lesbian, and bisexual citizens. Every chance we have to educate a person in a powerful position is an opportunity to create change. Even if the response is not positive, the fact that a conversation occurred is noteworthy. We failed to change our mayor's opinion, but he continues to speak with us and at least hears from us about who we are rather than only hearing from our opposition. Clearly, there is a danger that someone could be hurt as a result of being in the media. We live in communities that are characterized by fear, and those who are different—especially when they are challenging the status quo—are at risk. We follow up with each person who has been public to see what kind of response there has been. So far everyone reports overwhelming support. Perhaps we underestimate the ability of our straight neighbors to accept us. Perhaps resistance is building and eventually someone will be attacked and hurt. But our silence will not protect us, and, in the long run, we believe that the time has come when we need to be more out, when we need to articulate our agenda in terms the larger community can understand, when we can make things change. Keeping focused on what has been accomplished and setting reasonable goals helps maintain both the energy and the commitment to this work. Every effort helps, and every effort brings us closer to the day when we will no longer be oppressed. That is the belief that calls us forward.

REFERENCE

Neill, R. 1992. "Gays Deserve Equal Rights." *Charlotte Observer*, August 30, p. 3C.

Peter M. Nardi

Changing Gay and Lesbian Images in the Media

The crowds gathered in the city streets and with anger and action brought the filming to a halt. For several days, protesters shouted and jeered as cameras rolled. The demonstration was a reaction to a script that many felt depicted gay men in negative and distorted ways. The film was *Cruising*, the city was New York, and the year was 1979. For the first time in history, protests by gays took place before the opening of a film (Russo 1987). The same scene was to be repeated in the streets of San Francisco. This time the film was *Basic Instinct*, the negative images were about lesbians, but the year was now 1991. Despite twelve years having passed, gay men and lesbians were still protesting media depictions of homosexuality as violent, pathological, and evil.

However, during these twelve years a growing social movement emerged among lesbians and gays who developed a variety of strategies and organizations to counteract the repeated verbal and visual bashings the media have inflicted. The movement's visibility reached a peak in the weeks leading up to the 1992 Academy Awards when rumors circulated about a possible disruption of the show by lesbian and gay activists protesting *The Silence of the Lambs* and other negative stereotypes in films. An estimated one hundred demonstrators and one hundred police (many in riot gear) stood outside the Dorothy Chandler Pavilion. Ironically, that evening, in front of an estimated billion viewers, Debra Chasnoff, a lesbian, acknowledged her lover after winning an Oscar for best documentary short, and Bill Launch, lover of the late Howard Ashman, who won for the lyrics of *Beauty and the Beast*, said: "Howard and I shared a home and a life together.... This is the first Academy Awards given to someone we've lost to AIDS" (Wiley and Bona 1993:846).

Lesbian and gay people within the media identified themselves publicly for the first time before a massive audience. Clearly, some changes had occurred since the protests against *Cruising*.

By the spring of 1993 the media were covering gay issues as never before, in part as a result of national attention about gays in the military. Within a two-month period lesbians and gays appeared on the covers of *Newsweek*, *Nation*, *New Republic*, *New York*, *U.S. News and World Report*, and *National Review*, and the coverage of the lesbian and gay march on Washington and of the rising influence of gay political power was unprecedented. This shift and the continuing struggle to maintain accurate and fair media attention through various strategies are the focus of this chapter.

The Way We Were

In order to develop effective strategies against defamatory media images, the historical and social context of these images first needs to be understood. The history of the depiction of gays and lesbians in movies, on television, and in newspapers and magazines is not a pretty one. Russo (1987:347–49), in an appendix to *The Celluloid Closet* under the heading "Necrology," lists over forty examples of the ways in which gay or lesbian characters in films have died. Almost all were murdered or committed suicide.

From 1930 to the late 1960s the Motion Picture Production Code was the major form of self-regulation of Hollywood movies. And in that code's list of forbidden topics was "any inference of sexual perversion," i.e., homosexuality. Before 1930 many precode films had explicit references to homosexuals and numerous depictions of cross-dressing (Russo 1987). But it wasn't until 1961 that the subject of homosexuality was again allowed on-screen and the tone of the portrayals of gay people shifted. From the humorous, innocent sissy images of failed masculinity typical of the 1930s and 1940s, gay characters became lonely, predatory, and pathological people by the 1960s and 1970s (Russo 1987).

Television also has been "a cultural mirror which has failed to reflect [gays'] images accurately. To be absent from prime time, to be marginally included in it, or to be treated badly by it are seen as serious threats to their rights as citizens" (Montgomery 1989:8). Historically, gay and lesbian characters have been shown in stereotypical ways (men as effeminate and women as masculine), as a social problem, or in terms of how the regular heterosexual characters deal with them. Rarely, is it from the perspective of the gay character and rarely is affection displayed between gay characters.

Yet television (and especially British TV) has been much more likely to take risks in the presentation of fair and balanced images of lesbians and gays. Partly in response to pressure from a growing gay activists' movement, ABC in 1973 became the first U.S. network to air a made-for-TV movie about gay men, *That Certain Summer*. Within a few years most major situation comedies, drama shows, and talk shows addressed gay topics, typically as a special issue, rarely in terms of an ongoing character or plot. By the mid-1980s any attention to gay issues was almost always framed in terms of AIDS, and then with gays as victim or villain (Gross 1991).

One of the explanations for the negative media images and the relative invisibility of gays and lesbians historically can be traced to social, economic, and political forces that structure the nature of the entertainment industry and the ways they construct images of people. As profit-making business corporations, media organizations reflect the economic marketplace and political climate of the culture; that is, content is often dictated by what prevents the least erosion of potential consumers. As Gitlin (1985:3) so colorfully phrased it, television's "primary customers are the advertisers whose business is to rent the eyeballs of the audience." Targeting the "typical viewer" who purchases sponsors' goods, the media tailor their products so as not to offend the least common demoninator. This is the argument routinely made when the media are asked to include more gay and lesbian characters.

Media Theory

That people are concerned enough to reform the depictions of certain images in the media should come as no surprise. For years a variety of advocacy groups have transformed entertainment media into political territory (Montgomery 1989). Issues of accessibility and accountability, as well as accuracy, have dominated these debates. At the core of these discussions is a belief that "how we view issues, indeed, what we even define as an issue or event, what we see and hear, and what we do *not* see and hear are greatly determined by those who control the communications world" (Parenti 1986:ix). The influence the media exert in defining, structuring, and delimiting public discourse is related to prevailing political and economic conditions. Essentially, the media recreate, systematically and systemically, a version of reality that often supports the status quo.

Gross (1994:144) argues that much of our knowledge of the real world comes from fictional representations, especially about "groups and phenomena about which there is little firsthand opportunity for learning, particularly when such images are not contradicted by other established beliefs and ideologies." Hence, there is a strong need to focus on the media's depiction of gays and lesbians as a top priority of our movement.

Gross (1984) found that heavier television viewing (defined as four or more hours a day) was related to negative attitudes toward homosexuality, even when controlling for education, age, religion, urban-rural, or race. That is, while higher educated people tended to be more tolerant toward homosexuality than lower educated people, among heavy-viewing higher educated people the percentage of negative attitudes was not significantly different from that of heavy-viewing lower educated people.

If, indeed, attitudes are shaped by the media and if the media persist in presenting images favorable to the status quo, then is it any wonder that a variety of groups with least access to the control of the media and least visibility in the media should be activists and advocates of reform? But reform strategies vary, and each has different methods and outcomes. They include the adoption of assimilationist strategies (gay images that are essentially variations of the white male middle-class, nonsexual character) as well as subversion and appropriation (such as "camp" responses that undermine the power of the media images). Other strategies involve active resistance and opposition (through organized demonstrations) as well as the cultivation of lesbian and gay voices and views through gay and lesbian media (Gross 1991).

Certainly these strategies have contributed to recent shifts toward more balanced and "positive" images. But what is considered positive is a changeable concept, depending on the era and the audience's viewpoint, something to keep in mind when arguing with the media about positive images. For example, early feature films of the 1960s with gay characters were viewed as welcome portrayals, since they at least acknowledged the existence of people with homosexual feelings, yet today are often seen as negative depictions. And many of today's "positive" depictions are simply nonsexualized lesbian or gay characters who do not pose a threat to heterosexuals (Hantzis and Lehr 1994).

How the media depict gays and lesbians relates to important changes brought about by twenty-five years of activist social movements and organizing by a variety of advocacy groups. The National Organization for Women, the National Association for the Advancement of Colored People, religious organizations, and antiviolence groups have all been campaigning for better representation in television (Montgomery 1989). Their work directly affects the strategies used by lesbians and gays.

Pressure against the movie industry by the Gay Activists Alliance in cooperation with the National Gay Task Force (NGTF) began in 1973. Two years later NGTF called for a boycott of sponsors of the *Marcus Welby* TV show. These early attempts at organizing resistance, the later street protests against the filming of antigay movies, and the more recent visibility of the Gay and Lesbian Alliance Against Defamation (GLAAD) have all contributed to significant changes in the media.

On the other hand, some argue that what changes have occurred in the media are nothing more than assimilationist forms of incorporation in which the dominant culture accommodates the radical perspective into its view and robs "the radical of its voice and thus of its means of expressing its opposition" (Fiske 1987:38). This viewpoint is similar to feminist theory, which has also contributed insightful ways of looking at media representations. Thus, an analysis of the content of the portrayals and of the language used to frame gay and lesbian issues might show that the changes continue to ignore a wider range of accuracy at the expense of depictions that are structured in terms of the dominant patriarchal perspective of mostly white, mostly heterosexual, and mostly middle-class men.

Changing Images of Gays and Lesbians in the Media

Many theories can be invoked to explain media depictions of gays and lesbians, but it is also important when developing strategies to combat heterosexism and homophobia in the media to analyze and understand the actual types of portrayals that exist and how they differ. Here are four ways to characterize most gay and lesbian images: (1) overt homophobic and negative stereotypic characterizations, (2) heterosexism and the more subtle forms of stereotyping, (3) invisibility and omission, and (4) accurate, fair, and balanced images.

Overt Homophobic and Negative Stereotypic Characterizations

Combating overtly homophobic images has dominated a good deal of the energies and time of many lesbian and gay activists. Luckily, some of the early strategies of protest and lobbying have resulted in a significant decline of such negative characterizations. Developing successful strategies of reform requires some familiarity with what has been done already.

As mentioned earlier, the history of the movies during the production code era is a history of gay people as one-dimensional, evil, or silly characters who get what they deserve in the end. But in an era when such production codes no longer exist and when increasing visibility of nonstereotypical gays and lesbians is evident, there still remains today overtly homophobic depictions. The repeated use of epithets, such as *faggot, dyke, queer, homo,* and *fruit,* while not used gratuitously as much as in the past, does continue in many media. When they are used they often signify a way of establishing evil or marginality about the character so labeled, although they are occasionally used to demonstrate the ignorance of the person using them. These words become a shorthand for underlining the pathology or villainy of the character.

Linking certain characters with homosexuality through nonverbal cues is a common way of signaling their evilness, even when explicit epithets are not used. This is one area that must be carefully monitored and resisted. The battle over the movie *Basic Instinct* centered on these issues, specifically in the depiction of lesbians and bisexual women as serial killers, using ice picks to murder their predominantly white male heterosexual victims. While the word *dyke* may not have been used, references to a lesbian as masculine were typical. Although some lesbians read this film as a feminist response to patriarchy, many others argued that the historical context of predatory killer lesbian depictions precluded a more positive interpretation. If there were already other depictions of lesbians, then this particular portrayal might not have been so bad. It is the absence of balance and accuracy that becomes the chief contextual concern.

While the use of overtly homophobic expressions in movies and on television dramas and situation comedies has declined significantly in recent years, ad campaigns and videos created and marketed by the radical right groups fighting to overturn antigay discrimination ordinances and to pass repressive legislation against gays and lesbians depend primarily on presenting the most stereotypical images in sensational and negative ways. Many conservative religious programs consistently attack gays and lesbians with bogus research data, misinformation, and fear.

Targeting these groups, however, is probably a Sisyphean task, and many activists would rather not waste their energy fighting the radical right. However, a useful strategy is to target the stations buying and scheduling these shows. Demanding equal time or informing them about the erroneous content can be a more successful technique.

By creating images of lesbians and gays as "other," or as foreign, the media perpetuate and contribute to people's homophobia. While the media may have come a long way from the earlier 1930s' and 1960s' characterizations of homosexuals as genial sissies or unhappy neurotics, there are remnants of these depictions that need continued monitoring.

Strategies   If such a homophobic slur should be broadcast, there are several levels of action that might be taken. A call should be placed immediately to a representative of the medium in which the incident occurred and should be very specific about the details of the incident. Be sure to note the time, date, and context of the occurrence and other relevant information. Ideally, a tape recording of the homophobic remark would be made. If negative remarks continue, organize a phone tree and/or a letter-writing campaign to protest the antigay characterizations.

The call to a senior-level manager should also request that something concrete be done to remedy the situation: a public apology, a request for equal time, and a face-to-face meeting with the parties involved. It is very useful to provide constructive suggestions rather than just a critique. A key idea to remember is that this stage is to inform people about what has happened and why the incident is considered inappropriate.

When meetings, apologies, or equal time are not provided and when monitoring of the medium demonstrates continuing homophobic remarks, several other strategies could be used. If it is a problem with a radio or TV station, one way is to write a letter to the station protesting the incidents, request that the letter be placed in their Federal Communications Commission (FCC) license file, and send a copy to the FCC in Washington, D.C. All stations must be licensed and are open to challenge of that license if discrimination can be demonstrated. Attempts to do this were very common during the 1970s; although few stations lost their license, Montgomery (1989:25) found that "the petition to deny became a powerful weapon of intimidation."

If licenses are not at issue (as in the cases of movies, magazines, or newspapers), suggest that a formal protest take place, as was done at the filming of *Basic Instinct* and *Cruising*. Of course, demonstrations have the risk of publicizing the act that just might have disappeared anyway, but the demise of Andrew Dice Clay's career can be attributed in part to the protests that followed his performances.

Heterosexism and More Subtle Stereotyping

In a response to a minister's question about gays in the military, President Bill Clinton, at a 1993 press conference, replied that he would not be endorsing the "gay lifestyle" by lifting the ban. Clinton framed his response in a way that is probably one of the most common forms of subtle defamation: assuming a heterosexual perspective and presenting gays as "others" whose complex concerns can be reduced to a "lifestyle." In language, images, and the way issues are structured a view that often excludes gays and lesbians or marginalizes them is subtly put forward. It is important to be cognizant of this form of heterosexism in order to develop a more focused strategy of education and reform.

When the media do decide to include lesbian and gay voices and perspectives, there are techniques and words often used that end up reinforcing the dominance of the heterosexual perspective and the outside status of the gay viewpoint. So, for example, calling a lesbian an "avowed homosexual" or nongay people the "general population" perpetuates the "otherness" of the gay person without using traditionally negative stereotypes. While these phrases are not overtly homophobic, note that certain heterosexist assumptions are indicated by them.

In addition to language, the subtle forms of heterosexual dominance can be seen in the ways lesbians and gays are depicted, even positively. The images are almost exclusively white, middle or upper class, disproportionately male, and desexualized. *Making Love, Longtime Companion,* and *An Early Frost* are all examples of the perpetuation of assimilationist images of incorporation in movies and the exclusion of gay (and, especially, lesbian) characters of other races and social classes. Many gay and lesbian characters also appear in sitcoms, usually isolated from other relationships, or in newspaper obituaries without reference to romantic partners, thereby reinforcing some stereotypes about gay people being alone or separate from the ways others lead lives embedded in networks of family and friends (cf. Nardi 1990, 1992).

Furthermore, when lesbians and gays are depicted, the characters usually appear only once and then disappear (Gross 1994). The focus of the stories tends to be "on the acceptance of gay characters by the regular heterosexual characters. Very few gay couples [are] shown, and they [are] not permitted to display physical affection" (Montgomery 1989:93). Usually gay or lesbian characters appear when the topic is a gay one; rarely are they part of the ongoing cast of characters. Typically, they look and act just like everyone else on the show and the humor stems from this misidentification.

These more subtle forms of stereotyping are probably the most common in today's media and deserve special attention and strategic responses. With good intentions the creators of these images and phrases believe they are contributing to the diversity in their work and are helping eliminate discrimination based on sexual orientation. However, we have yet to see many stories dealing with people after they are already openly gay or, more radically, about the ways many lesbians and gays resist dominant heterosexual ideologies.

Strategies   Convincing people in the creative arts to alter their depictions is a difficult process. A typical response from those who are informed that they are using heterosexist language or characterizations is to invoke a charge of political correctness. Yet, the *New York Times* did finally listen to gay activists and dropped the cumbersome and problematic term *homosexual* and its ban against using *gay*. Repeated pressure can indeed be effective.

Again, education is the goal. A media guide was published by GLAAD in 1990 that provided writers with the differences in meanings between various phrases. A clear distinction is made, for example, between "avowed homosexual" and "an openly gay man or lesbian." One strategy, thus, is to compile a list of phrases and words and submit the glossary to the local media with an offer to conduct a workshop explaining the reasons behind the language. When information about the expressions is presented along with the glossary, writers are much more likely to consider the changes as something more than "political correctness."

Calls and letters to writers and producers are useful strategies, since each one usually represents hundreds of others who have not communicated. For example, when Barbara Walters interviewed Martina Navratilova on *20/20*, the ABC newsmagazine show, in 1991, Walters asked her if she could ever see herself married and referred to a husband and children as a "normal" life. Letters were written to the producers and to Walters complaining that she would never think to ask a heterosexual woman if she wished she were lesbian and reminding her that "normal" is not limited to heterosexual families. While no overt homophobic slur was made, the remark is an excellent example of a heterosexist perspective and a more subtle form of stereotyping (in other words, that every lesbian or gay person really wishes to be "normal" and heterosexual). In other segments she did on gay issues later on, Walters generally avoided such heterosexisms.

Critiquing these depictions requires alternative and constructive ways to alleviate the heterosexism. When one sitcom writer remarked at a meeting with GLAAD representatives that he did not know how to communicate quickly to the audience that his character was gay except by using stereotypical signs (more effeminate voice or mannerisms), it was suggested that he review the ways he communicates how characters are heterosexual. By simply allowing people to refer to a same-sex partner, by placing a photo of same-sex couples on a desk, or by having the characters discuss participation in an important gay event, the message could be communicated without resorting to stereotyping or overt declarations. Providing people in the media with specific suggestions and topics is an essential strategy when working with them to correct inaccurate characterizations or situations.

Invisibility and Omission

In 1991 about one hundred Public Broadcasting Service (PBS) stations refused to carry Marlon Riggs's award-winning documentary on African American gay men, *Tongues Untied*, and in 1994 PBS announced it would not financially support a sequel to *Tales of the City*, one of its highest-rated shows of all time. The actions of PBS not only sent a clear message that gay topics are too controversial to schedule but also contributed to keeping lesbians and gays invisible, perhaps the single greatest problem in contemporary media.

Nonreporting of major gay events is a form of distortion that seriously affects lesbian and gay images in the news media. For example, the 1994 Gay Games in New York were ignored in almost all sports coverage, even though they are the largest amateur sporting events in the world. What little was done often appeared in nonsports TV news segments or lifestyle sections of newspapers. Overt cases of omission are matched by routine exclusion from the everyday discourse of entertainment television, movies, newspapers, and magazines. Unless they are an exotic topic on one of the talk shows, a focus of a movie of the week, or a special theme of a sitcom, gays and lesbians are rarely part of the ongoing depiction of everyday life usually portrayed in most movies and TV shows.

With the 1995–1996 television season, there were few continuing gay or lesbian characters on American prime-time TV shows. *Roseanne* and *My So-Called Life* from ABC-TV and *Melrose Place* from Fox-TV were once the only shows with regular lesbian or gay characters. But their characters have been mostly homogenized; in fact, in a show filled with all sorts of sexual escapades, *Melrose Place*'s gay man has rarely been seen dating and his kiss with another man was edited from the final version. While appearances of gay characters have occurred on many shows, they have either appeared once or irregularly, thereby emphasizing their invisibility throughout the rest of the series' shows. And, along the way, they have been depoliticized, desexualized, and made nonthreatening to the status quo (Moritz 1994).

As Gitlin (1985) illustrates, however, the production of certain kinds of images is rarely a result of some conscious planned conspiracy; rather, it is a function of corporate bureaucracy and multiple hands involved in a development process that pursues safety and novelty without risk for the benefit of advertisers and economic profit. But, as Gross (1991:21) reminds us, "nonrepresentation maintains the powerless status of groups that do not possess significant material or political power bases." Those in power rarely require media visibility, while those at the bottom are "symbolically annihilated" through relative invisibility and kept distant from the ordinary lives of the majority of viewers.

Strategies   Monitoring invisibility is as elusive as tracking a ghost; it is much easier to deal with what is there than what is not. Thus, organizing to combat omission requires working with those who directly produce and write the material and educating them to see the world from a perspective often outside their own.

One way is to communicate through calls and letters about what was left out. It is very useful to know the names of the people who are in charge rather than to communicate with some anonymous person. But to write a major film studio executive, for example, and suggest that the company make an action film like *Speed* with a lesbian hero may not get very far. Since profits govern decisions, you need to point out other financially successful examples in which gay or lesbian characters were central to the story, such as *The Birdcage, Philadelphia, The Crying Game, Go Fish,* and *Four Weddings and a Funeral.* In fact, gay-themed *The Wedding Banquet* was the most profitable (cost to ticket sales ratio) film of 1993, proportionately outranking *Jurassic Park.*

Television and film are commercial industries and they are not about to jeopardize millions of dollars by doing something too risky. A lead gay or lesbian character is still considered too innovative and fraught with potential political and economic danger. Thus, suggestions to include a lesbian or gay character in secondary and supporting roles are much more likely to be heeded. As Moritz (1994:141) concludes:

> While it may be argued that these scripts are by design relatively unconcerned with gay rights and more concerned with ratings, it is also true that once-taboo subjects in both cinema and television have gained acceptance only gradually. This may not be the first choice of feminists and lesbians, but it is a first step in working toward at least a small measure of social change.

Thus, it may be an important strategy to work with the media in small but significant steps. Encouraging them to include a gay or lesbian character in any capacity, even as a one-shot event in a secondary role, is still a good start. And it does not hurt to suggest plot lines and ways of doing so. Working with them later on to expand the characters and story lines becomes less difficult.

Accurate and Balanced Portrayals

While invisibility continues to characterize media images, there has been a relative increase in the media representation of gays and lesbians in recent years and a trend toward more accurate and fair images. Some of this is due to an increase in the production of media by gays and lesbians themselves, such as the lesbian and gay film festivals regularly held in many major cities, gay newspapers and magazines that increasingly attract mainstream advertisers, and gay public access television. But nongay media are also increasingly devoting more attention to gay images, especially in light of major social, legal, and political issues that have focused on gays and lesbians.

One of the best examples is ABC-TV's *Roseanne*, which features a lesbian character played by Sandra Bernhart and Martin Mull in the role of Roseanne's gay boss. Their sexual orientation is an integrated aspect of their portrayals, without problematizing. Furthermore, they are depicted as people who have a network of friends and family.

With the exception of Tom Hanks in *Philadelphia* and Whoopi Goldberg in *Boys on the Side* there has not been any major studio feature film with "positive" gay or lesbian characters in lead roles in the past decade. A gay character did appear in *Frankie and Johnny* and another in *The Prince of Tides*. They both were kindly, good supportive neighbors of the lead female character, not too dissimilar to the traditional depictions of the effeminate best friend in the 1930s movies, only more openly acknowledging and stating they were gay. However, many independent films have had gay characters in central roles, in particular *My Beautiful Laundrette, Maurice, My Own Private Idaho, The Adventures of Priscilla, Queen of the Desert, The Sum of Us*, and *Strawberry and Chocolate*.

British television has produced several important gay-themed films, ironically based on American novels, including *Tales of the City, And the Band Played On*, and *The Lost Language of Cranes*. However, in each of these cases a director or writer has been openly gay, lending support to the importance of having open lesbian and gay people in positions of power to produce and regulate images. And while they have been more accurate and balanced in their portrayals, with few exceptions, the representations from Britain continue to emphasize white middle-class men.

Strategies   Essential to changing negative media images is acknowledging when positive ones occur. Too often the media hear only when people complain. Thus, PBS refused to support the production of the *Tales of the City* sequel, perhaps as a result of a barrage of calls from the radical right protesting the original show. Those who supported the miniseries were less likely to call to praise. Hence it is a very important strategy to let the media know when something is good.

However, when writing or calling the media to thank them for a fair appearance of a gay or lesbian character or theme, it is essential to signal that token presentations are insufficient. It is best to acknowledge the depiction and then quickly add an encouragement to do more of the same or to expand the way lesbian and gay characters are portrayed. Providing concrete ideas and situations adds strength to an otherwise dull thank-you letter. Be careful of appearing to accept small crumbs of visible and sanitized gay and lesbian characters.

Since the emergence of more accurate images can be traced in part to more openness among lesbian and gay media people, an indirect method of achieving less heterosexism and homophobia is to work with the media in developing internal policies that make gays and lesbians more likely to be open at work. One example of this is Hollywood Supports, an entertainment industry-founded organization in Los Angeles devoted to countering workplace fears and discrimination based on sexual orientation and HIV status. Through workshops, seminars, employee benefits counseling, and technical advice, this organization has been effective in creating climates supportive of gays and lesbians in the entertainment media. As a result of their work, in 1992, MCA/Universal became the first studio to create benefits for domestic partners.

Many other studios and media organizations now have such benefits, nondiscrimination statements that include sexual orientation, and gay/lesbian employee support groups. In so doing, gay writers, producers, directors, and script readers are much more likely to be open and to speak up when dealing with antigay images. One gay writer told the story about how—when he was closeted because of an antigay climate on the set of a TV sitcom—he was less likely to speak out against inaccurate stereotypes. But when he got a job working on the *Roseanne* show, where the mood was much more supportive, he felt comfortable being open about his sexual orientation and was able to provide important information and advice when the show dealt with gay issues and characters.

So, in addition to praising and encouraging the writers and producers directly about positive depictions of gays and lesbians, it also becomes salient to develop strategies for assisting media in creating a workplace climate that allows gay and lesbian employees to be visibly present and open with their comments and creative skills.

Organizing Responses

While individuals can have a big effect on the media through letters and calls, it often helps to have the clout and legitimacy of larger organizations and media. Several strategies that have been very successful in combating homophobia and heterosexism include the development of media watchdog organizations and the creation of media by and for lesbian and gay people.

In 1973 the Gay Activist Alliance (GAA) in New York was one of the first organizations to take on the media when it confronted executives at ABC-TV about unfavorable treatment of homosexuality (Montgomery, 1989). A group of GAA members later split to form the National Gay Task Force (NGTF), which then formed a Gay Media Task Force (GMTF) in Los Angeles, under the direction of Newt Deiter. The Association of Gay and Lesbian Artists (AGLA) also started in the early 1980s as a support group of gay media people to lobby the industry, consult on projects, and present awards for positive depictions of gays and lesbians.

Although GMTF and AGLA no longer exist, their efforts led to the formation of the Gay and Lesbian Alliance Against Defamation (GLAAD), begun in New York in 1985, then in 1988 in Los Angeles. Today GLAAD is the largest and most influential national organization, with chapters around the country devoted to monitoring the media's portrayals of gays and lesbians, responding with organized letter-writing actions and protest marches, and consulting with executives and creative staff.

In addition to organizations structured to resist and change stereotypical images, another form of response has been the creation of lesbian and gay media. From cable TV public access shows to computer E-mail, the Internet, newspapers, and slick magazines, gays have developed an impressive communications network.

With the beginning of the modern homophile movement in the early 1950s in Los Angeles, *ONE* became the first widely circulated homosexual magazine, selling two thousand copies a month (D'Emilio 1983), although earlier attempts included a 1924 Chicago newsletter called *Friendship and Freedom*, the 1934 newsletter *Chanticleer*, and *Vice Versa*, a 1947 Los Angeles lesbian magazine (Kepner 1994). Along with the *Ladder*, published by the Daughters of Bilitis from 1956 to 1970, and the *Mattachine Review*, published from 1955 to 1964, these early and important magazines invented a new form of discourse and helped create "an incipient sense of community" (D'Emilio 1983:110). The tradition carries on with such widely circulated national magazines as the *Advocate* (the longest continuously published gay magazine, since 1967) and many local lesbian and gay newspapers.

With the growing power of openly gay and lesbian filmmakers, television and newspaper reporters, and writers, a "most effective form of resistance to the hegemonic force of the dominant media" is occurring, namely "to speak for oneself" (Gross 1991:40). However, there is no lesbian or gay equivalent to the Christian cable networks or the numerous syndicated conservative religious radio and television shows that mobilize thousands of followers to write or call politicians instantly.

For gays and lesbians, access remains limited, especially in the powerful electronic national media. As Russo (1987:323) so forcefully said about homophobia in the movies (but as applicable to television, radio, print, and other media): "This will change only when it becomes financially profitable, and reality will never be profitable until society overcomes its fears and hatred of difference and begins to see that we're all in this together."

NOTE

Comments by Ken Plummer and Beth Schneider on earlier drafts helped shape my arguments. Thanks to them and to the people at GLAAD/Los Angeles who provided me with the opportunity to work with the media in changing gay and lesbian images.

REFERENCES

D'Emilio, J. 1983. *Sexual Politics, Sexual Communities*. Chicago: University of Chicago Press.
Fiske, J. 1987. *Television Culture*. New York: Routledge.
Gay and Lesbian Alliance Against Defamation (GLAAD). 1990. *Media guide to the Lesbian and Gay Community*. New York: GLAAD.
Gitlin, T. 1985. *Inside Prime Time*. New York: Pantheon.
Gross, L. 1984. "The Cultivation of Intolerance." In G. Melischek, K. Rosengren,

and J. Stappers, eds., *Cultural Indicators: An International Symposium*, pp. 345–64. Vienna: Austrian Academy of Sciences.

—— 1991. "Out of the Mainstream: Sexual Minorities and the Mass Media." In M. Wolf and A. Kielwasser, eds., *Gay People, Sex, and the Media*, pp. 19–46. New York: Harrington Park.

—— 1994. "What Is Wrong with This Picture? Lesbian Women and Gay Men on Television." In R. J. Ringer, eds., *Queer Words, Queer Images*, pp. 143–56. New York: New York University Press.

Hantzis, D., and V. Lehr. 1994. "Whose Desire? Lesbian (Non)Sexuality and Television's Perpetuation of Hetero/Sexism." In R. J. Ringer, ed., *Queer Words, Queer Images*, pp. 107–21. New York: New York University Press.

Kepner, J. 1994. "Our Movement Before Stonewall." Los Angeles: International Gay and Lesbian Archives.

Montgomery, K. 1989. *Target: Prime Time*. New York: Oxford University Press.

Moritz, M. 1994. "Old Strategies for New Texts: How American Television Is Creating and Treating Lesbian Characters." In R. J. Ringer, ed., *Queer Words, Queer Images*, pp. 122–42. New York: New York University Press.

Nardi, P. M. 1990. "AIDS and Obituaries: The Perpetuation of Stigma in the Press." In D. Feldman, ed., *Culture and AIDS*, pp. 159–68. New York: Praeger.

—— 1992. "That's What Friends Are For: Friends as Family in the Gay and Lesbian Community." In Ken Plummer, ed., *Modern Homosexualities: Fragments of Lesbian and Gay Experience*, pp. 108–20. London; Routledge.

Parenti, M. 1986. *Inventing Reality: The Politics of the Mass Media*. New York: St. Martin's.

Russo, V. 1987. *The Celluloid Closet: Homosexuality in the Movies*. Rev. ed. New York: Harper and Row.

Wiley, M., and D. Bona. 1993. *Inside Oscar: The Unofficial History of the Academy Awards*. New York: Ballantine.

Contributors

James T. Sears is professor of educational leadership and policies at the University of South Carolina. He is also a teaching professor for the South Carolina Honors College and a 1995 Southeast Asian Fulbright Senior Research Scholar on sexuality and culture. Author of six books, including *Growing Up Gay in the South* (1991), *Sexuality and the Curriculum* (1992), *When Best Doesn't Equal Good* (1994), and *Conversations for an Enlarging Public Square* (1996), Sears is currently completing an oral history of lesbian and gay Southern life. He serves on the editorial boards of several journals, including the *Journal of Homosexuality* and the *Journal of Gay/Lesbian Identity*.

Walter L. Williams is professor of anthropology at the University of Southern California, where he teaches courses on gay, lesbian, bisexual, and transgender studies. Of his seven books the most notable is *The Spirit and the Flesh: Sexual Diversity in American Indian Culture* (1986, revised 1992), based on his research in many Native American communities from Yucatan to Alaska. While Fulbright senior research scholar in Indonesia, he did research on gender variance and homosexuality in Southeast Asian cultures, followed by similar fieldwork research in Polynesia. His most recent book was coedited with the late gay pioneer W. Dorr Legg, *Homophile Studies in Theory and Practice* (1994). He is also president of the ONE Institute International Gay and Lesbian Archives and editor of the *International Gay and Lesbian Review*.

James Andre is chair of the development committee of the ONE Institute International Gay and Lesbian Archives. He is also vice president and chief financial officer of Alluvial Entertainment, Inc., and has taught courses on personal finance at the University of Southern California.

Lourdes Arguelles is professor of education at the Claremont Graduate School Center for Educational Studies. She is also a psychotherapist in private practice, working primarily with people of color and sexual minorities, and is active in community organizing in southern California's Inland Valley.

Robert Barret is professor of counselor education at the University of North Carolina at Charlotte and a psychologist in private practice. He serves as chair of the board of North Carolina PridePAC for Gay and Lesbian Equality and on Project HOPE of the American Psychological Association, which provides traning in HIV-related psychotherapy to psychologists throughout the nation. He is a father and a grandfather and the coauthor of *Gay Fathers* (1991).

M.V. Lee Badgett is executive director of the Institute for Gay and Lesbian Strategic Studies, in Washington, D.C. She is a labor economist in the School of Public Affairs at the University of Maryland and has also taught as a visiting professor of lesbian and gay studies at Yale University. Her research focuses on sexual orientation discrimination and family policy.

Warren J. Blumenfeld is editor of the *Journal of Gay, Lesbian, and Bisexual Identity,* and coauthor of *Looking at Gay and Lesbian Life* (1988). He also co-produced the documentary film *Pink Triangles* and edited *Homophobia: How We All Pay the Price* (1992). Currently in the social justice educational program at the University of Massachusetts, Amherst, he has for more than two decades facilitated diversity workshops relating to homophobia, anti-Jewish prejudice, racism, classism, ableism, and sexism.

Dee Bridgewater is an assistant professor of communication studies at UCLA, following completion there of a dissertation on homophobia. He has extensive experience as a consultant on gay and lesbian issues for nongay groups and in teaching courses for Southern California gay and lesbian communities.

Diane BuBose Brunner is associate professor of English and director of English education at Michigan State University. She is author of *Inquiry and Reflection: Framing Narrative Practice in Education* (1994) and essays on the coconstruction of identity based on sexuality, gender, race, and class.

Elizabeth Cramer is assistant professor of social work at Virginia Commonwealth University. Her research focuses on domestic violence and on services to lesbians and gay males. She has conducted many diversity training programs and presentations about lesbian identity and homophobia.

Louie Crew is professor of English at Rutgers University in Newark, New

Jersey. As founder of Integrity in the Episcopal Church, and as author of nearly a thousand works, he is a pioneer gay activist both in academia and in religious and community organizations.

J. Eileen Durgin-Clinchard is a veteran member and officer of Parents and Friends of Lesbians and Gays (PFLAG). She wrote her dissertation at the University of Nebraska on the characteristics of strong and successful local PFLAG chapters and now serves as a diversity consultant while conducting many classes and workshops on heterosexism.

Toby Emert is a counselor in private practice and also served as a staff counselor at the Career Center of the University of Texas at Austin.

Manuel Fernandez, a native of Chile, is a Ph.D. candidate in anthropology at the University of Southern California, where he is doing research on gender variance and heterosexismo in Honduras, Chile, and other Latin American countries. He is active in the Latin America Project of the ONE Institute International Gay and Lesbian Archives.

J Craig Fong is a civil rights attorney in Los Angeles and chair of the board of advisors of the Asian Pacific AIDS Intervention Team. Formerly he was chief policy analyst for the Los Angeles Gay and Lesbian Center, director of the immigration project of the Asian Pacific American Legal Center of Southern California, and director of the western regional office of the Lambda Legal Defense and Education Fund.

Patricia Hulsebosch is associate professor of elementary education at National Louis University in Chicago, where she does research on teacher development, cultural identity, and home-school relationships. She is currently chair of the Lesbian/Gay Studies Special Interest Group of the American Educational Research Association.

Suzanne Iasenza is associate professor of counseling at John Jay College of Criminal Justice and is also affiliated with the Center for Lesbian and Gay Studies at the City University of New York. She has been developing diversity programs for over a decade and has written extensively on lesbian and gay psychology. She is coeditor of *Lesbians and Psychoanalysis: Revolutions in Theory and Practice* (1996).

Diana Kardia completed her Ph.D. dissertation in education at the University of Michigan on "Diversity's Closet: Student Attitudes Toward Lesbians, Gay Men, and Bisexual People on a Multicultural Campus." She is currently an educational consultant for the Center for Research on Learning and Teaching and also consults with the Program on Intergroup Relations and Conflict, both at the University of Michigan.

Melissa Keyes is president of Keyes Consulting, Inc., in Madison, Wisconsin. She has served as a sex equity consultant at the Wisconsin Department of Public Instruction and teaches a graduate seminar for educational administrators on equity issues at the University of Wisconsin.

Mari E. Koerner is associate dean of the college of education at Roosevelt University in Chicago, where she is also associate professor in teacher education. Her research focuses on teachers' awareness of multicultural concepts and how this influences classroom instruction.

Donald N. Mager is associate professor of English and codirector of the liberal studies program at Johnson C. Smith University. He is author of volumes of poetry, including *To Track the Wounded One* (1986) and *Glosses* (1996).

Rita M. Marinoble is associate professor of counselor education at California State University, Sacramento. Formerly she spent fourteen years as a school counselor with the San Diego Unified School District. While presently focused on raising two adopted daughters from Mexico, she remains active in homophobia reduction in school and university settings.

Brian McNaught is a corporate consultant, author, and sexuality educator. He is author of *Gay Issues in the Workplace* (1900) and *On Being Gay* (1900) as well as the producer of numerous educational materials and videotapes on homosexuality.

Lynne Milburn is director of the Career Center at the University of Texas-Austin, which offers a supportive environment for the university's diverse population, and also maintains a private counseling practice.

Patricia Myers has been facilitating workshops and discussion groups on lesbian, bisexual, and gay men's issues for almost two decades and is coeditor of *A Certain Terror: Heterosexism, Militarism, Violence, and Change* (1996). She recently completed her Ph.D. coursework in American culture at the University of Michigan.

Peter M. Nardi is professor of sociology at Pitzer College, coauthor of *Growing Up Before Stonewall: Life Stories of Some Gay Men* (1994), and editor of *Men's Friendships* (1992). He is coeditor of *In Changing Times: Gay Men and Lesbians Encounter HIV/AIDS* (1997), *Looking Out: Sociological Contributions to Lesbian and Gay Studies* (1997), and *GLQ: A Journal of Lesbian and Gay Studies*. He served as chair of the Sociologists' Lesbian and Gay Caucus of the American Sociological Association, cochair of the Los Angeles Gay Academic Union, and copresident of the Los Angeles chapter of the Gay and Lesbian Alliance Against Defamation.

Robert Nugent is editor of *A Challenge to Love: Gay and Lesbian Catholics in the Church* (1983), coeditor of *The Vatican and Homosexuality* (1983), and coeditor of *Building Bridges: Gay and Lesbian Reality and the Catholic Church* (1992). Drawing upon more than twenty years of experience working with clergy and laity in areas of homophobia and pastoral ministry, his articles have been published in many journals and books.

Eric Estuar Reyes taught a course on the Asian Pacific Islander lesbian, gay, and bisexual experience at the UCLA Asian American Studies Center, after receiving his M.A. in urban planning at UCLA with a thesis on "Queer Spaces: The Spaces of Lesbians and Gay Men of Color in Los Angeles." He is currently a Ph.D. student in American civilization at Brown University.

Sylvia Rhue is coproducer of the antihomophobia documentary film *All God's Children*, as well as media director at ONE Institute International Gay and Lesbian Archives. She was a founding member of the National Black Lesbian and Gay Leadership Forum and an affiliated scholar at the University of Southern California Center for Feminist Research. Currently she conducts antihomophobia workshops in various African American religious and community organizations around the country.

Thom Rhue is former director of African and Afro-American studies at Stanford University, where he was a professor of sociology. During the 1970s he was deputy assistant secretary of the United States Department of Education and currently works as a survey research consultant. He and Sylvia Rhue are brother and sister.

Paula Alida Roy is a diversity consultant to several school districts in New Jersey as well as chairperson of the English department in a suburban high school. She is producing a videotape on sexual harassment with a grant from the New Jersey Division of Women. Her work has appeared in *Women's Studies Quarterly*.

Glenda M. Russell is a faculty associate in women's studies and a clinical instructor in psychology at the University of Colorado, as well as a psychologist in private practice in Boulder. She has worked in antihomophobia training for two decades, teaching classes for counselors, psychologists, and educators. She collaborated on the production of a musical oratorio for a Colorado chorale in which she sings about the harmful psychological effects of Colorado's antigay Amendment Two.

Sue Sattel is the educational equity specialist for the Minnesota Department of Children, Families, and Learning, where she focuses on sexual harassment curriculum development and training for schools.

Chuck Stewart received his Ph.D. in education from the University of

Southern California with a dissertation on the efficacy of sexual orientation training in law enforcement agencies. He has been a consultant for several police departments and universities, designing antiprejudice training programs. Drawing on his experience as a high school teacher, he has authored curricula and teaching packages to reduce the oppression of stigmatized communities within schools. He is cochair of the Los Angeles Gay and Lesbian Scientists, and an affiliated scholar of ONE Institute International Gay and Lesbian Archives.

Robert Sulek is dean of academic affairs at Lake Highland College and formerly rector of the honors college at Johnson C. Smith University. He is the author of *Hoosier Honor* (1986) and is currently writing a book on honors students at an African American university.

Mark H. Townsend is assistant professor of psychiatry at the Louisiana State University School of Medicine in New Orleans. He has published several articles on homosexuality and mental health.

Pat Tupper is a librarian and educator for the Minnesota Department of Children, Families, and Learning. She was president of the Minnesota chapter of Parents, Families, and Friends of Lesbians and Gays and cofounded a support group for nongay spouses.

Paul Van de Ven is a high school principal in New South Wales, Australia, and completing his doctoral studies in educational psychology at the University of Sydney.

Jane E. Vennard is ordained in the United Church of Christ to a special ministry of teaching and spiritual direction. She is an adjunct professor at the Iliff School of Theology in Denver, serving as a resource for lesbian and gay concerns.

Mollie M. Wallick is professor of psychiatry at the Louisiana State University School of Medicine in New Orleans, where she is director of Social Issues in Medicine and serves as faculty liaison to gay and lesbian medical students and residents. She has published several articles on homosexuality and mental health.

Gust A. Yep is associate professor of speech and communication studies at San Francisco State University. He has written many articles in scholarly journals and books on effective cross-cultural communications strategies for AIDS education and prevention, especially as affecting communities of color.

Index

Lesbian and Gay Studies

Lillian Faderman and Larry Gross, Editors

Edward Alwood, *Straight News: Gays, Lesbians, and the News Media*

Corinne E. Blackmer and Patricia Juliana Smith, editors, *En Travesti: Women, Gender Subversion, Opera*

Alan Bray, *Homosexuality in Renaissance England*

Joseph Bristow, *Effeminate England: Homoerotic Writing After 1885*

Beverly Burch, *Other Women: Lesbian Theory and Psychoanalytic Narratives*

Claudia Card, *Lesbian Choices*

Joseph Carrier, *De Los Otros: Intimacy and Homosexuality Among Mexican Men*

Terry Castle, *Noël Coward and Radclyffe Hall: Kindred Spirits*

John Clum, *Acting Gay: Male Homosexuality in Modern Drama*

Gary David Comstock, *Violence Against Lesbians and Gay Men*

Laura Doan, editor, *The Lesbian Postmodern*

Allen Ellenzweig, *The Homoerotic Photograph: Male Images from Durieu/Delacroix to Mapplethorpe*

Lillian Faderman, *Odd Girls and Twilight Lovers: A History of Lesbian Life in Twentieth-Century America*

Linda D. Garnets and Douglas C. Kimmel, editors, *Psychological Perspectives on Lesbian and Gay Male Experiences*

Richard D. Mohr, *Gays/Justice: A Study of Ethics, Society, and Law*

Sally Munt, editor, *New Lesbian Criticism: Literary and Cultural Readings*

Timothy F. Murphy and Suzanne Poirier, editors, *Writing AIDS: Gay Literature, Language, and Analysis*

Noreen O'Connor and Joanna Ryan, *Wild Desires and Mistaken Identities: Lesbianism and Psychoanalysis*

Don Paulson with Roger Simpson, *An Evening in the Garden of Allah: A Gay Cabaret in Seattle*

Judith Roof, *Come As You Are: Sexuality and Narrative*

Judith Roof, *A Lure of Knowledge: Lesbian Sexuality and Theory*

Claudia Schoppmann, *Days of Masquerade: Life Stories of Lesbians During the Third Reich*

Alan Sinfield, *The Wilde Century: Effeminacy, Oscar Wilde, and the Queer Moment*

Jane Snyder, *Lesbian Desire in the Lyrics of Sappho*

Chris Straayer: *Deviant Eyes, Deviant Bodies: Sexual Re-Orientations in Film and Video*

Ruth Vanita, *Sappho and the Virgin Mary: Same-Sex Love and the English Literary Imagination*

Thomas Waugh, *Hard to Imagine: Gay Male Eroticism in Photography and Film from Their Beginnings to Stonewall*

Kath Weston, *Families We Choose: Lesbians, Gays, Kinship*

Kath Weston, *Render Me, Gender Me: Lesbians Talk Sex, Class, Color, Nation, Studmuffins . . .*

Carter Wilson, *Hidden in the Blood: A Personal Investigation of AIDS in the Yucatán*